The Structure of Intellectual Property Law

ATRIP INTELLECTUAL PROPERTY

Series Editor: Annette Kur, *Max Planck Institute for Intellectual Property and Competition Law, Germany* and Jan Rosén, *Stockholm University, Sweden*

The ATRIP series present the fruit of annual meetings held by the International Association for the Advancement of Teaching and Research in Intellectual Property (www.atrip.org). Yielding unique opportunities for IP scholars from a global community to explore together the different facets of one overarching topic, the essence of those meetings is captured in the edited compilation of selected contributions contained in the volumes. Rather than employing a traditional, compartmentalized view of the different areas of IP, the ATRIP series typically apply a horizontal approach, cutting across the usual boundaries of legal categorization, with the aim to uncover hidden commonalities, and accentuate the need for differentiation where that is called for. As ATRIP counts among its members leading IP scholars from all parts of the world, and actively encourages participation of highly talented young researchers, the panel of authors contributing to the volumes does not only guarantee excellence, but also represents a full and vibrant picture of contemporary, high-level IP research in an international setting.

The Structure of Intellectual Property Law

Can One Size Fit All?

Edited by

Annette Kur

Max Planck Institute for Intellectual Property and Competition Law, Munich, Germany

Vytautas Mizaras

University of Vilnius, Lithuania

ATRIP INTELLECTUAL PROPERTY

Edward Elgar

Cheltenham, UK • Northampton, MA, USA

Published by
Edward Elgar Publishing Limited
The Lypiatts
15 Lansdown Road
Cheltenham
Glos GL50 2JA
UK

Edward Elgar Publishing, Inc.
William Pratt House
9 Dewey Court
Northampton
Massachusetts 01060
USA

A catalogue record for this book
is available from the British Library

Library of Congress Control Number: 2010939257

MIX
Paper from responsible sources
FSC® C018575
FSC
www.fsc.org

ISBN 978 1 84844 876 6 (cased)

Typeset by Servis Filmsetting Ltd, Stockport, Cheshire
Printed and bound by MPG Books Group, UK

Contents

Contributors

Dr Maciej Barczewski, Head of Postgraduate Studies in Intellectual Property and High Technology Law, Faculty of Law and Administration at the University of Gdansk (Poland)

Melissa A. Brown, Scholarly Communications Librarian at New York University (USA)

Professor Michael W. Carroll, Director, Program on Information Justice and Intellectual Property, American University, Washington College of Law (USA)

Professor Andrew F. Christie, Davies Collison Cave Professor of Intellectual Property at the Melbourne Law School, and Research Associate of the Intellectual Property Research Institute of Australia (IPRIA), University of Melbourne (Australia)

Professor Kenneth D. Crews, Director, Copyright Advisory Office, Columbia University Lecturer in Law, Columbia Law School (USA)

Professor Graeme B. Dinwoodie, Professor of Intellectual Property and Information Technology Law, Faculty of Law, University of Oxford; Director, Oxford Intellectual Property Research Centre; Professorial Fellow, St. Peter's College, University of Oxford (United Kingdom)

Professor Stefan Enchelmaier, LL.M. (Edinburgh), MA (Oxon), Professor of European and Comparative Commercial Law, York Law School, University of York (United Kingdom)

Associate Professor Christophe Geiger, Director of the Centre for International Intellectual Property Studies (CEIPI), University of Strasbourg (France); Senior Researcher, Max Planck Institute for Intellectual Property and Competition Law, Munich (Germany)

Dr Henning Grosse Ruse-Khan, Senior Research Fellow, Max Planck Institute for Intellectual Property and Competition Law, Munich (Germany)

Professor Ansgar Ohly, LL.M. (Cantab.), Professor of Civil Law and Intellectual Property Law at the University of Bayreuth (Germany), Visiting Professor at the University of Oxford (United Kingdom)

Professor Rudolph J.R. Peritz, Professor of Law and Director, IProgress Project, New York Law School (USA)

Professor Ulf Petrusson, Professor at University of Gothenburg, Director of Department at Institute for Innovation and Enterpreneurship (Sweden)

Professor Alexander Peukert, Professor of Law, Chair for Civil Law, Commercial Law and Intellectual Property Law, Goethe University Frankfurt am Main (Germany)

Dr Claudia Schmidt, Research Assistant, Chair of Economic Policy, Philipps University of Marburg (Germany)

Professor Martin Senftleben, Professor of Intellectual Property, VU University Amsterdam; Senior Consultant, Bird & Bird, The Hague (Netherlands)

Professor Jerzy Zajadło, Head of the Chair of Theory and Philosophy of State and Law, Faculty of Law and Administration at University of Gdansk (Poland)

Foreword

This book is the fruit of two congresses held in Munich (2008) and Vilnius (2009) under the common theme 'Can One Size Fit All?'. Whereas the first year focused on the commonalities in the structure of intellectual property (IP) throughout the various disciplines, the second year addressed specific topics which were analysed in the same horizontal manner. Selected contributions from both years are joined together in this volume, in a deepened and expanded form.

The congresses were arranged by the International Association for the Advancement of Teaching and Research in Intellectual Property (ATRIP, www.atrip.org), which is a unique community of IP scholars from all parts of the world, congregating annually so as to exchange ideas, receive inspiration, and gather information in a truly academic atmosphere and environment. The editors were involved in the organisation of the congresses as president of ATRIP and as local host. It is their wish to express their sincere gratitude to those persons and institutions without whose support a successful arrangement of the meetings would not have been possible, among them the World Intellectual Property Organisation (WIPO), the International Association for the Protection of International Property (AIPPI), and the International Federation of Patent Agents (FICPI). Generous support was further provided by the Academy of the European Patent Office (EPO) and by a number of sponsors from private practice. Special thanks also go to the academic institutions acting as co-organisers of the meetings, namely the Max Planck Institute for Intellectual Property and Competition Law in Munich and the Faculty of Law at the University of Vilnius. Last but not least, we are deeply indebted to the many persons who dedicated time and effort, with much enthusiasm, to the plethora of tasks behind the scenes, so as to ensure that the events took place smoothly and efficiently.

It has always been a crucial part of ATRIP's work to distribute the harvest gathered at the annual congresses to its members in the form of publications. Nevertheless, this book marks a new phase in those activities, as it is the first volume in an ATRIP series edited under the auspices of Edward Elgar Publishing. It is our hope that the series will find its place in the market, so as to attract a new and broader array of persons interested in topical issues of contemporary IP. In full awareness of this ambitious goal, the book has been given a concise structure and theme, so as to resemble a handbook rather than a mere compilation of congress papers. Our ultimate thanks go to the contributors who have understood and acted according to those ambitions. The last word on this, of course, needs to be spoken by the reader.

Munich and Vilnius, July 2010

Annette Kur and Vytautas Mizaras

Introduction

Annette Kur*

Is there a coherent system underlying the entire field of intellectual property (IP), or are the different constituent areas only loosely connected with each other? Have the foundations on which the different rights were originally grounded converged, or are they drifting apart? Does the fact that the law must react to a host of problems characterised by an ever-increasing degree of sophistication necessarily entail fragmentation ultimately leading to inconsistency, or are the principles informing legal choices sustainable enough to provide a solid and resilient frame? Vice versa – are those principles too rigid and inflexible, and therefore incapable of responding to novel challenges? To what extent, and where, should the system make room for more differentiation? Which tools does the law provide for the adjustment of protection to different needs and circumstances, and how much flexibility exists in employing those tools? *Can One Size Fit All?*

The idea of focusing on these and other issues at ATRIP meetings was born out of the *Intellectual Property of Transition* project, to which Graeme Dinwoodie refers in the first chapter of this book. The clue was taken from two seemingly antagonistic tendencies that were considered characteristic of contemporary IP law. As their overall coverage broadens, legal fields such as patent and copyright law become increasingly compartmentalised: pharmaceutical patents have little in common with patents in 'classical' technical fields such as machinery, and copyright in works of fine art is quite another discipline than copyright in news articles or computer programs. In order to attain and keep up expert status on a particular subject, a high degree of specialisation is needed, which may impede a full view on IP as one coherent field. On the other hand, there is also an increasing inclination towards overlaps, both as regards the way in which one and the same object may attract cumulative protection under different laws, and regarding the legal objectives underlying the different fields.

* Senior Researcher and Head of Unit, Max Planck Institute for Intellectual Property and Competition Law, Munich; President of ATRIP 2007–09.

While patent and copyright protection were originally based on quite distinct motives and concepts, patent law – in some parts of the world – has ventured out of the field of technology, while copyright long ago left the sphere of purely artistic creations. Although traditional rhetoric may still convey more idealistic views, legal developments in all fields are predominantly driven by utilitarian motives. Protection and encouragement of financial investment have become the primary rationale for the creation of new and extension of existing rights. Protection is frequently tailored so as to prevent third parties from taking commercial advantage of achievements made by the first investor, irrespective of whether or not a risk of market failure is created thereby. The problem with that approach is that it lacks an inherent balancing element, and that it tends to respond in an ad hoc fashion to needs and demands which are voiced strongly enough to create political pressure.

One possible response to those trends would be to embark on a quest for a 'One Right' system, which could provide the groundwork for establishing a well-calibrated IP regime. The task would be to identify the features of a core right which extends from a nucleus of unconditional power to exclude others from accessing and using the protected subject matter over various forms and degrees of attenuation to full accessibility and free use for everyone. The architecture of such a system would have to be elaborated on the basis of a holistic approach, investigating the commonalities in the foundations as well as in the existing and/or desirable limitations of different types of rights. For instance, an attempt could be made to draw up a charter of 'users' rights' forming the baseline for third-party conduct which must regularly be deemed permissible, irrespective of the kind of right invoked.

Of course, the outcome of that exercise would be deplorable if it left less room than at present for the finetuning of protection. However, depending on the details of implementation, the system might even allow for an optimum of flexibility and differentiation, with the appraisal being based on a common catalogue of evaluation factors interacting with each other. In its ideal form, the system could be compared to a tree, where one strong and massive trunk grows out of a meshwork of roots, then separates into different branches which sprout a large number of twigs, and finally end up in smaller and smaller sprigs which are too numerous to be counted. Translated into law, this means that full room is given for consideration of the specificities found in individual cases, while nevertheless, all solutions must respond, and must conform to, the common objectives and principles that provide the backbone of the system, so as to avoid arbitrary and inconsistent decisions.

While flexibility would thus be preserved or even enhanced, an obvious drawback of such a system would be that it tends to reduce legal certainty and foreseeability, and that it imposes a very high burden on those who are responsible for its application. It would also require the revisiting and, where necessary, the adaption of the legislative techniques traditionally employed in intellectual property law in order to give more room to individual evaluations.

Apart from such ambitious goals, a modest and probably more realistic aim for a holistic approach towards IP would be to promulgate an enhanced form of an Intellectual Property Code, which contains common rules on (administrative) procedures and sanctions as well as, for example, on IP rights as objects of property, where that is feasible. This might also help to sharpen the perception of the common features of legal fields which have remained separate up till now, and of the need for more differentiated treatment in others.

The contributions in this book address various aspects on the spectrum of issues arising from one or another form of a 'One Right' approach. They look into the underlying policies and economic foundations of intellectual property right, the principles governing limitations and exceptions, ownership, transfer and other contractual matters. Finally, they also address the question of whether one size can fit all with regard to its implications for intellectual property law. The conclusions drawn and suggestions made may differ in their potential to question current legal concepts and solutions. However, they are all proof of the fact that to conceive of intellectual property as one common area lending itself to horizontal thinking is a valuable exercise in legal analysis, and may foster new insights.

PART I

The general framework: foundation and limits of IP protection

1. Remarks: 'one size fits all' consolidation and difference in intellectual property law

Graeme B. Dinwoodie*

1. INTRODUCTION

This volume is dedicated, like the two ATRIP congresses on which it is based, to the overall theme of whether 'one size fits all' in intellectual property law. Are there sufficient commonalities among the component parts of our field that we could realistically construct a unitary body of intellectual property law?

More specifically, this contribution will consider whether the 'one size fits all' inquiry might be informed by an assessment of changes in the objectives or purposes of intellectual property protection. Have such changes made a 'one size fits all' solution more or less likely, and more or less desirable?

2. ONE SIZE FITTING ALL

Before getting to the specific questions of 'purpose' and 'objectives', I would like first to introduce the different dimensions to the overall question of 'one size fitting all', which will be explored in greater detail in later chapters.

There are a number of different inquiries that might be subsumed by the question of whether 'one size fits all' in intellectual property law.

* Professor of Intellectual Property and Information Technology Law, Faculty of Law, University of Oxford; Director, Oxford Intellectual Property Research Centre; Professorial Fellow, St. Peter's College, University of Oxford.

2.1. A Single Intellectual Property Right?

First, as perhaps best reflected in a project undertaken by the Intellectual Property in Transition team,[1] who starting in 2001 sought to develop a 'one-right-system', we might ask whether the historically distinct regimes of patent, copyright and trademark law have developed sufficient commonality that a single notion of an 'intellectual property right' can be formulated. This unified right, so the argument goes, would provide a greater economy of doctrine and thus greater certainty than the current mish-mash of separate, but increasingly overlapping, intellectual property rights that often provide multiple layers of protection to the same commercial product.

Thus, the Intellectual Property in Transition project explanatory memorandum from 2005 suggested that market actors no longer differentiated among IP rights along the lines suggested by formal legal doctrine. Indeed, the drafters of that memorandum went so far as to suggest that 'the only significant difference between modern copyright and patent law is the droit moral'.[2]

In the abstract, the idea of pursuing a one-size-fits-all philosophy, and collapsing the mélange of existing intellectual property systems into a single, clean IP right, might be attractive. Certainly, guaranteeing commercial actors that their rights in the products of their innovative activity, and their dealings with respect to the products of others, would be regulated by a single set of principles would substantially reduce the uncertainty and the compliance costs caused by multiple layers of protection.[3] It might also minimize the circumvention of legislative intent that often

---

[1] This project, with a heavy Nordic leadership, met in Stockholm in November 2005 with Friends of the Project, in connection with which a memorandum detailing proposed revisions of the TRIPS Agreement was prepared. *See* IPT Conference, 11–12 November 2005: TRIPS Amendments – Explanatory Memorandum (copy on file with author) ('Stockholm 2005 Memorandum'); IPT Conference, 11–12 November 2005 Intellectual Property in Transition Research Programme – Background ('IPT Background'). The project was the subject of a further conference in Helsinki in October 2008, the proceedings of which will be published; the project's findings relating to the TRIPS are published in Kur, A., and Levin, M. (eds) (2011), *Intellectual Property Rights in a Fair World Trade System: Proposals for Reform of TRIPS*, Edward Elgar.

[2] *See* ibid. at 2.

[3] The US Supreme Court is particularly aware of these concerns. *See, e.g., TrafFix Devices, Inc. v Marketing Displays, Inc.*, 532 US 23 (2001); *Dastar Corp. v Twentieth Century Fox Film Corp.*, 539 US 23 (2003); *see generally* Dinwoodie, Graeme B. (2004), 'The Trademark Jurisprudence of the Rehnquist Court', 8 *Marq. Intell. Prop. L. Rev.*, p. 187.

accompanies opportunistic exploitation of the slight differences among intellectual property regimes.

And, to be sure, there have been theoretical, doctrinal and strategic convergences that might suggest such a possibility. Let me give only a few examples. Theoretically, expansions in the scope of trademark protection, to cover both confusion as to association and endorsement,[4] on the one hand, and non-confusing dilution,[5] on the other, have changed the nature of trademarks. Once essentially defensive devices used to preclude rival traders from appropriating one's goodwill, trademarks have been transformed into commercial assets to be used affirmatively to create and control new, secondary markets.[6] Historical assertions that trademarks do not confer rights in gross might appear somewhat tenuous. Very often, trademark claims closely resemble those that one might typically have found in copyright law or patent law: the defendant has 'reproduced' my mark or is 'selling, or making use of' my mark.[7]

And one can pursue this assimilationist line of thought in some degree of detail: for example, the protection of trademarks on so-called 'related goods' could be reconceptualized as a variant on the adaptation right in copyright law;[8] the moral right of integrity can likewise be seen as an alternative formulation of the adaptation right (as indeed it was by the US courts, allowing the United States to fake adherence to the Berne Convention);[9] attribution rights can, to some extent, be protected through recasting the lack of attribution as an act of passing off.[10]

Likewise, as I mentioned above, the drafters of the Intellectual Property in Transition project suggested that 'the only significant difference

---

[4] *See* 15 USC § 1125(a)(1)(A)(2009); Directive 2008/95/EC of the European Parliament and of the Council of 22 October 2008 to Approximate the Laws of the Member States Relating to Trade Marks (codified version), OJ (L 299) 25 (8 Nov. 2008) ('Trade Mark Directive'), art. 5(1)(b); *see also* Directive 2008/95/EC of the European Parliament and the Council of 22 October 2008 to approximate the laws of the Member States relating to trade marks (codified version).

[5] *See* 15 USC § 1125(c) (2009); Trade Mark Directive, art. 5(2).

[6] *See* Dinwoodie, Graeme B. (2009), 'The Ninth Annual Distinguished IP Lecture: Developing Defenses in Trademark Law', 13 *Lewis & Clark L. Rev.*, pp. 99, 120.

[7] *Cf. Boston Professional Hockey Ass'n, Inc. v Dallas Cap & Emblem Mfg., Inc.*, 510 F.2d 1004 (5th Cir. 1975).

[8] *See* McKenna, Mark P. (2009), 'Testing Modern Trademark Law's Theory of Harm', 95 *Iowa L. Rev.*, p. 63.

[9] *See Gilliam v American Broadcasting Co.*, 538 F.2d 14 (2d Cir. 1976).

[10] *But see Dastar Corp. v Twentieth Century Fox Film Corp.*, 539 US 23 (2003); *see generally* Ginsburg, Jane C. (2004), 'The Right to Claim Authorship in U.S. Copyright and Trademarks Law', 41 *Hous. L. Rev.* p. 263.

between modern copyright and patent law is the droit moral'.[11] That is, for reasons perhaps of internationalization that I will come to later in my remarks, some see copyright and patent as purely instrumental rights; the development of the law is taking place without much consideration of other justifications for authorial rights.[12] The theoretical basis for the different rights is, under this reading, largely the same; and the (arguably baneful) dominance of law and economics in our field[13] makes any diminution in the influence of instrumentalism unlikely.

Thus, perhaps it is time to recognize that the theoretical bases of the different rights have substantially converged, rather than repeating historical formulations that are increasingly divorced from what the law actually confers.

A number of doctrinal changes might encourage this possibility. For example, each of the major discrete intellectual property regimes has expanded the subject matter that it will potentially protect, such that few creative or commercial products are not simultaneously freighted with a host of intellectual property rights. Almost anything under the sun made by man can be patented, with any gaps that might have existed in some developing countries slowly being filled;[14] anything capable of carrying meaning (and in the European Union, capable of graphic representation) can be a trademark;[15] close to all original works of authorship can be protected by copyright or related rights; and design protection is no longer confined to the purely aesthetic parts of a product.

Strategically, as intellectual property becomes a more dominant economic tool and as its ownership becomes centralized through unregulated corporate consolidation, each different form of intellectual property

---

11 *See supra* text accompanying note 2.

12 *See* Agreement on Trade-Related Aspects of Intellectual Property Rights, Apr. 15, 1994, Marrakesh Agreement Establishing the World Trade Organization, Annex 1C, Legal Instruments – Results of the Uruguay Round, vol. 31, 33 ILM. 81 (1994) ('TRIPS Agreement'), art. 9(1) (excluding compliance with Article 6*bis* of the Berne Convention from the scope of the WTO Dispute Settlement System).

13 *See* Dinwoodie, Graeme B. and Janis, Mark D. (2007), 'Confusion Over Use: Contextualism in Trademark Law', 92 *Iowa L. Rev.*, pp. 1623–32, 1638–41 (noting incompleteness of law and economics, whether as explanatory or normative tool, in trademark and unfair competition law); Barron, Anne, 'Copyright Infringement, "Free-Riding" and the Lifeworld', in Bently, Davis and Ginsburg (eds), *Copyright and Piracy: An Interdisciplinary Critique*, Cambridge University Press (2011).

14 *See* TRIPS Agreement, art. 27.

15 *See Qualitex Co. v Jacobsen Prods., Inc.*, 514 US 159 (1995); Trade Mark Directive, art. 1; *cf. Sieckmann v Deutschespatent-und Markenamt,* 2003 ETMR 37 (ECJ 2002).

comes to assume a common strategic value, namely, as a means of extracting or generating compensation. Those realists who see the 'compensation principle' as the central pillar of the real intellectual property creed thus might view the historical distinctions as rather beside the point.

However, there are good reasons to resist an attempt to pursue a unitary intellectual property right under the thinking that, in this era of convergence, 'one size might fit all'. Most practically, as indeed the drafters of the Intellectual Property in Transition project recognized, such an approach would discard the accumulated common understandings of over a century of developed law, and would generate substantial uncertainty (with attendant costs) as new concepts were fleshed out by courts. And, of course, this is to say nothing of the difficulty of finding political agreement on the content of such a system. It is difficult enough to secure consensus among the stakeholders involved in reform of copyright, patent or trademark, without inviting all of these parties into the same room to fight it out among themselves. It is incumbent on academics to view many of the questions in our field not only through the lens of theory or doctrine, but with an eye to the realities of political economy.

One of the more interesting (though not altogether helpful) changes in copyright lawmaking in the last decade has between the increased involvement of technology companies, more used to detailed regulatory systems such as those governing telecommunications.[16] It should not be a surprise, therefore, that copyright laws have in turn evolved (if that is the word) from elegant, if sometimes ambiguous and incomplete, statements of principle to detailed, backward-looking, narrow rules more akin to those promulgated by administrative agencies . . . rules that, we should not be astonished to learn, are equally as ambiguous and incomplete, but lack any of the elegance.[17]

But the reasons that doom any effort to create a single system are not merely practical. Some of the developments I mentioned above have not been uncontested. For example, the US courts might in fact produce some constraints on patent subject matter;[18] litigation of cases involving the application of technological protection measures (TPM) have forced courts to draw distinctions (reflective of pre-Software Directive impulses in Europe), between TPM-protected functional works, such as software

---

16 *See* Dinwoodie, Graeme B. (2000), 'A New Copyright Order: Why National Courts Should Create Global Norms', 149 *U. Pa. L. Rev.*, pp. 469, 483 n.38.

17 *See* Dinwoodie, Graeme B. (2003), 'Transcript of the Symposium on Digital Rights on the Law and Technology of Management', 18 *Berk. Tech. L. J.*, pp. 697, 764.

18 *See Bilski v Kappos*, 130 S. Ct. 3218 (2010).

embedded in garage door openers, and TPM-protected core creative copyright works.[19] And the compensation principle might be waning in a number of contexts where (in part induced by such things as certain Creative Commons licenses) authors seem to value attribution over immediate compensation.[20] Perhaps it is, after all, about 'respect', suggesting a bridge between the belief systems of the nineteenth century and the twenty-first.

Moreover, justifications for a 'one size fits all' system tend to ignore the somewhat different questions that arise with respect to trademark law, on the one hand, and copyright and patent law, on the other. Although expansions in the scope of trademark law have clearly strengthened the hand of the producer, trademark questions tend to be consumer-centered; the perception of consumers matters for the establishment and, with respect to core infringement claims, scope of rights.[21] That focus informs both doctrinal tests and evidentiary questions, as well as relief that can be provided to mitigate potential harms to competition. Article 21 of TRIPS prohibits compulsory licensing of trademarks;[22] but compulsory licensing of copyright and patents are seen as essential tools in mitigating potentially anti-competitive exercises of rights.[23] Trademark law might use different policy levers to avoid trademarks creating anti-competitive situations,[24] but these different doctrinal devices reflect real differences in the nature of the right, not mere historical contingency.

Moreover, much of the claim about the convergence of different IP regimes focuses on the substantive scope of rights. If one looks at questions of acquisition, there has been much less convergence. And, as the

---

19 *See, e.g., Chamberlain Group, Inc. v Skylink Techs., Inc.*, 381 F.3d 1178 (Fed. Cir. 2004); *Lexmark Int'l, Inc. v Static Control Components, Inc.*, 387 F.3d 522 (6th Cir. 2004); *Storage Tech. Corp. v Custom Hardware Eng'g & Consulting, Inc.*, 421 F.3d 1307 (Fed. Cir. 2005); *see generally* Reichman, Jerome H., Dinwoodie, Graeme B. and Samuelson, Pamela (2007), 'A Reverse Notice and Takedown Regime to Enable Public Interest Uses of Technically Protected Copyrighted Works', 22 *Berk. Tech. L.J.*, p. 981.

20 *See* www.creativecommons.org.

21 *See* Dinwoodie, Graeme B., 'Third Annual Lecture on International Intellectual Property Law: Ensuring Consumers "Get What They Want" – The Role of Trademark Law', Emmanuel College, University of Cambridge, May 13, 2008 (copy on file with author).

22 *See* TRIPS Agreement, art. 21.

23 *See* ibid. art. 31; *see also Magill v Commission*, [1995] All ER (EC) 416 (ECJ 1995).

24 *Cf.* 15 USC § 1064(3) (cancellation of registrations on ground of a mark becoming generic); 15 USC § 1115(b)(7).

debate about the Community Patent has shown, these are some of the most important questions to commercial actors.

Thus, in the strong form of replacing our diverse, although often similar, intellectual property regimes with a single system, a single IP right, there is surely little likelihood of such an approach being adopted.

However, that is not to say that the intellectual exercise of contemplating the common essence of intellectual property is not without merit. Inquiring about the common features of the different regimes may help to identify the topics upon which scholars and reformers should concentrate, and learning in one regime might helpfully inform the development of others. There is much to be said for intramural comparative analysis.

I will not say much in detail about the topics that might be the subject of that analysis; later chapters address some of the prominent examples. But it is clear that the development of exceptions and limitations (which will be addressed below), the role of unauthorized third-party use in the information and innovation ecosystem, and how contracts can override default principles of the different regimes, are all questions that pervade the field. Identifying commonalities will surely be useful.

2.2. Protection without Discrimination within an Intellectual Property Regime[25]

A second dimension to the question of whether 'one size fits all' in intellectual property law is in fact explicitly raised by the TRIPS Agreement. Article 27 of the TRIPS Agreement requires that 'patents shall be available and patent rights enjoyable without discrimination as to the . . . field of technology'.[26] The *travaux préparatoires* of the TRIPS Agreement emphasize that the provision was intended to guarantee protection for a variety of subject matter previously unprotected by patent rights in many countries.[27] But in Canada – Protection of Pharmaceuticals Patents, a dispute settlement panel of the WTO gave article 27 broader (structural) effect, and required exceptions to patent protection in Canadian law to

---

[25] The first part of Section 2.2 of these remarks draws on arguments elaborated in greater detail in Dinwoodie, Graeme B. and Dreyfuss, Rochelle Cooper (2007), 'Diversifying without Discriminating: Complying with the Mandates of the TRIPS Agreement', 13 *Mich. Tel. & Tech. L. Rev.*, p. 445.

[26] *See* TRIPS Agreement, art. 27.

[27] *See* Dinwoodie, Graeme B. and Dreyfuss, Rochelle Cooper (2004) *International Intellectual Property Law and the Public Domain of Science*, 7 J. *Int'l Econ. L.*, p. 431 (citing Canada – Patent Protection of Pharmaceutical Products, WT/DS114/R 4.6 fn.27 (WTO Dispute Settlement Panel 2000)).

comply not only with the demands of article 30, which explicitly regulates permissible exceptions from patent protection, but also with article 27's prohibition of technology-based discrimination.[28]

This broad reading, which might appear to impose a one size fits all mandate on patent law, might be problematic. Although the technological community was once fairly united in its needs, the recent debate over patent reform has made it clear that this is no longer the case. For example, the broad patents available for basic science present different problems from those associated with the thickets of narrow rights awarded in fields where advances are incremental. In the last few years, it has become increasingly difficult to believe that a one-size-fits-all approach to patent law can survive.[29]

Rochelle Dreyfuss and I have argued that even if one were to accept the possibility that the Canada – Pharmaceuticals panel reached the right conclusion and that article 27 is in some respects structural, strong arguments can be made that there is still considerable room for tailoring in national patent laws.[30] I won't rehearse all the arguments for allowing departures from one size fits all. Suffice it to say that under a normal meaning of the term 'discrimination', treating different cases differently is not discrimination. For example, it may not be discrimination to create exceptions to broad patents out of the concern that they dominate too broad a swath of the technological frontier, while giving the holder of a narrow patent the right to exploit the entire domain of his claim. At the end of the day, the value of the exclusivity offered to different technologies is similar.[31]

Although patent law is the only regime to have this type of provision imposed as a matter of international law, the impulse is one that is strong in national systems of copyright and trademarks operating without the constraint of international law. Thus, courts in copyright cases frequently disclaim any attempt to make aesthetic judgments in making assessments of creativity or infringement.[32] Likewise, the European Court of Justice has suggested that the distinctiveness of any claimed trademark must be determined according to the same nominal doctrinal rules, whether the mark be a word, a shape or a color.[33]

Of course, in both these cases, we know that protection is not conferred

---

28 *See* Dinwoodie and Dreyfuss, *supra* note 25.

29 *See* ibid.

30 *See* ibid.

31 *See* ibid.

32 *See Bleistein v Donaldson Lithographing Co.*, 188 US 239 (1903) (Holmes J.).

33 *See Linde, Winward Indus., & Rado Uhren v Deutsches Patent- und Markenant*, 2003 ETMR 78 (ECJ 2003).

on a one-size-fits-all basis. In many countries, an empirical observation of outcomes suggests that courts exhibit more solicitude for representational art over abstract art, for works of literature over functional text, and perhaps for certain types of music that conform more closely to the classical canon.[34] This is the application of a 'one-size' rule to different types of creativity. Likewise, although the European Court of Justice has nominally committed to a common test for distinctiveness of marks, it has explicitly recognized that certain types of marks (e.g., words) are more likely to be perceived by the public as indications of source than other types of marks (e.g., product shapes).[35]

Thus, the argument that Rochelle Dreyfuss and I made in the context of article 27 is hardly a departure from normal modes of analysis in intellectual property law. Indeed, Dan Burk and Mark Lemley had already shown persuasively that certain common doctrinal concepts in patent law operate differently on inventions in different industries.[36]

So there is a 'one size fits all' inquiry that is imposed on us by international law, at least in the context of patent law. But even that provision does not preclude our thinking about whether certain types of creativity or innovation or mark should be treated differently within particular intellectual property regimes.

2.3. One Size Fits All in the International Context

A third way in which the concept of 'one size fits all' might arise, and indeed has arisen, in intellectual property debates, is in thinking through the demands imposed on national forms of protection by international law. International intellectual property developments increasingly consist of efforts to harmonize national regimes, thus to some extent invoking the notion that one size might fit for all nations within the international system at issue. Within the European Union, of course, the 'harmonization' impulse is even stronger, in part because of a central, quasi-federal political apparatus.

---

[34] *See* Arewa, Olufunmilayo B. (2006), 'From J.C. Bach to Hip Hop: Musical Borrowing, Copyright and Cultural Context', 84 *N.C. L. Rev.*, p. 547; Carter, James H. (1991), 'They Know It When They See It: Copyright and Aesthetics in the Second Circuit', 65 *St. Johns L. Rev.*, p. 773.

[35] *See Linde, Winward Indus., & Rado Uhren v Deutsches Patent- und Markenant*, 2003 ETMR 78 (ECJ 2003).

[36] *See* Burk, Dan L. and Lemley, Mark A. (2003), 'Policy Levers in Patent Law', 89 *Va. L. Rev.*, p. 1575; Burk, Dan L. and Lemley, Mark A. (2002), 'Is Patent-Law Technology-Specific?', 17 *Berk. Tech. L.J.*, p. 1155.

So, there are a number of different dimensions to the question of whether 'one size fits all'. However, it is this third dimension – the question of movements toward uniformity internationally – that I wish to focus on as I turn to the more specific question of whether the 'one size fits all' inquiry might be informed by an assessment of changes in the objectives or purposes of intellectual property protection.

3. THE PURPOSES OF INTERNATIONAL INTELLECTUAL PROPERTY PROTECTION[37]

What about the purposes of protection from an international perspective? Have the purposes of international intellectual property law changed since the late nineteenth century? The Berne and Paris Conventions were aimed at developing an international system designed to constrain rampant piracy, and slowly expand core forms of protection. Given that political imperative, it is hardly surprising that the focus of the conventions was limited to minimum levels of protection for rightholders and national treatment to ensure basic protection in foreign markets.

Whatever balance was needed between the interests of different stakeholders was ensured politically at the national level, facilitated by relatively low levels of mandated protection, and buttressed by loose enforcement of international standards. And the international system was primarily a codifying device: norms tended to be mandated internationally after some positive experience in a number of countries' national laws.[38] But has any change in the purpose of international intellectual property law made this bare level of commonality less appropriate? Let's skip forward a century. The TRIPS Agreement contains important flexibilities with respect to implementation that allow countries to resist a one-size-fits-all approach. But the standards were clearly more detailed and extensive, and more effective enforcement mechanisms restricted national latitude.[39]

Although these changes reduced the range of choices open to its members, TRIPS largely followed the structural framework of minimum norms established by Berne and Paris. Is this structure appropriate in light

---

[37] The arguments in Section 3 of this chapter draw on Dinwoodie, Graeme B. (2007), 'The International Intellectual Property System: Treaties, Norms, National Courts and Private Ordering', in Gervais, D. (ed.), *Intellectual Property, Trade and Development: Normative and Institutional Aspects*, Oxford University Press, p. 61.

[38] *See* Dinwoodie, Graeme B. (2000), 'A New Copyright Order: Why National Courts Should Create Global Norms', 149 *U. Pa. L. Rev.*, p. 469.

[39] *See* Dinwoodie, *supra* note 37.

of the purposes of TRIPS? International intellectual property law has become an integral component of trade policy. Although part of the political impetus for international intellectual property lawmaking has long come from the economic gains that particular countries could secure in the global market, the recent situation of intellectual property within the institutional apparatus of the trade regime has been an important factor in the transformation of the system of international intellectual property law.

Arguments in favor of more rapid and intrusive international law making have been assisted by viewing intellectual property through the prism of international trade. The enhancement of international intellectual property obligations has been bolstered, in particular, by invocation of contemporary free trade philosophies, most notably that of comparative advantage. If one country has a comparative advantage in knowledge-based products then, the argument goes, global protection of intellectual property rights is essential to permit exploitation of that comparative advantage. This requires more international commonality.

Moreover, international exploitation and the effect of digital communication technologies on the ease of cross-border flow of information products means that the balance between national autonomy and universal standards – that is, how far, we might appropriately need to move toward one size fits all – might now need to be struck differently.

However, this need for international commonality is occurring in a climate where there are now 180 countries committed in national law to core (and more than basic) levels of protection. Moreover, new international norms are being discussed that have not been the product of widespread national deliberation. As a result, the backwards-looking aspect of the classical system, which tended to favor national autonomy and keep internationally mandated levels of protection low, has been somewhat disrupted.

It is in this context that we are beginning to see the current demand for internationally mandated user rights, or what I call substantive maxima, in a number of venues.[40] That is to say, the substantive pressures created by minimum standards that are more real and less minimal need to be countered by ceilings that constrain in the other direction. In the current political economy, highlighted by TRIPS-plus bilaterals, enabling balance through flexibility is not enough, and something more – whether we call

---

40 *See* Dinwoodie, Graeme B. (1996), 'Federalized Functionalism: The Future of Design Protection in the European Union', 24 *Am. Intell. Prop'y L. Ass'n Q. J.*, pp. 611, 715 n.274; Dreyfuss, Rochelle Cooper (2004), 'TRIPS-Round II: Should Users Strike Back?', 71 *U. Chi. L. Rev.*, p. 21.

them users' rights or substantive maxima – is necessary. The development of users' rights is a natural evolution of the international intellectual property system to reflect the exigencies of the present era.

Later chapters specifically examine exceptions and limitations, so I will not address the topic in too much detail. But I want to make one final observation that connects this changed focus of the international intellectual property system to the one-size-fits-all question.

Advocates of mandatory exceptions have often, in the past, been among those invoking the mantra that one size does not fit all. This is as true for exceptions as it is for exclusive rights. Nations should, at some level, be permitted room for choice as to the exceptions they wish, and as to the form of implementation. There has to be a users' rights parallel to article 1(1) of TRIPS.

4. CONCLUSION

Clearly, one size does not fit all – whether we are talking about a single intellectual property regime, whether we are talking about eradicating differences in the application of the rules within a single regime, or whether we are talking about the level of commonality to be imposed on nations by international law.

But it is also clear that there is much to be gained by seeking commonality in an intellectual property system where the major forms of protection are converging. And, if we look at the purposes of the international system, it is clear that its contemporary trade focus might cause us to require greater commonality among nation states.

But if the focus of the current international system requires greater commonality – greater attention to a one-size-fits-all approach on certain issues – it does so both with respect to the rights conferred on IP right holders and with respect to the new rights that might potentially be conferred on users.

2. A framework for tailoring intellectual property rights

Michael W. Carroll*

1. INTRODUCTION

The literature concerning intellectual property rights has grown considerably in the past few decades, reflecting the growing importance of patents and copyrights as components of national and international trade regulation as well as domestic innovation and cultural policy. Nonetheless, two large questions require further attention. First, when and why grant intellectual property rights? From the economic perspective, granting exclusive rights is only one of a number of options available to stimulate investments in innovation and cultural production. There is no generally accepted framework for assessing the trade-offs between granting intellectual property rights, investing public funds directly in innovation through grants or prizes or indirectly through tax policy, or some combination of these to encourage desired levels of inventive and creative activity.[1]

Second, why grant patents and copyrights as usually one-size-fits-all bundles of rights? Theoretically, it would be better to tailor intellectual property rights to reduce the social costs imposed by one-size-fits-all patents and copyrights – uniformity cost. This is not to say that tailoring intellectual property rights well is easily done. On the contrary, the practical obstacles are substantial, and it is for this reason that the conceptual frames of unitary patent and copyright systems dominate the literature. But intellectual property rights have been tailored before, and they will be tailored again. It is time to have a framework for analyzing this activity

* Director, Program on Information Justice and Intellectual Property, American University, Washington College of Law.

[1] Stiglitz, J. (2008), 'The Economic Foundations of Intellectual Property', *Duke Law Journal*, 57 (6), pp. 1693–1724; Gallini, N. and Scotchmer, S. (2002), 'Intellectual Property: When Is It the Best Incentive System?', in Jaffe, Adam, Lerner, Joshua and Stern, Scott (eds), *Innovation Policy and the Economy*, 2, Cambridge, MA: MIT Press, pp. 51–78.

and to recognize its potential value in rendering intellectual property rights better suited to their task(s).

This chapter shows the conceptual connections between the general economic case for intellectual property rights and the specific case for uniform rights. It then argues that three general criteria should frame the analysis of when and why intellectual property rights should be granted and whether these rights should be tailored for specific industries, innovators or purposes. First, policymakers should assess the relative abilities of government officials and potential authors, inventors and their financial backers, to predict innovative success, recognizing that investments in technological and cultural progress are uncertain. Second, they should assess the 'administrability' of a proposed policy option. This criterion combines assessments of relative administrative cost and robustness against attempts to game the system. Finally, considerations of political economy should be given due weight. Theoretical models of innovation policy trade-offs have their place, but the historical concentration of innovative and creative production in certain industries has given them influence with public officials that must be acknowledged when fashioning policy that is supposed to do real and important work in the real world.

2. WHY INTELLECTUAL PROPERTY?

In a competitive economy, we should expect underinvestment in creative and inventive endeavors because once an author, inventor or their respective financial backers have paid for the creation of a valuable creative or innovative work, competitors can reproduce and distribute that work at prices too low for those who invested in the creation to recoup their investments. The standard economic solution to this public goods or appropriability problem is government assistance to creators and innovators.

Government-created patents and copyrights are one form of such assistance, designed to stimulate investments in creative and innovative activities by excluding direct competition with the rightsholder in the marketplace. The owner of such rights will enjoy the reward of monopoly pricing if there is sufficient demand in the market for the underlying creative work or invention. However, while solving one problem, intellectual property rights create another by supplying rightsholders with powerful weapons against end-users, direct competitors and follow-on innovators who seek to bring socially beneficial innovations to market.

To promote progress, intellectual property law must strike a balance, providing sufficient incentives for innovation without unduly stifling the efforts of follow-on innovators or the liberties of end-users. Many proponents of intellectual property rights treat this move from problem to property as automatic, but it is not. Administering an intellectual property regime is socially costly, and the intellectual property strategy is merely one option that policymakers may deploy to encourage investments in creation and invention in the face of competition.

Government also can invest directly in innovation or creation through grants, contracts or prizes, or it can indirectly subsidize innovation through tax policy. When the options are parsed more closely, policymakers may select from or combine six strategies to solve the appropriability problem:

1. direct provision of useful information by government employees or grantees, such as government research scientists;
2. direct compensation ex ante to the innovator for producing the information (leaving the costs of reproduction and distribution to be borne by participants in a competitive market), such as the grant of a prize to a promising innovator;
3. direct compensation to the innovator ex post through a reward or prize system for innovations already created, such as prizes awarded by a number of federal government science agencies;
4. indirect compensation to the innovator through tax policy, by for example giving tax credits for investments in research and development;
5. protection of innovators from competition through the grant of exclusive production and distribution rights (thereby encouraging monopoly pricing), by creating patent and copyright law; or
6. other forms of protection from competition or misappropriation by increasing excludability of valuable information, by for example prohibiting circumvention of technological protection measures.[2]

The intellectual property strategy must compete with these others for the attention and favor of policymakers. Theoretically, direct investment strategies are superior to intellectual property because once the costs of creating and commercializing a creative or inventive work have been financed, the work can be commoditized. Competitive markets efficiently produce and distribute commodity goods, such as personal computers, generic drugs or books that no longer are under copyright. In the modern context, an emerging literature advocates for a range of institutional forms of direct compensation.[3] This pressure on the traditional case for

---

[2] Fisher, W. (2004), *Promises To Keep: Technology, Law, and the Future of Entertainment*, Stanford, Calif.: Stanford Law & Politics, pp. 200–01.

[3] Stiglitz, J. (2006), 'Scrooge and Intellectual Property Rights: A Medical

intellectual property is most welcome, and there are reasons to expect that this analysis may help alter the mix of government policies in favor of direct compensation to some extent.

Nonetheless, the case for intellectual property is likely to retain its vitality for some time. The intellectual property strategy demonstrates some practical advantages in some domains of innovation. Three practical considerations guide the analysis when assessing the feasibility and desirability of the various strategies for solving the appropriability problem: (1) policymakers' ability to value certain types or classes of creation or innovation; (2) the comparative administrative cost of a strategy; and (3) considerations of political economy associated with a particular strategy. By testing the case for intellectual property in relation to these practical metrics, the empirical and practical premises of the case are laid bare. Once exposed, the case for uniform intellectual property rights articulated in Section 2 and the responsive framework for tailoring in Section 3 follow as logical extensions.

2.1. The Innovation Lottery – Ignorance and Risk Spreading

What creative works or inventions will most benefit society? Who will create or invent them? Must the government promise some form of reward to induce these creators and inventors to bring these creations or inventions into being and to share them with the public or find a distributor to do so? What kind of reward and how much of it is needed?

Policymakers can answer some of these questions some of the time, but usually they must respond that they do not know. In particular, the challenge is exacerbated because the distribution of returns to investments in research and development is highly skew.[4] Thus, creativity and innovation usually are *uncertain*. These observations limit the utility of any ex ante compensation policy. While, in theory, the government can manage this uncertainty through post hoc rewards or prizes, the government will have difficulty in many circumstances calibrating the reward to the social value contributed by the creator or inventor.

Prize Fund Could Improve the Financing of Drug Innovations', *British Medical Journal*, 333 (7582), pp. 1279–84; Shavell, S. and van Ypersele, T. (2001), 'Rewards versus Intellectual Property Rights', *Journal of Law and Economics*, 44 (1), pp. 525–48; Abramowicz, M. (2003), 'Perfecting Patent Prizes', *Vanderbilt Law Review*, 56 (1), pp. 115–236.

[4] Scherer, F.M. (2001), 'Economics of Innovation and Technological Change', in Smelser, Neil J. and Baltes, Paul B. (eds), *International Encyclopedia of the Social and Behavioral Sciences*, UK: Pergamon, pp. 7530–6.

These observations give rise to the *ignorance justification* for intellectual property rights. On this view, government's ignorance about the incentives required to lure particular creators or innovators into the information production and distribution game and to keep them in it justifies the social costs imposed by intellectual property rights. These rights of exclusion underwrite a system of innovator control that finances innovation through the prospect and the occasional reality of monopoly profits in the marketplace.

Information theory supplies the reason. While the ignorance justification holds that the government is largely in the dark ex ante about the value of any particular invention or creation, the inventors or creators will have, on average, marginally better information about the potential success in the market of their intellectual outputs. For this reason, the consensus view among economically oriented commentators is that increasing an innovator's ability to exclude (or at least deter) competitors through exclusive rights is superior to reward because the system is driven by the marginally superior private information that innovators enjoy.[5]

Intellectual property rights are also supported by the cognate *risk-spreading* justification. Uncertainty about innovation poses unquantifiable risks for at least some innovators. While they may, on average, enjoy better information than the government, this margin of superiority is at times quite slim. Indeed, as anyone who watches any of the talent competitions currently in vogue on television knows, in individual cases, many artists or inventors are mistaken if not deluded about the market potential of their talent, their newly composed song or new invention.

This standard argument in favor of decentralization through private investment and market exchange has a significant drawback, however, which receives insufficient attention in the literature. The intellectual property strategy relies on users' ability to pay rather than willingness-to-pay in valuing innovation, and so those innovations or innovators selected for reward by 'the market' will skew toward the interests of the rich. The starkest example is in the financing of drug discovery. The patent system directs significant resources to the discovery and development of so-called 'me-too' and 'lifestyle' drugs for which wealthy consumers in industrialized economies are able to pay a hefty premium.[6] These resources are not directed toward discovery and development of cures for tropical diseases

---

5 Lunney, Jr., G. (2003), 'Patent Law, the Federal Circuit, and the Supreme Court: A Quiet Revolution', *Supreme Court Economic Review*, 11, pp. 1–80.

6 Love, J. and Hubbard, T. (2007), 'The Big Idea: Prizes to Stimulate R&D for New Medicines', *Chicago-Kent Law Review*, 82 (3), pp. 1519–54.

because the likely beneficiaries lack the ability to pay such premiums[7] even though their willingness to pay for a drug that would keep a child alive almost certainly is greater than what an aging consumer in the industrialized world would be willing to pay to enhance his (and, perhaps soon, her) sexual performance. The likely distortionary effects on resource allocation that follow from the gap between willingness-to-pay and ability-to-pay for innovation should serve as a signal for policymakers when choosing the right mix of intellectual property and direct compensation approaches. For fields of creativity or innovation in which the gap is significant, the direct compensation strategy, coupled perhaps with a tax strategy, is likely to perform better.

In sum, as against a centralized government compensation scheme or prize fund, the intellectual property strategy offers the benefits of decentralization. This strategy harnesses the sometimes superior private information that creators and innovators have about the value of their cultural or technological contributions and spreads the risk that they and their financial backers may be mistaken about the practical feasibility of a creative or innovative idea and about its market valuation if realized. The social cost of this strategy is that resources are channeled to innovations likely to serve those with an ability to pay, and these innovations are likely to be underutilized by those who are priced out of the market by monopoly prices or by those who are denied licenses because the transaction costs are too high or the rightsholder refuses to license. After balancing these costs and benefits, policymakers must then assess whether whatever net benefits this strategy yields are comparatively worth the administrative cost.

2.2. Administrative Cost

Any strategy for financing innovation comes with a price. Someone must be paid to perform an adjudication function to identify those deserving to receive entitlements or to enforce entitlements already granted. In addition, a policy must support a transaction structure. Under a direct compensation strategy, the government directly finances a greater share of total administrative costs by supplying one or more agencies responsible for identifying and rewarding innovators. Some of these personnel costs would be borne by existing agencies, such as those who administer the tax system, while others might be borne by agencies that would have to be created to implement a particular approach. If the compensation scheme

[7] Fisher, W. and Syed, T. (forthcoming), *Drugs, Law, and the Global Health Crisis*, Stanford, Calif.: Stanford University Press.

is ex ante, then a grants mechanism would be required similar to that used by granting agencies such as the National Institutes of Health. If a reward or bounty were offered for innovation, an agency would be required to determine when a reward had been earned. Under post hoc compensation schemes, the agency would also be responsible for metering value to calculate the reward. These direct adjudication or examination costs would likely be higher than those associated with an intellectual property strategy, even if the government were to deploy some form of examination prior to granting rights.

In exchange for substantial direct administrative costs associated with identifying those innovators deserving financial reward and administering the associated financing, direct compensation policies involve minimal costs associated with supporting a transaction structure. Information would be in the commons and would not require administrative support for licensing and litigation.

In contrast, the intellectual property strategy leaves most of the total administrative costs in private hands. Traditionally, the costs of deciding which innovators deserve financial reward has been borne by intermediaries with access to capital who fund a variety of screening mechanisms through which a creative work or innovation must pass before gaining access to substantial capital. In addition, the total costs of the transaction structure are far higher than under a direct compensation scheme because users must obtain licenses or permissions, and the boundaries of these transactions must be policed. Measuring these transaction costs is quite difficult because they are borne by a substantial number of persons and entities. In addition, the intellectual property strategy also requires courts to enforce rights and licenses, and, in the case of patents, requires an agency to administer the examination scheme through which the entitlement vests.

In the end, the direct compensation strategy likely involves lower total administrative costs than the intellectual property strategy. Both require financing of an adjudication function to identify which creators or innovators deserve financial reward. With respect to this cost component, the intellectual property strategy probably performs in a more cost-effective manner, leaving aside for the moment the normative differences in the criteria for selecting which innovators or innovations should receive financing. Although some arbitrariness and corruption may occur in the process by which books are selected for publication, movies for production, or music for recording, the financiers are by-and-large publicly traded multinational companies subject to discipline in the global capital markets. So it is likely that these actors are likely to perform the identification function more cost-effectively than government employees subject to public fiscal oversight.

However, when the total costs of intellectual property licensing and litigation are added to the equation, the intellectual property strategy becomes quite expensive. With respect to total transactional costs, only the roughest of estimates can be ventured. Litigation costs are somewhat easier to estimate,[8] although the costs of pre-litigation threats and responses are fairly elusive.

2.3. Political Economy

Even when direct financing of innovation is more efficient, three political considerations render the intellectual property strategy more attractive to policymakers than the direct compensation strategies. First, imposing taxes on the public indirectly through the creation of exclusive rights is politically far cheaper than having to justify direct taxation and direct expenditure of government funds on innovation. For example, when the United States Congress extended the term of existing copyrights by 20 years,[9] it passed a tax increase. The proposal pending at this writing for the European Union to extend the term of existing sound recording copyrights would do the same. Consumers of those copyrighted works subject to the term extension will pay a copyright premium that is analogous to the prize or reward that would be paid had the government collected the funds through taxation and paid out in the form of rewards or prizes.[10] However, because rights tax the public in an indirect means to an uncertain magnitude ex ante, the rights are (spent) with far less administrative evaluation of the social return on investment than is the case with direct procurement.

Second, the risk-spreading rationale reappears in a new guise. Recall that this argument holds that some failure in attempted innovation is certain and that markets are better suited to finance the costs of failure. Government can withstand a fair degree of criticism for failed investments in biomedicine or national defense technologies, but, at least in the United States, taxpayers would be far more skeptical of a scheme in which the government hired inventors of consumer goods or storytellers (such as

---

[8] Lanjouw, J. and Lerner, J. (2000), 'The Enforcement of Intellectual Property Rights: A Survey of the Empirical Literature', in Encaoua, David, Hall, Bronwyn H., Laisney, François, and Mainesse, Jacques (eds), *The Economics and Econometrics of Innovation*, The Netherlands: Kluwer, pp. 201–24.

[9] Sonny Bono Copyright Term Extension Act of 1998, Pub. L. No. 105–298, 112 Stat. 2827 (1998), *codified as amended at* 17 USC § § 108, 203(a)(2), 301(c), 302, 303 and 304.

[10] See, e.g., *Eldred v Ashcroft*, 537 US 186, 802, 804 (2003) (Breyer, J., dissenting).

filmmakers) and songwriters to supply the public's needs. Taxpayers in other industrial economies have shown far greater acceptance of direct government funding of cultural production and cultural institutions,[11] and thus some of the observations about comparative political economy made herein are necessarily culturally specific to the United States.

Nonetheless, however financed, we know that these investments will sometimes be wasted.[12] The direct compensation strategy invites greater negative political pressure from failure because it will be more visible and palpable to voters and because they are likely to react far more negatively to the centralization of risk in a set of government agencies than they are to the consequences of self-deluded or mistaken inventors and creators who seek wealth through intellectual property rights. The risk-spreading concern can be addressed through rewards rather than grants to avoid the problem of paying for what is unwanted. However, prizes risk being set too high or too low to induce the desired level of investment in innovation. Rewards tied to market success are the closest approximation to the beneficial risk allocation features of the intellectual strategy.

Third, while reward tied to market success would effectively neutralize the risk-spreading concern, this design choice for direct compensation highlights the most politically troublesome comparative disadvantage for the direct compensation strategy – agency costs. A mechanism for direct government pay-outs to innovators could be attractive to policymakers as a means of personal enrichment or as a means to reward political supporters or to threaten opponents. Even if direct investment were adopted for public-spirited reasons, administrative corruption or incompetence could lead to manipulation for personal gain by private actors. Finally, for rewards to be tied to market success, some form of metering must be created to measure how strong the winners in the innovation game are. Any metering regime would be susceptible to self-interested manipulation by the innovator and would be likely to require widespread deployment of privacy-invasive technologies and systems.

With respect to the intellectual property strategy, public sector agency costs (in the economic sense of the term) are of two types. The first and most often discussed is the problem of legislative and administrative capture.[13] This phenomenon results from the frequency and energy with which

---

11 Schuster, J. (1985), *Supporting the Arts: An International Comparative Study. Canada, Federal Republic of Germany, France, Italy, Great Britain, Netherlands, Sweden, United States*, US: National Endowment for the Arts.

12 Scherer (2001), *supra* note 4.

13 North, D. (1990), *Institutions, Institutional Change and Economic Performance*, Cambridge: Cambridge University Press.

rightsholders can make their case, which can lead to skewed perspectives about the interests at stake. Legislators, administrators and their staff members may favor proposals by rightsholders for self-interested reasons such as the hope or expectation of well-compensated employment by a rightsholder or rightsholder organization even when such proposals effectively increase taxes on the public without a corresponding return in creation or innovation. While interest groups clearly have an outsize influence on intellectual property legislation and administration,[14] there are countervailing checking forces in the process. The relative independence of the judiciary limits the agency costs associated with interpretation of the law.

Less well-recognized is the fact that the capacity for more directly corrupt self-dealing by administrative officials in an exclusive rights regime is cabined. Copyrights are granted without any government intervention, eliminating opportunities for self-dealing at the entitlement-granting stage. While a copyright owner of a US work must attempt to register her claim to copyright before enforcing her rights, the rules are designed so that even if registration were refused by a corrupt official seeking a bribe or other benefit from the copyright owner, such a strategy would likely be unsuccessful.

The current design of the patent system entails somewhat greater risk of self-dealing or corruption, but this risk is still relatively minimal. The potential entry points for corruption are in the processes of patent examination, re-examination, continuation, or re-issue. Certain obvious risks, such as a patent examiner's potential conflicts of interest are addressed by PTO rules, and these rules generally appear to be followed. Other forms of graft or corruption in which patent examiners or other officials in the PTO accept cash or in kind payments to deviate from their duties appear to be rare. Finally, the risk of insider trading by officials also seems to be in check. This risk is probably more significant among private sector insiders.[15]

3. WHY ONE-SIZE-FITS-ALL PATENTS AND COPYRIGHTS?

Accepting that intellectual property rights have a place in any overarching innovation policy, this section now turns to the question of how the

---

[14] Merges, R. and Reynolds, G. (2000), 'The Proper Scope of the Copyright and Patent Power', *Harvard Journal on Legislation*, 37 (1), pp. 45–68.

[15] Ahuja, G., Coff, R. and Lee, P. (2005), 'Managerial Foresight and Attempted Rent Appropriation: Insider Trading on Knowledge of Imminent Breakthroughs', *Strategic Management Journal*, 26 (9), pp. 791–808.

ignorance and risk-spreading rationales influence the definition of the subject matter, scope and duration of these intellectual property rights. As a general matter, the law in most nations delineates patents and copyrights uniformly without regard to context of invention or creation. This is due, in part, because the Agreement on Trade-Related Aspects of Intellectual Property Rights ('TRIPS')[16] requires certain minimum standards that constrain some of the tailoring flexibility that policymakers might otherwise enjoy. Nevertheless, TRIPS itself tailors protection, and its minimum standards still permit a significant amount of flexibility for downward tailoring in the form of limitations and exceptions to one-size-fits-all rights. Currently, trade negotiators appear to believe that there is no ceiling on upward tailoring.[17]

One-size-fits-all patents and copyrights necessarily are inefficient because the magnitude of the appropriability problems that these rights are designed to remedy varies considerably across and even within industries, and private ordering often fails to match these rights with those who would make best use of them.[18] As a result, this policy imposes *uniformity cost* on society by failing to supply fine-grained rights tailored to the economic circumstances of different classes of authors and inventors. According to the argument for uniform rights, the same ignorance and risk-spreading justifications for the intellectual property rights strategy supply the basis for one-size-fits-all as an initial *domestic* policy.

3.1. Public and Private Information

For the government to tailor rights according to subject matter or the status of the innovator, the government would require some basis for distinguishing among classes of innovation or innovators. The ignorance justification for intellectual property rights also justifies adopting uniform rights targeted at the average level of exclusion needed to stimulate the desired level of investment in innovation throughout the economy. The government initially lacks the information necessary to make principled distinctions among innovators or classes of innovation.

---

16 Agreement on Trade-Related Aspects of Intellectual Property Rights, Apr. 15, 1994, 33 ILM 81 (1994).

17 Grosse Ruse-Khan, Henning and Kur, Annette (2008), 'Enough is Enough – The Notion of Binding Ceilings in International Intellectual Property Protection', *Max Planck Institute for Intellectual Property, Competition & Tax Law Research Paper* Series No. 09-01, available at SSRN: http://ssrn.com/abstract=1326429.

18 Burk, D. and Lemley, M. (2003), 'Policy Levers in Patent Law', *Virginia Law Review*, 89 (7), pp. 1575–696.

Moreover, innovation is inherently dynamic.[19] The case for uniformity argues that even if the government were able to gather information sufficient to make a principled distinction between the rights accorded to innovation category *A* and innovation category *B*, the boundaries of those categories are likely to change. Technology-specific or subject matter-specific laws will become outdated quickly and therefore fail to provide the efficiency gains sought by tailoring. These practical obstacles to tailoring provide support for uniform rights as a second-best solution. Thus, uniform patents and copyrights are second-order second-best, or, in other words, a second-best solution nested within the second-best solution of intellectual property rights.

3.1.1. Tailoring through market exchange

The case for one-size-fits-all also holds that the intellectual property strategy has built-in features to reduce uniformity cost. The argument starts with a general proposition that generally defined rights are easy to ascertain ex ante and that any social costs arising from the choice of uniform rights do not warrant concern because once the rights vest, private ordering ensures that rewards generated by ownership of intellectual property rights flows to those who deserve the rewards.

As I previously have discussed at greater length, intellectual property rights harness three market-based features that reduce uniformity cost: demand elasticity, price discrimination and Coasean bargaining.[20] The social costs of intellectual property rights arise only when there is demand for protected information. If demand for a novelty toy that would have been invented in the absence of protection is 0, then even though granting uniform patent rights was unnecessary, uniformity cost is 0 because no potential buyers have been excluded. Uniformity cost rises with demand.

Even when uniformity cost arises, under traditional economic analysis, perfect price discrimination *theoretically* would eliminate the underdistribution of protected information. As others have shown, however, even as a matter of theory perfect price discrimination would not eliminate all social costs of intellectual property rights.[21] Moreover, even if perfect price discrimination would theoretically avoid reduction in social value,

---

[19] Merges, R. and Nelson, R. (1990), 'On the Complex Economics of Patent Scope', *Columbia Law Review*, 90 (4), pp. 839–917.

[20] Carroll, M. (2006), 'One for All: The Problem of Uniformity Cost in Intellectual Property Law', *American University Law Review*, 55 (4), pp. 845–900.

[21] Lunney, Jr., G. (2008), 'Copyright's Price Discrimination Panacea', *Harvard Journal of Law and Technology*, 21 (2), pp. 387–456; Frischmann, B. (2005), 'An Economic Theory of Infrastructure and Commons Management', *Minnesota*

perfect first-degree price discrimination in the intellectual property context is a practical impossibility.[22]

Finally, when demand is positive and price discrimination is imperfect, the Coase Theorem asserts that uniformity cost will affect *allocative* efficiency only if reallocation or reapportionment of uniform entitlements by contract is too costly.[23] Through licensing and non-enforcement of intellectual property rights, those who need to use another's information will obtain access and the practical ability to use it. Consequently, the theoretical advantages of publicly tailored rights are minimized by tailoring through private ordering supported by judicial and other public enforcement.

While licensing and enforcement practices undoubtedly relieve some of the pressure that a one-size-fits-all approach produces, it is not a complete solution. Most commentators agree that difficulties in valuing patents and copyrights raise transaction costs to the point that allocative efficiency will depend upon the subject matter, scope and duration of intellectual property entitlements.[24] This is particularly true because the externalities that justify patent and copyright law differ fundamentally from those that inspired Coase, and the law's choice is not between granting an entitlement to party *A* or to party *B* but between granting an entitlement to party *A* or to the public at large, comprised of an unknown and often unknowable proportion of higher- and lower-valued users. Consequently, allocative inefficiency in intellectual property law potentially imposes a far more significant social cost than it does with respect to tangible property. Uniformity cost is then a real problem in intellectual property law.

3.1.2. Tailoring through real options and standards

Recognizing uniformity cost, the proponent for one-size-fits-all patents and copyrights is likely to call attention to two strategies that patent and copyright law currently deploy to reduce the costs of one-size-fits-all rights. First, both bodies of law use real options by placing conditions

---

Law Review, 89 (4), pp. 917–1030; Meurer, M. (2001), 'Copyright Law and Price Discrimination', *Cardozo Law Review*, 23 (1), pp. 55–148.

22 Yoo, C. (2004), 'Copyright and Product Differentiation', *New York University Law Review*, 79 (1), pp. 212–80.

23 Coase, R. (1960), 'The Problem of Social Cost', *Journal of Law and Economics*, 3 (1), pp. 1–69.

24 Bessen, J. (2004), 'Holdup and Licensing of Cumulative Innovations with Private Information', *Economic Letters*, 82 (3), pp. 321–6; Long, C. (2000), 'Proprietary Rights and Why Initial Allocations Matter', *Emory Law Journal*, 49 (3), pp. 823–36.

on the full enjoyment of these rights. These options force potential rights owners to self-sort, thereby reducing social costs by tailoring the number of entitlements granted and producing coarse-grained information about the private valuation of the entitlement. Patent law uses the strategy more vigorously, requiring an inventor to undergo examination prior to acquiring a patent and further requiring payment of maintenance fees to retain rights during the full statutory duration of a patent.[25] By placing an option filter at both the front and back ends of the patent term, the law causes many inventions that satisfy the statutory subject matter criteria either not to be patented or to enter the public domain prior to expiration of the full term of protection.

Regrettably, in copyright law, the hostility to 'formalities' expressed in the Berne Convention as incorporated into TRIPS limits some uses of real options – such as a registration requirement or renewable terms of periods less that the life of the author plus 50 years.[26] In the United States, the only uses of the real-option design that remain are the registration requirement for initiating an infringement action with respect to US works and the conditional remedies tied to registration.[27] For this reason, the problem of uniformity cost has intensified in copyright law.

Second, when taken off the rack, a patent or a copyright appears to be only one size. But the fabric of both entitlements is elastic because the rights are defined by standards rather than rules. Thus, when measured by a court in the context of a particular case, the scope or size of a patent or copyright is necessarily tailored in some respects to conform often to industry-specific, technology-specific, or innovator-specific characteristics. Legal standards confer interpretive discretion on adjudicators. This interpretive discretion can be deployed ad hoc or systematically. With respect to the scope of intellectual property rights, courts can choose to use flexible doctrines to strike the incentives-access balance either on a per-work or per-invention basis, or more broadly along industry-specific or technology-specific lines.[28] In the case of patent injunctions, for example,

---

[25] Utility patents that issue from applications filed on and after December 12, 1980 are subject to the payment of maintenance fees necessary to maintain the patent in force. Fees are due 3½, 7½ and 11½ years from the date the patent is granted. 35 USC 41(b) (2000). A six-month grace period is provided during which the maintenance fee may be paid with a surcharge. 37 CFR § 1.362(e) (2005). Failure to pay the current maintenance fee on time may result in expiration of the patent.

[26] Springman, C. (2004), 'Reform(aliz)ing Copyright', *Stanford Law Review*, 57 (2), pp. 485–568.

[27] See 17 USC §§ 411, 412 (2006).

[28] Wagner, P. (2003), 'Of Patents and Path Dependency: A Comment on Burk and Lemley', *Berkeley Technology Law Journal*, 18 (4), pp. 1341–60.

the flexibility in the standard for relief should lead to industry-specific patterns because of industry-specific differences in facts that are salient under the standard.[29] Finally, after acknowledging that uniformity cost is real, the proponent would further defend uniform rights for the following reasons.

3.2. Administrative Cost

The uniform rights proponent, acknowledging difficulties in measuring the total social costs of intellectual property rights, is likely to have an intuitive sense that evidence of robust intellectual property licensing activity combined with legal entrepreneurship to reduce transaction costs through innovative licensing structures means that the magnitude of uniformity cost is not significant enough to justify very much tailoring. Digging in a little deeper, the proponent is likely to argue that broadly defined uniform rights facilitate licensing and enforcement, and so the policy choice really is one between tailoring through public or private ordering. On this view, the intellectual property system is rendered more administrable through broadly defined rights.

3.3. Political Economy

Certain considerations of political economy counsel in favor of uniformity as the default position for *domestic* policy. The strongest argument is that domestic uniformity disciplines or increases the costs of rent seeking by industries and other interest groups. Copyright and patent legislation serves for some as a paradigm public choice case because such legislation generally is the product of bargaining among industry groups with little or no consumer representation.[30] Commentators suggest that interest group involvement in copyright and patent legislation has intensified in recent years.[31] The argument for uniform rights holds that uniform patents or copyrights limits potential industry-based rent seeking because all

---

[29] Carroll, M. (2007), 'Patent Injunctions and the Problem of Uniformity Cost', *Michigan Telecommunications and Technology Law Review*, 13 (2), pp. 421–44.

[30] Litman, J. (2001), *Digital Copyright: Protecting Intellectual Property on the Internet*, Amherst, NY: Prometheus Books; Patry, W. (1996), 'Copyright and the Legislative Process: A Personal Perspective', *Cardozo Arts and Entertainment Law Journal*, 14 (1), pp. 139–52.

[31] Merges, R. (2000), '100 Years of Solicitude', *California Law Review*, 88 (6), pp. 2187–240.

industries affected by a proposed change must agree for an amendment to pass successfully through the many veto points in the legislative process. The argument then falls back. Even if a particular tailoring measure would have improved the efficiency of copyright law, legislative practice that would routinely grant additional rewards or create special carve-outs for individual interest groups would intensify the problems of rent seeking already apparent in the process.

It is very important to note that the topic of geographic or international uniformity should be kept quite distinct from the political economy argument for uniform rights in domestic law. Evidence that would support the discipline argument for domestic legislative policy does not equally support the argument for international harmonization. On the contrary, the average level of exclusion needed in any particular economy will vary in part depending on the extent to which it is a net importer or exporter of goods or services embodying protected information.[32] Thus, the push for international harmonization, which imposes the same average level of exclusion and is now encoded in the TRIPS Agreement, is best understood as successful rent seeking spearheaded by multinational rightsholding corporations headquartered in the United States, Europe and Japan.

4. A FRAMEWORK FOR TAILORING

Although proponents for domestic uniformity and international harmonization largely have the law on their side at the moment, the numerous multilateral treaties that specify minimum standards for patent and copyright law have tailored standards for certain subject matter. In addition, in the United States, for example, Congress has tailored rights granted by patent and copyright law in the United States along industry- or technology-specific lines in a number of instances, and the federal courts and relevant administrative agencies have further tailored the nominally uniform rights granted by patent and copyright law to apply differently with respect to certain kinds of invention and works of authorship.

Tailoring is not exclusively a matter of amending legislation. Instead, intellectual property law can be, and has been, tailored by (1) legislation, (2) judicial interpretation and evidentiary presumptions, and (3) administrative rules, statutory interpretation and adjudication. The point is important because judges and agency officials do not always view their

---

[32] Scotchmer, S. (2004), 'The Political Economy of Intellectual Property Treaties', *Journal of Law, Economics and Organization*, 20 (2), pp. 415–37.

interpretive practices as having the effect of tailoring the general standards of patent and copyright law, but in practice they have and, the framework proposed herein suggests, they should. In particular, the considerations of political economy within the framework suggest that judicial tailoring is likely to be the most efficiency-promoting form of tailoring patent and copyright law.

The framework proposed herein requires that three conditions be met for tailoring to be successful. First, the 'knowledge corollary' to the ignorance justification for intellectual property rights must be satisfied. Policymakers must have sufficiently reliable information about eliminable uniformity costs. It is likely that tailoring will have to be done on an industry-specific or technology-specific basis.[33] Second, any measures to tailor intellectual property rights so as to eliminate such uniformity costs should be administratively feasible and cost-effective – i.e., 'administrable'. Finally, considerations of political economy should influence the final design of any tailoring proposal with respect to its institutional form.

4.1. Substantial Evidence of Uniformity Cost

To satisfy the knowledge corollary, what kinds and how much evidence must a tailoring proponent adduce? The proponent's burden increases in rough proportion to the degree that a proposal calls for disaggregation of rights. For a proponent to establish a prima facie case that tailoring is appropriate under the first element within this framework, the proponent need only adduce substantial evidence of identifiable uniformity cost. The substantial evidence is evidence of a quantity and quality that 'a "reasonable mind might accept" a particular evidentiary record as "adequate to support a conclusion"'.[34] The quality and quantity of this evidence also will be relevant when assessing whether any added costs associated with administering tailored rights are justified, but these matters should be kept analytically distinct. Before we know when to tailor or whether existing tailoring promotes efficiency, we need a better idea of the kinds of evidence likely to support a particular case for tailoring. This subsection suggests the kinds of evidence likely to support a tailoring argument. The strength of that support varies with the scope of the proposal.

---

33 Levin, R., Klevorick, A., Nelson, R. and Winter, S. (1987), 'Appropriating the Returns from Industrial Research and Development', *Brookings Papers on Economic Activity*, 3, pp. 783–831.

34 *Dickinson v Zurko*, 527 US 150, 162 [1999].

4.1.1. Innovator incentives – when rights are wrong

Innovative activity appears to have many complicated motivations, and society may receive the benefits of certain forms of innovation even without extending rights sufficient to induce a rational, selfish actor to innovate.[35] Moreover, in some cases anticipated prestige, notoriety or other 'nonpecuniary income' would serve as a sufficient return on the investment to induce initial production in the absence of copyright or patent. Alternatively, the investment in initial production may serve as a loss-leader to increase other revenue streams, such as speaker's fees. Finally, firms in a competitive economy are under constant pressure to innovate to differentiate their products and services from their competitors even without the promise of exclusive rights.[36]

Using this kind of evidence to support a tailoring proposal may be difficult, however. One complication for the next stage of the analysis – administrability – is that there may be no feasible way to differentiate between those who would have created or innovated in a particular field without the promise of exclusive rights and those who require such a promise. Compare and contrast, for example, the numerous musicians who would compose and perform in a world without copyright with those creators driven by the thought of riches and fame underwritten by copyright. Similarly, consider those free and open source software programmers motivated by nonpecuniary factors – and these are not all such programmers – and those who rely on a proprietary strategy as their motivation.[37] With this kind of evidence of uniformity cost, the solution may be to place an option filter on otherwise uniform rights rather than seek to differentiate legislatively or judicially. Alternatively, policymakers could tailor the real options to apply only to certain classes of work.

4.1.2. Alternative appropriability mechanisms

Even for those creators and innovators who seek control over others' use of their creations and innovations as a means of extracting compensation, patents and copyrights usually supplement a range of other tools or strategies. Evidence that these other tools are particularly effective or ineffective in light of relevant cost structures would tend to show that uniform

---

[35] Cohen, J. (2007), 'Creativity and Copyright Theory', *University of California, Davis, Law Review*, 40 (3), pp. 1151–206; Amabile, T. (1996), *Creativity in Context*, US: Westview Press.

[36] Baker, J. (2007), 'Beyond Schumpeter vs. Arrow: How Antitrust Fosters Innovation', *Antitrust Law Journal*, 74 (3), pp. 575–602.

[37] Bitzer, J., Schrettl, W. and Schröder, P. (2007), 'Intrinsic Motivation in Open Source Software', *Journal of Comparative Economics*, 35 (1), pp. 160–69.

intellectual property rights are misaligned. In particular, evidence related to the following alternative mechanisms is likely to be highly probative.

Although granting exclusive rights remains the dominant policy tool, the government also directly and indirectly subsidizes some forms of information production through grants, rewards and tax incentives.[38] In the United States, the federal government funds approximately 25% of research and development, and in OECD countries, public sector investment approaches 50%.[39] Because the standard model recognizes that optimal protection must trade off solutions to the underproduction and underutilization problems, where the underproduction problem is solved through direct or indirect government investment, the level of protection should decrease to minimize deadweight losses from underutilization.

The other form of direct subsidy that should be squared with uniform intellectual property rights is prizes and rewards. Many of the modern implementations of this option, however, use it as a supplement rather than a substitute for intellectual property protection. The uniformity cost perspective suggests that this approach makes sense only if uniform rights are insufficiently robust to attract certain types of creative or innovative activity. As a middle ground, policymakers might permit winners to pursue or to retain intellectual property rights but might either require that the government receive a license to use and to sublicense or require the winner to agree to pursue open licensing.

Lead-time advantage and network effects are two market-specific economic phenomena that affect appropriability and innovator incentives and would therefore independently provide evidence relevant to a tailoring proposal. Lead-time or first-mover advantage is the most common market-specific appropriability feature that could be the basis for tailoring. Research indicates that the value of lead time often is industry specific,[40] and that in product markets with patentable goods, incumbents often enjoy significant market-share advantages even after competitors

---

38 Warda, J. (2006), 'Tax Treatment of Business Investments in Intellectual Assets: An International Comparison', OECD Directorate of Science Technology and Industry Working Paper 2006/4, available at http://www.oecd.org/dataoecd/53/4/36764076.pdf.

39 Menell, P. and Scotchmer, S. (2007), 'Intellectual Property', in Mitchell Polinsky, A. and Shavell, S. (eds), 2 *Handbook of Law and Economics*, Amsterdam: North-Holland pp. 1473–570.

40 See generally Lieberman, M. and Montgomery, D. (1998), 'First-Mover (Dis)Advantages: Retrospective and Link with the Resource-Based View', *Strategic Management Journal*, 19 (12), pp. 1111–25; Robinson, W., Kalyanaram, G. and Urban, G. L. (1994), 'First-Mover Advantages from Pioneering New Markets', *Review of Industrial Organization*, 9 (1), pp. 1–23.

have entered a market.[41] The value of the lead-time advantage is affected not only by its duration but also by competitors' copying costs. One study shows that imitation costs for patentable goods can run to about 65% of the costs of innovation.[42] However, about 70% of the goods studied were patented and 'imitation costs' included the costs of inventing around the patent. Consequently, this data does not translate immediately into the costs of competition in markets without intellectual property rights. If expected profits derived from this lead-time or first-mover advantage are sufficient to recoup the costs of initial production, the case for government intervention largely disappears. The best case for tailoring based on lead-time profits would be one in which intellectual property rights should be treated as superfluous on both sides of the ledger, but rightsholders use the rights to engage in strategic litigation that squeezes additional rents from competitors and consumers with no offsetting social benefits.

A second market-based feature that might justify tailoring is the presence of strong network effects. A tailoring proponent relying on evidence of network effects would likely argue that a producer in a market with network externalities may have a number of ways to recoup the costs of initial production even in the absence of exclusive rights.[43] Economists distinguish between markets involving actual networks, virtual networks and positive feedback effects, and these distinctions could impact the strength of a tailoring proposal.[44] Evidence of network externalities may support a shift from a property to a liability rule to provide a form of rate-of-return regulation of a 'natural' monopoly.[45] For example, evidence of a market exhibiting strong network effects because of demand for standardization may support proposals to permit reverse engineering to allow competitive entry. Patent law currently does not recognize a reverse-engineering defense, although some scholars have offered proposals either for a generalized fair use defense that could be adapted to market circumstances or more tailored proposals to permit reverse engineering.[46]

---

[41] Barnett, J. (2004), 'Private Protection of Patentable Goods', *Cardozo Law Review*, 25 (4), pp. 1251–314.

[42] Mansfield, E., Schwartz, M. and Wagner, S. (1981), 'Imitation Costs and Patents: An Empirical Study', *Economic Journal*, 97 (388), pp. 907–18.

[43] Frank, R. and Cook, P. (1995), *The Winner-Take-All Society: Why the Few at the Top Get So Much More Than the Rest of Us*, US: Free Press.

[44] Lemley, M. and McGowan, D. (1998), 'Legal Implications of Network Economic Effects', *California Law Review*, 86 (3), pp. 479–612.

[45] Lemley, M. and Weiser, P. (2007), 'Should Property or Liability Rules Govern Information?', *Texas Law Review*, 85 (4), pp. 783–842.

[46] Samuelson, P. and Scotchmer, S. (2002), 'The Law and Economics of Reverse Engineering', *Yale Law Journal*, 111 (7), pp. 1575–664; O'Rourke, M.

Evidence of strong network effects pose one particular challenge to tailoring proponents, however. If network effects coupled with exclusive rights confer substantial market power, is tailoring intellectual property rights superior to policing abuses of such market power through competition law instead? A tailoring proponent would have to account for the role of competition law in network markets, and it may be more efficient to leave uniform intellectual property rights intact and to adapt their actual reach through judicial application coupled with enforcement under competition law.

4.1.3. Overlapping rules and rights

Two common legal features that intellectual property owners factor into their appropriability calculus is the availability of other legal rights of exclusion, such as trade secret, trademark, or contract law, and regulatory requirements in the marketing and distribution of creations or innovations. Patent and copyright law already have been tailored to respond to these features in some respects. For example, with respect to overlapping rights, trade secret law provides a liability rule substrate to the property-rule regimes of patent and copyright.[47]

As important, product differentiation strategies supported by trademark law supply an important source of power over price. The effects of trademark and trade secret protection may be sufficient to induce the desired level of investment even in the absence of copyright or patent rights in some cases.[48] Moreover, the exclusivity provided by copyright or patent rights facilitates the producer's ability to establish strong, highly distinctive marks.[49]

4.1.4. Fragmentation and market failure

The flipside of overlapping rights are rights that are too finely grained to support the innovative investments or activities in a particular industry or context. In such cases, problems of anticommons may emerge. Tailoring proponents may propose measures that consolidate rights, increase limitations or exceptions to the rights, or tailor remedies to offer only liability rule protection of the rights.

(2000), 'Toward a Doctrine of Fair Use in Patent Law', *Columbia Law Review*, 100 (5), pp. 1177–250.

47 Reichman, J. (1994), 'Legal Hybrids between the Patent and Copyright Paradigms', *Columbia Law Review*, 94 (8), pp. 2432–558.

48 Kieff, S. (2006), 'Property & Intellectual Property: An Unconventional Approach to Anticompetitive Effects & Downstream Access', *Emory Law Journal*, 56 (2), pp. 327–438.

49 Parchomovsky, G. and Siegelman, P. (2002), 'Towards an Integrated Theory of Intellectual Property', *Virginia Law Review*, 88 (7), pp. 1455–528.

4.1.5. Demand-side features – positive spillovers

Even if uniform rights suited information producers to a tee, a good argument for tailoring rights could be derived from evidence of certain positive externalities, or spillovers, on the demand side. Where the evidence shows that patented or copyrighted information serves as an input to a range of private and public goods, a tailoring proponent may seek to propose limitations or exceptions for the producers of public goods while leaving exclusive rights intact as against the producers of private goods. Much of the recent commentary calling for revitalized experimental use exception to patent infringement or for tailoring of patent law with respect to university researchers follows this line.[50]

4.1.6. Industrial innovation decision structures

Economic analysis to date suggests that the magnitude of appropriability problems varies by industry, and tailoring proposals are likely to call for line drawing along industry lines. Policymakers should recognize the effect on industry structure and degree of competitive entry influenced by the subject matter and scope of intellectual property rights, and policymakers should tailor rights to modulate the degree of entry depending upon industry maturity and other competitive conditions.[51] Where intellectual property rights are robust, innovation decisions are likely to be made within hierarchal firms that own these rights, and the willingness of these firms to grant licenses to follow-on innovators who may become competitors is suspect. In contrast, where intellectual property rights are subject to significant limitations or exceptions, innovation decisions are likely to be made polyarchically.[52] Evidence of industry maturity, licensing incentives, and other factors effecting competitive entry would be relevant to tailoring proposals along industry-specific lines.

4.2. Administrability

Tailored provisions of the law succeed when the distinctions drawn are jurisprudentially stable and administratively cost-effective. I combine these two measures into the metric of administrability. If the economic

---

[50] Hagelin, T. (2006), 'The Experimental Use Exemption to Patent Infringement: Information on Ice, Competition on Hold', *Florida Law Review*, 58 (3), pp. 483–561.

[51] Merges, R. and Nelson, R. (1990), 'On the Complex Economics of Patent Scope', *Columbia Law Review*, 90 (4), pp. 839–917.

[52] Wu, T. (2006), 'Intellectual Property, Innovation, and Decision Architectures', *Virginia Law Review*, 92 (1), 123–48.

evidence from the first step of the analysis shows that uniformity cost is particularly problematic with respect to certain subject matter, a particular industry, or a particular class of innovator, such as employees of universities, then the legal analysis turns to the question of institutional form.

Once specific uniformity costs have been identified, the proponent must also show that it would administratively feasible to tailor rights and that doing so would be cost justified. Demonstrating feasibility means showing (1) that the law can adequately delineate the subject matter governed by tailored rights and (2) that such distinctions will be stable enough in practice to defeat arbitrage by clever attorneys.[53] If tailored rights result in significantly differential treatment of works under copyright law or inventions under patent law, parties would have an incentive to characterize works in a less protected category as works belonging to a category with greater protection.

Demonstrating that tailored rights are cost-justified also requires attention to the costs of complexity, including impacts on licensing and litigation as the parties and the courts incur greater education costs to master the more complex rules. The working assumption for many lawyers appears to be that greater complexity in the law necessarily leads to greater administrative costs. However, where a proponent has shown that the risk of arbitrage can be minimized because legal terminology has relatively stable meanings, greater complexity may actually reduce licensing and litigation costs by creating better-tailored default rules.

Nonetheless, concerns about greater administrative costs and legal arbitrage rightly counsel caution when analyzing the desirability of tailoring. These concerns also lead one to favor the more flexible approach of judicial tailoring when a desirable change in the law can be accomplished either judicially or legislatively. But some dimensions of the current rights structure can be altered only legislatively, and we should opt for this approach when the costs of uniformity are particularly high in a given context.

4.3. Political Economy

Tailoring proposals will likely hit their toughest sledding when faced with the political economy defense for uniformity. On balance, considerations of political economy support an argument that tailoring through judicial or administrative interpretation is more likely to succeed than legislative tailoring. As public choice theory suggests, the risk of an environment

---

53 Gallini and Scotchmer (2002), *supra* note 1.

more conducive to special pleading is highest when expanded rights would increase private profits for the majority of industry players while increasing social cost. The fear that this will routinely be the case should be diminished by recognition that all information-intensive sectors treat information as both input and output. As long as a substantial subset of industry players is more concerned about access to inputs than control over outputs, the public choice risks associated with a more tailoring-friendly legislative environment are lower than advertised.

Since overall the legislative record shows a trend toward expansion of the subject matter, scope and duration of intellectual property rights resulting from consensus among information-intensive industry groups that greater control is worth more than easier access, the discipline argument must show that this trend would be steeper in a tailoring-friendly environment. As with the rest of the framework, arguments about the likely effects of political economy on any particular tailoring proposal or class of proposals should be based on evidence. Categorical dismissal of legislative tailoring as efficiency-promoting is not supported by the evidence.

The reason to be skeptical about the likelihood that legislative tailoring will succeed is not so much that industry groups will more successfully seek rents, but that interest groups will be more successful than in the courts at killing or diluting tailoring measures that would improve the efficiency of the law by constraining subject matter, scope or duration. This is because the current subject matter, scope and duration provisions of patent and copyright law indicate that most uniformity costs result from overprotection rather than underprotection. Starting from this statutory baseline, industry-specific legislative tailoring pursuant to the knowledge corollary likely would involve reducing protection for given industries. Because political economy raises particular risks for legislative tailoring, a more immediately attainable goal for using the knowledge corollary to reduce deadweight loss is to improve industry-specific tailoring in the courts.

5. CONCLUSION

The framework proposed herein refines the empirical questions that should be asked and answered to improve intellectual property policy. One-size-fits-all patents and copyrights are necessarily inefficient even after one accounts for the various ways in which market measures, real options and flexible standards can be used to reduce uniformity cost. Ultimately, intellectual property law still needs tailoring, and it has been tailored by legislatures, courts and administrative agencies over time. The framework for tailoring focuses analysis on the relative abilities of government officials or private creators or innovators to pick winners in the innovative and creative fields of endeavor, the administrability of a particular policy and the considerations of political economy that should influence any ultimate policy proposals.

3. Patents and progress: the economics of patent monopoly and free access: where do we go from here?

Rudolph J.R. Peritz*

Some chapters in this collection discuss the grounds for protecting intellectual property rights. This chapter is one of several that investigate the other side – the public domain and free access. It takes an economic perspective, taking as its point of departure a landmark article about patents written in 1950 by two economists, Fritz Machlup and Edith Penrose.

Questions about the public domain and free access span the entire array of intellectual property rights – from patent to copyright to trademark, and beyond. For advocates of free access, patents present a more difficult policy problem than copyright and trademark, in my view, because patents do not have an obvious free expression connection or cultural component to invite open access. Both copyright and trademark have fair use defenses that, in the US, stand shoulder to shoulder with freedom of expression and a socio-political marketplace of ideas. US patent law has no fair use defense and its experimental use defense is only a mirage. Patent's marketplace of ideas stands in the shadow of commercial markets for goods and services, and for technology transfer.

That is not to say there is no overlap or common ground; perhaps the most interesting and challenging overlap involves computer software, although, even there, inventors look more like authors of textual invention.

In any event, patent scholarship, if not patent protection, has been a breed apart. When patent scholars have written about access and the public domain, they have addressed technological development and economic growth. Thus access and the public domain in patent policy have been synonymous with commercial competition policy rather than freedom of expression.

* Professor of Law and Director, IProgress Project, New York Law School.

And so this chapter takes up the harder question – What do we know better about free access to patented inventions in the 60 years since Fritz Machlup and Edith Penrose wrote about it?

Let's begin with what the article taught us. Machlup and Penrose[1] wrote an article entitled 'The Patent Controversy in the Nineteenth Century' for an American readership because they wanted to dispel the widespread American misperception that patent protection had always been accepted as an unquestionable benefit to society. As the title suggests, the article demonstrated that the belief was historically inaccurate.

What is stunning about the article is that the arguments and policy questions they raised remain front and center almost 60 years later. The article recounts the four major arguments posed to justify patent protection. Two can be understood as moral arguments about the distributive justice, the fairness, of a patent regime and two as economic arguments about its social utility.[2] One of the social utility arguments is that patents provide inventors with the best incentive to invent. This familiar argument is the constitutionally inscribed basis for patent protection in the United States, and although all four arguments retain some appeal around the world, patent policy analysts have focused almost entirely on the incentive theory for patent protection.

Yet economics scholars and researchers have not resolved the fundamental question whether society is better off with patent protection than with free access to copy, imitate, improve, and surpass the inventive work of others.

So what have they been doing for 60 years? To address this question, the chapter takes a quick look at the theoretical work and empirical studies

---

1 Machlup, Fritz and Penrose, Edith (1950), 10 *Journal of Economic History* 1.

2 This chapter is a lightly edited version of the talk presented at the Munich conference. The underlying research paper, entitled 'Patents and Progress: The Incentive Conundrum', is a work in progress that was distributed at the conference. Send requests to Rudolph.Peritz@nyls.edu. For available work that includes bibliographic materials referenced in this chapter, see Peritz, Rudolph (2009), 'Thinking about Economic Progress: Arrow and Schumpeter in Time and Space', in Drexl, Josef (ed.), *Liber Amicorum for Hanns Ullrich*, Bruxelles: Larcier Pub.; Peritz, Rudolph 'Competition *within* Intellectual Property Regimes – The Instance of Patent Rights', in Ezrahi, Ariel and Anderman, Steven D. (eds), *Intellectual Property and Competition Law: New Frontiers*, Oxford, UK: forthcoming 2011. For a narrower law and economics approach that reaches similar conclusions, see Landes, William and Posner, Richard (2003), *The Economic Structure of Intellectual Property Law*, Cambridge, MA: Harvard University Press 9–10, pp. 294–333 (discussing economic indeterminacy of patent regime as means to promote economic progress).

about patents and progress. It concludes with a few observations about scholarly work that seeks to expand the debate about free access beyond the mainstream economic analysis.

First, the theoretical literature.

Two works by economists laid the foundation – one by Fritz Machlup himself and the other by Nobel Laureate Kenneth Arrow.

In 1958, Machlup delivered a report to Congress entitled 'An Economic Review of the Patent System'. The 90-page document synthesized two centuries of economic scholarship and then developed a framework for future empirical research. Here is the Report's conclusion:

> None of the empirical evidence at our disposal and none of the theoretical arguments presented either confirms or confutes the belief that the patent system has promoted the progress of the technical arts and the productivity of the economy.

What's to be done? 'Muddle through', he wrote. Why? Because 'we have had a patent system for a long time,' he declared, 'it would be irresponsible, on the basis of our present knowledge, to abolish it'. And so to 'muddle through', as he called it, Machlup developed a nine-step analysis for evaluating the economic links from patent protection to technological development and economic growth. Despite some shortcomings, this remarkable template remains an insightful and useful guide for 'muddling through' an economic analysis of patent policy.

As a general matter, 20th century patent theorists have divided into two camps – one calling for stronger patent rights for current inventors and the other for more access for future inventors. Both sides claim their proposals would encourage inventive activity and promote progress. Surprisingly perhaps, both have taken their cue from the same 1962 paper by Nobel Laureate Kenneth Arrow.[3]

Arrow questioned the impact of competition on incentives to invent. For economists, perfect competition is the Holy Grail. Its miraculous power produces allocative efficiency by taking society's resources and putting them to their highest and best uses. But Arrow argued that perfectly competitive markets fail. They fail to encourage inventors to invent.

You've heard Arrow's story before. Without patent protection, inventions are easily copied or imitated. Free access to their ideas discourages inventors from inventing and, thus, harms society. Patent rights correct

---

[3] Arrow, K.J. (1962), 'Economic Welfare and the Allocation of Resources for Invention', in Nelson, R. (ed.), *The Rate and Direction of Inventive Activity: Economic and Social Factors*, Princeton, NJ: Princeton University Press.

this market failure by allowing inventors to profit and society to benefit from increased invention. Patent protection and the profits it generates are the means to an end. Patents are private rights that produce the public benefits of technological advancement and economic progress.

And so Arrow postulates a trade-off between perfect competition and patent protection from competition. In the short run, patent protection raises prices from competitive levels and thus misallocates society's resources. But in the long run, those higher prices create the very incentives needed for more invention and, with it, the technological progress and economic growth that benefit society most. Patent protection is a trade-off between current costs and future gains.[4]

Theoretical analysis of patent protection has largely taken Arrow's trade-off as its point of departure and, for the most part, has focused on the long-run effects. In addition to the body of work elaborating the social benefit side of Arrow's trade-off, four major clusters of theoretical scholarship have developed.

One group has focused on particular industrial sectors. Two sets of sectoral studies present an interesting contrast. The pharmaceuticals literature asserts that the high costs of research and low costs of imitation make patent protection particularly important there, while the information technology literature claims that patent protection is counterproductive in that sector because invention depends on collaboration and free access to prior art. Still, it's important to recognize that any sectoral analysis must be understood in the context of broader economic circumstances. If, for example, we take as plausible the arguments in both the pharmaceuticals and software literatures, a change in patent policy that benefits one sector might harm others. But it's the overall effect we're interested in.

A second group of scholars *has* explored the broader economic circumstances. They point out that the social costs of patent rights run high for many reasons. Perhaps the greatest is the opportunity cost. Resources drawn to research by the promise of patents would have been put to any number of other uses and would have produced other social benefits, perhaps greater benefits. Determining these opportunity costs is particularly troublesome because experimental design of empirical studies has presented intractable problems.

In their 2003 book, law and economics practitioners William Landes and Richard Posner conclude that 'the high social costs of intellectual property rights create uncertainty as to whether on balance such rights are,

---

4 Arrow poses several hypothetical situations that mix competition and monopoly, situations that are discussed in the research paper.

from an overall social standpoint, cost-justified at all'. They acknowledge the indeterminacy of Arrow's trade-off and stitch together an appealing patchwork of narrow economic objectives, objectives which are themselves plausible but debatable. Nevertheless, Landes and Posner assemble a useful economic toolkit that advances policy analysis beyond an ill-conceived reliance on traditional incentive theory.

A third segment of the theoretical literature has emerged from the work of economist Edmund Kitch,[5] who took Arrow's trade-off as the starting point for what he called prospect theory. Like the prospector who discovers gold, the inventor should be rewarded with extensive control over her discovery. Prospect theory has elicited a wide array of views about the optimal scope and depth of patent rights. In any case, it raises a fundamental policy question insofar as it proposes that patents should encourage commercialization of existing inventions rather than discovery of new ones. The problem, of course, is that given scarce capital resources, more investment in commercialization leaves less for invention.

Fourth and finally, a cluster of economists questions Arrow's very formulation of a trade-off. In particular, they argue that patent protection is not necessary because competitive markets tend to produce sufficient invention. This view is particularly appealing to those who want free access to use other's inventions. I take this up in my concluding remarks.

In summary, the theoretical literature presents a series of reasonable but contestable arguments for both patent protection and free access to use.

Perhaps the theoretical impasse should be taken as an invitation to transform the question into an empirical matter. What of the empirical literature?

A wide array of studies has developed various data sets to investigate different proxies for economic progress. Researchers have interviewed corporate decision makers; they have measured research and development expenditures or patenting activity on the input side, and productivity gains or economic growth on the output side. Studies have looked at single sectors, individual countries, and across countries.

The longest series of studies developed interview data from senior executives in the research and development departments of commercial firms. Five studies between 1959 and 2001 all reached the same conclusion: The prospect of patent protection was typically a factor of third or fourth order importance to research and development decisions, with the

---

5 Kitch, Edmund (1977), 'The Nature and Function of the Patent System', 2 *Journal of Law and Economics* 266 (describing the prospect theory of reward to encourage commercialization).

exception of the drug industry and perhaps chemicals. It should be remembered that these studies investigate the private value of patents; public benefits are not addressed.

Other recent studies have inquired into the public benefits by looking at the relationship between changes in patent protection and changes in research and development expenditures. Japanese and US studies found the data inconclusive. One study across 29 countries found a positive correlation and another across 60 countries found a weak negative one. Moreover, there have been mixed findings in studies of the impact of patent protection on the ultimate economic goal of increasing growth. In sum, the empirical literature on public benefits is inconclusive.

Regardless of their findings, all of the empirical work confronts methodological difficulties. Here are two. First, the variables used are controversial. The uses of patent counts, citations, or renewal rates as measures of technological progress have all been criticized, as has the use of research and development expenditure data. Simply counting patents, for example, does not take into account differences in their importance and social value. And more R&D spending does not necessary lead to more or better inventions or, further, to economic progress.

There is a second methodological difficulty – the intractable problem of disentangling patent or R&D data from other sources of economic growth. Arthur Leff,[6] a noted American legal scholar put the general problem of disentanglement this way: 'If a state of affairs is the product of *n* variables, and you have knowledge of or control over less than *n* variables, if you think you know what's going to happen when you vary "your" variables, you're a booby'.

The empirical literature's indeterminacy is no less daunting than the theoretical impasse that accompanies it. Small wonder, then, that so many policy makers have turned to what seems to be the next best alternative, the simplistic and mistaken focus on the means itself – on strengthening patent protection.

Why have so many policy makers in the US been persuaded to champion stronger patent rights? An easy answer comes from the public choice literature, from economist George Stigler's[7] conception of government as a market in which private interests purchase favorable regulation, such

---

[6] Leff, Arthur A. (1974), 'Economic Analysis of Law: Some Realism about Nominalism', 60 *Virginia Law Review* 451, 476 (reviewing Richard Posner (1973), *Economic Analysis of Law*).

[7] Stigler, George J. (1956), 'Industrial Organization and Economic Practice', in White, Leonard D. (ed.), *The State of the Social Sciences*, Chicago: Chicago University Press.

as patent protection. But that answer is partial at best, because private interests and their lobbyists need more than money. At the very least, they need intellectual capital. They need rationales that can be expressed in the rhetoric of public interest.

Private interests have such a rationale for expanding patent protection and closing public access to use. It is a public interest rhetoric that stems from a widespread misunderstanding which equates private value and public benefit. Simply put, the misunderstanding is that the public benefits whenever inventors and their firms benefit from patents. But inventors can be better off, firms more profitable, but society worse off when, for example, the resources applied to invention could have been put to a better use. I call this gap between public benefit and private value, patent's incentive conundrum. The incentive conundrum confuses or provides rhetorical cover for too many patent apologists.

If this confusion of public benefit with private gain can be lifted, what's to be done? Four interesting alternatives have been put forward.

First, some scholars believe that patent policy should be kept much as it is, that the best we can do is to make the patent system more efficient by clarifying the judicial rules and improving the administrative procedures. Beyond the spate of articles and books about it, one notable effort to effect change is New York Law School's ongoing pilot project at the US Patent Office. The project takes a Wiki approach to improving the process of determining non-obviousness by inviting outside experts to submit prior art references to assist patent examiners, references which are publicly available and contestable.

A second approach seeks to expand the competition side of Arrow's trade-off by opening access to patented inventions. In this view, competition and not patent monopoly is the preferable means for promoting progress. This open access approach has had several variants.

The best-known variant of the open access approach takes up Isaac Newton's image of standing on the shoulders of giants, an image Newton himself borrowed. These scholars reason that free access improves the conditions for invention because, as one economist[8] put it, 'the higher the level of disembodied knowledge, the more "soil" exists upon which innovation . . . can work and the higher the rate of technical progress'. The mixed metaphor of disembodied soil is unfortunate but the clear intent is to justify free access.

In a slight variation, other economists have concluded that wider access

---

[8] Romer, Paul (1990), 'Endogenous Technological Chance', 98 *Journal of Political Economy* 71 (October).

to patented inventions benefits society because multiple points of invention improve the conditions for technological improvement. To invent a solution, two heads are better than one, three better than two, and so on. These scholars all call for more widespread access to patented inventions, again to encourage competition and thereby improve the conditions for invention.

In another variant of the open access movement, some economists reject Arrow's trade-off as the proper analytical framework. For example, in a recent book and a series of articles, two economists[9] have demonstrated that patent protection is not necessary because real markets naturally produce time lags that allow inventors to collect 'competitive rents' – meaning higher than competitive profits – long enough to attract adequate resources for future invention. In this view, the best trade-off for improving social welfare is to minimize patent protection, and to maximize open competition and free access to use.

Some policy analysts have moved beyond traditional economic formulations to a third alternative. They urge consideration of exogenous alternatives, exogenous in that they reject entirely the terms of Arrow's efficiency trade-off between competition and patent monopoly. Perhaps best known is the open-source movement, which emerged from the communitarian ethic that produced Linux software and the early Internet culture. The communitarian credo of open-source production is that cooperation and sharing create better software as well as better social relations than competition and proprietary ownership.

This communitarian logic is not limited to the open-source movement. It encompasses as well the work of activists and economists like Nobel Laureate Amartya Sen,[10] for whom distributional goals rather than efficiency concerns are central tenets that should guide human rights, trade, and development policies. The three policies have coalesced most visibly in the initiatives to distribute life-saving pharmaceuticals to third-world countries, particularly AIDS drugs in southern Africa.

I close by mentioning a final approach, a growing body of scholarship that takes the indeterminacy of the Arrow trade-off as an opportunity to expand the scope of patent policy beyond economic metrics of both efficiency and distribution. To economists, this approach is truly radical. Here progress means more than technological improvement, and free

---

9 Boldrin, Michele and Levine, David (2005), 'The Economics of Ideas and Intellectual Property', 102 *Proceedings of the National Academy of Sciences*.

10 Sen, Amartya (1999), *Development as Freedom*, Oxford: Oxford University Press.

access means more than competitive markets, more even than equitable distribution of society's material resources. It extends the meaning of open access to embrace a social process for determining what *should* be encouraged – for example, for asking why patent policy rewards equally those who invent life-saving drugs, new tobacco products, and garbage bags with holiday designs. It means respecting the cultural and religious values of indigenous peoples, as well as acknowledging their contributions. The daunting challenge here is to respect local decision making and at the same time satisfy worldwide needs for technological advancement and economic growth.

In a nutshell, what do we know? First, the economics literature is inconclusive on whether patent protection is more effective than competition in promoting technological improvement and economic growth. In other words, even if patents provide incentives for inventors to invent more and they get rich, we don't know whether that promotes society's progress. It's a conundrum. Second, there is a plausible economic rationale to support open competition and free access over patent protection. Third, there is a growing socio-economic literature that rejects the entire formulation, the trade-off between competition and patent monopoly, in favor of other social values, such as fair distribution of society's resources, and cooperation and sharing as the best model for technological advancement and social welfare more generally.

The economic logic of dynamic efficiency cannot deliver technical solutions to patent policy questions of economic progress. It turns out that patent policy is best understood as 'muddling through' hard choices based on economically informed estimates and qualitative judgments about social welfare broadly conceived.

4. Comment: some economic considerations regarding optimal intellectual property protection

Claudia Schmidt*

1. INTRODUCTION

Since the landmark articles of Fritz Machlup[1] and Edith Penrose,[2] economic scholars and researchers have put a lot of effort into further illuminating and deepening the economic analysis of the social value of patents. However, although a lot of research has been undertaken, lawyers and legal scholars often complain that no significant advancements have been made in the literature. According to these complaints, although in some cases economics proves positive for the patent system, both empirical and theoretical results in economic theory on (overall) social benefits are indecisive: On the one hand we can assume that patent incentives attract resources to the production of patentable inventions, that is, patents offer incentives to innovators. At the same time, we cannot be sure that society will be better off because of the patents. In other words, critics of the economic theory of patents argue that the results are rather inconclusive.[3]

I strongly disagree with this conclusion. The results of economic works are not necessarily inconclusive; rather it is not possible to make an overall assessment of the intellectual property system in general or the patent system in detail. Instead, economic results show an inevitable differentiation. In certain cases and to a certain extent, patents are not necessary to promote innovation, that is, to appropriate the returns of research

* Research Assistant, Chair of Economic Policy, Philipps University of Marburg, Germany.

1 Machlup, Fritz (1958), *An Economic Review of the Patent System*. Washington: US Government Printing Office.

2 Penrose, Edith (1959), *The Theory of the Growth of the Firm*. London: Basil Blackwell.

3 Compare the contribution of Rudy Peritz (Chapter 3) in this publication.

and development efforts. In these cases, incorrectly defined intellectual property rights create inefficiencies and thereby lead to a reduction in social welfare.[4] Rather than focussing on the question as to whether we need a patent or intellectual property rights system at all, we should use our knowledge to minimize welfare losses caused by inefficiently designed intellectual property rights.

In the following section, I will give a few examples to explain why we should redefine our intellectual property rights system before going on to explain what should be considered in achieving this redefinition.

2. DIFFERING RELEVANCE OF INTELLECTUAL PROPERTY RIGHTS

In economics, we generally argue that intellectual property rights are justified because they aim at the promotion of innovation or, in other words, at the enhancement of total welfare. Still, intellectual property rights provide not only benefits for the innovator, but induce a reduction of welfare due to monopoly-pricing, at least in the short run.[5] Thus, to avoid an unduly broad welfare loss, an efficient design of intellectual property rights demands a balancing between the rights of the innovator, the rights of competing or later innovators and, of course, the rights of the public.

What is often overlooked is that, besides intellectual property rights, firms and investors also make use of a range of other instruments and mechanisms to appropriate the fruits of their labour. Several empirical studies show that IP protection, especially patents, play only a minor role in securing the returns of investments in innovation. For example, a study of Mansfield found out that, aside from pharmaceutical and chemical industries, 80 to 90 per cent of inventions would have been made in the absence of patent protection.[6]

---

4 Kerber, Wolfgang and Schmidt, Claudia (2008), 'Microsoft, Refusal to License Intellectual Property Rights, and the Incentives Balance Test of the EU Commission', Working Paper, http://papers.ssrn.com/sol3/papers.cfm?abstract_id=1297939, accessed 15 January 2009; Schmidt, Claudia (2010), *Refusal to License Intellectual Property Rights as Abuse of Dominance*, Frankfurt am Main: Peter Lang.

5 For a more sophisticated description of this economic problem, see Menell, Peter S. and Scotchmer, Suzanne (2007), 'Intellectual Property Law', in Polinsky, A. Mitchell and Shavell, Steven (eds), *Handbook of Law and Economics,* vol. 2, Oxford: Elsevier, pp. 1476–8.

6 Mansfield, Edwin (1986), 'Patents and Innovation: An Empirical Study', *Management Science*, 32 (2), pp. 173–81.

The use of patents also differs between 'complex' and 'discrete' product industries. Complex products industries are those in which a product is protected by a large number of patents, while discrete product industries are those in which a product is relatively simple and therefore associated with a small number of patents. In complex product industries, patents are used to block rival use of components and to acquire bargaining strength in cross-licensing negotiations. In contrast, discrete product industries use patents to block substitutes by creating patent 'fences'.[7]

Moreover, these empirical studies show that firms also rely on other appropriability instruments like first-mover advantages (or lead-time) and secrecy. The first-mover advantage describes the benefits of being first on the market, for example, the possibility of establishing publicity and profiting from learning curve effects. These results can be illustrated by a survey in Cohen, Nelson and Walsh (2000).[8] In their survey, they asked firms to rate the effectiveness of different appropriability mechanisms and furthermore, to specify why they patent innovations at all.

Table 4.1 reflects the mean percentage of product innovations for which the different appropriation mechanisms were evaluated to be effective.[9] In studying the table, at least two facts become obvious: first, the importance of patents varies greatly. In some industries, the value of patents seems to be decisive for innovation, whereas in other industries their value seems negligible. In the motor industry, for instance, patents are rated to be effective for approximately 25 per cent of innovations, whereas in the drugs industry or in the industry for medical equipment they were evaluated as effective for more than 50 per cent of innovations.[10] Second, we can

---

[7] Dosi, Giovanni, Marengo, Luigi and Pasquali, Corrado (2006), 'How Much should Society Fuel the Greed of Innovators? On the Relations between Appropriability, Opportunities and Rates of Innovation', *Research Policy*, 35, pp. 1110–21.

[8] Cohen, Wesley M., Nelson, Richard R. and Walsh, John P. (2000), 'Protecting their Intellectual Assets: Appropriability Conditions and Why U.S. Manufacturing Firms Patent (or Not)', Working Paper 7752, www.nber.org/papers/w7742, accessed 15 January 2009.

[9] This table shows only a small subset of the interviewed firms. I chose the industries in order to show how patents are important over a broad range of sectors. For the complete results, compare Cohen et al. (2000), *supra* note 8, p. 32.

[10] As Cohen et al. point out, even though the numbers can tell us the percentage of effective appropriability mechanisms, these numbers do not say anything about the importance of innovation. For example, even if in the motor industry patents are only effective for 25 per cent of inventions, we do not know the extent to which the firms' volume of sales or revenue depends on this 25 per cent. It might well be that this 25 per cent of inventions accounts for 75 per cent of all inventions (Cohen et al. (2000), *supra* note 8, p. 6).

Table 4.1 Effectiveness of appropriability mechanisms for product innovations

Industry	N	Secrecy	Patents	Other Legal	Lead Time	Complementary Sales/ Service	Complementary Manuf.
Food	89	58.54	**18.26**	21.18	53.37	39.83	51.18
Chemicals	65	52.7	**37.46**	21.62	48.62	44.92	41.31
Drugs	49	53.57	**50.20**	20.82	50.10	33.37	49.39
Medical Equipment	67	50.97	**54.70**	29.03	58.06	52.31	49.25
Aerospace	48	55.10	**39.92**	16.15	58.02	34.58	46.88
Motor/ Generator	22	50.91	**25.23**	19.09	48.86	47.27	45.23
Computers	25	44.20	**41.00**	27.20	61.40	40.20	38.00

Source: Cohen et al. (2000) (emphasis).

say that firms rely on a bundle of appropriability mechanisms, rather than just one.[11] No firm seems to rely exclusively on patents; even pharmaceutical industries like the drugs industry, which rely heavily on patents, also profit from lead-time or secrecy to a high degree.[12] Generally, the survey found that even though in some industries patents are very important, in no industry are they rated as the most important appropriability mechanism.[13] Figure 4.1 illustrates these results.

According to Figure 4.1, patents generally play only a minor role in appropriating the returns of research and development investments. On average, for product innovations, lead-time and secrecy seem to be the most important appropriation mechanisms. These results differ slightly in relation to process innovations but, once again, the role of patents is negligible, whereas secrecy and complementary manufacturing are on average the most important appropriability mechanisms.[14]

---

[11] Cohen et al. (2000), *supra* note 8, p. 8.

[12] Cohen et al. (2000), *supra* note 8, p. 9.

[13] Ibid.

[14] Besides these empirical findings, there are also theoretical models highlighting the role of (prior) knowledge, path dependencies and other firm-specific characteristics that influence a firm's capability of appropriating the returns of research and development efforts or of imitating other firms. For a discussion of this compare Cohen, Wesley W. and Levinthal, Daniel A. (1990), 'Absorptive

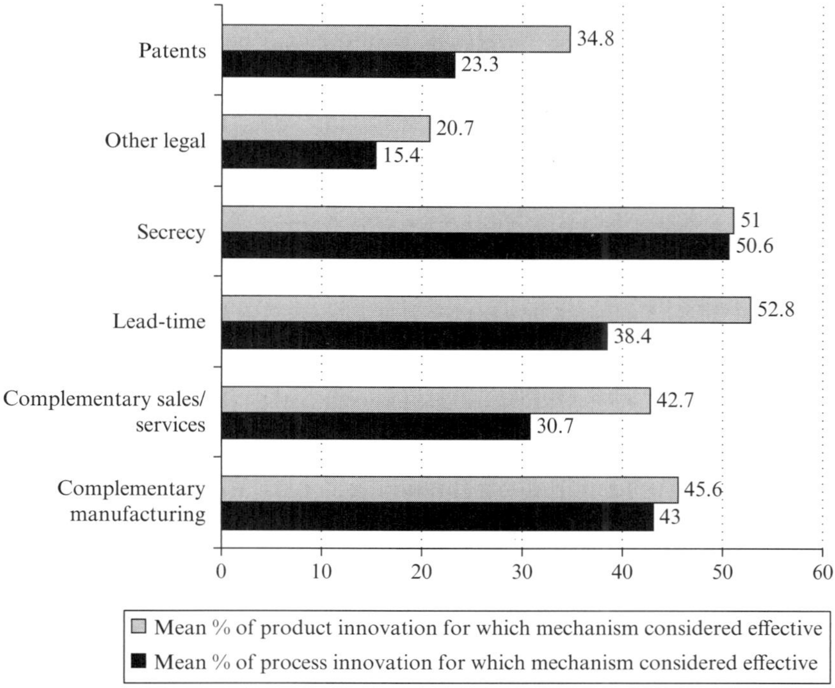

Source: Cohen et al. (2000).

Figure 4.1 Effectiveness of appropriability mechanisms for product and process innovations

3. EFFICIENT DESIGN OF INTELLECTUAL PROPERTY RIGHTS

This brings us finally to the question of how to design a 'better' or 'more appropriate' patent system or intellectual property rights system in general. Economic literature actually provides a broad range of models concerned with the design of *the* efficient patent system, starting with very

Capacity: A New Perspective on Learning and Innovation', *Administrative Science Quarterly*, 35, pp. 128–52; Saviotti, Pier Paolo (1998), 'On the Dynamics of Appropriability, of Tacit and of Codified Knowledge', *Research Policy*, 26, pp. 843–56; Teece, David J. (1986), 'Profiting from Technological Innovation: Implications for Integration, Collaboration, Licensing and Public Policy', *Research Policy*, 15, pp. 285–305.

basic assumptions of stand-alone innovations in a perfect market, progressing through to more complex cumulative and follow-on innovations in an imperfect market.

The classic model by Nordhaus, upon which most subsequent economists base their analyses, shows that the optimal patent duration depends on the buying behaviour of the consumers (that is, how sensible consumers react to changes in prices), and on the 'ease' of invention.[15] An 'easy' invention leads to a larger inventive output for a given level of resources. Based on this, Nordhaus draws the following conclusions: first, the fewer the number of consumers that react to increases in price, the longer the patent duration should be as this would only evoke a small static loss of social welfare. Second, the easier an invention is to make, the shorter the protection should be.[16] This simple static model illustrates that a general patent lifetime cannot be optimal, but is related to differences in industries.[17]

Since its inception, the model has been subject to various extensions. For example, optimal patent duration is longer when enforcement is incomplete[18] or when compulsory licensing at low rates is possible.[19] Duration is shorter when rivalry among firms raises the costs of invention, or when competitors may waste resources to invent around the patent.[20]

Other arguments have to be considered if the invention is not a stand-alone innovation, but serves as the basis for future inventions, that is, cumulative innovation. In this case, we also have to consider the conflicting interests of the inventors. The first innovator would prefer broad protection to appropriate the full social value (that is, the stand-alone value and the value for the succeeding invention), whereas the second innovator prefers less protection to avoid high licensing fees. Thus, the broader

---

15 Nordhaus, William D. (1969), *Invention, Growth, and Welfare: A Theoretical Treatment of Technical Change*, Cambridge, MA: MIT Press, p. 79.

16 Ibid., pp. 76 et seq.

17 Kerber and Schmidt (2008), *supra* note 4, p. 22.

18 Scherer, Frederic M. (1984), *Innovation and Growth: Schumpeterian Perspectives*, Cambridge, MA: MIT Press.

19 Tandon, Pankaj (1982), 'Rivalry and the Excessive Allocation of Resources to Research', *Bell Journal of Economics*, 14, pp. 152–65.

20 The preconditions for the efficient design of patents become even more complex if we want to determine, not only the length, but also the scope of protection. For a discussion of the optimal scope, compare Gilbert, Richard and Shapiro, Carl (1990), 'Optimal Patent Length and Breadth', *The RAND Journal of Economics*, 21, pp. 106–12; Klemperer, Paul (1990), 'How Broad Should the Scope of Patent Protection Be?', *The RAND Journal of Economics*, 21, pp. 113–30; Wright, Donald J. (1999), 'Optimal Patent Breadth and Length with Costly Imitation', *International Journal of Industrial Organization*, 17, pp. 419–36.

the protection for the first inventor, the higher the incentives for her to innovate, whereas the second innovator has only reduced incentives to innovate because the licensing fee would diminish the expected return on the inventive effort.[21]

Similar problems occur in the area of copyright. Here again we face a trade-off between access and incentives. Higher protection provides more incentives and thus more innovation. Simultaneously, higher protection raises the access costs of later authors and therefore the costs of creation. This leads to reduced incentives for creation.[22] A more recent study of Pollock demonstrates that optimal copyright protection decreases with a decline in costs of production and distribution of the protected work. According to his model, the optimal length of copyright protection would be about 15 years (after creation).[23] Nevertheless, our copyright system provides protection for 70 years after the death of the creator.

4. CONCLUSION

Returning to my initial thesis, from an economic perspective, a definitive statement on an overall efficient design of intellectual property rights is not possible. As illustrated briefly above, empirical and theoretical economic works show that the importance of patents and intellectual property rights varies depending on products, industries and alternative appropriability instruments. It follows that a differentiated (that is, industry-specific) intellectual property rights system would be more efficient. The existing patent and copyrights systems are designed uniformly, largely ignoring the various differences between sectors. Consequently, inefficiencies arise and with them, an increase in social welfare losses.

Thus, the main question is not whether we need intellectual property protection at all. Instead, we should focus our attention on the question of how we can use these economic insights to create a more differentiated and therefore more efficient intellectual property rights system.

---

21 Scotchmer, Suzanne (1991), 'Standing on the Shoulder of Giants: Cumulative Research and the Patent Law', *The Journal of Economic Perspectives*, 5, 29–41.

22 Landes, William M. and Posner, Richard A. (1989), 'An Economic Analysis of Copyright Law', *The Journal of Legal Studies*, 18, pp. 325–63.

23 Poilock, Rufus (2007), 'Forever Minus a Day? Some Theory and Empirics of Optimal Copyright', Discussion Paper, http://mpra.ub.uni-muenchen.de/5024/, accessed 11 November 2008, p. 26.

5. Patents and open access in the knowledge economy

Ulf Petrusson*

1. INTRODUCTION[1]

This chapter discusses patents and the patent system in a knowledge economy, looking at the positive and negative consequences of patents for society, and asking the question: to what extent does it appear possible to build a patent system that serves its intended purpose of promoting both open access to technology and the creation and utilization of innovation, when the economy is changing. In doing so, I examine how the patent system supports the use and incorporation of patents into business and market constructions, and how this system interacts with and structures open access to technology, in the context of an economy that is no longer industrial but knowledge-based. Especially interesting is how the patent system interacts with open science, open innovation,[2] distributed innovation[3] and open technology platforms.

Even though the debate on the contribution of patents per se, and of the patent system, to societal development and welfare is not in any way new, we can still argue that there is growing controversy over the role of the patent system in a knowledge economy.[4] The advocates of the patent system in the industrial setting have argued that it is a crucial prerequisite

* Professor at University of Gothenburg, Director of Department at Institute for Innovation and Entrepreneurship.

1 I would like to thank Henrik Rosen, Tobias Thornblad and Caroline Pamp for their help and contributions.

2 In the academic discussion, the concept of open innovation is very much introduced by Chesbrough, Henry (2003), *Open Innovation: The New Imperative for Creating and Profiting from Technology*, Boston: Harvard Business School Press.

3 Regarding the concept of distributed innovation, see Von Hippel, E. (1988), *The Sources of Innovation*, Oxford: Oxford University Press.

4 Regarding the big 19th century patent controversy, see Machlup, F. and Penrose, E., 'Patent Controversy in the Nineteenth Century', 10(1) *Journal of Economic History* pp. 1–29.

for protecting and rewarding human development, going so far as to call it 'one of the greatest of all elements which have contributed towards the expansion of industry and the development of science and the useful arts'.[5] Conversely, there are those who consider the patent system a significant threat, or at least as an impediment, to both human development and welfare, and not only as a sweeping, ideological statement against encroaching globalization and capitalism. Patent opponents have started a lively and relevant discussion in the last few decades about whether or not patents, and more specifically the current patent system, could actually be an obstacle to useful research efforts, entrepreneurial initiatives and new ventures, knowledge sharing and technology transfer, new market creation, and the development of new treatments and therapeutic methods.[6] This has been particularly prominent in new and evolving markets, as has been seen in the 'patent thicket' discussion in relation to the field of biotechnology, which has generated significant debate and interest.[7]

The amount, and intensity, of debate on these issues is not surprising in itself. How society chooses to construct and relate to the patent system will have an unavoidable impact on fundamental values, such as the freedom of research, information, and competition, among others. Yet this does not explain how it is possible that there is still no widespread consensus on whether the patent system as an institution actually generates wealth, or if its net contribution to the economy is destructive of value. This uncertainty was also very much the conclusion of Machlup's famous study of the patent system in 1958.[8] Machlup concluded that we do not have

---

5 Fox, Harold (1947), *Monopolies and Patents: A Study of the History and Future of the Patent Monopoly*, Toronto: University of Toronto Studies, p. 212. Compare the conclusions on the role of property rights in Rosenberg, Nathan and Birdzell, L.E. Jr. (1986), *How the West Grew Rich – The Economic Transformation of the Industrial World*, London: Tauris.

6 See for example Stiglitz, J., 'Making Globalization Work', 139 *South Bulletin* 2007, pp. 67–75. Stiglitz, J., 'How to Fix the IP Imbalance: Too Much IP Protection Bad for the Economy', *Managing Intellectual Property*, October 28, 2004, pp. 35–9. Ostergard, R.L., Tubin, M. and Altman, J., 'Stealing from the Past: Globalization, Strategic Formation and the Use of Indigenous IP in the Biotech Industry', 22(4) *Third World Quarterly* 2001, pp. 643–60. M. Perlman, 'IPR and the Commodity Form: New Dimensions in the Legislated Transfer of Surplus Value', 35 *Review of Radical Political Economics* 2003, pp. 304–20.

7 Heller, M.A. and Eisenberg, R.S. (1988), 'Can Patents Deter Innovation? The Anticommons in Biomedical Research', 280 *Science* 1988, pp. 698–701.

8 Machlup, Fritz, An Economic Review of the Patent System, *Study of the Subcommittee on Patents, Trademarks and Copyrights of the Committee on the Judiciary*, United States Senate 85th Congress, 2nd Session, 1958, pp. 79–80.

enough knowledge to decide whether the patent system has an altogether positive or negative impact on society. 'None of the empirical evidence at our disposal and none of the theoretical arguments presented either confirms or confutes the belief that the patent system has promoted the progress of the technical arts and the productivity of the economy. The best we can do is to state assumptions and make guesses about the extent to which reality corresponds to these assumptions.'[9]

An important observation is that most of the analysis is based on an understanding of patents as regulatory interventions in market behavior, and in competition; interventions that need to be motivated and legitimized.[10] The patent itself is historically often understood as a monopolistic position granted by the government.[11] Those who are positive towards the patent system tend to describe the patent as a necessary restriction of competition that will stimulate invention, and thereby also competition in the long run.[12] This view is especially prevalent within the field of economics, but it is also quite common within the legal field to describe patents in terms of a public intervention in market competition.[13] Translating Machlup's conclusion into this context, we could say that discussion of the impact of the patent system can be characterized as 'a failure to understand complex systematic effects of regulatory interventions'.[14]

Thus, a crucial step to enable a constructive discussion of the roles of the patent system in a knowledge economy is to develop a theoretical framework that will enable an understanding of the systemic effects. As I see it, if we are to go beyond the conclusion of Machlup, we will need to recognize how patent law from a legal point of view is both an *internal*

---

9 Ibid.

10 I have analyzed this thoroughly in Petrusson, U. (1999), *Patent och Industriell Omvandling: En studie av dynamiken mellan rättsliga och ekonomiska idésystem*, Stockhalm: Norstedts Juridik.

11 See for example Fox, above note 5. Dutton, H.I. (1985), *The Patent System and Inventive Activity, During the Industrial Revolution 1750–1852*. Manchester: Manchester University Press, p. 17. Kaufer, Erich (1989), *The Economics of the Patent System*, Great Britain: Harward Academic Publishers GmbH, pp. 6–8. Walterscheid, Edward C. (1994), 'The Early Evolution of the United States Patent Law (Part 1)', 76(9), *Journal of the Patent and Trademark Office Society*, p. 706.

12 See below section 2.1.

13 In the Nordic discussion, Alf Ross and Mogens Koktvedgaard have played important roles in defining intellectual property within a market competition context. See for example Koktvedgaard, Mogens (1965), *Konkurrencepraegde Immaterialretspositioner*, Kobenhavn: Juristforbunders forlag, p. 190.

14 Sunstein, Cass R. (1990), *After the Rights Revolution*, Cambridge: Harvard University Press, p. 91.

as well as an external constructionist process.[15] We need to understand how the internal transformation of what is patent law interacts with how patents, patentable inventions, patent licenses etc. operate in the external construction of business and the enabling of access to technology. In terms of theoretical approach, the aim of this chapter is to apply a *socio-legal approach* to patents and the patent system.[16] It is the understanding of the interaction between the external and internal that will help us to avoid the failure to understand the complex systematic effects of regulatory interventions, self-regulatory mechanisms and also the regulatory construction of planned systems. When focusing on the 'internal' dimension of law an overall challenge is how the external understanding of law can be used internally when describing and analyzing law. Thus, external insights into the role of patents in knowledge-based business help us to reconstruct the internal approaches, for example, how to understand and interpret legal concepts such as 'patent', 'invention', 'discovery', 'research use', 'exhaustion of rights' etc. Understanding of the interactions of the external and internal is obviously fundamental when discussing patent reform.[17]

The external theoretical framing in this chapter is the role of the concept of the patent as a tool for building business in the knowledge economy.[18] It is clear to anyone with professional experience of patents that not even the most extensive patent portfolio will by itself grant its owner a monopoly

---

15 Tuori elaborates on the distinction between the internal and the external: 'Legal-scientific and social-scientific research on law understands the law as the object of study in different ways. The law shows to legal scholars its symbolic normative side, whereas social scientists primarily focus on social practices related to the law . . . The legal scholar approaches the law from a participant's internal point of view, whereas the social scientist adopts an observer's external point of view.' Tuori, Kaarlo (2002), *Critical Legal Positivism*, Aldershot: Ashgate, p. 285.

16 I have more thoroughly discussed the importance of a sociolegal approach in Petrusson, U and Glavå, M. (2008). 'Law in a Global Knowledge Economy – Following the Path of Scandinavian Sociolegal Theory', in Wahlgren, P. (ed.), *Law and Society: Scandinavian Studies in Law*, vol. 53. Stockholm: Jure.

17 I agree with the Danish legal theorist Dalberg-Larsen when he explains that by examining the sociological character of law, lawyers can formulate new sociolegal theories to be used in legal practice.

18 The school of evolutionary economic thought, significantly developed by Nelson and Winters, opens up a new development direction, wherein economic and legal theory are far more capable of cross-pollination within the field of patent theory. An illuminating example of this type of cross-pollination can be found in Merges, Robert and Nelson, Richard (1990), 'On the Complex Economics of Patent Scope', *Columbia Law Review*, 90, pp. 839–916.

on the market.[19] However, the negative right conferred by the patent to exclude others and prevent specific behavior generates a position of control that can be used to block, but also to build.[20] Much like contracts, patents can be used both to construct and to enable open access.[21] Patents, as well as patentable inventions, can be managed as property, and can be transacted upon more or less openly.[22] The assumption in this chapter is that in an external setting of knowledge-based business the legal concepts related to patent law are and can be used in a different way than in an industrial setting. In this external legal context, patent regulation is not only a governmental intervention, but a way to provide self-regulatory instruments to be used by inventors, firms and other actors to establish, use, and determine the validity of tradable properties. Are they as self regulatory instruments used to promote open access? As tools, they will be governed by patent law. It is therefore necessary, from my point of view, to also apply an *internal sociolegal approach.* We need to critically analyze how the transformation of business affects the balance of the patent institution, through its effect on the criteria of patentability, rules on scope, rules on which activities will infringe and which will not, etc. To what extent does patent law provide self-regulatory tools that will enable a constructive development of the knowledge economy and how does the legal profession, which controls the internal construction process, respond to the external development?

Thus, in this chapter I will analyze how the transformation of business in a knowledge economy will also transform how patent regulation

---

19 Compare David, Paul (1993), 'Intellectual Property Institutions and the Panda's Thumb: Patents, Copyrights, and Trade Secrets in Economic Theory and History' in Wallerstein, Mitchel B., Mogee, Mary Ellen and Schoen, Roberta A. (eds), *Global Dimensions of Intellectual Property Rights in Science and Technology*, Washington, DC: National Academy Press, p. 21.

20 Compare Berger, Peter L. and Luckmann, Thomas (1966), *The Social Construction of Reality: A Treatise in the Sociology of Knowledge*, Garden City, NY: Doubleday.

21 Machlup's work, in conjunction with among others Nelson and Arrow's articles from the 1960s, seems to have played a significant role in establishing interest in the patent system within economic theory. Cf. Arrow, Kenneth (1962), *Economic Welfare and the Allocation of Resources for Invention: The Rate and Direction of Economic Activity. Economic and Social Factors*, Conference No. 13, Universities-National Bureau of Economic Research, Princeton University Press, p. 609, and Nelson, Richard (1959), 'The Simple Economics of Basic Scientific Research', 67, *Journal of Political Economy*.

22 It was at the end of the 1800 that the concept of 'intellectual property' started to get used: Walterscheid, above note 11 p. 702.

operates as a set of self-regulatory norms/tools.[23] In doing this, I will view the patent system from an internationalist perspective, primarily addressing the aspects of the modern patent system that are held in common by most countries, but I will also provide examples of national legislation and patent use to make the discussion more concrete. I will discuss patents and the patent system in the interaction between the proprietary sphere of knowledge that is kept private and the openly available sphere of knowledge that is public. I will discuss how the interaction of the external and internal result in areas that earlier were part of the public domain being privatized and in access to knowledge being increasingly regulated by intellectual property rights (IPRs). I look at the structured development of the public domain as one of the goals of a working patent system and at how patents and the use of patents can build a public domain of knowledge and technology in a knowledge-driven economy.

A major assumption to be pursued in the chapter is that if a knowledge economy is to promote open access to technology and thereby be sustainable, patents and other IPRs have to be used to construct open technology platforms. To illustrate this, two such platforms, which I will describe as 'open IP platforms', will be analyzed: the Innovative Medicines Initiative (IMI), a European initiative that aims to improve the competitive situation of the European Union in the field of pharmaceutical research by supporting faster discovery and development of better medicines for patients, and the Global System for Mobile Communications (GSM).

---

[23] When elaborating on the sociolegal approach to law as a norm, it is quite usual to begin this by categorizing different norms. Hydén has undertaken the elaboration of a general theory on norms, in which he elaborates on norms from both an external as well as an internal point of view. In his external analysis he focuses, for example, on how norms are created as a result of practical actions and vice versa. Especially interesting for this chapter is his theory on how legal systems provide norms for self-regulation in other systems, and how legal norms act as intervening norms and solve inter-system conflicts. Closely related to this, and thus also of considerable interest, are his theories on how legal norms constitute and govern the rules of market interactions and power games. Hydén, Håkan (2002), *Normvetenskap*, Lund: Sociologiska institutionen, Univ., p. 109. Cf. Hydén, Håkan (1989), 'Retssociologiens relevans vid behandlingen af formueretlige spørgsmål', in Basse, E.M. (ed.) *Regulering og styring – en jurisdisk teori- og metodebog*, Kobenhaven, Gad, p. 126.

2. OPEN ACCESS AS PURPOSE AND GROUNDS FOR JUSTIFYING THE PATENT SYSTEM

2.1. A Monopoly to Incentivize both Innovation and Open Access

The question on how to balance the right to exclude and the promotion of openness in patent legislation is in no way a new one. In, for example, the preparatory work from 1919 preceding the Swedish Patents Act it is stated that 'the purpose of all patent regulation is to encourage inventive activities by offering inventors opportunity to make profit on their work, to stimulate that created inventions are made public and thereby promote the engineering sciences and the development of business'.[24] According to the Swedish preparatory work, it is the combination of the incentive to invent and the disclosure of the technology together that is supposed to promote both science and innovation within a country. Even though it is quite a strong claim that this is the purpose of all patent regulation, there is no question that considerations of this character have played a significant role in justifying patent legislation around the world. [25]

Going back in history, the incentive element has historically been of particular relevance in motivating the need for a patent system.[26] Classical philosophers such as Smith, Bentham and Mill, for example, are among those who motivated the creation of the patent institution with the argument that a time-limited exclusivity would function as a reward and incentive for inventiveness. According to Smith, incentive and reward were essential, as the actual value of such an incentive was dependent on the commercial success of the invention according to the principles of supply and demand.[27] Mill recognized the moral dimension and argued that 'it would be a gross immorality in the law to set everybody free to use a person's work without his consent and without giving him an equivalent'.[28]

---

24 Patentlagstiftningskommitténs betänkande VI, 1919. Förslag till Lag om patent m. m. p. 161.

25 See for example Machlup, and Penrose, above note 4, p. 10. Machlup, above note 8, p. 21. Basber, Björn L. (1984), *Patenter og teknologisk endring i Norge 1840–1980, en metodediskusjon om patentdata anvendt som teknologi-indikator*, Bergen: NHH, p. 13. Dutton, above note 11, p. 17.

26 One alternative to patents which has been discussed since the introduction of the patent system is that government should recognize successful inventors with a direct monetary reward; see for example Machlup, above note 8, p. 15.

27 Smith, Adam (1978), *Lectures on Jurisprudence*, Oxford: Clarendon Press, p. 83 (first published 1762–3).

28 Mill, John Stuart (1985), *Principles of Political Economy*, Books IV and V, London: Penguin Books, p. 296 (first published 1848).

Bentham underlined the importance of patents to avoid the discouraging effect of free riders: 'A man will not be at the expense and trouble of bringing to maturity an invention unless he has a prospect of an adequate satisfaction, that is to say, at least of such a satisfaction as to his eyes appears an adequate one, for such troubles and expense'.[29]

The element of disclosure, on the other hand, does not seem to have played the same role in justifying the patent system, at least in its early history. As early as 1775, however, Edmund Burke argued on these grounds for the legitimacy of the system. 'Monopoly is an odious term . . . [but a patent] . . . is not making a monopoly of what was common. It is the direct reverse, for the condition of the patent, compelling a discovery, makes that common which was private before.'[30] The argument for creating public access is often used to balance and legitimize the reward and incentive argument. Patents, i.e. rewards, are granted in exchange for the inventions being made available to the public.[31] The assumption is that if the government does not provide a patent system, inventors would endeavor to keep their inventions secret. The exclusive right offered through the patent is considered to be the basis for the willingness of inventors to accept that their inventions are made public.

Thus, the historical justification of the patent system has very much centered on the importance of the monopoly-like position offered by the patent.[32] In relation to the creation of public access, the incentive of the exclusive position that the patent confers is viewed as being what motivates inventors to patent inventions that otherwise would be kept secret. Discussion within the field of economics often ends up in a cost-benefit analysis in relation to the patent as a monopoly.[33] The starting point is that monopolies in general are negative and create a deadweight loss, while the patent is more sophisticated because of its double nature as both a monopoly and an incentive for

---

29 Bentham, Jeremy (1952), 'Manual of Political Economy', in Stark, W. (ed.), *Bentham's Economic Writings*, Vol. 1, New York: Burt Franklin, p. 262 (the original is published 1793–5).

30 The citation is from the secondary source Dutton, above note 11, p. 23.

31 Patentlagstiftningskommitténs betänkande VI, 1919. Förslag till Lag om patent m. m. p. 161.

32 Dam, Kenneth W. (1994), 'The Economic Underpinnings of Patent Law', 23(1) *The Journal of Legal Studies*, pp. 241–71.

33 A few examples among many include F Beck, Roger (1981), 'Competition for Patent Monopolies', 3, *Research in Law and Economics*, pp. 91–110. Harris, Christopher and Vickers, John (1985), 'Patent Races and the Persistence of Monopoly', 33 *The Journal of Industrial Economics*, pp. 461–81.

new inventions.[34] Rosenberg describes the cost-benefit relation created by the patent: 'the benefits of the patent system are the increase in output which society owes to that class of inventions which would not have been made at all in the absence of the system, plus the increase in output owing to the earlier introductions of inventions which would have come anyway, but at a later date. The costs of the system are the restrictions in output for which the patent laws are responsible by allowing all holders of patent inventions to exclude others from their use during the period of patent protection'.[35] The motivation for the patent system is, according to Rosenberg, that we, by accepting the delay in the diffusion and broader usage of new inventions, are able to spur the creation of new inventions.

For those who are skeptical towards the patent system it is of course open to us to question if it is necessary 'to endure the output-restricting effects of patent monopolies in order to stimulate invention'.[36] The incentive dimension has been questioned from a number of different perspectives, as has the patent system's use as a means to create public access. It has been claimed that if it is possible to keep an invention secret, that invention will be kept secret regardless of the existence of a patent system. This argument holds that the patent itself is not sufficient incentive to surrender the possibility of secrecy.[37] It has even been questioned whether the possibility of patenting does not, in fact, stimulate increased secrecy. Because an invention requires novelty for patentability, inventors and firms wanting to safeguard patentability will keep their inventions secret under the development stage. Without the possibility of patenting, it would become strategically important to get the invention onto the market as soon as possible and thereby secure recognition and competitive advantage.[38]

A general conclusion, nowadays widely accepted, is that the focus on the patent system as provider of monopolistic positions granted by governments, does not necessarily help us see the full picture.[39] Instead, if we

---

34 See for example Cooter, Robert and Ulen, Thomas (1988), *Law and Economics*, Glenview, IL: Scott, Foresman; London: HarperCollins, p. 135.

35 Rosenberg, Nathan (1972), *Technology and American Economic Growth*, New York: Harper and Row, p. 188.

36 Eisenberg, Rebecca (1991), 'Patents and the Progress of Science – Exclusive Rights and Experimental Use', 23, *Marquette Intellectual Property Law Review*, p. 76.

37 Bowman, Ward S. (1973), *Patent and Antitrust Law*, Chicago: University of Chicago Press, p. 13. Scherer, F.M. (1970), *Industrial Market Structure and Economic Performance*, Chicago: Rand McNally, p. 381. Eisenberg, above note 36, p. 79.

38 Machlup and Penrose, above note 4, pp. 1–29. Machlup, above note 8, p. 24.

39 Godenhielm describes the approach in the context of legal theory as the 'economics theory' (my translation). Godenhielm, B. (1994), *Patentskyddets*

are to understand the role of patents in creating open access, a good starting point might be the role of the patent system in providing a public and international source of patent documentation to be used in science, business development etc.[40]

2.2. The Institutional Order of the Public Domain

The public domain, a widely used concept with a long legal tradition, represents the space where the public is in control and where there should be no private property claims. Open access and freedom to use are fundamental attributes of the public domain. In relation to the patent system, a public domain can be described as a legal concept used to balance the rights conferred by the patent, and a check on the privatization of technology.[41] However, public domain could also be described as a sophisticated institutional order, created over centuries, where the patent system is an important enabler in the construction process.

Instead of approaching the public domain from the traditional perspective, in which patent regulation constitutes a regulatory intervention in the context of a norm that all knowledge, if not kept secret, belongs to the public domain, we can approach the concept of the public domain as a legally planned and constructed global storage of open and available science, R&D results and other knowledge. Recognized in this perspective as a global institutional endeavor, the public domain can be seen as including all patent information and scientific information documented,

---

omfattning i europeisk och nordisk rätt, Helsingors: Juristförbundets förlag, p. 6. See further Petrusson, above note 10, p. 107.

40 In his 1958 study, Machlup concludes his analysis of the discussion within economics: 'The most perplexing and disturbing confusions occur in discussions about the "value of patents". This is no wonder, what with the large number of possible meanings in the minds of the writers on the subject: they may be talking about (a) the value of patents to their owners, (b) the value of patents to society, (c) the value of the patent system to society, (d) the value of patented inventions to their users, (e) the value of patented inventions to society, (f) the value of the patent induced inventions to society. But even that is not all, because the social value of inventions may depend on the degree to which they are used, and the value of patents to their owners on the way they are exploited.' Machlup, above note 8, p. 54. An example of a less illuminating empirical analysis in this regard is Harris, James (1979), *Comments on the Use of Patent Statistics with Recommendations for Further Studies*. DECD: Second Workshop on the Measurement of R&D Output.

41 'Public domain' is an Anglo-American concept and it is of course important to recognize that in some jurisdictions the concept of public domain per se has not had such an importance. Still, I will argue that discussion of the concept is relevant in all jurisdictions.

published, archived and made freely accessible over the years. It is obviously not that difficult to argue that the existence of such a public domain is of great importance for human creativity. To what extent patent information is important in relation to other information such as scientific publications is obviously not self evident, however. Patent information is today not only considered to be an important source for clarifying legal issues such as novelty, state of the art, invalidation risks, freedom to operate, infringement risks etc, but also an important source for supporting inventive and innovative activities in different respects.[42] We have also seen reports etc. on how patent information can be used in business intelligence in a number of different ways. USPTO, EPO and other patent offices around the world offer a number of different services in relation to patent information. The EPO, for example, provides visitors with access to esp@cenet, a free online searchable database comprising over 50 million patent documents from around the world.

Further, a number of firms have been formed in recent decades around the business concept of providing access to patent information together with different reporting and analysis tools, for example, Questel's Qpat, Minesoft's Patent Tracker, Thomson Reuters' Derwent and Delphion. Of these, the most interesting solutions are those that are able to apply the same search and information management tools to both patent information and scientific records, for example, Thomson Innovation. The greater the number of databases and different tools available to use the data, the more advanced the institutional order which is created in the public domain.

In this way, the phenomenon of the public domain cannot only be viewed as the bulk of knowledge which is not controlled in the private sphere, but can also be viewed as an institutional order, with said order becoming increasingly advanced and accessible. The creation of an open and accessible public domain is more than just the purpose and grounds for justification; it has become a regulated institution. In this respect, patent regulation cannot be seen as simple governmental intervention, or as government-provided self-regulatory instruments: the patent system comprises elements in a legally planned systematic order. By analyzing just how the institution has emerged, it is possible, as I see it, to distinguish four regulatory pillars on which the patent-related public domain is built: (1) regulation of patent information, (2) regulation of patenting procedures, (3) regulation of the patent, and (4) regulation of interfaces toward other sources of information.

---

[42] See for example 'Dissemination of Patent Information' (2009), prepared by the WIPO secretariat.

The first and most obvious pillar is the *regulation of patent information*. It is easy to recognize that we need regulation and/or other norms on how to document patent information, organize archives, access archives, create search systems, use search systems, interpret and use data, train people in how to act in different respects etc. This is probably what most people not within the patent profession would recognize as crucial if we are actually to construct an institution in this regard. As I have already mentioned, the potential generated by the near-global spread of the internet and advances in information technology in general has proven to be extraordinary. A problem that will be discussed below is whether this development makes the information more accessible to the public, or whether the public domain is becoming more exclusively accessible only to those actors who are able to afford the technology for patent information access and processing, and who have the skills necessary to be able to manage and interpret the information, and create value from it.

Just as important as regulating patent information is *the regulation of patenting procedure*. Without the obligation to submit appropriate descriptions, drawings, summaries, deposits of biological materials etc., we would not have the documents and information necessary to build the system. Further, regulation of the examination procedure and documentation of the same creates an efficient system for quality control of the information going into the system, while simultaneously adding valuable information to the system, for example, the citations by the examiner of other patent documents. The same could be said about regulation on how to make objections and how these should be governed. It is obvious that regulation on when patent applications are made public is directly decisive in determining when data could and should be open. It is also quite obvious that regulation on how to organize the patent procedure in national and international patent offices, etc., will have a direct impact on who controls the interface with the public domain in different ways.

The third pillar is *the regulatory construction of the right*. The criteria on what is patentable have a direct as well as indirect effect on what kind of information will be included in the system, i.e. both in relation to what will be included as information on the field of existing patents, and in relation to what information applicants will find interesting and necessary actually to submit. The limitation on the chronological scope of patent protection determines when information enters the public domain and becomes free to use. The seemingly simple construction of limiting the scope of the patent, and of the patented invention, to what is stated in the claims of the application, is an extraordinarily creative means of assisting the interpretation of what is actually included in the public domain.

The importance of the *regulation of the interface with other information systems* is not as obvious, even for those of us working with patent information on a daily basis. The importance of this pillar will obviously grow as more systems and more advanced systems for patent information access and management are created. A classic example, as I see it, is the Bayh-Dole Act in the United States, where universities have a responsibility to file for patents as a means of ensuring that important R&D results are part of patent documentation. This establishes regulatory pressure on the continued maintenance and active use of an interface between scientific research and the patent information system, which in due course will lead to the construction of an increasingly systematized public domain.

Thus, I consider that the question of to what extent the patent system will promote open access is very much dependent on the scope of the 'public domain' that we are able to build through regulations and other means. As an institution, this constructed public domain will represent public value in the form of a structured knowledge repository for the public good. In the knowledge society, this public value will grow rapidly, and opens up a number of ways of creating private value.[43]

2.3. Patents as Tools to Govern Openness in the Private Domain

In line with what has been stated above, one of the major grounds for justification of the patent system, which is not always made clear, is that the patent system provides self-regulatory tools to be used by inventors and other business actors.[44] Concepts such as the patentable invention, the patent, and the patent license, are all tools which can be used to govern R&D collaborations, commercialization, strategic partnering, technol-

---

43 Merges concludes in relation to this development that 'all of these major private investments in the public domain reveal a self-correcting feature of the intellectual property system that has been overlooked until now, and signal that public lawmaking is not the only arena in which the excesses of intellectual property may be addressed'. Merges, Robert P., 'A New Dynamism in the Public Domain', 71, *University of Chicago Law Review* 2004, pp. 183–203 (available at SSRN: http://ssrn.com/abstract=558751).

44 'If intellectual property is viewed as a tool of exploitation, it is easy to follow this argument. If, on the other hand, intellectual property is viewed as a tool of development, as suggested here, then a different perspective emerges. Viewed from the perspective of opportunity gains and losses for the development process, intellectual property can be seen as part of a country's infrastructure', Sherwood, Robert, (1993) 'Why a Uniform Intellectual Property System Makes Sense for the World' in Wallerstein, M.B., Mogee, M.E. and Schoen, R.A. (eds), *Global Dimensions of Intellectual Property Rights in Technology and Science*. Washington, DC: National Academy Press, p. 81 (1993).

ogy standardization, etc. By focusing only on the regulatory aspects of the patent system, we tend to approach the patent as a static right with negative implications – primarily a right to block others. This is of course a legally correct observation, and the patent is not constructed as a positive right nor does it ensure the owner's right to use the patented invention in any way – the primary feature of the patent remains the right to exclude. Still, even in situations where the owner of a patent is dependent on access to someone else's patents to be free to use the invention, the own patent is a means in the negotiation to set up a business solution. Restating the definition from this perspective, the patent can described as a dynamic right to regulate openness, rather than solely constituting a means to exclude, meaning regulating who should have access to which aspects of the patented invention, and on which terms.[45] This reversal of the traditional perspective can also be seen within economics, in those discussions where the patent has been seen as a mechanism for rent seeking.[46] When we recognize that the concept of the patent as well as the concept of the patentable invention, are tools that can be used to create structural order in business and increasingly also in research, we can start to talk about how to govern:

- openness with as few limitations as possible (openness for everybody),
- openness within one's own R&D group,
- openness within R&D collaboration projects,
- openness within a certain community, and
- structural arenas for openness (open IP platforms).[47]

Thus, one of the major conclusions in this chapter is that the question of whether patents and the patent system will block open access will always be dependent on how patents are used in the self-regulation of openness in the private domain. The increasing use of patents by patent holders to ensure openness, for example, by using collective cross-license transactions under, for example, (F)RAND (Fair, Reasonable and Non Discriminatory)

---

45 '[I characterize IPRs as a] binding commitment to openness as the right to include – by analogy with the traditional notion of property as involving at its core a right to exclude.' Merges, Robert (2008), *IP Rights and Technological Platforms*, University of California, Berkeley, School of Law, Working Paper Series.

46 'As a result of the invention, protected by the patent, the inventor has a cost advantage that allows him to make more money – economic rent – than his competitors.' Dam, above note 32, p. 6.

47 Petrusson, U. and Pamp, C (2009), 'Intellectual Property, Innovation and Openness, in Arup, C. and Van Caenegem, W. (eds), *Intellectual Property Policy Reform*, Cheltenham, UK and Northampton, MA, USA: Edward Elgar.

terms, increasingly supports a claim that the patent system actively promotes openness. If, on the other hand, the specific market or field is characterized by a competitive climate where business actors use their patent portfolios to block creative efforts other than facilitating their own efforts as far as possible, it obviously becomes very difficult, even for the most ardent patent advocates, to argue that the system is not harmful to achieving open access. If the competitive climate is such that firms use their patent portfolios to block all creative efforts as far as possible, the situation will obviously be bad in this respect. Consequently, it is important which elements the business cultures consist of and also how business models are developed in relation to patents. An emerging business climate where we see more and more of the so-called patent trolls, which increasingly spring up with profitable business models, is not necessarily an attractive future.

When approaching the patent as a tool, it also becomes clear that it is not necessarily obvious how the self-regulatory mechanisms operate. In his 1958 report, Fritz Machlup made an important remark about the concept of intellectual property: 'The meaning and object of "property" and "property rights" are shrouded by confusions, which however are more troublesome to lawyers than to economists. But it is almost embarrassing how often the controversial idea of property right in invention is confused with the noncontroversial idea of a property right in a patent.'[48] Machlup realized that there exists a fundamental uncertainty, as well as lack of awareness, regarding the self-regulatory mechanisms of the patent regulation. As I see it, there is an obvious risk that this uncertainty has a negative impact in a fundamental way, especially in the context of knowledge-based business.[49] In business practice, patents are not governed in the same way as monopolies. Most likely, the prevailing approach is to consider patents as a form of legal protection, and as a means of excluding specific behavior. In a setting of contractual negotiations, it is open to us to approach patents both as rights to exclude as well as rights to regulate openness. When it comes to the usage of the property concepts, my understanding is that the observation of Machlup remains correct.[50]

---

48 Machlup, above note 8, p. 53.

49 I have elaborated this uncertainty in Petrusson, U. (2003), 'Patents as Structural Capital – Towards Legal Constructionism', in Granstrand, O. (ed.), *Economics, Law and Intellectual Property*, Dordrecht: Kluwer Academic Publisher, pp. 363–94.

50 According to Machlup and Penrose, the characterization of patents as property was very much a political endeavor. 'It was strategically essential for the latter (patent advocates) to separate as far as possible the idea of patent protection from the monopoly issue and from the free trade issue. This was attempted by

Thus, we can historically recognize that patent regulation will offer a number of different approaches to patents as self-regulatory instruments. Legal uncertainty is obviously negative. Still, it is important to recognize that a pluralistic approach can be very constructive, and the flexibility to alternate between an approach to the patent as (1) protection, (2) a right to exclude behaviors, (3) a right to govern openness, and (4) a property, is also probably quite constructive. In addition, the patentable/patented invention could also be considered to have the characteristics of a property. It is striking how sophisticated are the solutions that patent regulation offers in this respect. Detailed rules on patentability criteria, scope, infringing and non-infringing actions, exempted behaviors, remedies etc., have a clear and direct impact in the form of norms for how business actors communicatively use such concepts as protection, rights, and properties when governing (typically self-regulating) open access.

3. KNOWLEDGE-BASED BUSINESS AND THE SHIFT IN BALANCE BETWEEN PUBLIC AND PRIVATE DOMAINS

3.1. Open Access in an Industrial Setting – The Starting-point

Building on what has been said in the preceding section, we can conclude that the question of the patent system's effect on open access will on the one hand depend on how the public domain is legally constructed, and on the other hand on how patents, patentable inventions etc. seen as self-regulatory tools, stimulate and enable open access in the private domain. It is actual usage and the business climate in the private domain that will decide to what extent actual openness will be constructed. Still, the regulatory design of these tools will have a direct impact on whether a specific piece of knowledge is likely to end up in the public or private sphere. Clearly, rules on patentability, publication, expiration and invalidation will have a decisive impact on the content and construction of the public domain.

The exemption rules in relation to the patent are especially interesting when it comes to the creation of openness in the private sphere.[51]

presenting the case of patent protection as one of natural law and private property, of man's right to live by his work and society's duty to secure him his fair share, and of society's interest in achieving swift industrial progress at the smallest possible cost.' Machlup and Penrose, above note 4, p. 9.

51 The exemption is normally labeled the experimental use exemption or the R&D exemption. The exemption is not necessarily an element in the patent

Even though patented inventions are controlled in the private sphere, the knowledge they contain can be available for use in specific contexts. An exemption of great importance in this respect is the so-called research exemption, which enables an open space in research processes. Another example is the so-called exhaustion of rights, which opens up product markets.[52] When the patented invention is implemented in a product and the product put on the market within a region where exhaustion of rights is legally established, the right to exclude most behaviors will be exhausted.

In this setting it is important to recognize that patent regulation is very much a product of industrialization. Patent regulation is developed in close interaction with what can be described as a research-adjusted material value chain, i.e. (1) R&D, (2) production, (3) distribution, (4) sales and (5) after-market services. In this industrial setting, therefore, we see how the patent as a self-regulatory tool is primarily adjusted through legislation to provide a means for preventing others from manufacturing, or as a means for governing how and whether others use the tool in manufacturing processes. Taking the research exemption together with the exhaustion of rights, the patent system has been designed to allow research on the patented invention without requiring permission or compensation, which strengthens the protection against commercial manufacture, and allows the design and maintenance of open markets, where buyers can trade with patented products without requiring additional licenses. Within this industrial logic, the patent guarantees exclusivity within a manufacturing context, and thus, for example, the setting of a standard in this context typically requires an unpatented technology.

The question is how the patent will operate as a self-regulatory tool in a more knowledge-oriented economy, where technology becomes the basis for a greater range of business activities and transactions, in a more diverse and strategic way. How will the exemptions operate? Will the balance between the public and private domains change? In what follows I will analyze and discuss how developments following from the transition to the knowledge economy, based on well-established sociological observations on what constitutes the knowledge economy, will impact patents and patents as self-regulative tools. My goal is to analyze to what extent this transition will lead to a shift in the balance between public

---

regulation; it could also be the outcome of the judges' considerations, for example on 'the rule of reason' (originally stated in *Standard Oil Co. of New Jersey v United States*, 221 US 1 (1911), but also reformulated in Article 28 (ex 30) of the Treaty of Rome).

[52] Another term used for the concept of exhaustion of rights is the first sale doctrine.

and private domains, in relation to the patent system, and what that shift might consist of.

3.2. Transaction-Based Research and Patent-driven Innovation in Early Phases

One of the characteristic features of the knowledge economy is that universities and public research organizations are becoming increasingly engaged in the utilization of research.[53] In relation to this, the question has been raised whether this also means that academic activities are increasingly affected by an 'ethos of commercial exploitation'.[54] Whether this is the case or not, it is clear that project leaders in research projects are beginning to focus on the packaging of research results as a means of extracting industry funding, and potentially commercializing results on a relevant market. Many universities take, and have for a long time taken, responsibility for providing industry with intellectual property through contract research. Another way that universities are changing their role and scope of activities is through the increasing development of license models as means to commercialize packaged research results.[55] A third way is to establish firms. University-linked company incubators are established in order to stimulate the creation of new ventures and entrepreneurship. Many of the firms build their business models on patented inventions and the intellectual packaging of research results emanating from the university. Increasingly, universities become platforms for new science-based business sectors, such as the biotech sector.

The acceptance of an IPR approach in research projects makes researchers and their project leaders more commercially oriented, i.e. it becomes possible to privatize the knowledge process, and thus increasingly it

---

53 For a more in-depth analysis of what is described in this section see Pamp, Caroline (2010), *Intellectual Property in Science*, Stockholm: Jure Förlag AB.

54 Regarding the use of this term see, for example, Sherman, Brad (1995), 'Governing Science – Patents and Public Sector Research in the United Kingdom', 26(1) *IIC* 1995, p. 24.

55 The so-called Cohen-Boyer patent is often discussed as an IPR that helped direct US universities toward a more commercial rationale. In 1973, Stanley Cohen of Stanford University and Herbert Boyer of the University of California discovered a process for recombining DNA to form biological chimeras (US4237224), leading to breakthroughs in industrially applicable recombinant DNA. The first patent application was submitted in 1974, with an agreement to assign the patent granted to Stanford University. Since the patents for the Cohen-Boyer process were granted, licensing agreements have generated more than $140 million in royalties.

becomes privatized. Actors promoting industry collaboration recognize the potential to fill the so-called gap between university and industry by promoting license-based business structures.[56] Databases and other ICT solutions become important means in the packaging of intellectual properties, as well as in governing research processes. It follows that fundamental academic activities and responsibilities, i.e. education and research, are also increasingly shifted towards the private domain, and governed through license transactions.

Biotechnology is perhaps the most obvious field illustrating this transition. The field is still very young, and entrepreneurs working on the development and commercialization of new advances seldom know which products and services, in which forms, are going to be offered to end-users.[57] Many firms are dependent on venture finance, and the concept of patents and patentable information are important tools used to present and illustrate the value of innovations to investors and innovation-supporting institutions. Consequently, business development tends to a large extent to be license-based – either to leverage the value of primary patent resources in small firms, or so that larger firms can navigate increasingly complex and crowded patent landscapes.

Biotech firms, as well as universities, are incentivized to patent prodigiously, and tend to patent up-stream, i.e. patent claims are drafted to cover research output rather than products based on research results, or manufacturing processes rather than existing products.[58] It makes sense

---

56 The transformation is, to a large extent, driven by developments in the United States. In 1980, the US Congress passed the Bayh-Dole Act. This act, among other things, established a new approach to publicly funded research. Under Bayh-Dole, universities still had an obligation to publish research results, but they were given the opportunity and encouraged to apply for any relevant patents before doing so. As this change in practice was implemented, universities increasingly became commercially oriented and began to establish license structures. Regarding the implications, see, for example, Mowery, David C., Nelson, Richard R., Sampat, Bhaven N. and Ziedonis, Arvids (1999), 'The Growth of Patenting and Licensing by U.S. Universities: An Assessment of the Effects of the Bayh-Dole Act of 1980', published in revised form in *Research Policy*, 30, 2001, pp. 99–119.

57 Compare White, Thomas and Sninsky, John (1999), 'Genomics and Intellectual Capital', in Imparato, Nicholas (ed.), *Capital for our Time: The Economic, Legal and Management Challenges of Intellectual Capital*, Stanford: Hoover Institution Press, pp. 270–81.

58 See Heller and Eisenberg, above note 7, pp. 698–701. Compare Cowan, Robin and Harison, Elad (2001), 'Intellectual Property Rights in a Knowledge-Based Economy', *MERIT-Infonomics Research Memorandum series*, 2001-027, p. 23. Collected from http://ideas.repec.org/p/dgr/umamer/2001026.html and Long,

for a commercial development actor to patent as early as possible, and the developments discussed so far help push the limits back for what is feasible in this regard. In, for example, the field of biopharmaceuticals, research within universities, as well as in associated innovation eco- and support systems, results in diagnostic tools to detect diseases, screening tools to select new molecular entities, research tools to measure toxicology, pharmacovigilance or the effect of a drug.[59]

Increasingly, we see international legal developments where exemption for research and experiments is called into question, or marginalized.[60] In some countries, only research that is not commercially motivated is exempted,[61] and in the US, for example, we have seen a development where the research exemption has more or less disappeared. Concerning biotechnology, this development has led to situations where a new invention may not be used at all in research or as an object of research, simply because it was originally developed to be a research tool. The rationale to

---

Clarisa (1999), 'Patents and Innovations in Biotechnology and Genomics', in Imparato (ed.), above note 57, pp. 251–69.

[59] 'The hottest new term in biotech.' Howard Schulman, Vice President, Biomarker Discovery Sciences, PPD, Inc.: http://www.ppdi.com/pdf/hottest_term_in_biotech.pdf.

[60] In most European countries, such an exemption has been adopted more or less verbatim from the Community Patent Convention (which has never been ratified), article 9 b, stating that 'acts done for experimental purposes relating to the subject-matter of the patented Invention' do not constitute infringement. In the Swedish Patents Act, this is expressed in § 3. This exemption extends to experimental use on a patented invention, but not experimentation with the help of a patented invention (i.e. a research tool). No distinction is made based on whether the actor using the exemption is a commercial entity or not. In Germany, this has been confirmed by case law in *Clinical Trials I&II*. In the US, the experimental use exemption has been defined in case law only (there is no statutory experimental use exemption except as regards clinical trials, so-called Bolar provisions). In recent cases, the constructed exemption has been narrowed down to acts done 'solely for amusement, to satisfy idle curiosity or for strictly philosophical enquiry'; see *Madey v Duke University*. In the decision, it was also stated that universities could not rely on an experimental use exemption because their research furthered their legitimate business purposes, i.e. attracting students and researchers. It is interesting to note that there is no experimental use exemption for copyright, including databases, except for a few provisions about special circumstances. This means that when copyright is claimed in software protected by copyright only, it is not possible to make a counterclaim of experimental use, but that it is possible to claim experimental use in relation to a granted patent in the same software.

[61] See further in Pamp, Caroline and Petrusson, Ulf (2004), 'Claiming Intellectual Property in Research – Towards an Entrepreneurial University'. Working Paper presented at the CIP Symposium 2004 on the Entrepreneurial University, June 1–3, 2004, Göteborg.

uphold these claims is that a research exemption, if applied to research tools, would make such patents useless. Consequently, researchers are not allowed to use some biotechnological solutions, even in non-commercial research. Licenses are required, which in turn tends to result in the reification of a commercial market in the academic sphere.

Thus, the development of increasing opportunities in claiming intellectual property in science, supported by developments in case and statutory law, which enables actors to 'patent up-stream', and which restricts the applicability of the experimental use exemption, etc., also opens up commercial solutions in the R&D sphere. The development is linked to the creation of new business models in relation to research tools, diagnostic tools, features, content and other more intellectual innovation. Biotechnology-based firms are created, and wealth is generated, in a knowledge-generation segment which has historically been open and included in the public domain, i.e. the academic research segment. In this situation, there is a definite shift in the balance between the public and private domains; one that goes so far that we can begin to question if even basic research can be performed any more without having to consider patent licensing or transferring and assigning IPRs.[62] Patents, and the expanded sphere of patentable inventions, become building blocks in the privatization of the science and research sphere.[63] The example of the biotechnology field shows that the transformation to the knowledge economy represents a clear shift in the traditional balance between the public and the private, which in a fundamental way will affect how we define freedom of research.

3.3. No Free Movement of Virtual Goods

Another of the major societal transformations that characterizes what we term the knowledge economy is the emergence of new business models that appropriate, incorporate, and depend on the emergence of the internet. New forms of agreements, such as various content provider and license agreements, are developed. Today, many managers and management scholars focus on knowledge and information as something the firm should produce, diffuse and employ on the internet. Information

---

[62] As long as the solutions are created taking the public interest into consideration, the development can be understood as what Merges describes as a 'self-correcting feature'. Merges, above note 43.

[63] Compare Merges, R. (1996), 'Property Rights Theory and the Commons – The Case of Scientific Research', in Frankel, Paul E., Miller, F.D. Jr. and Paul, J. (eds), *Scientific Innovation, Philosophy, and Public Policy*, Cambridge: Cambridge University Press, pp. 145–67.

and knowledge are increasingly characterized as the raw material for the construction of new innovations.[64] As a resource, knowledge is often described as the most important type of resource for generating market value and economic rent.[65] A major development, directly related to what we experience as knowledge-based business, is that physical products and services are complemented by virtual products and innovations that are entirely intellectually conceptualized.[66]

Over the last decade we have seen a development where computer software, virtual solutions and even business models have become patentable inventions in some geographies.[67] Even though this legal development has been questioned and criticized, the number of patents granted in these fields has increased drastically. Today patents, together with copyrights and database protection, are tools to control the virtual.

As discussed above, the principle of exhaustion of rights (first sale doctrine in the US) is an exemption that has a direct normative impact on the creation of an open sphere, enabling the reification of markets for physical goods.[68] If there is no exhaustion of rights within a specific geographic territory, the creation of markets within said territory must be the result of license structures, i.e. you will need a license to distribute, re-sell and even use the product. This in turn means that the principle of exhaustion of rights will also impact whether product markets are national, regional or international. If the legal exemption, extracted from regulation or court cases, stipulates national exhaustion, it is possible to consider the national area to be one market. A consequential norm is that it is possible to set differentiated prices without considering international competition and thus parallel imports, i.e. it will be possible to divide markets. If, on the other hand, the exemption stipulates international exhaustion, it will not be possible to use the patent to establish different geographical markets.

---

64 Castells describes this as one of the primary features of what he considers to be the information technology paradigm in business. Castells, Manuel (1996), *The Information Age: Economy, Society and Culture, vol. 1: The Rise of the Network Society*, Malden, Mass.: Blackwell, p. 61.

65 See, for example, Grant, Robert (1997), 'The Knowledge-based View of the Firm: Implications for Management Practice', in Bontis, Nick and Choo, Chun Wei (eds) (2002), *The Strategic Management of Intellectual Capital and Organizational Knowledge: A Collection of Readings*, New York: Oxford University Press.

66 An interesting example that very much clarifies this development is DRM. See Schollin, Kristoffer (2008), *Digital Rights Management: The New Copyright*, Stockholm: Jure.

67 http://en.wikipedia.org/wiki/Business_method_patent.

68 A European case of great importance regarding patents was *Centrafarm v Sterling Drug*, case 15/74, 1974 ECR 1147.

Innovations such as features, software tools and systems etc. are of a different nature from innovations that relate primarily to physical implementation.[69] They typically constitute platform technologies and network innovations, i.e. the value of the innovation for the user increases as more users also get access to the same innovation. The value of a software tool is dependent on the utilities it enables for the individual user, one such utility being interoperability with other software tools, operating systems etc., and another the possibility of implementing the tool on different hardware.

When we consider the trading space for virtual goods, however, we do not make reference to the same principle of exhaustion of rights.[70] For example, the sale of a virtual product over the internet will not result in any exhaustion. The character of the virtual makes it impossible to even discuss exhaustion in the same way as we do with physical products; the usage of the digital will include copying. The more patenting that we see of virtual tools, systems and features, the more business models we will see that are driven not only by copyright licensing, but also by patent licensing. The fact that we increasingly include virtual features in physical offerings thus makes it possible also to control distribution of physical goods without exhaustion.[71] Development of the so-called services, through for example internet-based service platforms, comes along with a push for license-based business models. Distribution and sales will in general

---

69 Compare Carroll, Ray and Tansey, Richard (2000), 'Intellectual Capital in the New Internet Economy – Its Meaning, Measurement and Management for Enhancing Quality', 1(4), *Journal of Intellectual Capital* 2000, p. 305.

70 See, for example, *Adobe Systems, Inc. v Stargate Software Inc.*: 'This Court notes that software is unique from other forms of copyrighted information. Technology and software, in particular, has radically transformed the way information is created and exchanged. Software fundamentally differs from more traditional forms of medium, such as print or phonographic materials, in that software can be both, more readily and easily copied on a mass scale in an extraordinarily short amount of time and relatively inexpensively. One of the primary advantages of software, its ability to record, concentrate and convey information with unprecedented ease and speed, makes it extraordinarily vulnerable to illegal copying and piracy. This Court finds that it is important to acknowledge these special characteristics of the software industry and provide enhanced copyright protection for its inventors and developers.' (*Adobe Systems, Inc. v Stargate Software Inc.* 216 F.Supp.2d 1051 N.D.Cal., 2002, p. 1059).

71 'The Court, therefore, concludes that based on the clear and unambiguous language of the relevant contracts, coupled with the multiple restrictions on title placed on the reseller in the above agreements, the transaction should be characterized as a license, rather than a sale.' (*Adobe Systems, Inc. v Stargate Software Inc.* 216 F.Supp.2d 1051 N.D.Cal., 2002, p. 1060).

become less open at the same time as we begin to see 'product markets' in new areas. Once again, we can see how patents and patentable inventions become building blocks in a sphere which has historically been open and thus how they will also affect market freedom.

3.4. The Dawn of Patent Markets

A general conclusion is that the transformation towards a knowledge economy as such is an expression of the expansion of the private domain.[72] We have seen how both the research sphere as well as the sphere of market transactions are being privatized, i.e. increasingly regulated by intellectual property rights. Obviously, the challenge in knowledge-based business is very much how to leverage knowledge into profits, which can be described as an 'objectification and privatization of knowledge'.[73] There is in this context not a shadow of a doubt that the transaction of intellectual property is one of the most fundamental means of achieving such leverage.[74] However, this does not mean that it is IPRs, e.g. patents and copyrights, that are expressed as value propositions in such transactions; rather, they consist of features, systems, contents, IT services, tools etc., being conveyed as explicit value propositions within the transaction. The roles of IPRs are often implicit.

Simplistically, we can state that structural transformation has accelerated and also pushed the economy into a situation where wealth creation is dependent on commodification and proprietization of information, knowledge, artistic and even moral processes. Developments on the internet show how digitalization, together with intellectual property claims, generate the potential to commercialize almost all human activities.

---

[72] We can also see how the concept of knowledge tends to exclude the dimension of power. Foucault concludes: 'No knowledge is formed without a system of communication, registration, accumulation, and displacement that is in itself a form of power, linked in its existence and its functioning to other forms of power. No power, on the other hand, is exercised without the extraction, appropriation, distribution, or restraint of knowledge.' Foucault, Michel (1997), *The Essential Works of Michel Foucault: 1954–1984, Vol. 1, Ethics: Subjectivity and Truth*. London: Allen Lane, p. 17.

[73] Compare Spender, J.C., 'Making Knowledge the Basis of a Dynamic Theory of the Firm', 17 *Strategic Management Journal* 1996, p. 52.

[74] See for example Krogh, von Georg and Grand, Simon (2002), 'From Economic Theory Toward a Knowledge Based Theory of the Firm – Conceptual Building Blocks', in Choo, Chun Wei and Bontis, Nick (eds), *The Strategic Management of Intellectual Capital and Organizational Knowledge*. Oxford: Oxford University Press, pp. 163–84.

Technical functions, biological findings, data, learning experiences, theoretical analyses and entertainment can all be transformed into structural objects. In conjunction with concepts of copyright, patents and other legal constructions, information technology makes it possible to relate to research tools, diagnostic tools, systems, virtual products, features, internet services etc., as value propositions for which we can predict and therefore also create one or several markets.[75]

At the same time, we do know that an increase in claims of patentable inventions, patents and other intellectual property might block knowledge-sharing, technology diffusion, R&D, production and distribution. The greater the number and scope of patent claims, the more difficult it is to achieve freedom to operate. As a negative right, a patent can be used to block firms from using technology they have developed themselves, i.e. to the extent it is possible to argue that the technology is covered by the patent claims. Increasingly, actors appear that are only focused on achieving patents that they aggressively use to claim patent infringement and thereby achieve incomes from 'offensive licensing'. The actual inventions and innovations are not necessarily interesting for these actors. It is the patent as a legal instrument that becomes the commodity in these emerging patent markets. Patents are purchased as a means to claim patent infringement, nothing more. It will be difficult to construct a sustainable knowledge economy if we end up in a continuous development where more and more actors (sometimes described as 'patent trolls') refrain from using their patents to govern and permit access to either technology or innovation, but instead accumulate patents to negotiate a stake in the revenue streams created by others.[76]

The conclusion from this section is that if patent systems are to enable sustainable wealth and welfare in a knowledge economy, patent tools have to be used to enable access to technology and innovation, rather than simply to block it. The more business or regulatory developments create patents as self-regulatory tools, which can be used to construct private

---

[75] 'The Digital Dilemma: Intellectual Property in the Information Age' (2000), Committee on Intellectual Property Rights and the Emerging Information Infrastructure, Computer Science and Telecommunication Board, Commission on Physical Sciences, Mathematics, and Applications, National Research Council. Washington, DC: National Academy Press. Stefik, Mark (1999), *The Internet Edge: Social, Legal, and Technological Challenges for a Networked World*, Cambridge, Mass. and London: MIT Press.

[76] The concept of the patent troll is fuzzy in many ways and many tend to dislike it nowadays. See for example http://www.rkmc.com/Patent_Troll_A_Self-Serving_Label_that_Should_be_Abandoned.html.

business solutions in what up until then were public domains, the more dependent we become on the creation of private structures that take collective and also public interests into consideration. A joint challenge for all stakeholders in the development of knowledge-based business is the use of patents as self-regulatory tools to construct platforms with more or less preset conditions under which access to technology and innovation is governed.[77] The extent to which this is possible, and how this challenge is met, will in many ways decide to what extent the patent system will be constructive, and of course also affect how that system will need to be revised over the years to come.

4. OPEN IP PLATFORMS – THE FOUNDATION OF A SUSTAINABLE KNOWLEDGE ECONOMY

4.1. Platforms for Governance of Openness

An important conclusion is consequently that if we are to understand whether or not patents promote open access or not in a knowledge economy, we need to understand how patent related norms operate as self-regulatory tools in the construction of open IP platforms. The characteristics which should define an open IP platform are of course far from obvious. Building on the analysis in the third section we can see platform developments emerging from commercial behavior based on *transactions of the results of R&D* (see section 3.2), or arising out of the *creation of virtual products* (see section 3.3).

In a discussion on how business is increasingly platform driven, the concept of platform technology often takes a central role as a description of open platforms where a number of stakeholders use the same system, software, protocol etc.[78] Platform technology is, in my terminology, a relatively sophisticated virtual product, defined by the degree of collective access, development, usage and control that it allows. Some platforms are developed by one actor and then made accessible to a collective, i.e. distribution and usage are more or less open, while other systems are developed

---

[77] For example, Fligstein concludes: 'social structures, social relations, and institutions have not been created automatically in market society. They have been long-run historical projects ongoing in all of the industrial societies that have worked through waves of crisis.' Fligstein, Neil (2001), *The Architecture of Markets: An Economic Sociology of Twenty-first-century Capitalist Societies*, Princeton, NJ: Princeton University Press, p. 4.

[78] Merges, above note 45.

collectively, even openly, i.e. development is carried out outside the hierarchical control of a corporate structure. When, for example, platforms are based on the principles of more or less unabridged freedom of information, they can be constructed as open-source platforms. The platform can be characterized as an innovation in itself, but also as a development cluster or distribution platform (even a market), depending on the context and the character of the technology that sustains the platform activity. What might constitute an innovation for one actor might be a platform for transactions for others, which is what enables a market for open platforms and related platform technologies. In some cases, the technology enabling the platform is made part of a technology standard. Sophisticated platform technologies, such as transmission and communication technologies in the cellular phone field, are often constructed as structural layers. In some cases, the layer can be constructed to enable both the inclusion and transaction of applications that are developed by external actors, more or less independently.

Still, it is also possible to describe a shared database, for example, as an open IP platform. More or less collective open development, gathering, access, usage and/or control of the content of the base make it purposeful to talk about it as a platform. We can distinguish between specific pieces of knowledge on the one hand, and the totality of knowledge, i.e. the platform, on the other.[79] Thus, a fundamental way to distinguish different platforms from each other is to analyze to what extent each platform is leveraged into a system, toolbox etc. We can ask ourselves: does the platform consist of

(1) collected data, R&D results etc.,
(2) packaged content and/or features,
(3) systematized toolbox(es),
(4) an operational system, or
(5) a multilayered system, where one layer generates a market-like platform for the next layer?

A good starting-point for discussing the role of patents and open IP platforms is multi-stakeholder R&D collaboration.[80] Existing IP plat-

[79] Compare Merges, R. *From Medieval Guilds to Open Source Software: Informal Norms, Appropriability Institutions, and Innovation*. Conference on the Legal History of Intellectual Property Madison, Wisconsin, 13 November 2004.

[80] For example, in the European Union public research organizations are increasingly encouraged to apply for patents with the purpose of directly promoting open innovation. 'To the question 'Why should [Public Research Organizations

forms have what can be described as a more collaborative rationale. Both development and usage tend to be open, at least to some extent. The first patent-related issue that tends to come up with a collaboration of this kind is who is going to own the results of the collaboration. Nowadays this typically means thinking in terms of who owns the 'background IP' and the 'foreground IP'. The second step thereafter is normally to discuss the rights of other parties to access and use the background of other parties and the foreground created in the projects. To what extent should they have the right to use the results in research, development, production, distribution and sales? The outcome of the negotiations establishing a collaboration, if it is a more extensive program, will define the regulatory framework under which a specific R&D project will have to operate. If one or several actors take on the responsibility, in a structured way, to collect the results of the collaboration and make them accessible, the results will also constitute a constructed platform – structurally as well as technically. If the R&D consortia are controlled by one or several firms, on the other hand, it might perhaps be more appropriate to talk about the construction of a cluster, rather than a platform. A way of characterizing a platform would be as a structured packaging of the technology that has the potential to make it available to innumerable users/ stakeholders.

Platforms will be constructed differently depending on whether they are driven by strictly private interests or if public interests are also taken into consideration, but also depending on whether the stakeholders participating in the platform are otherwise normally competitors or if the platform is a community effort. The unifying reason for focusing on platform construction is the structured order of a great number of intellectual assets that can be made openly accessible in a structured way, and the fact that the construction of the platform itself can be carried out in an open way. Focusing on the assets as building blocks in the construction of the platform, or as objects that users derive from the platform, helps clarify how platforms can be expressed as the structured governance of a potentially unlimited number and variety of IP transactions.

(PROs)] protect intellectual property' appropriate answers are 'To encourage the economic applications of their discoveries for the benefit of the public' and 'To make the research function more attractive and better supported'. To the question 'How should this property be protected', it is appropriate that the PRO takes steps itself, provided that these steps reflect good understanding of where and how the benefits can accrue.' 'Responsible Partnering. Joining forces in a world of open innovation. A guide to better practices for collaborative research and knowledge transfer between science and industry', Report, January 2005, p. 3.

4.2. A Research Consortium Platform Logic – The Example of Innovative Medicine

The Innovative Medicines Initiative (IMI) is a European initiative that aims to improve the competitive situation of the European Union in the field of pharmaceutical research by supporting faster discovery and development of better medicines for patients. IMI will implement innovative patient-centered projects that address the principal causes of delay or bottlenecks in the current biomedical R&D process. These bottlenecks have been identified as predicting safety, predicting efficacy, bridging gaps in knowledge management and bridging gaps in education and training.[81] The IMI calls for project proposals that are open to anyone that in the first stage express their interest in the topic (e.g. from academia, small and medium-sized enterprises (SMEs), patient organizations, etc.). In the second stage, following the first stage peer review, a full project consortium is formed by combining applicants with an European Federation of Pharmaceutical Industries and Associations (EFPIA) consortium already associated with the topic.[82]

Participants bring R&D data, know-how and information, in addition to intellectual property rights pertaining to such data, collectively defined as 'Background' onto the IMI platform for utilization in specific projects to generate 'Foreground'. Ownership of Foreground belongs in the first instance to the individual participant who generated it, but different allocations of ownership may be agreed upon through contractual means.[83] Information related to Foreground is expected to be disseminated by participants, but other participants have the right to review the material in time to protect patentable information or request that the information is kept secret.[84] The initiative is governed by the European Commission, which presents policies and enters into contracts with platform stakeholders. The portfolio of assets is controlled by a two-tiered contrac-

[81] Innovative Medicines Initiative, 'The Innovative Medicines Initiative (IMI) Research Agenda – Creating Biomedical R&D Leadership for Europe to Benefit Patients and Society', 9 February 2008 (Version 2.0), viewed on 9 August 2009, http://www.imi.europa.eu/docs/imi-gb-006v2-15022008-research-agenda_en.pdf.

[82] Innovative Medicines Initiative website, viewed on 9 August 2009, http://www.imi.europa.eu/.

[83] Innovative Medicines Initiative, 'The IMI – IPR Policy', IMI IP Policy Version 1 August 2007, viewed on 9 August 2009, http://www.imi.europa.eu/docs/imi-ipr-policy01august2007_en.pdf.

[84] Innovative Medicines Initiative, 'Clarification Note – IMI IP Policy', viewed on 15 September 2009, http://www.imi.europa.eu/docs/clarification-note-imi-ip-policy.pdf.

tual control where the 'Grant Agreement' is between the IMI Joint Undertaking and the individual projects, whereas the 'Project Agreement' is between participants in one of the projects. The latter also regulates secrecy obligations between parties while collaborating. This contractual control is further supported by an IPR policy. IMI is a Public-Private Partnership between the pharmaceutical industry, represented by the EFPIA and the European Communities represented by the European Commission (EC).[85] These two founding members also constitute the governing board of the initiative.

Utilization of Background or Foreground outside of the scope of the project has been categorized as either Direct Exploitation (DE) or Research Use (RU). Direct Exploitation can broadly be defined as 'to develop for commercialization or to commercialize Foreground itself' whereas Research Use is defined as 'use of Foreground or Background necessary to use Foreground for all purposes other than for completing the project or for Direct Exploitation'. A commercialization path under DE is unrestricted in regard to a participant's own results, IP and IPRs, but is determined through negotiation in regard to results, IP and IPRs that belong to other participants. RU is made available non-exclusively under fair and reasonable terms both to other participants and to third parties. Although platform content is only available to developers, access to Foreground is open to anyone on request. RU rights are available to third parties on non-exclusive fair and reasonable terms and DE rights are negotiated on commercial terms. Both Background and Foreground are available on a royalty-free basis to participants for the purpose of and to the extent necessary to undertake and complete an IMI project.[86] Improvements are not explicitly defined in the IMI IPR policy except for the fact that generated results are included under the Foreground definition. All IMI projects must have at least two partners from each of the categories of academia, SMEs and large pharmaceutical companies. Collaborative relationships can be described as being driven by a subset of the actors since the research agenda is set by the directors of research of the EFPIA.

---

[85] Nunes Correia, F., 'Council Regulation (EC) No 73/2008 – Setting up the Joint Undertaking for the implementation of the Joint Technology Initiative on Innovative Medicine', *Official Journal of the European Union*, 20 December 2007, viewed on 9 August 2009, http://eur-lex.europa.eu/JOHtml.do?uri=OJ%3AL%3A2008%3A030%3ASOM%3AEN%3AHTML.

[86] PR-Helpdesk, 'IP policy in IMI Actions', last updated July 2008, viewed on 9 August 2009, http://www.imi.europa.eu/docs/ipr-helpdesk-doc-on-imi-ipr-policy.pdf.

As IMI aims to boost Europe's biomedical R&D base by improving the predictability of safety and efficacy evaluation, an essential component to make this process efficient is the establishment of a Knowledge Management (KM) pillar. Projects will have an information management and data modeling component, a KM platform, which is integral to the project and is deliverable. The KM platform will be a set of enabling technologies and processes to process data and information that allow knowledge creation, sharing and reuse. To enable flexibility in such a complex system, the KM platform will be a federated, multilayered architecture in which independent components, data sources, scientific services and the like can be configured dynamically and articulated by rules and ontologies. One of the aims of the KM platform is to support complete compatibility between heterogeneous data such as proprietary experimental data (e.g. from pharmaceutical companies), highly curated, experimental public domain data (e.g. SwissProt) and publicly available documentary data (e.g. Medline). Such openness will ideally allow data to be searched, queried, extracted, integrated and shared across both public and proprietary sources, ranging from chemical structures to clinical trials data.

IMI can be concluded to be a multilayered structure in terms of openness ranging from a relatively closed level of platform governance to a comparatively open approach to usage of the platform content that falls under 'Research Use'. A multileveled structure is also present in the portfolio logic where ownership and management of intellectual property rights reside with individual stakeholders, which stands in contrast to intellectual assets (e.g. biomedical data) that are managed in a centralized KM platform. Having experience and skills in intellectual asset and property management (IAM/IPM) will play an important role in access to new projects when defining which data and IP are brought in as 'Background', managing what information from 'Foreground' needs to be delayed in publication for novelty reasons and how to carefully draft the definition of 'Sideground' in the project agreement to open up new commercialization paths. Other related aspects that will require contract drafting experience are the definition of 'Fair and Reasonable' that is to be defined upfront in the project agreement, as well as segmenting the field of 'Research Use', which goes beyond the legal concepts of research use or research exemptions in most patent laws. Clearly participants with advanced capabilities in IAM/IPM are in an advantageous position to successfully extract value from participation in IMI.

4.3. A System Platform Logic – The Example of GSM

The Global System for Mobile Communications (GSM) is, at the time of writing, the most popular based on use technology standard for mobile telecommunications in the world.[87] GSM combines and standardizes interfaces between several different technologies into a single platform for cell phone communication, and provides a standard for intercompatibility and interconnectability that has helped usher in the modern age of telecommunications. As the standard builds on contributions from several different actors, the GSM standard functions as both a technology platform for intercompatibility and as an IP platform for collaboration and technology exchange.

The development of the GSM standard was the result of a directed effort to create a pan-European standard to harmonize the technologies being developed for the rapidly expanding cellular networks of the different member states, which were too incompatible to provide simple, international communication, and too fragmented to allow the realization of the significant economies of scale that could theoretically be captured otherwise. While the European telecommunications market had recently been deregulated to allow free competition to replace the state telecommunications monopolies, the need for collaboration to standardize the incompatible technologies was understood, and supported by European Commission directives prompting harmonization.[88]

The Groupe Spécial Mobile, and later the European Telecommunications Standards Institute, was formed as a consortium of technology developers within telecommunications, working to develop a telecommunications standard that was pan-European, increased existing network capacity, allowed for advanced subscriber authentication, improved voice clarity, simplified and standardized the process of non-voice data transmission, and provided easy international roaming between network providers and operators, among other benefits. The GSM standard became a significant success, both in terms of adoption and in terms of developing a blueprint for technology standardization within telecommunications, but at the same time featured several conflicts and uncertainties, among other things regarding patents and access to technology.

The GSM platform was formally designed as a hierarchical grouping of project groups with different areas of responsibility, creating contributions for an open selection process sometimes known as a 'beauty contest' – comparative hearings to determine a winner based on stated and perceived merits, as opposed to selection by lottery or auction. This organization

87 According to statistics on bearer technologies provided by GSMA Mobile Infolink on 8 July 2009, the GSM standard has been implemented by 80.02% of all mobile telecommunications bearers.

88 See White Paper COM (84) 277 and Green Papers COM (87) 290 and COM (94) 145.

was formally specified in the procedural regulations of GSM bodies, such as the European Telecommunications Standards Institute (ETSI), to minimize bureaucracy and promote direct and efficient technology development collaboration, yet there was no provision to provide a central body with a hierarchically supported mandate to govern the collaboration. The result was that the GSM platform was built up to provide governance in the form of technology direction and collaboration support, where there were clear roles, self-evaluation and evolution of roles in terms of development contributions.

In terms of the governance of technology development within GSM, activities were primarily governed by a common vision of quality. While there were obvious competing goals in terms of which technologies were to be standardized, there was a common vision of the level of quality to be attained, as well as the overall purpose of standardization. Each actor, regardless of their specific product niche, was aware that the market as a whole would benefit from increased user adoption, interoperability, and quality.

In terms of IP and IPR governance, however, there was no such joint vision or commonality of purpose, and the GSM platform, and more specifically ETSI, opted for a minimum of IPR governance. Despite the conflicts experienced in the setting and implementation of the GSM standard, the telecommunications standardization actors have not attempted to substantially limit the use of patents to control contributions to standards, and the numbers of patents reading on standards have only increased since then.[89] It is unlikely that a patent-free policy could ever be successfully established for a telecommunication standard, given industry practice.

The consequences of a minimal IP governance structure for a standardization platform have led to a number of mechanisms being proposed to manage resulting problems without significantly hampering the standards setting and implementation process, with varying results. The concept of Fair, Reasonable, and Non-discriminatory licensing (FRAND, often referred to as Reasonable and Non-discriminatory, or RAND) is one such mechanism, attempting to hold adherents to a standard for licensing

---

[89] For example, according to Lévêque, F. and Ménière, Y. (2008), 'Patents, Anti-trust and Standards', 9(1) *Competition and Regulation in Network Industries* 2008, the technology constituting the MPEG-2 video and audio compression standard is covered by 425 patents with 28 different assignees, and the WCDMA standard, at the time of their study, was linked to over 6000 patent applications owned by more than 30 firms (for more on the increase in patenting in standards, see Simcoe, T. (2005), 'Explaining the Increase in Intellectual Property Disclosure', Joseph L. Rotman School of Management, University of Toronto.

terms that does not put the standard at risk of prohibitive licensing and transaction costs. Briefly and superficially explained, the Fairness commitment of FRAND can be seen as a commitment to avoid anti-competitive terms; Reasonable refers mainly to a royalty rate that is not out of proportion with the utility of the license or the value of the technology, and Non-discriminatory refers to a commitment to apply similar or equivalent terms in all licenses relating to the standard (the obligations of FRAND are usually only applicable between members of the standardization body in question).

Further, FRAND can be seen as a useful compromise in an industry that would most likely not accept a royalty-free (RF) licensing policy, but the specific meaning of the terminology of FRAND is undefined, and suffers from a lack of authoritative backing, either through court room precedent or standardization body regulation that would effectively define and enforce it.[90] Among the complex issues that are not yet resolved in establishing a joint understanding of FRAND is the debate over whether FRAND should be based on proportionality and dynamically adjusted to take into account new contributions and prevent royalty stacking.[91] FRAND terms applied to essential patents covering the GSM standard.

Access to the primary output of GSM standardization activities – the GSM specification – was entirely open to members. Implementation of the specification in products and market actions, however, required, as already mentioned, access to a number of patents on the technologies in the standard. Patents on those technologies that were considered central to the standard – patents that would unavoidably be infringed by implementation of the standard – were usually subject to FRAND commitments, as discussed earlier, in order to encourage licensing and the widespread adoption of the standard, but the fact remained that access to the essential patents of the GSM standard was closed and required negotiation and compensation.

Access and implementation in telecommunication standards, including GSM as well as others, are regulated and limited by both formal and

---

90 For more on the definition of FRAND as a tool for mitigating access problems in standards, see Bekkers, R., Iversen, E. and Blind, K. (2006), 'Patent Pools and Non-assertion Agreements: Coordination Mechanisms for Multi-party IPR Holders in Standardization', Paper for the EASST 2006 Conference, Lausanne, Switzerland, 23–26 August.

91 For a discussion on the effects of royalty stacking of otherwise reasonable royalty rates, see Lemley, M.A. and Shapiro, C. (2007), 'Patent Holdup and Royalty Stacking', 85 *Texas Law Review* 2007, Stanford Law and Economics Olin Working Paper No. 324.

informal costs. Formally, actors are required to pay a fee for membership; the level of participation and influence over the standard is limited to members and sometimes based on the size of the contribution.[92] These fees can in and of themselves prevent smaller actors from participating in the standards-setting process. Informally, actors are required to devote significant time and manpower to participation if they are to have any significant influence. Due to the nature of the processes with the Standard Setting Organizations (SSOs) during the standardization of GSM, exerting an active influence on the standard required numerous meetings in person, contributions on several different occasions, and careful scrutiny of hundreds or thousands of other contributions before each session. This cost itself is prohibitive for several actors.

Finally, as already alluded to, successful implementation of the GSM standard typically incurred royalty costs. Implementing the standard is in itself costly – as mentioned earlier, the telecommunications standards allow and typically expect members to charge royalties for access to essential IP, which means that there is a cost not only for access to the collaborative platform surrounding the standard, but for practical market application of the standard itself. Due to the power dynamic of the telecommunications standards organizations, as mentioned above, there is an identifiable risk that smaller actors with significant technology investments will use their patent holdings as the basis for large royalty fees. While the literature has not identified this behavior as prevalent during the standardization of GSM, it has since become a well-recognized risk in telecommunications standardization.

4.4. The Role of Patents in the Creation of Open IP Platforms

First we have to recognize that markets for intellectual property differ drastically from markets for physical property. As has already been mentioned, it is far from common for patents to be packaged as the visible and primary value propositions of a given transaction. Instead, the value of the transaction is often offered as a technology, tool, system, feature etc., and it is obvious that patents and patentable inventions can be more or less explicit in the discussion of the value proposed. Still, when analyzing these transactions, especially when applying a sociolegal perspective,

---

92 Membership fees within ETSI range from €2000/annum for universities and non-profit associations to over €150 000/annum. Observers pay a flat fee of €4000/annum. Http://www.etsi.org/WebSite/Membership/fees.aspx last accessed 2009-10-03.

the role of the self-regulatory patent tool is normatively important, and sometimes even fundamental, in setting up transactions. The contract tool is of course even more fundamental, but by itself, the contract is not necessarily sufficient for the task of establishing sustainable knowledge markets. Developing, let alone creating, a market for knowledge based only on the use of contracts would require a knowledge provider to be in bilateral contractual relationships with every user of the specific piece of knowledge that the knowledge provider wants to put on the market. Merges discusses the Creative Commons license in this respect: 'Though contract is an incredibly flexible and robust legal institution, it carries with it some built-in limitations. The primary problem is that contract binds parties through mutual bilateral consent. So to be effective, a Creative Commons license must "flow through" or somehow apply to every "downstream user" who comes in contact with a piece of content whose authors wants (*sic*) it to carry Creative Commons licensing restrictions. To put it conceptually, there must be an unbroken chain connecting the creator of content with an ultimate user whose activities challenge the limitations meant to accompany that content. If licensing restrictions become severed from the content, the status of intended restriction will become uncertain.'[93]

Focusing on how the patent tool can be used to create access, the patent, as well as the claim of the patentable invention, is an important tool to be used in *claiming the object of the transaction* as well as *in regulating the market transaction.*[94] With regard to the role of the patent in normatively defining/claiming/creating the object of the transaction, we can see how the patent tool can be used to package (1) the technical solution, (2) the commercial utility/innovation enabled by the technical solution and (3) the legal control position.[95] If we instead focus on the role of the patent in governing the transaction we can in a similar way see how the patent tool can be used to (1) govern access to the technology and support the implementation of the technology, (2) govern access to different utilities

---

[93] Merges, above note 45.

[94] Regarding the role of copyrights in this respect, see Radin, Margaret Jane (2000), 'Humans, Computers, and Binding Commitment', 75 *Indiana Law Journal*, pp. 1125–62.

[95] Adorno draws the conclusion: 'An object can be conceived only by a subject but always remains something other than the subject, whereas a subject by its very nature is from the outset an object as well. Not even as an idea can we conceive a subject that is not an object, but we can conceive an object that is not a subject. To be an object also is part of the meaning of subjectivity; but it is not equally part of the meaning of objectivity to be a subject.' Adorno, Theodor W. (1973), *Negative Dialectics*, London: Routledge & Kegan, p. 183.

and market solutions, and (3) govern the right to exclude actions, behavior etc. Depending on what the customer wants, such as access to technology, access to new innovations, or access to a position of control, patent tools will play a different role in the contractual setting.

It is important to distinguish between open IP platforms, where the value propositions governed by the patents are technology and innovation, and platforms where the value propositions governed are limited to control. In the examples of both the IMI and the GSM platforms, all three dimensions are included, and the platforms are constructed to govern technical solutions and innovations. In IMI, open access is in different aspects supposed to enable learning through R&D, implementation in different quality processes, innovation and other forms of value creation. Conversely, a platform for building, trading and governing control positions would normally only include patents and would be described as an open patent platform. These kinds of platforms, without technology and utilities, can be created for defensive purposes – an interesting example is the open patent initiative to defend Linux against lawsuits.

Regardless of the overall purpose of the platform, any construction where technology and research are managed in interactions places emphasis on patents as important tools in the construction of the platform per se. Patents then become tools to be used when the stakeholders decide whether the platform should be:

- project oriented and controlled ad hoc through project contracts,
- driven by network control according to a contractual model implemented in a web of contracts,
- controlled by a jointly created and relatively informal organization,
- controlled by a formally strong and hierarchical organization, which presents policies and enters into contracts with stakeholders, or
- controlled by a formally strong structure supported by the public and acknowledged in public policy/regulation.

The greater the level of formality and independence in the governance structure of the platform, the easier it becomes to establish control through means other than patents. This becomes especially clear if we limit our analysis to the internal transactions within the platform, where we can see how an advanced platform construction makes it possible to govern the transactions through standardized contractual solutions similar to the Creative Commons License. Further, the platform construction allows for transactions not only with IPRs, but also with other intellectual assets. In the IMI platform, we see that 'data' can simply be defined as background and foreground IP. This means that on the one hand it becomes possible to extract financial value from intellectual assets in a much broader sense, and on the other hand that the access to and openness of these assets needs to be governed through the platform, as the patent system becomes inadequate as the only means of enabling the necessary transactions.

It is very much the creation of a formal organization encompassing and governing the platform that generates this new logic where more or less all creative activities can become IP transactions. A crucial question, therefore, when analyzing the more organized platforms is to what extent the platform per se assumes responsibilities for ownership/control. To what extent does the platform governance take on ownership/control of intellectual assets created? Is the ownership/control of the platform content:

- placed on the individual stakeholders who govern access, development and usage,
- placed on the stakeholders who contractually have decided how they jointly should govern ownership issues,
- placed on the stakeholders, but the formal platform organization has on behalf of the stakeholders the organizational capacities and formal procedures on how to overview and govern the intellectual assets in the platform,
- assumed by a formal organization that takes over ownership and control of the intellectual assets included in the platform?

In the case of GSM, I have already mentioned that actors were able and in many cases expected to patent their technology contributions to the standard, and to use these patents as a means of claiming exclusion rights. In a collaborative standard, it is difficult to claim results through confidentiality or similar means, as each contribution will have been highly scrutinized, and so the claims on the content of standards will often be entirely dependent on claims made by virtue either of market position, or IPR-based control (typically through patents). In the case of GSM, as has been the case with subsequent telecommunications standards, there was no possibility for the technology platform itself to make claims on the valuable results of development activities.

Typically, standardization platforms, such as those building the GSM standard are designed to minimize platform ownership in the results of the joint process. In the case of GSM, whether in the Groupe Spéciale Mobile or the ETSI platform, actors took responsibility for the structure of the technology specification design process, but there was no ambition to create a platform capable of ownership, commercial management, market strategy, etc. in relation to the technology that was being developed. While it is unlikely that it would have been possible, or in any way desirable, to create a platform based on this level of ownership responsibility for such a wide range of market activity, geographical influence, and technological development, it is also clear that many of the conflicts and uncertainties that arose in the standardization of GSM did so at least partly due to the lack of a strong and structured central ownership responsibility.

Unlike platforms established on the basis of, for example, open source technology development,[96] the telecommunications standardization platforms have never prevented members from litigating based on IPRs covering a standard – even essential patents that are required for implementing the standard in the first place. The result in telecommunication standardization, including the GSM standard, is that the IPR-based right to exclude has not only been a driving force in prompting negotiations and license constructions, but also in directly preventing market implementations of the technology.[97] The result is an openness supported by the very real threat of being shut out from accessing the technology.

5. CONCLUSIONS

A general and unavoidable conclusion is that the shift to a knowledge-oriented economy is closely linked to the patent system. In the fields of biotechnology as well as of communication technology, patents have played a crucial role in development where business has become more knowledge based. Patents are fundamental self-regulatory tools in the construction of more network- and open-innovation-based development processes. They are also important tools in the construction of new

---

[96] For examples of how open-source standardization differs, see for example West, Jowel and Dedrick, Jason (2001), 'Open Source Standardization: The Rise of Linux in the Network Era', Center for Research on Information Technologies and Organizations (CRITO), University of California, Irvine.

[97] As an example, Simcoe (2009) has looked at litigation rates for a sample of 949 US patents disclosed in standards-setting contexts between 1984 and 2004, and found that '[standards-disclosed] patents have a very high litigation rate – about 5.5 times greater than a random sample from the same vintage and technology class'. Simcoe concludes that this is not a result of the litigiousness of the standardization context as much as it is a selection effect, stemming from the fact that firms are more likely to disclose their most valuable patents, and are thus more willing to go to the expense of enforcing them by litigation. See Simcoe, T.S., Graham, S.J.H. and Feldman, M.P. (2009), 'Competing on Standards? Entrepreneurship, Intellectual Property and Platform Technologies', available at: http://www.rotman.utoronto.ca/timothy.simcoe/papers/CompetingOnStandards.pdf, accessed 10 March 2010.

knowledge-based business models. At the same time, the patent system poses a number of fundamental challenges in relation to the future of the knowledge economy. The new business models of the knowledge economy capitalize on the practice of up-stream patenting and the fact that research itself can no longer necessarily be exempt from patentability, and are built around research tools, diagnostics tools, etc. This use of patent-related self-regulatory tools has a striking effect – not only on freedom in research, but also in altering the boundaries of the market economy and the sphere of the public domain.

A major conclusion of this chapter is that for this development to be constructive, we are dependent on the development of open IP platforms. In the sphere of public research, platforms have to be constructed as public/private-hybrids, i.e. private domain solutions need to be used to promote the public interest. Platforms like the IMI need to include public interest among their motivating rationale, and also become an element in the construction of an 'IP-based public domain'.

Another conclusion is that the use of patents and other IPRs in relation to the virtualization of technology-driven innovation has changed the foundation of the market economy. In the external setting, a large number of new license-based business models have been developed around the simple fact that transactions with innovations controlled through patents and copyright always require permission, and give rise to a web of agreements. This has had a drastic impact on the freedom of competition. In the virtual sphere, markets are not 'out there', but need to be constructed by actors with an incentive to participate in those markets once they have been constructed. Much as stated above in regard to the expanded use of patents, if this development of new permission-based business models is to be constructive, we are dependent on the development of open IP platforms. The GSM platform is an example of how open IP platforms become integrated in markets as such, once it becomes impossible to participate in the (in this case European) telecommunications market without also taking part in the creation and claiming of the GSM platform.

As I see it, it is most likely that the patent system will have to be reformed in the setting of the now maturing knowledge economy. There is no guarantee that IPRs in a knowledge economy will not be capable of preventing creative destruction. However, at this stage, we still lack enough knowledge to understand and see how the patent system will operate as a fundamental element in the rules of the game for a more knowledge-driven economy. Perhaps the most important conclusion in this context is that the need for reform will be completely different if there is no constructive development of open IP platforms. Our collective abilities to develop open IP platforms will in many ways define which kinds of businesses will be created and what business climate we will generate. The concept of the open IP platform, for me, very much represents our collective challenge in 'institutionalizing' the public domain, as well as the private domain.

6. Free access, including freedom to imitate, as a legal principle – a forgotten concept?

Ansgar Ohly*

1. GRETCHEN'S QUESTION

In Goethe's drama *Faust*, Gretchen asks Dr Faustus: 'Now tell me: how do you take religion?'[1] Gretchen's question is naïve, but also fundamental, directly to the point, and it is answered in an evasive way. If we try to rephrase Gretchen's question in relation to intellectual property law, it might be: 'Now tell me: how about imitation?' What sounds like a question asked by a student in an introductory course is in fact a fundamental issue about which there is a surprising degree of disagreement.

If imitation is unfair, it follows that intellectual property protection against misappropriation is appropriate, even where there is no evidence that such protection is beneficial for society. The protection of well-known marks against dilution and misappropriation of goodwill, for example, can easily be justified. Overlaps between intellectual property rights are generally acceptable, and unfair competition law can be relied on in order to fill gaps between intellectual property rights. If, however, imitation is a necessary and welcome process in a market economy, the argumentative threshold for justifying intellectual property rights is significantly higher. Broad anti-dilution laws, for example, are more difficult to justify because consumer interests are only marginally affected and because there is no evident need to create incentives for the creation of luxury images. Overlaps between intellectual property rights can be worrying where the accumulation of rights can undermine exceptions.[2] Seen from

* Dr. iur. (Munich), LL.M. (Cantab.), Professor of Civil Law and Intellectual Property Law at the University of Bayreuth, Visiting Professor at the University of Oxford.

1 Goethe, *Faust I*, Marthens Garten, verse 3415.

2 Cf. on this issue Dinwoodie, Graeme (2002), 'Trademark and Copyright:

this perspective, the area between intellectual property rights should not be referred to as a 'gap' but rather as a free space which should not be restricted by unfair competition law.

Two diametrically opposite positions can be distinguished. According to one view, 'reaping without sowing' is unfair. The classical exposition of this attitude can be found in the opinion of the US Supreme Court in *INS v AP*:

> In doing this [i.e. rewriting news gathered by the plaintiff and publishing the news as its own] defendant, by its very act, admits that it is taking material that has been acquired by complainant as the result of organization and the expenditure of labor, skill, and money, and which is salable by complainant for money, and that defendant in appropriating it and selling it as its own is endeavoring to reap where it has not sown, and by disposing of it to newspapers that are competitors of complainant's members is appropriating to itself the harvest of those who have sown. Stripped of all disguises, the process amounts to an unauthorized interference with the normal operation of complainant's legitimate business precisely at the point where the profit is to be reaped, in order to divert a material portion of the profit from those who have earned it to those who have not; with special advantage to defendant in the competition because of the fact that it is not burdened with any part of the expense of gathering the news. The transaction speaks for itself and a court of equity ought not to hesitate long in characterizing it as unfair competition in business.[3]

At least in Continental Europe, many courts and academic lawyers have adopted the same attitude. One year before the Supreme Court decision in *INS v AP* was handed down, the German judge and academic *Adolf Lobe* characterised 'ploughing with someone else's calf' as unfair.[4] In present-day Europe, it is in particular the French courts which grant broad

---

Complements or Competitors?', in Ginsburg, Jane C. and June M. Besek (eds), *Adjuncts and Alternatives to Copyright*, New York: ALAI-USA, pp. 498 et seq.; Kur, Annette, 'Exceptions to Protection Where Copyright and Trademarks Overlap', in Ginsburg and Besek (eds), *ibid.*, pp. 594 et seq.; Ohly, A., 'Areas of Overlap between Trade Mark Rights, Copyright and Design Rights in German Law', GRUR Int. 2007, 704 et seq.; Quaedvlieg, A. (2009), 'Overlap/relationships between Copyright and other Intellectual Property Rights', in Derclaye, Estelle (ed.), *Research Handbook on the Future of EU Copyright*, Cheltenham: Edward Elgar, pp. 408 et seq.

[3] 248 US 215, 239–40 (1918); see also Callman, R., 'He Who Reaps Where He Has Not Sown: Unjust Enrichment in the Law of Unfair Competition', 55 *Harvard Law Review* 595 (1942). For a critical analysis of Callmann's line of argument, see Wadlow, C., 'Rudolf Callmann and the Misappropriation Doctrine in the Common Law of Unfair Competition' (2008), forthcoming in IPQ 2011.

[4] Lobe, A., 'Der Hinweis auf fremde gewerbliche Leistung als Mittel zur Reklame', MuW XVI (1916–17), 129.

protection against 'parasitic competition'.[5] This approach is based on the conviction that 'it is unfair to attain a competitive advantage resulting from the (. . .) investment of another'.[6] Many other jurisdictions provide for protection against 'slavish imitation' or misappropriation, often on the basis of unfair competition law.[7]

In common law jurisdictions, however, the majority opinion in *INS v AP* has not been widely followed. It has been referred to as an island rather than a landmark.[8] Today, most common lawyers are more likely to subscribe to the vigorous dissent given by Justice Brandeis, who warned against interfering with free competition:

> That competition is not unfair in a legal sense, merely because the profits gained are unearned, even if made at the expense of a rival, is shown by many cases besides those referred to above. He who follows the pioneer into a new market, or who engages in the manufacture of an article newly introduced by another, seeks profits due largely to the labor and expense of the first adventurer; but the law sanctions, indeed encourages, the pursuit.[9]

According to this position, imitation as such is not only unobjectionable, it is 'the very lifeblood of a competitive economy'.[10] Competition by imitation drives down prices. Since consumers 'want the best deals they can get',[11] vigorous competition is in their best interest, at least as long as there is no deception. In Europe, English judges are probably the strongest proponents of the freedom of imitation.

---

5 See Le Tourneau, Philippe (1998), *Le Parasitisme*, Paris: Litec; Lucas, André and Henri-Jacques Lucas (2006), *Traité de la propriété littéraire et artistique*, 3rd ed., Paris: Litec, para. 20; Malaurie-Vignal, M., 'Le parasitisme des investissements et du travail d'autrui', *D.*1996, *chron.* p. 177.

6 Cour d'appel de Paris, 14 June 2006, *Propr. Industr.* 2006, comm. 81 with case-note *Gasnier – Cartier v Raymond Weil.* This judgment is discussed by Christian Le Stanc in his comment to this paper.

7 See Kaufmann, Peter Joachim (1986), *Passing Off and Misappropriation*, Weinheim: VCH, pp. 73 et seq; Kamperman Sanders, Anselm (1997), *Unfair Competition Law*, Oxford: Clarendon Press, pp. 22 et seq. and the country reports by Henning-Bodewig, Frauke (2006), *Unfair Competition Law, European Union and Member States*, The Hague: Kluwer.

8 High Court of Australia, *Moorgate Tobacco v Philip Morris* [1985] RPC 219, 237–8 per Deane J, quoting Morison, W.L., 'Unfair Competition at Common Law', (1951–3) 2 *University of Western Australia Law Review* 34, 37.

9 248 US 215, 248, 259 (1918).

10 US Supreme Court, *Bonito Boats, Inc. v Thunder Craft Boats, Inc.*, 489 US 141, 146 (1989).

11 English Court of Appeal, *L'Oréal v Bellure*, [2007] EWCA Civ 968, para. 139 per Jacob LJ.

The position of many Continental European jurisdictions is somewhere between these extremes. Art. 11 (1) of the Spanish Code against Unfair Competition explicitly stresses the freedom of imitation, but imitation is considered unfair in certain situations, in particular where the imitation results in an association with another trader's products or where another trader's reputation is misappropriated (Art. 11 (2)). Along the same lines, German law recognises the freedom of imitation (Nachahmungsfreiheit) outside the scope of intellectual property law as a principle,[12] but the sale of imitated products is considered as unfair, when (a) consumers are deceived, (b) the reputation attached to the original products is damaged or unduly exploited or (c) the imitation was made possible by a breach of confidence.[13] Under the Italian Civil Code, the slavish imitation of products is unfair when it creates confusion,[14] whereas the mere misappropriation of reputation can be enjoined under the general clause of unfair competition law,[15] as long as such protection does not conflict with the limits of intellectual property protection.[16] The Dutch Supreme Court (Hoge Raad) stresses the freedom of trade as a principle,[17] but is prepared to protect results of skill and labour against slavish imitation in exceptional cases.[18] In several countries, a certain discrepancy between theory and practice can be observed: while in theory imitation is free, judges often seem to have the hunch that it is wrong to imitate someone else's products without reasonable efforts of one's own.[19]

---

[12] Reichsgericht, RGZ 73, 294, 297 – *Schallplatten*; Bundesgerichtshof (BGH) GRUR 1952, 516, 520 – *Hummelfiguren*; BGH GRUR 2000, 521, 523 – *Modulgerüst*; BGH GRUR 2006, 79. para. 19 – *Jeans I*; BGH GRUR 2007, 795, para. 22 – *Handtaschen*; Ohly, Ansgar, in Piper, Henning, Ansgar Ohly and Olaf Sosnitza (eds) (2009), *Gesetz gegen den unlauteren Wettbewerb (UWG)*, 5th ed., Munich: Beck, § 4 para. 9/2; Wiebe, Andreas, in Heermann, Peter and Günter Hirsch (eds) (2006), *Münchener Kommentar zum Lauterkeitsrecht*, Munich: Beck, § 4 No. 9, paras 15 et seq.

[13] § 4 No. 9 of the German Act against Unfair Competition.

[14] Art. 2598 (1) Codice civile.

[15] Tribunale di Milano, 27 July 2005, Giurisprudenzia annotata di diritto industriale 2005, B 13, and 10 July 2006, Giurisprudenzia Annotata di diritto industriale 2006, M 81.

[16] See the Italian LEGO case, Corte di Cassazione, 28 February 2008, No. 5437; this judgment is analysed by Alberto Musso in his comment to this paper.

[17] Hoge Raad, 26 June 1953, *Machinefabriek Thole v Hyster Company*, NJ 1954, 90, 180.

[18] Hoge Raad, 27 June 1986, *Holland Nautic/Decca,* NJ 1987, No. 191, p. 664; Quaedvlieg, A., 'Leistungsschutz in den Niederlanden – Schutz des "sweat of the brow"?', GRUR Int. 1997, 971.

[19] See Kur, A., 'Der wettbewerbliche Leistungsschutz: Gedanken zum

2. INTELLECTUAL PROPERTY AND THE FREEDOM OF IMITATION: THE NEED FOR A FAIR BALANCE

One of the fundamental tasks of intellectual property research is the search for the right balance between effective intellectual property protection and free competition.

Over recent decades, intellectual property protection has been extended and strengthened both at the international level and in national jurisdictions. The TRIPS Agreement not only sets out minimum standards of intellectual property protection, it also puts an obligation on member states to provide for enforcement procedures which permit effective protection against infringement (Art. 41 (1)). In the European Union and elsewhere, intellectual property protection has been extended to new types of subject-matter. At the same time, the Enforcement Directive has harmonised the remedies available in cases of infringement at a high level. It is not the intention of this chapter to criticise these developments. Indeed, where intellectual property protection is justified, it must keep pace with new developments and it must be efficient.

It seems, however, that the political drive towards more and stronger intellectual property protection has relegated the countervailing principle of free competition to the second division. The need for a balance of rights and obligations (Art. 7 TRIPS), the necessity to prevent practices which unreasonably restrain trade (Art. 8 (2) TRIPS) and the principle of proportionality (Art. 3 (2) EC Enforcement Directive) feature less prominently in the international political arena than the need for strict intellectual property protection. In particular, the principle of freedom of imitation is often considered as outdated or unjustified. Sometimes such criticism is made explicit.[20] As already noted above, however, courts and authors often pay rhetorical tribute to this concept, while nevertheless restricting imitation on the basis of well-established intellectual property or tort law doctrines.

---

wettbewerbsrechtlichen Schutz von Formgebungen, bekannten Marken und Characters', GRUR 1990, 1. This point will be explored in more detail below at Sections 3.2 and 3.3.

20 See Fezer, K.-H., 'Modernisierung des deutschen Rechts gegen den unlauteren Wettbewerb auf der Grundlage einer Europäisierung des Wettbewerbsrechts', WRP 2001, 989, 1007; Glöckner, Jochen (2006), *Europäisches Lauterkeitsrecht*, Munich: Beck, p. 595; Lubberger, A., 'Grundsatz der Nachahmungsfreiheit?', in Ahrens, Hans-Jürgen, Joachim Bornkamm and Hans-Peter Kunz-Hallstein (eds) (2006), *Festschrift für Eike Ullmann*, Saarbrücken: Juris, pp. 737 et seq.

Against this tendency, the crucial importance of the freedom to imitate should be stressed. There are two reasons why imitation must be free. First, there is a strong policy argument: imitation is the lifeblood of a competitive economy. This is evident when the imitation is one step in the process of creating a new product. But even the non-innovative or non-creative imitation has a central function in a market: it enhances competition and reduces prices. To be sure, the economic analysis of intellectual property shows that there may be good reasons for restricting competition by imitation in order to advance competition by innovation.[21] But this justification is also a limitation: propertisation is no end in itself; it is only justified as far as it is necessary to ensure the proper functioning of markets.[22] The second argument is of a systematic nature. Exceptions, thresholds of protection and the limited duration of rights reflect the result of a legislative balancing exercise.[23] These limits of protection must be respected in other areas of intellectual property and unfair competition law, if this field of law is to be construed as a coherent whole. This is generally recognised with regard to patent law: few courts would be prepared to protect inventions once patent protection has lapsed. Surprisingly, however, courts often do not approach design protection with the same systematic rigour. At least European courts seem more willing to grant protection against the imitation of product shapes, regardless of whether design protection is still available.

As indicated above, the tension between propertisation and the freedom of imitation could be analysed with regard to many issues of intellectual

---

[21] For a summary of the current economic justifications of patent law, see Guellec, Dominique and Bruno van Pottelsberghe (2007), *The Economics of the European Patent System*, Oxford: Oxford University Press, pp. 49 et seq.; Landes, William M. and Richard A. Posner (2003), *The Economic Structure of Intellectual Property Law*, Cambridge, MA: Belknap Press, pp. 13 et seq., 294 et seq.; Scotchmer, Suzanne (2004), *Innovation and Incentives*, Cambridge, MA: MIT Press, 2004, pp. 34 et seq.

[22] See Lemley, M., 'Property, Intellectual Property, and Free Riding', 83 *Texas Law Review* 1031, 1057 (2005).

[23] This point is emphasised vigorously by Deane J in *Moorgate Tobacco v Philip Morris* [1985] RPC 219, 240 (High Court of Australia): 'Those limits, which define the boundary between the area of legal or equitable restraint and protection and the area of untrammelled competition, increasingly reflect what the responsible Parliament or Parliaments have determined to be the appropriate balance between competing claims and policies. Neither legal principle nor social utility requires or warrants the obliteration of that boundary by the importation of a cause of action whose main characteristic is the scope it allows, under high-sounding generalizations, for judicial indulgence of idiosyncratic notions of what is fair in the market place.'

property law. One could ask whether intellectual property law should protect investment as such, one could investigate the overlap between several rights and one could certainly look at substantive and methodological questions concerning exceptions. Taken together, these issues could easily fill a monograph. I will have to make a selection. Thus I will focus on one area where the conflict between protection against imitation and free competition is evident, both in theory and in everyday practice: the relationship between intellectual property and unfair competition law.

3. INTELLECTUAL PROPERTY AND UNFAIR COMPETITION LAW

3.1. Towards a European Perspective

Can unfair competition law fill gaps in the intellectual property system? The answer will obviously depend on the national legal background. In many continental European jurisdictions, unfair competition law is regularly invoked in intellectual property cases. For a German or Dutch lawyer, it is not unusual to take action against product imitation not only under trade mark or design law, but also on the basis of doctrines of unfair copying or slavish imitation. When the reputation of a luxury brand is exploited by another trader, a French lawyer will regularly rely both on trade mark law and on the unfair competition law doctrine of parasitic competition. A common lawyer, on the other hand, is likely to insist that the limits of intellectual property protection should not be undermined by the application of unfair competition law. From a Continental perspective, however, the tort of passing off grants protection against a particular type of unfair competition, and it supplements the law of registered trade marks in a way which is partly equivalent to the intellectual property law protection of unregistered trade marks, which exists in many Continental jurisdictions. Thus it is difficult to find a jurisdiction which rigorously excludes any type of supplementary unfair competition protection.

Within the EU, the national perceptions of what is fair and unfair are converging due to the approximation of law by means of EC Directives, which are in turn interpreted by the ECJ. Since 2005, the law of unfair commercial practices in business-to-consumer relations has been harmonised. While there is no general directive which would protect traders against unfair competition, the Community law provisions on comparative advertising have been interpreted so broadly by the ECJ that they have gained significant importance for the protection of goodwill. Thus I will look at the freedom of imitation and the issue of misappropriation from a Community law perspective rather than from the viewpoint of national law. It will emerge that European courts restrict copying in three typical situations, which will be analysed in turn: (1) consumer deception, (2) exploitation or tarnishment of another trader's image, (3) identical or 'slavish' copying.

3.2. Consumer Deception

Regardless of the respective legal backgrounds, there seems to be general agreement that the sale of imitated products can be enjoined when it misleads consumers as to the trade source of goods. Causing confusion is listed as one category of unfair competition by Art. 10bis (3) No. 1 of the Paris Convention. According to Art. 4 (h) of the EC Directive 2006/114/EC on Misleading and Comparative Advertising, comparative advertising must not 'create confusion among traders', whereas Art. 6 (2)(a) of the EC Unfair Commercial Practices Directive (2005/29/EC) provides that 'any marketing of a product, including comparative advertising, which creates confusion with any products, trade marks, trade names or other distinguishing marks of a competitor' is to be regarded as misleading and hence as unfair.

Indeed, there are evident and undisputed economic reasons for protecting both traders and consumers from deception as to the trade origin.[24] Consumers can only choose if they can distinguish between goods. Rules against confusion safeguard market transparency and reduce consumer search costs, while at the same time making it worthwhile for traders to invest in the quality and the image of their products. Trade marks, in particular, create protected 'channels of communication' between traders and consumers.[25]

Most, if not all, European legal systems prohibit the sale of imitated products where it results in consumer confusion. Several countries have explicit statutory provisions to this effect,[26] other jurisdictions have general

---

[24] See Landes and Posner, *supra* note 21, pp. 166 et seq.; Griffiths, Andrew, in Bently, Lionel, Jennifer Davis and Jane C. Ginsburg (eds) (2008), *Trade Marks and Brands*, Cambridge: Cambridge University Press, pp. 241, 245 et seq.; Kaufmann, *supra* note 7, pp. 121 et seq.

[25] Lehmann, M., 'Unfair Use of and Damage to the Reputation of Well-Known Marks, Names and Indications of Source in Germany: Some Aspects of Law and Economics', (1986) 17 *IIC*, pp. 746, 763.

[26] E.g. Art. 2598 (1) of the Italian Civil Code; § 4 No. 9 (a) of the German Act against Unfair Competition. Art. 11 (2) of the Spanish Act against Unfair Competition, which prohibits imitations which import an 'association', is interpreted to cover the risk of confusion; see STS, 17 July 2007, RJ 2007, 5140, FJ 4;

statutory provisions along the lines of Art. 10bis (3) No. 1 of the Paris Convention,[27] in a third group of jurisdictions, the courts have developed actions against market practices which cause consumer deception. This third group comprises jurisdictions as diverse as French law, where 'confusion' is recognised as one of the categories of 'concurrence déloyale',[28] and English law, where the tort of passing off serves the same function.[29]

The general rule, however, requires three qualifications. First, there may be situations in which countervailing interests trump the principle that confusion should be avoided. According to the doctrine of functionality, which is well-established both in trade-mark law[30] and in the law of passing off[31] or unfair competition,[32] technical product features should remain free, even if consumers attribute these features to one particular manufacturer.

Secondly, monopoly use, which can be the result of intellectual property protection, of state monopolies or may just result from the market structure, may result in the mark being associated with a particular manufacturer. When a competitor starts offering 'postal' services after the deregulation of the market for mail delivery, consumers will tend to associate these services with the former state monopolist,[33] and when a competitor takes up the idea of selling lemon juice in squeezable lemon-shaped containers, consumers will be likely to be confused into thinking that all containers of this type are offered by one company.[34] Although the ECJ did not recognise an anti-monopoly defence with regard to the regis-

---

García Pérez, Rafael, *Ley de Competencia Desleal* (2008), Aranzadi: Cizur Menor, p. 278.

27 E.g. Art. 3 (d) of the Swiss Act against Unfair Competition; Art. 6 of the Spanish Act against Unfair Competition.

28 See Henning-Bodewig, *supra* note 7, p. 123; Kamperman Sanders, *supra* note 7, p. 26.

29 On the relationship between passing off and unfair competition, see Wadlow, Christopher (2004), *The Law of Passing-Off*, 3rd ed., London: Sweet & Maxwell, paras 1-49 et seq. and chapter 2.

30 See Art. 3 (1)(e)(ii) Trade Mark Directive; Art. 7 (1)(e)(ii) Community Trade Mark Regulation.

31 See Wadlow, *supra* note 29, paras. 8-120, 8-121; Supreme Court of Canada, *Kirkbi v Ritvik Holdings*, [2005] 3 SCR 302, 2005 SCC 65, para. 58.

32 For German law, see BGH GRUR 2008, 790, para. 36 – *Baugruppe*; Ohly (*supra* note 12), § 4, para. 9/41.

33 Hence the German Federal Supreme Court 'BGH GRUR 2009, 669 – *Post II*' considered the trade mark 'Post' as descriptive, but considered it likely that the mark had acquired distinctiveness (Art. 3 (3) Trade Mark Directive = § 8 (3) of the German Trade Mark Act).

34 See House of Lords, *Reckitt & Colman v Borden* [1990] RPC 341.

tration of shapes as trade marks,[35] courts should be wary of perpetuating monopolies on the basis of anti-confusion rules.

Thirdly, courts sometimes have the tendency to imply confusion in cases of 'slavish imitation'. The German Federal Supreme Court, for example, presumes consumer confusion in cases of exact or almost exact copying.[36] A typical example is the *Jeans* case decided in 2005.[37] The defendant had sold almost identical copies of G-Star's 'Elwood' jeans. Apparently, the design of the jeans was not protected by an intellectual property right.[38] The Court of Appeal gave judgment for the claimant on the basis of unfair competition law. This judgment was upheld by the Supreme Court, which held that the jeans were very distinctive, that there had been almost exact copying and that hence consumers were likely to be misled. The Court added that unfair competition protection did not conflict with the policy of Community Design law, according to which unregistered design rights expire after three years, because the prevention of confusion was not the purpose of design law. The risk involved in this argument is evident: by implying confusion in cases of identical copying, design protection is granted through the back door, even where a design right would have lapsed. The Court covered this inconsistency by attaching the tag 'confusion' to the defendant's practice. This problem can only be avoided by taking two principles of European Community law seriously. First, the perspective from which the existence of a likelihood of confusion is determined should be the perspective of a reasonably well-informed and reasonably observant and circumspect consumer.[39] Secondly, as is recognised in European trade mark law,[40] shapes may lack distinctiveness because

---

35 ECJ, case C-299/99, [2002] ECR I-05475, *Phillips v Remington*, para. 65.

36 BGH GRUR 1999, 751, 753 – *Güllepumpen*; BGH GRUR 2004, 941, 943 – *Metallbett*; BGH GRUR 2007, 984, para. 36 – *Gartenliege*; see the criticism by Kur, A., '(No) Freedom to Copy? Protection of Technical Features under Unfair Competition Law', in: Prinz zu Waldeck und Pyrmont, Wolrad et al. (2008), *Patents and Technological Progress in a Globalized World, Liber Amicorum Joseph Straus*, pp., 521, 527.

37 BGH GRUR 2006, 79 – *Jeans I*.

38 This point is not discussed in the judgment. Apparently a registered design right did not exist. Since the jeans had first been marketed in 1996, the protection of unregistered designs under the Community Design Regulation did not apply. Trade mark protection for the shape of the jeans was excluded, because the shape gives substantial value to the product (Art. 3 (e)(iii) Trade Mark Directive), as the ECJ has decided in a case concerning this very jeans model: ECJ, case C-371/06, [2007] ECR I-7709, *Benetton v G-Star*.

39 Recital 18 of the Unfair Commercial Practices Directive.

40 ECJ, joined cases C-53-55/01, [2003] ECR I-3161 *Linde, Winward, Rado*, para. 48.

consumers do not normally regard shapes as indications of origin. Hence consumers will normally attach particular importance to the labelling of products. Courts in several jurisdictions have accepted this argument in cases concerning the sale of toy bricks which are compatible with LEGO products: while the shape of the bricks is identical, appropriate labelling at the point of sale will normally avoid confusion.[41] The same is true for jeans: young purchasers of fashion are extremely brand-oriented. It seems highly unlikely that these consumers take their decision without first looking at the label.

To sum up, there seems to be considerable agreement in Europe that a remedy against confusion should be available, but that it needs some qualification. Should Directive 2006/114/EC on Misleading and Comparative Advertising ever be extended to cover all unfair commercial practices in business-to-business relations, the new directive should arguably contain a provision drafted along the following lines:

> (1) The offer of imitated products shall be regarded as unfair where it is likely to deceive an average consumer, who is reasonably well informed and reasonably observant and circumspect, by creating confusion with any products of a competitor.
> (2) The imitation of product features shall not be regarded as unfair where it is necessary in order to obtain a technical result.
> (3) When assessing the risk of confusion, regard shall be had to the extent to which the consumers' perception is the result of a dominant position held by the original producer.

3.3. Exploitation or Tarnishment of Product Image

A much more controversial issue is whether the copying of luxury products is unfair in cases in which there is no consumer confusion but in which the imitator 'piggybacks' on the goodwill of the original manufacturer.

The laws of the EU member states differ considerably in this respect. English courts, on the one hand, have not been prepared to enjoin misappropriation without misrepresentation.[42] Under the French doctrine of 'parasitic competition',[43] on the other hand, the non-confusing imitation

---

[41] See, for German law, BGH GRUR 2005, 349, 352 – *Klemmbausteine III*; for Italian law, Corte di Cassazione, 28 February 2008, No. 5437; for Canadian law, *Kirkbi v Ritvik Holdings*, [2005] 3 SCR 302, 2005 SCC 65, para. 61.

[42] As is stressed by Jacob LJ in *L'Oréal v Bellure*, [2007] EWCA Civ 968, paras 137 ff. (CA), and Jacob J (as he then was) in *Hodgkinson Corby v Wards Mobility Services* [1995] FSR 169, 174 (Ch).

[43] See the references *supra* note 5.

of luxury products is regularly considered as unfair. The courts not only enjoin the sale of 'lookalike' no-name products, but also the imitation of well-known product shapes by other manufacturers of luxury goods. In the *Tank* case,[44] Raymond Weill, a highly reputed producer of luxury watches, had offered square-shaped watches which bore a reminiscence to the 'Tank' watch, a classic Cartier model. The Paris Court of Appeal held that this amounted to an unfair act of parasitic competition, although the defendant enjoyed a high reputation itself. Most European jurisdictions have adopted positions between these two extremes. In German law, Art. 4 No. 9 (b) of the German Act against Unfair Competition prohibits the offer of product imitations where the reputation of the imitated product is unduly exploited or damaged. In some recent judgments, however, the German Supreme Court has interpreted this provision restrictively. In a case concerning cheap knock-off copies of Hermès handbags,[45] the Court held that the differences between the prestigious original and the cheap copy were so evident that no consumer would transfer the luxury image to the cheap copies. According to the Court, unfair competition law did not prohibit the creation of an association with a luxury product. In the latest LEGO decision,[46] the Supreme Court allowed the sale of toy bricks which were compatible with LEGO bricks. Where one manufacturer had dominated a market for a long time, consumers created a link between the original product and the newcomer's goods almost as a matter of course. If the newcomer avoided confusion by clearly labelling its products, the entry into a formerly monopolistic market did not amount to unfair competition, even if the newcomer benefited from the positive reputation of the original product. Art. 11 (2) of the Spanish Act against Unfair Competition provides that the imitation of another trader's products is unfair where it results in an association or an unjustified appropriation of another trader's reputation. Unfairness is excluded, however, where these practices are inevitable. Italian courts have also enjoined the offer of imitated products for reasons of misappropriation,[47] but the Italian Corte di Cassazione has recently allowed the marketing of toy bricks which were exact imitations of LEGO bricks.[48]

In view of these differences between the national traditions, the level of protection against pure misappropriation in European Community law is surprisingly high. The proprietor of a well-known trade mark can prohibit

---

44 *Supra* note 6.
45 GRUR 2005, 349 – *Klemmbausteine III.*
46 GRUR 2007, 795 – *Handtaschen.*
47 *Supra* note 15.
48 *Supra* note 16.

the use of identical or similar signs where such use without due cause takes unfair advantage of, or is detrimental to, the distinctive character or the repute of the mark.[49] In this respect, European law goes further than US law,[50] which only protects famous marks against dilution by blurring or by tarnishment.[51]

Another piece of Community legislation is even more protective. Art. 4 of the Directive on Misleading and Comparative Advertising is on its face a provision which liberalises the law of comparative advertising. According to this article, comparative advertising is *permitted* when the conditions set out in the article are met. One of the conditions is that comparative advertising does not take unfair advantage of the reputation of a trade mark, trade name or other distinguishing marks of a competitor or of the designation of origin of competing products (Art. 4 (f)). What is more, the advertisement must not present goods or services as imitations or replicas of goods or services bearing a protected trade mark or trade name (Art. 4 (g)). It is probably fair to say that the relevance of these provisions has been underestimated by many European lawyers. Meanwhile, for three reasons, the Community rules on comparative advertising have become an important tool in the luxury industry's arsenal. First, the ECJ has decided that Art. 4 not only permits comparative advertising, but also obliges member states to prohibit comparisons which do not meet the criteria set forth in the article.[52] Secondly, the ECJ has given a very broad definition to the term 'comparative advertising'.[53] Thirdly, the Court of Justice has held that the use of another trader's mark in unfair comparative advertising may infringe that mark, even if the mark is not well known and if the origin function remains unaffected.[54] Hence the provisions

---

49 Art. 9 (1)(c) Community Trade Mark Regulation; Art. 5 (2) Trade Mark Directive. The latter provision is optional, but to the best of my knowledge, all member states have made use of this option.

50 Although the difference is reduced by the US doctrine of post-sale confusion, *see Hermès Int. v Lederer de Paris Fifth Avenue Inc.*, 219 F.3d 104, 108 (2nd Cir., 2000).

51 Sec. 43 Trademark Act 1946 ('Lanham Act') as changed by the Trademark Dilution Revision Act 2006; see also the criticism by Tushnet, R., 'Gone in Sixty Milliseconds: Trademark Law and Cognitive Science', 86 *Texas Law Review* 507 (2008).

52 ECJ, case C-44/01, [2003] ECR I-3095, *Pippig Augenoptik v Hartlauer*, para. 44.

53 See ECJ, case C-112/99, [2001] ECR I-7945, *Toshiba Europe v Katun*, paras 35 et seq.; ECJ, case C-381/05, [2007] ECR I-3115, *De Landtsheer Emmanuel v CIVC*, paras 28, 42.

54 ECJ, case C-487/07, [2009] ECR I-5185, *L'Oréal v Bellure*, para. 65.

against unfair comparative advertising are regularly enforceable by means of a civil action, although the directive itself allows the member states to choose between private and administrative enforcement.[55]

While there may be good reasons for protecting trade marks against dilution by tarnishment or blurring, the broad protection against misappropriation which is granted by both European trade mark law and the Directive on Misleading and Comparative Advertising is difficult to justify.[56] While there seems to be a widespread sense that 'reaping without sowing' or 'plowing with someone else's calf' is wrong, this intuition is rarely rationalised. Consumer protection cannot be invoked, since consumer interests are not affected unless there is some element of deception. On the contrary, laws against 'knock-off copies' reduce consumer choice. Indeed, Recital 14 of the Unfair Business Practices Directive stresses that 'it is not the intention of this Directive to reduce consumer choice by prohibiting the promotion of products which look similar to other products unless this similarity confuses consumers as to the commercial origin of the product and is therefore misleading'. The incentive paradigm does not provide a convincing justification either.[57] There is no reason to assume that manufacturers would not invest in the creation of product images without protection against misappropriation. As long as there is efficient protection against confusion as to source, consumers can distinguish high-image products from cheap imitations. Indeed, since US law only provides protection against dilution,[58] the US experience militates against the assumption that the market for luxury products would collapse without broad anti-misappropriation provisions. One may even doubt whether the state should actively support the 'hidden persuaders' by enhancing the creation of luxury reputation.[59]

Finally, deontological approaches are also bound to fail. The *Lockean* labour theory has been criticised, both generally and in its application

---

[55] Art. 5 (1) of Directive 2006/114/EC on Misleading and Comparative Advertising.

[56] See Lemley, M., 'The Modern Lanham Act and the Death of Common Sense', 108 *Yale Law Journal*, 1687, 1705 (1999): 'One can understand why trademark owners want these things, of course, but we must look to the public interest, not private interests, to decide whether trademark owners should get them'.

[57] See Lemley (*supra* note 56) at pp. 1706 et seq.; Griffiths (*supra* note 24), pp. 421, 263.

[58] It needs to be acknowledged, though, that the lack of a full misappropriation doctrine in US trade mark law is partly compensated by the doctrine of post-sale confusion; see *supra* note 50.

[59] See the critique of the legal protection of product image by Assaf, Katya (2007), *Image in der Werbung*, Cologne, etc.: Carl Heymanns, pp. 332 et seq.

to intellectual property.[60] But even apart from this criticism, it does not provide a convincing justification for a misappropriation theory where the object of protection is not a one-off creation (such as a copyrightable work) but the result of continuing investment.[61] It has been suggested that an argument based on expressive autonomy might justify anti-misappropriation protection, as the owner of goodwill is forced to fund someone else's message.[62] But this approach does not explain why the law should recognise such an autonomy right in the first place. The same objection can be made against approaches based on unjust enrichment,[63] which cannot explain by themselves[64] why the enrichment should be unjust.[65] It seems that these issues have not been investigated in greater detail before European anti-misappropriation legislation was passed. At least from the travaux préparatoires of the Comparative Advertising Directive it is evident that the main aim of the drafters was the liberalisation of advertising law in Europe. The other side of the coin – prohibition of unfair comparative advertising – seems not to have been discussed in detail.

But even if the present state of the law is accepted in principle, it should be stressed that neither under Art. 5 (2) of the Trade Mark Directive nor under Art. 4 (f) of the Directive on Misleading and Comparative Advertising is taking advantage of another trader's reputation prohibited as such. It must be 'unfair'. The wording of both provisions suggests a two-step test. The law of comparative advertising, in particular, highlights that not every advantage is necessarily unfair. Claims of equivalence between an unknown and a well-known product may provide consumers

---

60 Locke himself did not apply his labour theory to intellectual property; see Oberndörfer, Pascal (2005), *Die philosophische Grundlage des Urheberrechts*, Baden-Baden: Nomos, pp. 48 et seq. For a criticism of the labour theory, see Stallberg, Gero (2006), *Urheberrecht und moralische Rechtfertigung*, Berlin: Duncker & Humbolt, pp. 79 et seq., 106 et seq.; Spence, M., 'Passing Off and the Misappropriation of Valuable Intangibles', (1996) 112 *Law Quarterly Review* 472, 493.

61 Scott, D., A. Oliver and M. Ley-Pineda, 'Trade Marks as Property', in Bently et al. (eds), *supra* note 24, pp. 285, 297 et seq.

62 See Gordon, W., 'On Owning Information: Intellectual Property and the Restitutionary Impulse', 78 *Virginia Law Review* 149, 211 (1992); Spence, M., 'An Alternative Approach to Dilution Protection', in Bently et al., *supra* note 24, pp. 306, 312 et seq.

63 See Gordon, *ibid.*; Kamperman Sanders, *supra* note 7, pp. 121 et seq.

64 As discussed below, there may be good arguments for granting low-level protection against unfair copying under certain restrictive circumstances. But the notion of unjust enrichment describes the consequences of these arguments rather than providing an independent justification.

65 Spence, *supra* note 60, p. 489.

with useful information. Hence they should be permissible, even if they take some advantage of the reputation of the well-known product. The *Siemens v VIPA* case is a case in point.[66] By adopting the serial numbers used by Siemens, VIPA had arguably taken advantage of the reputation which Siemens products enjoyed in the market.[67] Nevertheless the Court of Justice did not consider this practice as unfair, since VIPA's practice made it easier for purchasers to identify compatible products.[68]

The recent ECJ decision in *L'Oréal v Bellure*,[69] however, is a cause for concern. According to the Court, a trader takes unfair advantage of the distinctive character or the repute of that mark, where it seeks 'to ride on the coat-tails of the mark with a reputation in order to benefit from the power of attraction, the reputation and the prestige of that mark and to exploit, without paying any financial compensation, the marketing effort expended by the proprietor of the mark in order to create and maintain the mark's image'. This test is highly reminiscent of the concept of 'parasitic competition'. It seems to suggest that taking advantage of another trader's reputation is by definition unfair, at least where the defendant is acting intentionally.

No distinction is made between the fact that a manufacturer of 'smella-like' perfumes certainly takes advantage of the reputation of luxury perfumes and the issue of whether this is unfair. The Court's metaphoric language ('riding on the coat-tails') conceals that according to the wording and the intention of Art. 5 (2) of the Trade Mark Directive and Art. 4 (f) of the Directive on Misleading and Comparative Advertising, the mere fact that skill, ingenuity and money need to be invested in order to create a product image is not by itself a sufficient reason for letting the trade mark owner's interests prevail.

While the draft anti-confusion provision suggested above probably reflects a broad European consensus, a draft provision against misappropriation is likely to be much more controversial. The following proposal is an extrapolation from Art. 5 (2) of the Trade Mark Directive and Art. 4 (f) of the Directive on Misleading and Comparative Advertising. I present it for discussion, but in the light of the objections discussed above I hesitate to support it.

---

66 ECJ, case C-59/05, [2006] ECR I-2147, *Siemens v VIPA*.

67 It could be objected, however, that the serial numbers also served a functional purpose and that, hence, they did not convey any quality image to consumers.

68 ECJ, case C-59/05, [2006] ECR I-2147, *Siemens v VIPA*, paras 22–4, 26.

69 ECJ, case C-487/07, [2009] ECR I-5185.

> The offer of imitated products shall be regarded as unfair where it without due cause takes unfair advantage of, or is detrimental to, the distinctive character or the repute of the trade mark, trade name or other distinguishing marks of a competitor or of the designation of origin of competing products.

4. SLAVISH IMITATION

Whereas provisions against confusion and misappropriation are on the borderline between unfair competition and intellectual property law, legal protection against 'slavish imitation' or 'imitation as such' has the same effect as an intellectual property right. Like copyright or design rights, it grants the original producer the exclusive right to prevent other traders from copying the external appearance of a product. Whereas provisions against misrepresentation leave a competing trader the possibility of marketing product imitations provided he or she avoids confusion, provisions against 'slavish imitation' prohibit the sale of exact imitations as such. Unfair competition law does not provide an independent justification for such protection. Since the imitator neither causes confusion nor misappropriates nor damages someone else's reputation, there are no additional factors of unfairness apart from the mere copying.

In theory, as seen above,[70] most European jurisdictions subscribe to the principle of freedom of imitation. But, as Gordon aptly notes, the 'notion that one deserves to keep the "fruits of his labor" seems so evidently correct, so evidently in accord with traditional notions of corrective justice and traditional conceptions of the judicial role, that giving legal protection to intellectual products appears to require no special justification'.[71] Thus in practice courts often find ways to protect products against types of imitation which they consider as unfair. As seen above,[72] German courts tend to presume consumer confusion in cases of identical copying. The Dutch Supreme Court, while stressing the freedom of imitation as a principle, has been prepared to protect fruits of labour against copying, which are comparable to products protected by intellectual property law.[73] This doctrine of slavish imitation seems to be relied on quite extensively by the courts of instance.[74] In countries without concepts of 'unfair copying', copyright has sometimes been relied on in order to protect the

---

70 *Supra* at section 1.
71 Gordon, *supra* note 62, p. 277.
72 *Supra* note 36.
73 *Supra* note 18.
74 See Quaedvlieg, *supra* note 18, p. 984.

results of skill and labour. The English law of industrial designs prior to 1988 is an example in point.[75] One of the few countries which explicitly prohibit 'slavish copying' is Switzerland. According to Art. 5 (c) of the Swiss Act against Unfair Competition, anyone acts unfairly who takes the marketable results of the work of another person and exploits them by means of technical reproduction procedures without an appropriate effort of his own. In practice, however, this provision seems to be applied rather restrictively.[76]

Given these differences between European jurisdictions, it is not surprising that the law of 'slavish imitation' has not been harmonized at Community level. Arguably, the Commission has by-passed this issue by including most relevant categories of unfair copying in intellectual property law. In some countries, non-original databases, unregistered designs and well-known marks were protected against imitation by unfair competition law before such protection was included in European intellectual property law. There remains one rather surprising provision in the Directive on Misleading and Comparative Advertising. According to Art. 4 (g), comparative advertising must not present goods or services as imitations or replicas of goods or services bearing a protected trade mark or trade name. Since this rule even applies in cases where the imitation as such is permitted,[77] its justification is unclear. English[78] and German[79] courts have tried to interpret the respective national provisions restrictively. The European Court of Justice, however, has construed it rather broadly in *L'Oréal v Bellure*. According to the Court, the ambit of the provision is not restricted to explicit claims of imitation. Even advertisements which only state that essential product characteristics have been imitated fall foul of this rule.[80] Taken to its extreme, the Court's understanding of Art. 4 (g) would result in a ban on advertisements for generic drugs,[81] although this may not have been the Court of Justice's intention. Art. 4

---

[75] See Cornish, William R., David Llewelyn and Tanya Aplin (2010), *Intellectual Property: Patents, Copyright, Trade Marks and Allied Rights*, 7th ed., London: Sweet & Maxwell, paras 15-04 et seq.

[76] See Hilty, R., '"Leistungsschutz" made in Switzerland? – Klärung eines Missverständnisses und Fragen zum allgemeinen Schutz von Investitionen', in Ahrens et al., *supra* note 20, pp. 643 et seq.

[77] ECJ, case C-487/07, [2009] ECR I-5185, *L'Oréal v Bellure*, para. 73.

[78] English Court of Appeal, *L'Oréal v Bellure*, [2007] EWCA Civ 968, para. 67 (warning that a broad interpretation of this provision may be overprotective).

[79] BGH GRUR 2008, 628, para. 26 – *Imitationswerbung*.

[80] ECJ, case C-487/07, [2009] ECR I-5185, *L'Oréal v Bellure*, paras 75, 76.

[81] See Ohly, Ansgar and Michael Spence (2000), *The Law of Comparative Advertising*, Oxford: Hart Publishing, p. 85.

(g), in its broad interpretation by the ECJ, seriously restricts the freedom of imitation by restricting the freedom to inform consumers about the identity of the features of the original and the imitation. It seems doubtful whether this restriction is compatible with the constitutional right to free speech, guaranteed by Art. 10 of the European Convention on Human Rights[82] and by Art. 11 of the Charter of Fundamental Rights of the European Union.

From an economic perspective, the case against anti-copying provisions is not as clear as it may seem at first sight. On the one hand, competition by imitation reduces market prices and enables the consumer to get good deals. On the other hand, the same considerations which justify intellectual property law may also justify protection against 'slavish imitation'. Although intellectual property protection may result in welfare losses, may obstruct product improvements and may give rise to undesired strategic behaviour,[83] it may be necessary in order to provide incentives for innovation in cases in which untrammelled freedom of imitation would prevent investment in research and development.[84] Since intellectual property law largely follows a 'one size fits all' logic, intellectual property protection tends to be inflexible and often too broad. Unfair competition law would allow a type of protection tailored to each individual case, a 'more economic approach' to imitation, which restricts welfare losses to what is inevitable. While this approach may result in legal uncertainty and may thus stifle unobjectionable competition, a legal realist will observe that the courts' unsystematic attempts to by-pass the freedom of imitation on the basis of consumer deception or copyright does not necessarily result in a higher degree of certainty. On the contrary, it may be better to give the courts a legal basis for openly discussing the arguments for and against protection in each case.

Thus the issue of protection against imitation as such is largely an institutional one. Does legislation alone have the capability and authority to create property rights, or can courts grant property-like protection on a case-by-case basis? In German law, the former 'general clause' of unfair competition law (§ 1 of the Act against Unfair Competition of 1909) has repeatedly been relied upon to grant protection in situations unforeseen by

---

82 These doubts were already expressed shortly after the entry into force of the directive; see Ohly and Spence, *ibid.*, p. 92; Kur, Annette, Lionel Bently and Ansgar Ohly, 'Sweet smells and a sour taste', *Max-Planck Research Paper Series No. 9/12*, http://papers.ssrn.com/sol3/papers.cfm?abstract_id=1492032.

83 Lemley, *supra* note 22, p. 1060.

84 See the references *supra* note 21.

legislation. Courts used to protect performances,[85] databases,[86] computer software[87] and unregistered designs[88] before legislation reacted. According to *Eugen Ulmer*, the tort of unfair competition served as a pacesetter for legislation.[89] Some of the judgments in which the courts were prepared to fill gaps in the intellectual property system are better reasoned[90] than many of those judgments in which courts have stretched the limits of the concept of confusion in order to reach the desired result. Such protection, however, must always respect the precedence of intellectual property legislation. Whenever intellectual property legislation has drawn a line between protection and free competition, the recourse to unfair competition law is blocked. Thus courts could not prevent the free use of inventions after the end of patent protection, but there may be a case for protecting sports broadcasting rights on the basis of unfair competition law in countries where legislation has not created such rights and where the basis of sports marketing rights is doctrinally uncertain.[91]

However, there are three powerful arguments against this approach.[92] First, in European law it would create a dilemma. The European Court of Justice, which only hears a very limited number of cases and which can only give preliminary rulings which do not decide on the full merits, may not be able fully to balance the competing interests and to weave a sufficiently dense web of precedents. If, however, the question is left to

---

[85] BGH GRUR 1962, 470 – *AKI*; and, based on personality rights, BGH GRUR 1960, 614 – *Figaros Hochzeit*.

[86] OLG Frankfurt GRUR 1983, 757 – *Donkey Kong Junior I*.

[87] BGH GRUR 1999, 923, 926 – *Tele-Info-CD*.

[88] BGH GRUR 1973, 478 – *Modeneuheit*.

[89] Ulmer, Eugen (1980), *Urheber- und Verlagsrecht*, 3rd ed., Berlin and Heidelberg: Springer, p. 40.

[90] See, e.g., the judgment BGH GRUR 1973, 478 – *Modeneuheit*, in which the Federal Supreme Court openly justified supplementary unfair competition protection for unregistered designs long before unregistered design rights were introduced by the Community Design Directive.

[91] See Lochmann, René (2005), *Die Einräumung von Fernsehübertragungsrechten an Sportveranstaltungen*, Tübingen: Mohr Siebeck, pp. 182 et seq. The OLG Stuttgart, MMR 2009, 395, recently enjoined the operators of an internet forum from enabling private football fans to upload video sequences showing scenes of amateur football matches. The reasoning was based on unfair competition law, but is open to fundamental objections; see Ohly, A., 'Hartzplatzhelden.de oder: Wohin mit dem unmittelbaren Leistungsschutz?', GRUR 2010, 487. Meanwhile, the judgment has been reversed by the Federal Supreme Court: judgment of 28 October 2010, case no. 1 2R 60/09 (still unpublished).

[92] For a critique of unfair competition law protection against slavish imitation see Peukert, Alexander (2008), *Güterzuordnung als Rechtsprinzip*, Tübingen: Mohr Siebeck, pp. 320 et seq., 811 et seq.

the member states, the present differences, which can result in barriers to intra-Community trade, remain. Secondly, there is the risk that the lower courts in particular may ignore the limits of intellectual property law and may tend to grant protection against 'unfair copying' even in cases where intellectual property rights have expired or where exceptions apply. Thirdly, intellectual property law has been extended continually over the past decades. It is difficult to find unintentional gaps in the intellectual property system. Arguably, academics should direct their efforts to cutting through the intellectual property thicket rather than suggesting new forms of protection. On the other hand a world of narrow and strong intellectual property rights, supplemented by flexible rules of unfair competition may be preferable to the present world in which many types of trivial intangible subject-matter receive broad, inflexible and long-term intellectual property protection. Thus, paradoxically, an unfair competition doctrine might play a role in the fight against the hypertrophy of intellectual property law.

Although I do have a certain sympathy for a flexible unfair competition approach to controlling imitation, I also take the counter-arguments seriously. But the arguments for and against should be discussed more openly. In particular, it should be acknowledged that there are good reasons against a rigid exclusionary rule in intellectual property law. Thus my final and certainly most controversial drafting proposal for a future European Directive on Unfair Competition is as follows:

> The imitation of products manufactured or marketed by a competing trader can be prohibited for a limited time. When granting such protection, a fair balance between the interests of the producer, the imitator and the interests of the general public must be sought. In particular the following factors should be taken into account: (i) the originality of the product, (ii) the degree of imitation, (iii) the public interest in the creation and provision of the product, (iv) the likelihood that the product would not be produced or marketed under conditions of free competition.

5. CONCLUSION

What, then, is the answer to Gretchen's question? It is that imitation is not unfair. Imitation may be prevented by intellectual property law for good reasons. Subject to certain exceptions, the offer of imitated products should also be prohibited when consumers are misled. I am sceptical about protecting 'image' against misappropriation. As far as 'slavish copying' is concerned, the present system of extensive intellectual property law makes it difficult to argue for additional regimes of anti-copying protection. But if we step back from the current political debate, we might find that a system of narrowly defined intellectual property rights for strong innovations or creations, supplemented by a flexible doctrine of unfair competition protection, may be preferable to the present world, where more and more types of intangible subject-matter are granted broad, long-term and strong intellectual property protection.

PART II

Finetuning the scope of protection: limitations and exceptions

7. Maximising permissible exceptions to intellectual property rights

Andrew F. Christie*

1. INTRODUCTION

Exceptions to intellectual property (IP) rights are of fundamental importance to achieving the policy objectives that justify the grant of IP rights. To the extent to which an IP right is considered to be 'too strong', the way to 'weaken' (or, to better 'balance') it is through the use of an exception to it. It is not surprising, therefore, that much attention has been paid in recent times by academics and policy-makers to the issue of exceptions, and in particular to the issue of the extent to which the 'three-step test' in international treaties restricts the ability of national legislatures to introduce new exceptions to IP rights.[1]

* Davies Collison Cave Professor of Intellectual Property at the Melbourne Law School, and Research Associate of the Intellectual Property Research Institute of Australia (IPRIA), University of Melbourne. This chapter is based on a presentation by the author at the 2008 Congress of the International Association for the Advancement of Teaching and Research in Intellectual Property (ATRIP), Munich, 22 July 2008, and describes research that was supported by IPRIA and by the Australian Research Council through its Linkage Project scheme as part of the project Cultural Collections, Creators and Copyright: Museums, Galleries, Libraries and Archives and Australia's Digital Heritage (Andrew Kenyon and Andrew Christie, LP0669566).

1 The following is a selective, but representative, sample of the more recent literature: Geiger, C., 'From Berne to National Law, via the Copyright Directive: The Dangerous Mutations of the Three-Step Test', (2007) 29 (12) *European Intellectual Property Review*, p. 486; Hugenholtz, P.B. and Okediji, R. 'Conceiving an International Instrument on Limitations and Exceptions to Copyright – Final Report', 2008 at http://www.ivir.nl/publicaties/hugenholtz/finalreport2008.pdf (last visited 6 March 2009); Kur, A., 'Of Oceans, Islands, and Inland Water – How Much Room for Exceptions and Limitations under the Three Step-Test?', (2008) *Max Planck Papers on Intellectual Property, Competition & Tax Law Research* No. 08-04 at http://papers.ssrn.com/sol3/papers.cfm?abstract_id=1317707 (last visited 6 March 2009); Ricketson, S., *WIPO Study on Limitations and Exceptions of Copyright and Related Rights in the Digital Environment*, 2003, Geneva:

Unfortunately, much of the published discussion on this topic suffers from a failure to properly conceptualise the nature of exceptions to IP rights. This failure is exemplified by a general tendency to talk about exceptions without defining them. The failure to properly conceptualise exceptions provides a significant constraint on the ability of commentators to provide insights about how national laws may be reformed to maximise the scope of permissible activities while remaining compliant with the TRIPS Agreement.

This chapter seeks to remedy some of these failures. In particular, it seeks to provide a reasoned conceptualisation of the nature of exceptions and limitations. Then, building on that conceptualisation, this chapter offers an insight into how, in a practical manner, a national legislature can maximise the scope of permissible activities in respect of IP rights while remaining compliant with the international constraints on exceptions to IP rights.

2. UNDERSTANDING EXCEPTIONS

The first step to understanding exceptions is to identify the context in which they operate. Accordingly, this section begins by explaining the hierarchy in which IP rights subsist, and by identifying the location of exceptions to those rights. It then defines an exception, and the related concept of a limitation.

2.1. Contextualising Exceptions

Put simply, in the absence of an IP right, the law does not preclude a competitor from exploiting the creation or innovation of another. Thus, the general rule is free competition. An IP right provides the owner of the IP subject matter with the entitlement of being the exclusive exploiter of that subject matter. IP rights are, therefore, an exception to the general rule of free competition. IP rights, where they do exist, are not absolute. Rather, IP rights are subject to certain exceptions. Thus, exceptions are a qualification to the exception to the general rule. By virtue of provisions in international treaties, and in particular the three-step test of the TRIPS

WIPO, (WIPO Doc. SCCR/9/7) at http://www.wipo.int/edocs/mdocs/copyright/en/sccr_9/sccr_9_7.pdf (last visited 6 March 2009); and Senftleben, M., *Copyright, Limitations, and the Three-Step Test: An Analysis of the Three-Step Test in International and EC Copyright Law*, The Hague: Kluwer Law International, 2004.

Agreement, exceptions to IP rights are only permitted under certain conditions. Thus, the TRIPS three-step test provides a constraint on the qualification to the exception to the general rule. Exceptions can only be effected by way of national law. Thus, the form of its implementation in national legislation determines the practical effect of an exception. To be valid, this implementation must comply with the constraints on exceptions contained in the relevant international treaties.

It follows from all of this that there is a distinct hierarchy to any IP right system, as follows:

Level 1. General rule: free competition
Level 2. Exception to the general rule: intellectual property right
Level 3. Qualification to the exception: permitted act
Level 4. Constraint on the qualification: TRIPS three-step test
Level 5. Implementation of the qualification within the constraint: permitted act in national law

2.2. Defining Exceptions

Both of the words 'exception' and 'limitation' have been used in international treaties, and in some writings about those treaties, with little in the way of reasoned definition.[2] To the extent to which writers do give reasoned meanings for these terms, there is no consensus.[3] This lack of principled analysis is surprising, given the major roles that exceptions and limitations play in IP law. This section provides a reasoned definition of the terms, from first principles.

The dictionary definitions of 'limitation' include 'a point or respect in which something is limited', 'a limit'. A 'limit', in turn, is defined as:

> one of the fixed points between which the possible or permitted extent, amount, duration, range of action, or variation of anything is confined; a bound which may not be passed, or beyond which something ceases to be possible or allowable.[4]

---

2 As Hugenholtz and Okediji note: 'While [international treaties] expressly refer to "limitations and exceptions" as the object of the three-step test, surprisingly little has been written, even in the *IMRO* WTO Panel Report, on what actually constitutes "limitations and exceptions".': Hugenholtz and Okediji, *supra* note 1, p. 19.

3 According to Kur: 'Concerning the terminological aspect, no agreement or uniform practice seems to exist on the international level' (Kur, *supra* note 1, p. 5).

4 *Oxford English Dictionary* (2nd edn), Oxford: Oxford University Press, 1989.

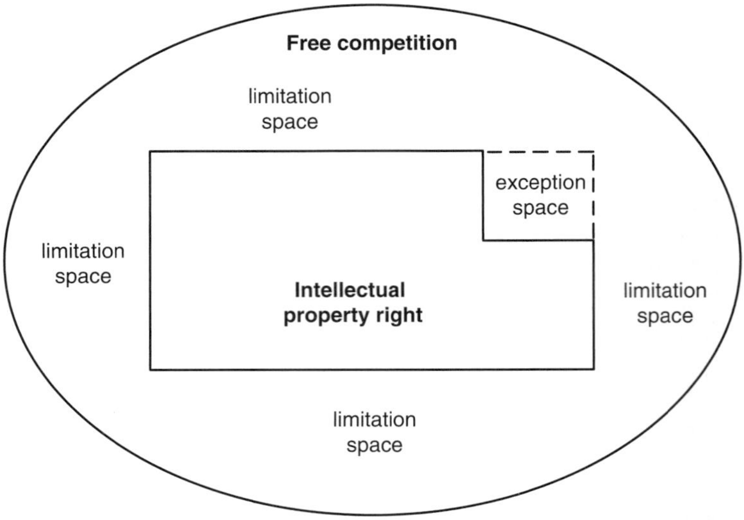

Figure 7.1 Nature of limitations and exceptions to IP rights

This provides support for the view that a limitation, properly conceived, is a *boundary* of the IP right-holder's right. That is to say, the IP right-holder's right does not extend into the space delineated by the limitation. Put another way, the limitation is an integral part of the definition of the IP right-holder's right.

An 'exception' is different. As dictionaries show, an exception is:

> something that is excepted; a particular case which comes within the terms of a rule, but to which the rule is not applicable.[5]

In terms of IP rights, an exception is a *carve-out* from the IP right-holder's right. That is to say, an exception cuts back on the IP right-holder's right, by removing a part of it, either partially (in the case of remunerated exceptions) or wholly (in the case of unremunerated exceptions). Put another way, an exception is a space into which the IP right-holder's right would extend *but for* the existence of the exception.

The general nature of limitations and exceptions to IP rights is illustrated in Figure 7.1.

Figure 7.1 conveys, diagrammatically, the relationship between an

---

[5] Ibid.

IP right, a limitation to an IP right and an exception to an IP right. As explained above, an IP right is an exception to the general rule of free competition. It is, in a sense, an island in a sea of free competition.[6] The boundary of the IP right (the shore of the island, so to speak) is delineated by the limitations to the right. Part of the IP right has been carved out, by an exception, from what is delineated by the limitations. This part of the right is returned to the space for free competition (it is, by analogy, land given up to the sea).

By this definition, limitations are general constraints on the scope of the IP regime. These constraints are contained in the legislation enacting the IP regime, and operate primarily by delineating the types of subject matter protected by the legislation, the types of exclusive rights provided to the protected subject matter, and the duration of the protection provided to the protected subject matter. Limitations operate at Level 2 in the hierarchy of an IP right.

Exceptions are more specific than limitations. They operate by removing liability for infringement for undertaking certain acts that would, but for the exception, be within the scope of the IP right-holder's exclusive rights. Exceptions may be remunerated or unremunerated. A *remunerated* exception is a partial carve-out of the IP right-holder's right – it removes the right-holder's entitlement to prevent use by third parties of the subject matter protected by the right, but leaves intact the entitlement to be compensated financially for any use by third parties of the subject matter.[7] An *unremunerated* exception, in contrast, is a complete carve-out of the IP right-holder's right – it removes the right-holder's entitlement both to prevent use by third parties of the subject matter and to be compensated financially for any use by third parties of the subject matter. Exceptions operate at Level 3 in the hierarchy of an IP right.

---

[6] A number of commentators have chosen to use the metaphor of islands in an ocean for explaining their conceptualisation of exceptions and limitations to IP right-holder's rights. Kur, for example, states: 'If IP rights in general are considered islands in a sea of freedom, the rules granting immunity for certain kinds of uses . . . might more adequately be described as pools of water forming within the island' (Kur, *supra* note 1, p. 6).

[7] A remunerated exception is often referred to as a 'compulsory licence' or an 'obligatory licence': see, e.g., Ricketson, *supra* note 1, p. 4. Other synonyms are 'non-voluntary licence' or 'statutory licence'.

3. CONSTRAINING EXCEPTIONS

3.1. The Three-Step Test

The three-step test qualifies the permissible scope of an exception to an IP right. The test was first incorporated into international IP law through the introduction, in 1967, of Article 9(2) into the Berne Convention for the Protection of Literary and Artistic Works of 1886 ('Berne'). Article 9(2) arose out of the debate concerning the introduction of a general right of reproduction into the text of the Berne Convention for the first time at the Stockholm Revision Conference in 1967. The issue had been discussed at the Diplomatic Conferences prior to the conclusion of the Convention in 1884 to 1886, and again in 1948, but the different definitions of a reproduction right that existed in the national legislation of participating states meant that agreement could not be reached on how it could be incorporated into the Convention. By the time of the 1967 Conference, however, the concern of participants 'lay not with the proposition that there should be a general right of reproduction, but with the formulation of the exceptions that should be made to it'.[8]

Therefore, it was the debate surrounding the formulation of appropriate exceptions to the new reproduction right, introduced as Article 9(1), that produced the wording of the current Article 9(2) of the Berne Convention. Article 9(2), in the form adopted by the Conference, states:

> It shall be a matter for legislation in the countries of the Union to permit the reproduction of such works in certain special cases, provided that such reproduction does not conflict with a normal exploitation of the work and does not unreasonably prejudice the legitimate interests of the author.

It is instructive to look at the drafting history of the article. The wording first proposed for Article 9(2) provided:

> . . . that it would be possible for national legislation to permit the reproduction of the works referred to in paragraph (1) in three cases: (a) for private use; (b) for judicial or administrative purposes; (c) in certain particular cases, provided (i) that reproduction is not contrary to the legitimate interests of the author, and (ii) that it does not conflict with a normal exploitation of the work.[9]

---

[8] Ricketson, S. and Ginsburg,, J. (2006), *International Copyright and Neighbouring Rights: The Berne Convention and Beyond* (2nd edn), Oxford: Oxford University Press, p. 639 (para. 11.19).

[9] 'Report on the Work of Main Committee I (Substantive Provisions of the Berne Convention: Articles 1 to 20)', (1967) *Records of the Intellectual Property Conference of Stockholm June 11 to July 14, 1967 Volume II*, para. 78.

During the debate, a number of submissions were made to Main Committee I regarding possible changes to the proposed wording, some seeking to restrict the scope of permissible exceptions and some to extend it. The United Kingdom submitted a proposal which removed criteria (a) and (b) and grouped all the exceptions into a single formula of 'in certain special cases'.[10] Main Committee I adopted this proposal.

Main Committee I also adopted a proposal from the Drafting Committee suggesting that, in this new general clause corresponding to item (c) above, the 'second conditions should be placed before the first, *as this would afford a more logical order* for the interpretation of the rule'.[11] The reasoning behind this was:

> If it is considered that reproduction conflicts with the normal exploitation of the work, reproduction is not permitted at all. If it is considered that reproduction does not conflict with the normal exploitation of the work, the next step would be to consider whether it does not unreasonably prejudice the legitimate interests of the author. Only if such is not the case would it be possible in certain special cases to introduce a compulsory license, or to provide for use without payment.[12]

It can be seen from this reasoning that Main Committee I understood that it was possible for a particular use of a work to not conflict with the normal exploitation of the work and yet be prejudicial to the legitimate interests of the author of the work. Furthermore, by choosing to reverse the order of steps (i) and (ii) in sub-paragraph (c) of the original proposal, it may be argued that the Main Committee I understood that the converse was not possible – that is, it was not possible for a particular use of a work to conflict with a normal exploitation of the work and yet not be prejudicial to legitimate interests of the author. Such an understanding may be implied from the explanation that reversing the order 'would afford a more logical order'. Presumably, the new order (where the legitimate interests of the author are considered after consideration of the normal exploitation of the work) is more logical because the set of all things that conflict with the normal exploitation of a work is a sub-set of the set of all things that are contrary to the legitimate interests of the author. If consideration of the legitimate interests of the author were undertaken before consideration of the normal exploitation of the work, there would be no work left for the last step to undertake. Reversing the order of the two steps ensures that there is always some work to be done by the last step.

---

10 Ibid, para. 81.

11 Ibid, para. 85 (emphasis added).

12 Ibid.

A number of other international instruments have adopted the three-step test that was introduced into the Berne Convention in 1967 as Article 9(2). This first adoption of the test occurred in 1994, in the Agreement on Trade-Related Aspects of Intellectual Property Rights ('TRIPS').[13] The TRIPS Agreement adopted the three-step test as a qualification on the exceptions that may be introduced by WTO member states in respect of copyright,[14] trademark,[15] industrial design[16] and patent rights.[17] Two years later, the test was adopted to qualify the exceptions that member states could introduce in respect of the rights provided in two World Intellectual Property Organization Treaties: the WIPO Copyright Treaty 1996 ('WCT'),[18] and WIPO Performances and Phonograms Treaty 1996 ('WPPT').[19] In more recent times, the three-step test has been used in supra-national instruments, such as European Union Harmonisation Directives[20] and in bilateral Free Trade Agreements.[21]

Whether deliberately or otherwise, the three-step test has not been incorporated into these international instruments in identical form. Rather, the test has been adopted with subtle – and, in some cases, not so subtle – differences. The differences in implementation do not just occur between the different international instruments in which the three-step test has been incorporated – there are differences in implementation *within* the same instrument. For example, of the four implementations of the test in the TRIPS Agreement, only two are the same: those in Articles 26(2) and 30. Thus, there are three different implementations of the three-step test in the TRIPS Agreement.

3.2. Operation of the Three-Step Test

A full understanding of the three-step test requires both a micro-level and a macro-level analysis. A micro-level analysis – a consideration of exactly

---

13 The TRIPS Agreement is Annexe 1C to the Agreement Establishing the World Trade Organization 1994.

14 TRIPS Article 13.

15 TRIPS Article 17.

16 TRIPS Article 26(2).

17 TRIPS Article 30.

18 WCT Article 10(1).

19 WPPT Article 16(2).

20 See, e.g., Directive 2001/29/EC of the European Parliament and of the Council of 22 May 2001 on the harmonisation of certain aspects of copyright and related rights in the information society, Article 5(5).

21 See, e.g., the Free Trade Agreement between the Government of the United States of America and the Government of Australia of 18 May 2004, Articles 17.2.5 (trademarks), 17.4.10(a) (copyright) and 17.9.3 (patents).

how each step operates – is beyond the scope of this chapter.[22] A macro-level analysis – a consideration of how the three steps operate with respect to each other – is provided below.

A superficial reading of the three-step test is that the steps are cumulative and, therefore, that each step must be satisfied if an exception is to be permitted under it. This seems incontrovertible.[23] Thus, the only exceptions permitted by the three-step test are those exceptions that are special cases, and that do not conflict with the normal exploitation of the protected subject matter, and that do not prejudice the legitimate interests of the right-holder.

What is debatable, however, is whether the steps need to be applied in a particular order – and, if so, what is that order.[24] It was noted above that the Main Committee I responsible for drafting Article 9(2) of the Berne Convention considered that one particular ordering of the three steps was more logical than another – namely, that consideration of the legitimate interests of the author should occur after consideration of the normal exploitation of the work. This seems to suggest that the Main Committee I considered that every use of a work that conflicts with the normal exploitation of it will be prejudicial to the legitimate interests of the author of the work; however, the legitimate interests of the author of the work go beyond the normal exploitation of the work, such that some uses of a work will be prejudicial to the legitimate interests of the author even though they do not conflict with the normal exploitation of the work.

If this reasoning is accepted – and if it is accepted as applying to the three-step test in the TRIPS Agreement and the other international treaties into which it has subsequently been introduced – there is a profound

---

22 For micro-level analyses, see Kur, *supra* note 1, pp. 22–31.

23 This was the view expressed in the report of the decision of the TRIPS Dispute Settlement Panel in the case *United States – Section 110(5) of the US Copyright Act*, WT/DS160/R, 15 June 2000, at §6.87: 'Failure to comply with any one of the three conditions results in the Article 13 exception being disallowed'.

24 Senftleben, amongst others, believes that the steps must be applied in the order in which they appear in the TRIPS Agreement provisions – because, in his view, there is 'a teleological line of argument' that substantiates this ordering (Senftleben *supra* note 1, p. 131). In Kur's opinion, the WTO dispute resolution panels 'emphasize that the test actually does consist of three . . . clearly discernible stages, which must be passed through cumulatively and in a strict order' (Kur, *supra* note 1, p. 22). Geiger, however, believes it is 'necessary to "re-think" the three-step test and to adopt a new reading of it', under which the third step of the test would be applied first. In his view, 'no text seems to forbid' applying the test in this way (Geiger, C. (2007), 'The Role of the Three-Step Test in the Adaptation of Copyright Law to the Information Society', January–March *e-Copyright Bulletin*, pp. 1, 18).

consequence for the way in which the test operates: step 2 is logically redundant. That is to say, it is only necessary to consider whether an exception satisfies steps 1 and 3. If it does, it will be permitted under the three-step test, because it will (in the eyes of Main Committee I) also not be in conflict with the requirements of step 2.

4. MAXIMISING EXCEPTIONS

Many commentators have expressed concern that the TRIPS three-step test is an undue restriction on the scope of exceptions that are permissible within any particular IP regime.[25] This concern is the motivation behind the 'Declaration on a Balanced Interpretation of the 'Three-Step Test' in Copyright Law' produced by a group of European copyright academics.[26]

It is also the motivation behind the call for an international treaty on mandated exceptions to copyright law.[27] There is, therefore, a desire amongst certain stakeholders to maximise the scope of permissible exceptions to IP rights. The final part of this chapter offers a conceptualisation of the three-step test that maximises the scope of exceptions permitted by the test, while remaining in compliance with existing international law.

4.1. Understanding Gervais' 'Reverse Three-Step' Test

Daniel Gervais's (2004) article, 'Towards a New Core International Copyright Norm: The Reverse Three-Step Test,'[28] introduces the concept

---

[25] See, e.g., Eckersley, P., 'Virtual Markets for Virtual Goods: The Mirror Image of Digital Copyright?', (2004) 18 *Harvard Journal of Law and Technology* 85, pp. 153–8; Koelman, K., 'Fixing the Three Step Test', (2006) 28 *European Intellectual Property Review*, pp. 407, 411; Okediji, R., 'Public Welfare and the Role of the WTO: Reconsidering the TRIPS Agreement', (2003) 17 *Emory International Law Review*, pp. 819, 822–23; and Oriola, T., 'Against the Plague: Exemption of Pharmaceutical Patent Rights as a Biosecurity Measure', (2007) 7 *University of Illinois Journal of Law, Technology and Policy*, pp. 287, 321–7.

[26] 'Declaration on a Balanced Interpretation of the "Three-Step Test" in Copyright Law', (2008) 39 *IIC*, p. 707.

[27] See the *Proposal by Chile on the Analysis of Exceptions and Limitations*, Standing Committee on Copyright and Related Rights, Thirteenth Session, Geneva, November 21–3, 2005 (WIPO Doc. SCCR/13/5) at http://www.wipo.int/meetings/en/html.jsp?url=http://www.wipo.int/edocs/mdocs/copyright/en/sccr_13/sccr_13_5.doc (last visited 6 March 2009). That proposal seeks an 'agreement on exceptions and limitations for purposes of public interest that must be envisaged as a minimum in all national legislations for the benefit of the community': 2.

[28] (2005) 9(1) *Marquette Intellectual Property Law Review* 1–35.

of reversing the three-step test to define the full scope of what copyright law protects. As Gervais explains:

> What I suggest is reversing the test, based on the assumption that what the exception (whether fair use in domestic U.S. law or the three-step test at the multilateral level) does not allow is what in fact copyright intended to protect. Expressed in mathematical terms, if fair use is the 'A' universe, then the 'non-A' universe contains uses that require a license.[29]

It appears that what Gervais is proposing is that the copyright-holder's entitlement can, and should, be defined by what the three-step test does not permit. Under this approach, the scope of the copyright holder's exclusive rights would be defined as:

> use that does not meet the two real steps of the Berne three-step test [i.e.] [u]se that interferes with normal commercial exploitation or unreasonably or unjustifiably prejudices the copyright holder's rights.[30]

This statement needs qualification, however. Read literally, it suggests that the scope of a copyright-holder's right is defined by that which the three-step test does not permit. Such a reading would be incorrect, however, because it fails to take account of the role of limitations. As noted in Section 2 above, limitations – that is, statutory restrictions on the subject matter of protection, the nature of the exclusive rights, and the duration of protection – are the boundaries of the IP right-holder's right. It cannot be that Gervais is suggesting that these limitations can be ignored and that all one needs to do to define the scope of the copyright-holder's right is to reverse the three-step test. This cannot be so because the three-step test does not operate to determine the subject matter of protection, nature of exclusive rights or duration of protection.

This author will suggest a variation on the literal reading of Gervais's reverse three-step test: reversing the three-step test defines the *minimum permissible* scope of the IP right-holder's right, assuming that the maximum permissible limitations to that right have been applied. The logic in support of this proposition is as follows. If the maximum permissible limitations have been applied to the IP right, then the scope of the IP right that remains is to be determined by the exceptions that have been applied to it. Given that the three-step test defines the maximum permissible carve-out from an IP right-holder's right, then the reverse of this test will define the

---

29 Ibid, 28.
30 Ibid, 29.

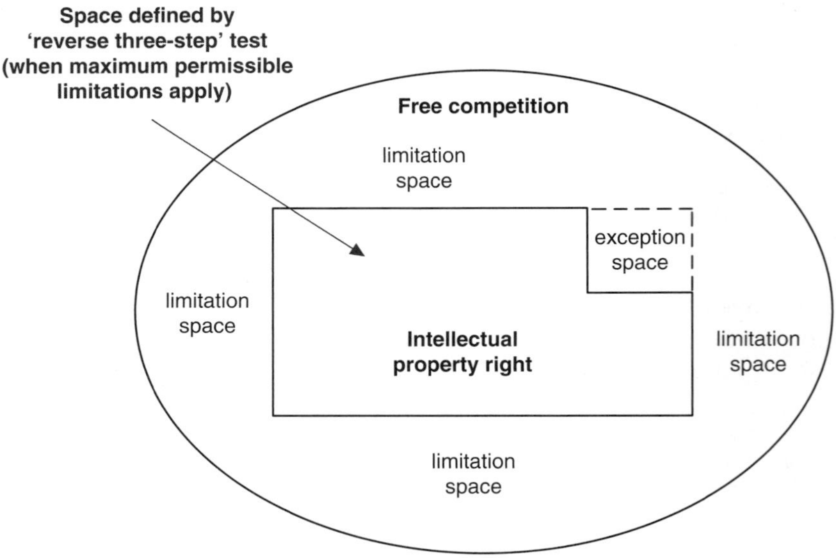

Figure 7.2 'Reverse three-step' test as definition of the scope of an IP right

minimum permissible scope of the right that remains after the maximum permissible exceptions have been applied (when the maximum permissible limitations have also been applied). This understanding of the Gervais reverse three-step test is illustrated in Figure 7.2.

4.2. Defining the Maximum Permissible Exception

Gervais's concept of reversing the three-step test to define the scope of the copyright-holder's right, while highly interesting, is rather impractical. Although there is much to be said in favour of simplifying the exclusive entitlements of the copyright holder, national legislatures in recent times have continued the historical trend of *increasing* the number of exclusive rights of copyright, not decreasing them. It is, therefore, rather unlikely that any national legislature in the short term will adopt the reverse three-step test as the definition of the exclusive rights of the copyright-holder. Thus, the reverse three-step test is not the practical solution to the existence of unduly wide exclusive rights – or, put another way, to the existence of unduly narrow exceptions – that concern those stakeholders who have made the 'Declaration' on the three-step test in copyright law or who have proposed an international treaty mandating certain exceptions in copyright law.

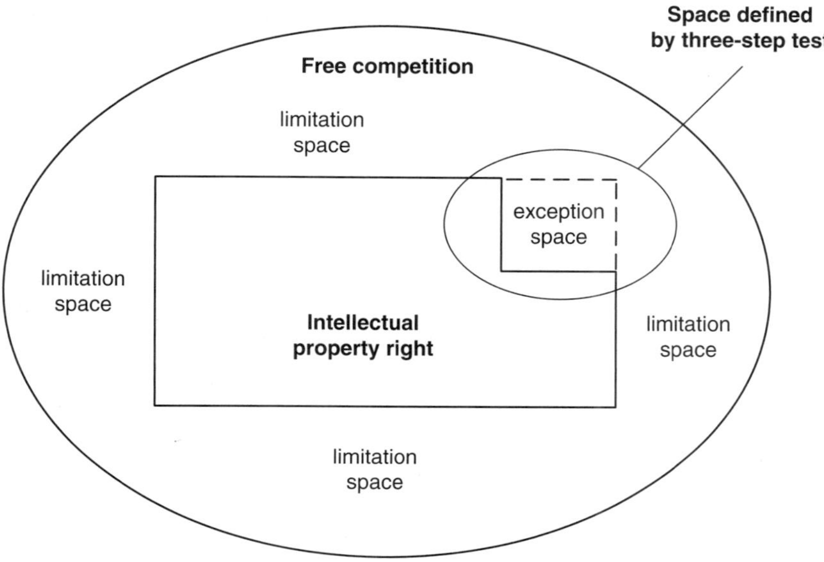

Figure 7.3 Three-step test as definition of maximalist exception to an IP right

However, even though the reverse three-step test does not provide a useful response to that concern, a related concept does. In particular, it is argued that there is a practical way in which a national legislature can maximise the scope of permissible exceptions to an IP right-holder's right – namely, by introducing an exception that adopts the very language of the relevant three-step test. Under this approach, the three-step test moves from being a *constraint on* the scope of an exception to an IP right to being a *definition of* the scope of an exception. An exception that uses the very language of the three-step test is, by definition, a 'maximalist exception' – that is, an exception that permits the maximum activities possible, while remaining in compliance with the three-step test's constraints. This role for the three-step test is illustrated in Figure 7.3.

Since most attention to date has been focussed on copyright, that regime will be used here as the example of how a national legislature can maximise the scope of permissible exceptions to an IP right-holder's right. It is to be noted, however, that an equivalent maximalist exception can easily be drafted for each of the other IP regimes.

A maximisation of the scope of permissible exceptions to copyright could be implemented in national legislation by the introduction of an exception worded along the following lines:

> In any particular case, it is not an infringement of copyright to do any act that does not conflict with a normal exploitation of the protected subject matter and that does not unreasonably prejudice the legitimate interests of the copyright owner.

An exception worded this way is, self-evidently, compliant with the relevant provisions in the international treaties,[31] since it uses the very concept of each of the three steps of the three-step test in those treaties. Further, by applying to 'any act' that would otherwise be an infringement, an exception worded in this way maximises the scope of permissible activities. Unlike the 'fair dealing' provisions of United Kingdom copyright law, for example, such an exception is not limited to acts done for a particular purpose, such as for research, private study, criticism, review or news reporting.[32] An exception worded in this manner 'fills the entire space' of exceptions permitted by the three-step test.

Although the idea of incorporating the words of the three-step test into national legislation is not new,[33] the proposal above is fundamentally different in nature. The national provisions that incorporate the three-step test apply the words as a constraint on specific permitted acts – that is, they limit the scope of the existing permitted exceptions by requiring them to comply with the three-step test. The maximalist exception proposed in this chapter permits all acts that are consistent with the three-step test. Thus, whereas the incorporation of the three-step test into the national legislation of European countries and China has the effect of further constraining the scope of permitted acts, the incorporation of the test in the proposed maximalist exception has the effect of expanding the scope of permitted acts.

There is no reason in principle or in practice why a maximalist exception

---

[31] The relevant provisions are Berne Article 9(2), TRIPS Article 13 and WCT Articles 10(1) and (2).

[32] See the UK Copyright, Designs and Patents Act 1988, ss 29 and 30.

[33] Various European jurisdictions have implemented the exceptions identified in Article 5 of the EU Copyright Harmonisation Directive in their national law with an express constraint along the following lines: 'the exceptions enumerated . . . may neither conflict with the normal exploitation of the work nor unreasonably prejudice the legitimate interests of the author': see the instances cited by Geiger, *supra* note 1 above, p. 486. China, too, has a provision in its copyright legislation stating that the acts permitted by specific provisions of its Act 'shall not impair the normal exploitation of the work concerned, nor unreasonably prejudice the legitimate interests of the copyright owner': Article 21 of the Regulations for the Implementation of the Copyright Law of the People's Republic of China, promulgated by Decree No. 359 of the State Council of the People's Republic of China on 2 August 2002, and effective as of 15 September 2002.

as proposed herein could not be implemented in a country's national legislation, in conjunction with that country's existing exceptions. When implemented with existing exceptions, the maximalist exception would operate as a 'catch-all' safety net, permitting acts that satisfy the three-step test even though there is no specific exception legislated in respect of that act. The effect of the maximalist exception, therefore, is to ensure that all otherwise infringing acts that, according to international treaties, *may* be permitted by the national law *are* permitted by the national law.

5. CONCLUSION

As noted in Section 4 above, much angst has been expressed in recent times about the unduly restrictive effect of the three-step test in international treaties, especially as they apply to copyright law. This has led to a declaration about how the copyright three-step test should be applied, and to initiatives for an international treaty mandating the exceptions that must be provided in national copyright laws. Because these developments require a change to the status quo, there is a substantial risk they will not succeed.

There is, however, an alternative to changing the international law, which may provide the outcome sought by those concerned about the three-step test. This alternative is to take full advantage of the flexibility permitted by the existing international law. As shown above, by using the very language and concepts of the current three-step test in international treaties, it is possible to craft exceptions in national legislation that maximise the range of permitted activities, while remaining compliant with the requirements of the three-step test.

8. Overprotection and protection overlaps in intellectual property law – the need for horizontal fair use defences

Martin Senftleben*

1. INTRODUCTION

During recent decades, intellectual property (IP) protection has been expanded continuously.[1] New technologies have been found to be eligible for patent protection.[2] New types of marks have been recognized in trademark law.[3] Copyright law is no longer confined to the cultural domain.[4] In parallel, the exclusive rights of IP owners have been broad-

* Ph.D.; Professor of Intellectual Property, VU University Amsterdam; Senior Consultant, Bird & Bird, The Hague.

[1] For an early critical assessment of this broader trend, see Spoor, J.H. (1990), *De gestage groei van merk, werk en uitvinding*, Zwolle: Tjeenk Willink.

[2] This tendency has been particularly strong in US patent law. For instance, see US Supreme Court, 447 US 303 (1980), *Diamond v Chakrabarty*, with regard to biotechnology. Cf. Maier, G.J. and Mattson, R. C. (2001), 'State Street Bank ist kein Ausreißer: Die Geschichte der Softwarepatentierung im US-amerikanischen Recht', *GRUR Int.*, p. 677; Merges, R.P. (1999), 'As Many as Six Impossible Patents before Breakfast: Property Rights for Business Concepts and Patent System Reform', *Berkeley Technology Law Journal* 14, pp. 577, 587. As to current, more cautious approaches in US patent law, see US Court of Appeals for the Federal Circuit, 545 F.3d 943, 88 USPQ.2d 1385 (Fed. Cir. 2008), in Bernard L. Bilski and Rand A. Warsaw.

[3] Cf. Gilson, J. and Gilson, A. (2005), 'LaLonde, Cinnamon Buns, Marching Ducks and Cherry-Scented Racecar Exhaust: Protecting Nontraditional Trademarks', *Trade Mark Reporter* 95, p. 773; Fezer, K.-H. (2005), 'Eine Theorie der variablen Marke – Zum Markenschutz für Markenbildungskonzeptionen', *GRUR*, p. 102.

[4] With the inclusion of computer programs, technical machine instructions have become part of the subject matter eligible for copyright protection. See Article 10(1) TRIPS and Article 4 WCT. As to the impact of this inclusion on the

ened. The TRIPS Agreement provides for a comprehensive portfolio of patent minimum rights.[5] The WIPO Copyright Treaty added new layers of protection to the standard reached under the Berne Convention.[6] As a result of protection against dilution, trademark rights have become instruments for the exploitation of brand image.[7]

Enhanced protection, however, gives rise to the question of appropriate counterbalances. Flexible rights are likely to require flexible limitations for at least two reasons. On the one hand, flexible limitations facilitate the task of maintaining a proper balance between protection and competing freedoms within individual protection regimes. On the other hand, flexible limitations can be employed to safeguard breathing space for unauthorized use when it comes to overlaps between different forms of IP protection. If an intellectual creation enjoys cumulative protection in different IP protection systems,[8] a network of corresponding, flexible limitations ensures that the freedom offered in one system is not eroded through protection granted in another system.

The flexibility required within and across IP protection regimes may be

---

copyright system, see Gordon, S.E. (1998), 'The Very Idea! Why Copyright is an Inappropriate Way to Protect Computer Programs', *EIPR*, p. 10; Quaedvlieg, A.A. (1987), *Auteursrecht op techniek*, Zwolle: Tjeenk Willink; Dietz, A. (1985), 'Copyright Protection for Computer Programs: Trojan Horse or Stimulus for the Future Copyright System?', *UFITA* 110, p. 57.

5 See Article 28 TRIPS. Gervais, D. (2003), *The TRIPS Agreement: Drafting History and Analysis*, 2nd edn., London: Sweet & Maxwell; Correa, C.M. (2007), *Trade-Related Aspects of Intellectual Property Rights – A Commentary on the TRIPS Agreement*, Oxford: Oxford University Press.

6 See Articles 11 and 12 WCT on the protection of technological measures and rights management information. Cf. Girsberger, M. (2007), *Schutz von technischen Maßnahmen im Urheberrecht: Die WIPO-Internetabkommen und deren Umsetzung in den Vereinigten Staaten, der Europäischen Union und der Schweiz*, Bern: Stämpfli; Arlt, C. (2006), *Digital Rights Management Systeme – Der Einsatz technischer Maßnahmen zum Schutz digitaler Inhalte*, Munich: C.H. Beck; Koelman, K. (2003), *Auteursrecht en technische voorzieningen*, Den Haag: SDU; Bechtold, S. (2002), *Vom Urheber- zum Informationsrecht: Implikationen des Digital Rights Management*, Munich: C.H. Beck; Wand, P. (2001), *Technische Schutzmaßnahmen und Urheberrecht*, Munich: C.H. Beck.

7 Cf. Senftleben, M.R.F. (2009), 'The Trademark Tower of Babel – Dilution Concepts in International, US and EC Law', *IIC* 40, p. 45; Fezer, K.-H. (2003), 'Entwicklungslinien und Prinzipien des Markenrechts in Europa – Auf dem Weg zur Marke als einem immaterialgüterrechtlichen Kommunikationszeichen', *GRUR*, p. 457.

8 Cf. Derclaye, E. and Leistner, M. (2010), *Intellectual Property Overlaps: A European Perspective*, Oxford: Hart Publishing; Cruquenaire, A. and Dussollier, S. (eds) (2009), *Le cumul des droits intellectuels*, Brussels: Larcier.

provided by open-ended fair use provisions that allow the courts to develop and adjust IP limitations case-by-case on the basis of abstract criteria. Against this background, the following analysis explores the notion of fair use (Section 2) and identifies factors indicating a need for fair use solutions (Sections 3 and 4) before embarking on a discussion of the situation in copyright (Section 5), patent (Section 6) and trademark (Section 7) law. Drawing conclusions, protection overlaps will be considered (Section 8).

2. DEFINITION

The term 'fair use' is often understood as a reference to the fair use doctrine that evolved in US copyright law.[9] However, it is not the purpose of the present inquiry to clarify whether this particular type of fair use legislation could serve as a model for the horizontal regulation of IP limitations. In the present context, the term 'fair use' merely indicates that limitations are regulated in a flexible way. Instead of a closed list of precisely defined exceptions to exclusive rights, a fair use system rests on abstract criteria allowing the judge to determine whether a given unauthorized use is to be deemed permissible.

While the fair use doctrine in US copyright law complies with this general description of the phenomenon,[10] it constitutes only one particu-

---

9 Section 107 of the US Copyright Act permits the unauthorized use of copyrighted material for purposes 'such as criticism, comment, news reporting, teaching [. . .], scholarship, or research'. To guide the decision on individual forms of use, four factors are set forth in the provision which shall be taken into account among other considerations that may be relevant in a given case:

(1) the purpose and character of the use, including whether such use is of a commercial nature or is for nonprofit educational purposes;
(2) the nature of the copyrighted work;
(3) the amount and substantiality of the portion used in relation to the copyrighted work as a whole; and
(4) the effect of the use upon the potential market for or value of the copyrighted work.

10 The list of purposes referred to in Section 107 of the US Copyright Act is understood as an open, non-exclusive enumeration. See Senate and House Committee Reports, as quoted by Seltzer, L.E. (1978), *Exemptions and Fair Use in Copyright – The Exclusive Rights Tensions in the 1976 Copyright Act*, Cambridge, and London: Harvard University Press, pp. 19–20: '. . . since the doctrine is an equitable rule of reason, no generally applicable definition is possible, and each case raising the question must be decided on its own facts . . . The bill endorses the purpose and general scope of the judicial doctrine of fair use [. . .] but there is no

lar example of conceivable fair use approaches. The fair use defence may feature less prominently in a system of IP limitations. The regulation of limitations may even rely predominantly on precisely defined exceptions and still qualify as a fair use system as long as the list of specific exceptions is supplemented with an open-ended clause for the identification of additional types of permissible unauthorized use in the light of the individual circumstances of a given case. For the purposes of the present analysis, the term 'fair use', thus, broadly refers to some flexible element in the regulation of IP limitations that opens up the system.[11]

Moreover, fair use need not be equated with use free of charge in the present context. While the US fair use doctrine does not provide for the payment of equitable remuneration, the inclusion of this feature will not be deemed incompatible with the notion of fair use in the following analysis. The payment of compensation enhances the breathing space that can be created in fair use systems.[12] When the permission of unauthorized use seems desirable even though the exemption impacts deeply on the position of the right owner, the payment of equitable remuneration constitutes an important balancing instrument broadening the scope of potential fair use solutions. Therefore, the following analysis includes the consideration of enhanced flexibility that follows from solutions based on compensation payments.[13]

3. RATIONALE

In copyright theory, the fair use approach is associated with the utilitarian foundation of the Anglo-American copyright tradition, perceiving copyright as a prerogative granted to enhance the overall welfare of

---

disposition to freeze the doctrine in the statute . . . Beyond a very broad statutory explanation of what fair use is and some of the criteria applicable to it, the courts must be free to adapt the doctrine to particular situations on a case-by-case basis'.

[11] For a detailed discussion of different types of fair use legislation, see Förster, A. (2008), *Fair Use*, Tübingen: Mohr Siebeck, pp. 211–22.

[12] This advantage outweighs the disadvantage of costs arising from the necessity to establish collective licensing bodies and ensure the appropriate distribution of collected compensation payments among right owners.

[13] This approach is in line with international standards. With regard to the three-step test in copyright law, for instance, it is recognized that the payment of equitable remuneration may be used to reduce an unreasonable prejudice to legitimate interests to a permissible, reasonable level. Cf. Senftleben, M.R.F. (2004), *Copyright, Limitations and the Three-Step Test – An Analysis of the Three-Step Test in International and EC Copyright Law*, The Hague, London and New York: Kluwer Law International, pp. 125–33.

society by ensuring a sufficient supply of knowledge and information.[14] This theoretical basis only justifies rights strong enough to induce the desired production of intellectual works. Therefore, the exclusive rights of authors deserve individual positive legal enactment.[15] Those forms of use that need not be reserved for the right owner to provide the necessary incentive remain free. Otherwise, rights would be awarded that are unnecessary to achieve the goals of the system. In sum, exclusive rights are thus delineated precisely, while their limitation can be regulated flexibly in open-ended provisions, such as fair use.[16] Oversimplifying the theoretical model underlying common law copyright, it might be said that freedom of use is the rule, rights are the exception.

The opposite constellation – rights the rule, freedom the exception – follows from the natural law underpinning of continental-European droit d'auteur. In the natural law theory, the author occupies centre stage.[17] A literary or artistic work is perceived as a materialization of the author's personality. Accordingly, it is assumed that a bond unites the author with the object of her creation.[18] Moreover, the author acquires a property right in her work by virtue of the mere act of creation. This has the corollary that nothing is left to the law apart from formally recognizing what is already inherent in the 'very nature of things'.[19] The author-centrism of the civil law system calls on the legislator to safeguard rights broad enough to concede to authors the opportunity to profit from the use of their self-expression, and to bar factors that might stymie their exploitation. In consequence, civil law

---

14 In this vein, the US Supreme Court, for instance, referred to copyright as an 'engine of free expression' in *Harper & Row v Nation Enterprises*, 471 US 539 (1985), III B.

15 Cf. Strowel, A. (1994), 'Droit d'auteur and Copyright: Between History and Nature', in Sherman, B. and Strowel, A. (eds), *Of Authors and Origins*, Oxford: Clarendon Press, pp. 235, 241–249; Calandrillo, S.P. (1998), 'An Economic Analysis of Property Rights in Information: Justifications and Problems of Exclusive Rights, Incentives to Generate Information, and the Alternative of a Government-Run Reward System', *Fordham Intellectual Property Media and Entertainment Law Journal* 9, pp. 301, 310.

16 See Geller, P.E., 'Must Copyright be For Ever Caught Between Marketplace and Authorship Norms?', in Sherman and Strowel, *supra* note 15, pp. 159, 170; Strowel, *supra* note 15, pp. 250–51.

17 Cf. Edelman, B., 'The Law's Eye: Nature and Copyright', in Sherman and Strowel, *supra* note 15, pp. 79, 82–7; Geller, *supra* note 16, pp. 169–70; Strowel, *supra* note 15, pp. 236–7.

18 Ulmer, E. (1980), *Urheber- und Verlagsrecht*, Berlin, Heidelberg and New York: Springer, pp. 110–11. See Desbois, H. (1973), *Le droit d'auteur en France*, 2nd edn., Paris: Dalloz, p. 538.

19 See Desbois, *supra* note 18, p. 538; Ulmer, *supra* note 18, pp. 105–6.

copyright systems recognize flexible, broad exclusive rights. Exceptions, by contrast, are defined narrowly and often interpreted restrictively.[20]

While this analysis on the basis of copyright theory may explain the evolution of fair use in common law jurisdictions, it fails to provide justifications for fair use. This is particularly true with regard to the ostensible antagonism between author centrism and flexible rights in civil law jurisdictions, and utilitarianism and flexible limitations in common law jurisdictions.[21] The particular advantage of fair use can hardly be derived from reflections on differences in legal theory. The merits of fair use come to the fore, however, once the costs of IP protection are factored into the equation. Intellectual property rights restrict fundamental freedoms, particularly freedom of expression and freedom of competition.[22] From an economic perspective, it has to be considered that IP monopolies, while spurring investment in new creations, also impede follow-on innovation requiring the use of pre-existing, protected material. Hence, there is a delicate balance inherent in all IP protection regimes.[23]

---

[20] Cf. Grosheide, W. (1986), *Auteursrecht op Maat*, Deventer: Kluwer p. 2; Geller, *supra* note 16, p. 170; Strowel, *supra* note 15, pp. 249–50; Förster, *supra* note 11, pp. 182–4. ECJ, case C-5/08, [2009] *Infopaq International v Danske Dagblades Forening*, paras. 56–8 (online available at www.curia.eu).

[21] From a historical perspective, this antagonism may not be overestimated anyway. See Ginsburg, J.C. (1994), 'A Tale of Two Copyrights: Literary Property in Revolutionary France and America', in Sherman and Strowel, *supra* note 15, pp. 131, 133.

[22] See Dommering, E.J. (2008), *De achtervolging van Prometheus – over vrijheid en bezit van informatie*, Amsterdam: Otto Cramwinckel; McGeveran, W. (2008), 'Four Free Speech Goals for Trademark Law', *Fordham Intellectual Property, Media and Entertainment Law Journal* 18, pp. 1205–27; Geiger, C. (2006), '"Constitutionalising" Intellectual Property Law? The Influence of Fundamental Rights on Intellectual Property in the European Union', *IIC* 37, p. 371; Strowel, A., Tulkens, F., and Voorhoof, D. (eds) (2006), *Droit d'auteur et liberté d'expression*, Brussels: Editions Larcier; Hugenholtz, P.B. (2002), 'Copyright and Freedom of Expression in Europe', in Elkin-Koren, N. and Netanel, N.W. (eds), *The Commodification of Information*, The Hague, London and Boston: Kluwer, p. 239; Dreier, T. (2001), 'Balancing Proprietary and Public Domain Interests: Inside or Outside of Proprietary Rights?', in Dreyfuss, R., Leenheer-Zimmerman, D., and First, H. (eds), *Expanding the Boundaries of Intellectual Property: Innovation Policy for the Knowledge Economy*, Oxford: Oxford University Press, pp. 295–316; Macciacchini, S. (2000), *Urheberrecht und Meinungsfreiheit*, Bern: Stämpfli; Benkler, Y. (1999), 'Free as the Air to Common Use: First Amendment Constraints on Enclosure of the Public Domain', *New York University Law Review* 74, p. 355; Netanel, N.W. (1996), 'Copyright and a Democratic Civil Society', *Yale Law Journal* 106, p. 283.

[23] Cf. Landes, W.N. and Posner, R.A. (2003), *The Economic Structure of Intellectual Property Law*, Harvard: Harvard University Press. With regard to

With regard to the maintenance of this balance, fair use has a crucial role to play. In advanced IP protection systems offering flexible, broad exclusive rights, it is wise to employ fair use as a counterbalance. In this way, the risk of counterproductive overprotection can be minimized. An IP regime with only a limited number of narrow exclusive rights, by contrast, does not necessarily require an open-ended fair use defence. In the absence of flexible rights, overprotection is less likely. Precisely defined exceptions may be sufficient.

Accordingly, the fair use discussion is not about the question of whether freedom of use should be the rule, and protection the exception. Instead, it concerns the question of appropriate balancing tools. Flexible rights necessitate flexible limitations. This becomes obvious at times of new technological developments that impact on the IP system. In these times of change, broad exclusive rights are likely to absorb and restrict new possibilities of use, even though this may be undesirable from the perspective of social, cultural or economic needs.[24] In this situation, abstract fair use factors ensure a fast reaction. They allow the courts to re-establish a proper balance between freedom and protection. A closed system of narrowly defined limitations, by contrast, is likely to react too slowly to unforeseen challenges. It requires the intervention of the legislator and the development of new, specific exceptions. This process of law making can hardly keep pace with rapid technological advances. As a result, the balance between freedom and protection will be lost.

---

copyright law, see from the same authors: Landes, W.N. and Posner, R.A. (1989), 'An Economic Analysis of Copyright Law', *The Journal of Legal Studies* 18, p. 325.

[24] With regard to the critical assessment of broad IP protection, see Assaf, K. (2009), 'Der Markenschutz und seine kulturelle Bedeutung', *GRUR Int.*, p. 1; Mazziotti, G. (2008), *EU Digital Copyright Law and the End-User*, Berlin and Heidelberg: Springer; Depenheuer, O. and Peifer, K.N. (eds) (2008), *Geistiges Eigentum: Schutzrecht oder Ausbeutungstitel?*, Berlin and Heidelberg: Springer; Hilty, R.M. (2007), 'Sündenbock Urheberrecht?', in Ohly, A. and Klippel, D. (eds), *Geistiges Eigentum und Gemeinfreiheit*, Tübingen: Mohr Siebeck, p. 111; Hilty, R.M. and Peukert, A. (2004), *Interessenausgleich im Urheberrecht*, Baden-Baden: Nomos; Geiger, C. (2004), *Droit d'auteur et droit du public à l'information, approche de droit comparé*, Paris: Litec; Kröger, D. (2002), *Informationsfreiheit und Urheberrecht*, Munich: C.H. Beck; Hoeren, T. (1997), 'Urheberrecht in der Informationsgesellschaft', *GRUR*, p. 866; R. Cooper Dreyfuss (1996), 'We are Symbols and Inhabit Symbols, so Should we be Paying Rent? Deconstructing the Lanham Act and Rights of Publicity', *Columbia-VLA Journal of Law & Arts* 20, p. 123.

4. HYPOTHESIS

The central advantage of fair use, therefore, is enhanced flexibility in the area of IP limitations to maintain an appropriate balance between freedom of use and protection of right owners. This counterbalance is particularly needed in IP protection systems offering flexible, broad exclusive rights. In particular, it becomes crucial when rapid technological developments impact on IP protection regimes and disturb their equilibrium between rights and limitations.

Given the continuous expansion of IP protection during recent decades, and the constant impact of new technologies, it can be hypothesized that these conditions for the introduction of fair use defences are fulfilled. Against this background, an attempt will be made to show that fair use defences are required in several branches of protection (Sections 5, 6 and 7). On the basis of this analysis, it will finally be considered whether a universal fair use infrastructure is needed to safeguard the inner consistency of the IP system in case of protection overlaps (Section 8).

5. COPYRIGHT

Flexible fair use defences can be found in the copyright legislation of many countries.[25] If the adoption of fair use elements is more than a relic of the Anglo-American copyright tradition, it should be possible to show that the factors identified as justifying a fair use approach weigh in favour of fair use in the case of the copyright system (5.1). Subsequently, it must be asked whether national fair use legislation complies with international copyright standards (5.2). To emphasize the current need for fair use, the shortcomings of restrictive EC legislation will finally be considered (5.3) before drawing conclusions (5.4).

5.1. Need for Fair Use

With regard to flexible, broad exclusive rights, a trend towards comprehensive entitlements can be inferred from developments at the international level. It was one of the major accomplishments of the 1967 Stockholm

---

[25] Moreover, new systems have been established recently. With regard to the introduction of fair use in Israel, see Fischman Afori, O. (2008), 'An Open Standard "Fair Use" Doctrine: A Welcome Israeli Initiative', *EIPR*, p. 85; Pessach, G. (2010), 'The New Israeli Copyright Act – A Case-Study in Reverse Comparative Law', *IIC* 41, pp. 187, 189–93.

Conference for the Revision of the Berne Convention to formally recognize a general right of reproduction in Article 9(1) BC.[26] In Article 8 WCT, a general right of communication to the public was later added to this portfolio of flexible, broad rights. Further grants of protection, such as public performance, translation and adaptation rights, complement these general rights.[27]

An additional factor to be considered is the openness of the copyright system with regard to subject matter eligible for protection. The Berne Convention contents itself with the clarification that the notion encompasses 'every production in the literary, scientific and artistic domain, whatever may be the mode or form of its expression', and provides an illustrative list of subject matter ranging from 'books, pamphlets and other writings' to 'works relative to geography, topography, architecture or science'.[28] Article 10(1) TRIPS and Article 4 WCT add computer programs. In most national jurisdictions, elastic tests of 'originality' are applied to identify the subject matter of copyright protection. In consequence, the doors to copyright protection are wide open.

Therefore, it is justified to speak of a flexible, broad grant of protection in copyright law – both in terms of exclusive rights and the subject matter of protection. In addition, copyright law is constantly challenged by new technological developments. The fast development of the Internet requires continuous recalibrations of the protection system. Advanced search engine services, user-created content and the digitization of cultural material can serve as examples of current phenomena requiring the reconsideration of the scope of protection.[29] Hence, both factors identified above

---

[26] The recognition of a general right aimed at redressing the anomaly that the Convention did not reflect the fundamental position held by the right of reproduction, whereas broad reproduction rights had become widespread in national legislation. See Doc. S/1, Records of the Intellectual Property Conference of Stockholm June 11 to July 14, 1967, Geneva: WIPO 1971, pp. 81 and 111–12.

[27] See Articles 11(1)(i), 11ter(1)(i), 11bis(1)(iii), Article 8 and Articles 12, 14 BC.

[28] See Article 2(1) BC.

[29] Cf. Knopp, M. (2010), 'Fanfiction – nutzergenerierte Inhalte und das Urheberrecht', *GRUR*, p. 28; Beunen, A.C. (2010), 'De Google Book Settlement nader beschouwd en bekeken vanuit bibliotheken', *AMI*, p. 38; Bechtold, S. (2010), 'Optionsmodelle und private Rechtssetzung im Urheberrecht am Beispiel von Google Book Search', *GRUR*, p. 282; Senftleben, M.R.F. (2009), 'Pacman forever – preservering van computergames', *AMI*, p. 221; Helberger N., Guibault, N., Janssen, E.H., Van Eijk, N.A.N.M, Angelopoulos, C., and Van Hoboken, J.V.J. (2009), 'Legal Aspects of User Created Content', available online at http://ssrn.com/abstract=1499333; Hugenholtz, P.B. (2009), 'De Google Book-schikking: de wereldliteratuur gelicentieerd', *Nederlands Juristenblad*, p. 2145; Elferink, M. and

– flexible, broad protection and new technological developments – tip the scales in favour of fair use in the case of copyright law.

5.2. Permissibility

International copyright law reflects the need for flexible solutions in the field of limitations. Article 9(2) BC offers national law makers the freedom

> . . . to permit the reproduction of such works in certain special cases, provided that such reproduction does not conflict with a normal exploitation of the work and does not unreasonably prejudice the legitimate interests of the author.

This three-step test – certain special cases (step 1), no conflict with a normal exploitation (step 2), no unreasonable prejudice to legitimate interests (step 3) – also made its way into Article 13 TRIPS and played a decisive role during the negotiations of the WIPO 'Internet' Treaties.[30] In Article 10(1) WCT, it paved the way to agreement on limitations of the rights newly granted under the WIPO Copyright Treaty, including the right of making available online as part of the general right of communication to the public.[31]

Ringnalda, A. (2009), *Digitale ontsluiting van historische archieven en verweesde werken*, Amstelveen: deLex; Van Hoboken, J.V.J. (2008), 'De aansprakelijkheid van zoekmachines. Uitzondering zonder regels of regels zonder uitzondering?', *Computerrecht*, p. 15; Van Gompel, S. (2007), 'Unlocking the Potential of Pre-existing Content: How to Address the Issue of Orphan Works in Europe?', *IIC* 38, p. 669; Sherman, D. B. (2007), 'Cost and Resource Allocation Under the Orphan Works Act of 2006: Would the Act Reduce Transaction Costs, Allocate Orphan Works Efficiently, and Serve the Goals of Copyright Law?', *Virginia Journal of Law & Technology* 12, p. 13.

[30] With regard to the evolution of this 'family' of copyright three-step tests in international copyright law, see Senftleben, *supra* note 13, pp. 43–98; Dittrich, N. (2005), 'Der Dreistufentest', in Dittrich, N. (ed.), *Beiträge zum Urheberrecht VIII*, Vienna: Mahz, p. 63; Bornkamm, J. (2002), 'Der Dreistufentest als urheberrechtliche Schrankenbestimmung – Karriere eines Begriffs', in Ahrens H.-J., Bornkamm, J., Gloy, W., Starck, J., and von Ungern-Sternberg, J. (eds), *Festschrift für Willi Erdmann zum 65. Geburtstag*, Cologne, Berlin, Bonn and Munich: Carl Heymanns, p. 29.

[31] As a consequence, the three-step test of Article 10(1) WCT is the central threshold for limitations on the right of making available online. As to the debate in the context of the WIPO 'Internet' Treaties, see Senftleben, *supra* note 13, pp. 96–8; Ficsor, M. (2002), *The Law of Copyright and the Internet – The 1996 WIPO Treaties, their Interpretation and Implementation*, Oxford: Oxford University Press; Reinbothe J. and von Lewinski, S. (2002), *The WIPO Treaties 1996 – Commentary and Legal Analysis*, London: Butterworths.

A line between the international three-step test and open-ended fair use provisions, such as the US fair use doctrine, can easily be drawn. The prohibition of a conflict with a normal exploitation, for instance, recalls the fourth factor of the US fair use doctrine 'effect of the use upon the potential market for or value of the copyrighted work'.[32] The drafting history of the three-step test confirms that the flexible formula has its roots in the Anglo-American copyright tradition.[33] In the context of the WIPO Copyright Treaty, it has moreover been confirmed that the international test, indeed, constitutes a means of enabling limitations and enhancing the flexibility of the copyright system:

> It is understood that the provisions of Article 10 permit Contracting Parties to carry forward and appropriately extend into the digital environment limitations and exceptions in their national laws which have been considered acceptable under the Berne Convention. Similarly, these provisions should be understood to permit Contracting Parties to devise new exceptions and limitations that are appropriate in the digital network environment.[34]

At the national level, the three-step test has been used in this enabling sense,[35] for instance, in decisions of the German Federal Court of Justice.

---

32 Cf. Section 107 of the US Copyright Act. With regard to the application of fair use analyses concerning the fourth factor in the context of the three-step test, see Senftleben, *supra* note 13, pp. 184–7.

33 See observation by the United Kingdom, Doc. S/13, Records of the Intellectual Property Conference of Stockholm June 11 to July 14, 1967, Geneva: WIPO 1971, p. 630. Senftleben, *supra* note 13, pp. 47–52.

34 See Agreed Statement Concerning Article 10 of the WIPO Copyright Treaty.

35 In fact, the three-step test has been understood in the sense of an 'enabling' provision allowing countries to satisfy their existing individual social, cultural and economic needs at the time when the test was first developed and incorporated in Article 9(2) BC. At the 1967 Stockholm Conference, the test was perceived as a flexible framework, within which national legislators would enjoy the freedom of safeguarding national limitations and satisfying the aforementioned domestic needs. See Doc. S/1, Records of the Intellectual Property Conference of Stockholm June 11 to July 14, 1967, Geneva: WIPO 1971, p. 81. Kur, A. (2008), 'Of Oceans, Islands, and Inland Water – How Much Room for Exceptions and Limitations Under the Three-Step Test?', *Max Planck Institute for Intellectual Property, Competition & Tax Law Research Paper Series* No. 08-04, online available at http://ssrn.com/abstract=1317707; Geiger, C. (2006), 'The Three-Step Test, a Threat to a Balanced Copyright Law?', *IIC* 37, pp. 683, 694–6; Senftleben, M.R.F. (2004), 'Grundprobleme des urheberrechtlichen Dreistufentests', *GRUR Int.*, pp. 200, 206–07. For an overview of national case law applying the three-step test as a flexible standard, see Griffiths, J. (2009), 'The "Three-Step Test" in European Copyright Law – Problems and Solutions', *Intellectual Property Quarterly*, p. 489,

In a 1999 case concerning the Technical Information Library Hanover, the Court underlined the public interest in unhindered access to information. Accordingly, it offered support for the Library's practice of copying and dispatching scientific articles on request by single persons and industrial undertakings.[36] The legal basis of this practice was the statutory limitation for personal use in § 53 of the German Copyright Act. Under this provision, the authorized user need not necessarily produce the copy herself but is free to ask a third party to make the reproduction on her behalf. The Court admitted that the dispatch of copies came close to a publisher's activity.[37] Nonetheless, it refrained from putting an end to the library practice by assuming a conflict with a work's normal exploitation. Instead, the Court deduced an obligation to pay equitable remuneration from the three-step test, and enabled the continuation of the information service in this way.[38]

In a 2002 decision concerning the scanning and storing of press articles for internal e-mail communication in a private company, the Court gave a further example of its flexible approach to the three-step test. It held that digital press reviews had to be deemed permissible under § 49(1) of the German Copyright Act just like their analogue counterparts, if the digital version – in terms of its functioning and potential for use – essentially corresponded to traditional analogue products.[39] To overcome the problem of the outdated wording of § 49(1) that seemed to indicate

---

available online at http://ssrn.com/abstract=1476968. For a proposal to use the three-step test as an instrument to delineate the exclusive rights of copyright owners, see Gervais, D. (2005), 'Towards a New Core International Copyright Norm: The Reverse Three-Step Test', *Marquette Intellectual Property Law Review* 9, p. 1.

[36] See German Federal Court of Justice (Bundesgerichtshof), 25 February 1999, case I ZR 118/96, *Juristenzeitung* 1999, p. 1000, with case comment by Schack, H. For an English description of the case, see Senftleben, *supra* note 13, pp. 206–8.

[37] See Bundesgerichtshof, ibid., p. 1004.

[38] See Bundesgerichtshof, ibid., pp. 1005–07. Baronikians, P., 'Kopienversand durch Bibliotheken – rechtliche Beurteilung und Vorschläge zur Regelung', *Zeitschrift für Urheber- und Medienrecht* 1999, p. 126. In the course of subsequent amendments to the Copyright Act, the German legislator modelled a new copyright limitation on the Court's decision. § 53a of the German Copyright Act goes beyond the court decision by including the dispatch of digital copies in graphical format.

[39] See German Federal Court of Justice (Bundesgerichtshof), 11 July 2002, case I ZR 255/00, *GRUR* 2002, p. 963; *Juristenzeitung* 2003, p. 473, with case comment by Dreier, T. Cf. Hoeren, T. (2002), 'Pressespiegel und das Urheberrecht', *GRUR*, p. 1022.

that the limitation was confined to press reviews on paper,[40] the Court stated that, in view of new technical developments, a copyright limitation may be interpreted extensively.[41] Taking these considerations as a starting point, the Court arrived at the conclusion that digital press reviews were permissible, if articles were included in graphical format without offering additional functions, such as a text collection and an index. This extension of the analogue press review exception to the digital environment, the Court maintained, was in line with the three-step test.[42]

Hence, the test can be used to strengthen limitations and enhance flexibility in copyright law. National legislation adopting a fair use approach, however, goes beyond the court decisions described. It allows the courts to create new limitations on the basis of abstract factors instead of entrusting them merely with the flexible interpretation of pre-defined, specific exceptions. In other words, national fair use legislation 'institutionalizes' the function of enabling limitations which the international three-step test has because of its open-ended wording. The abstract criteria of the three-step test may be regarded as a model for national fair use factors in this context.[43]

However, doubt has been cast upon the permissibility of fair use legislation on the grounds that a national fair use system could not be qualified as a 'certain special case' in the sense of the three-step test.[44] This counter-

---

40 § 49(1) of the German Copyright Act, as in force at that time, referred to 'Informationsblätter'.

41 See Bundesgerichtshof, ibid., p. 966–6.

42 See Bundesgerichtshof, ibid., pp. 966–67. The Court referred to the three-step test of Article 5(5) of the EC Copyright Directive 2001/29. The EC three-step test enshrined in this provision, however, does not deviate from the international three-step test.

43 As to the application of the three-step test criteria in the framework of a fair use weighing process, see Koelman, K.J. (2006), 'Fixing the Three-Step Test', *EIPR*, p. 407. However, see also the conclusions drawn by Griffiths, *supra* note 35, who doubts that the three-step test offers an appropriate basis for fair use provisions.

44 As to the debate on the impact of the three-step test on open-ended limitations, such as the US fair use doctrine, see Förster, *supra* note 11, pp. 191–201; Senftleben, *supra* note 13, pp. 133–7 and 162–8; Bornkamm, *supra* note 30, pp. 45–6; Cohen Jehoram, H. (2005), 'Restrictions on Copyright and their Abuse', *EIPR*, p. 359; Ricketson, S. (2002), 'The Three-Step Test, Deemed Quantities, Libraries and Closed Exceptions', Strawberry Hills, NSW: Centre for Copyright Studies, available online at http://www.copyright.com.au/assets/documents/CC50202Berne.pdf; Senftleben, M.R.F. (2003), 'Beperkingen à la carte: Waarom de Auteursrechtrichtlijn ruimte laat voor fair use', *AMI*, p. 10; Leaffer, M. (2001), 'The Uncertain Future of Fair Use in a Global Information Marketplace', *Ohio State Law Journal* 62, p. 849; Okediji, R. (2000), 'Toward an International Fair

argument is based on the three-step tests of Article 13 TRIPS and Article 10(2) WCT. In contrast to the aforementioned Article 9(2) BC and Article 10(1) WCT, these tests do not primarily serve as the basis for national limitations. Article 13 TRIPS and Article 10(2) WCT rather constitute additional safeguards seeking to ensure that all kinds of copyright limitations keep within the limits of the three-step test.[45] Interpreting the TRIPS test, however, the WTO Panel reporting on Section 110(5) of the US Copyright Act did not endorse the view that fair use, by definition, was incompatible with the requirement of 'certain special cases'. Instead, the Panel followed a more cautious approach:

> However, there is no need to identify explicitly each and every possible situation to which the exception could apply, provided that the scope of the exception is known and particularised. This guarantees a sufficient degree of legal certainty.[46]

In this way, the Panel left room for national copyright laws providing for fair use. Legal certainty is not necessarily an exclusive task of the legislator. It may be divided between law makers and judges. In fair use systems, the degree of legal certainty need not be lower than in systems with specific, statutory limitations. The open factors constituting the fair use criteria allow the courts to determine 'certain special cases' of permissible unauthorized use in the light of the individual circumstances of a given

---

Use Doctrine', *Columbia Journal of Transnational Law* 39, pp. 75, 116–30; Cohen, J.E. (1999), 'WIPO Copyright Treaty Implementation in the United States: Will Fair Use Survive?', *EIPR*, p. 236; Newby, T. (1999), 'What's Fair Here is not Fair Everywhere: Does the American Fair Use Doctrine Violate International Copyright Law?', *Stanford Law Review*, p. 1633.

45 For a discussion of the different functions of the three-step test, and the difference between Articles 9(2) BC and 10(1) WCT on the one hand, and Articles 13 TRIPS and 10(2) WCT on the other, see Senftleben, *supra* note 13, pp. 118–25.

46 See WTO Document WT/DS160/R, available online at www.wto.org, para. 6.108. For comments on the report, see Senftleben, M.R.F. (2006), 'Towards a Horizontal Standard for Limiting Intellectual Property Rights? – WTO Panel Reports Shed Light on the Three-Step Test in Copyright Law and Related Tests in Patent and Trademark Law', *IIC* 37, p. 407; Ficsor, M. (2002), 'How Much of What? The Three-Step Test and its Application in Two Recent WTO Dispute Settlement Cases', *RIDA* 192, p. 111; Oliver, J. (2002), 'Copyright in the WTO: The Panel Decision on the Three-Step Test', *Columbia Journal of Law & the Arts* 25, p. 119; Brennan, D.J. (2002), 'The Three-Step Test Frenzy – Why the TRIPS Panel Decision might be considered Per Incuriam', *Intellectual Property Quarterly*, p. 213; Ginsburg, J. (2001), 'Toward Supranational Copyright Law? The WTO Panel Decision and the "Three-Step Test" for Copyright Exceptions', *RIDA*, p. 13; Hugenholtz, P.B. (2000), 'De wettelijke beperkingen beperkt. De WTO geeft de driestappentoets tanden', *AMI*, p. 197.

case. With every court decision, a further 'special case' becomes known, particularized and thus 'certain' in the sense of the three-step test. A sufficient degree of legal certainty follows from established case law instead of detailed legislation. For instance, a sufficient degree of legal certainty can be attained in a system with a long-standing fair use tradition, such as the US copyright system.[47]

Moreover, it is to be recalled that flexible law making in the field of copyright limitations is a particular feature of the Anglo-American copyright tradition. At the international level, a WTO Panel can be expected to take into account both the continental-European and the Anglo-American tradition of copyright law. The Panel's formula of 'a sufficient degree of legal certainty' can thus be understood to ensure that not only precisely defined civil law exceptions but also common law fair use limitations are capable of passing the test of 'certain special cases'. Otherwise, an entire tradition of legal thinking would be discredited and declared incompatible with international standards.

In national systems switching from a closed list of statutory exceptions to an open-ended fair use approach, the required degree of legal certainty can be secured by applying case law established under the old system as the basis of the new fair use system. In mixed systems combining several statutory exceptions with an open fair use clause, the listed statutory exceptions can be regarded as examples of permissible fair use that can serve as a reference point for the courts. Considering the standard set forth by the WTO Panel, international copyright law, therefore, does not preclude any variant of fair use. With the open-ended factors of special cases, normal exploitation, legitimate interests and unreasonable prejudice, the international three-step test itself can be perceived as a source of inspiration for flexible law making in the field of copyright limitations rather than an obstacle to the introduction of national fair use systems.

5.3. EC Worst-Case Scenario

In the current online environment, enhanced flexibility in the field of copyright limitations is indispensable. From a social and cultural perspective,

---

[47] In this sense, see Senftleben, *supra* note 13, pp. 162–8. Beebe, B. (2008), 'An Empirical Study of U.S. Copyright Fair Use Opinions, 1978–2005', *University of Pennsylavania Law Review* 156, p. 549. However, see the critical comments by Förster, *supra* note 11, pp. 197–201, on the unrestricted openness of the US system. With regard to the predictability of fair use decisions, see also Nimmer, D. (2003), '"Fairest of Them All" and Other Fairy Tales of Fair Use', *Law and Contemporary Problems* 66, p. 263.

the web 2.0 promotes and enhances freedom of expression and information with its advanced search engine services, interactive platforms and various forms of user-generated content.[48] From an economic perspective, it creates a parallel universe of traditional content providers relying on copyright protection, and emerging Internet industries whose further development depends on robust copyright limitations. In particular, the newcomers in the online market – social networking sites, video forums and virtual worlds – promise remarkable potential for economic growth that have already attracted the attention of the OECD.[49]

The inefficiency of systems ignoring the merits of flexible copyright limitations can currently be observed in the EC. The adaptation of EC copyright law to the digital environment has led to a legislative framework that imposes a heavy burden on users of copyrighted material. Elements of both traditions of copyright law have been combined in the most unfortunate way. In the Copyright Directive 2001/29/EC, paragraphs 1, 2, 3 and 4 of Article 5 set forth a closed catalogue of exceptions. This enumeration is in line with the continental-European copyright tradition. The listed exceptions, however, are subject to a three-step test laid down in paragraph 5.[50] This inclusion of a provision with open-ended criteria recalls the Anglo-American copyright tradition.[51] However, the interplay between the two elements – the closed catalogue and the open three-step test – is regulated as follows:

---

48 See the literature indicated *supra* note 29.

49 See OECD, Participative Web: User-Created Content, document DSTI/ICCP/IE(2006)7/Final, dated 12 April 2007, available online at http://213.253.134.43/oecd/pdfs/browseit/9307031E.PDF. Cf. Dreier, T. (2001), 'Primär- und Folgemärkte', in Schricker, G., Dreier, T., and Kur, A. (eds), *Geistiges Eigentum im Dienst der Innovation*, Baden-Baden: Nomos, p. 51; Geiger, C. (2008), 'Die Schranken des Urheberrechts als Instrumente der Innovationsförderung – Freie Gedanken zur Ausschließlichkeit im Urheberrecht', *GRUR Int.*, p. 459.

50 As to the drafting history of this hybrid framework for copyright exceptions, see Hart, M. (1998), 'The Proposed Directive for Copyright in the Information Society: Nice Rights, Shame about the Exceptions', *EIPR*, p. 169; Hugenholtz, P.B. (2000), 'Why the Copyright Directive is Unimportant, and Possibly Invalid', *EIPR*, p. 499; Visser, D.J.G. (2001), 'De beperkingen in de Auteursrechtrichtlijn', *AMI*, p. 9; Bayreuther, F. (2001), 'Beschränkungen des Urheberrechts nach der neuen EU-Urheberrechtsrichtlinie', *Zeitschrift für Urheber- und Medienrecht*, p. 828; Reinbothe, J. (2001), 'Die EG-Richtlinie zum Urheberrecht in der Informationsgesellschaft', *GRUR Int.*, p. 733.

51 As pointed out, *supra* note 32, a line between the criteria of the three-step test and open fair use factors can easily be drawn. The criterion of 'no conflict with a normal exploitation', for instance, resembles the fourth fair use factor 'effect of the use upon the potential market for or value of the copyrighted work'.

> The exceptions and limitations provided for in paragraphs 1, 2, 3 and 4 shall only be applied in certain special cases which do not conflict with a normal exploitation of the work or other subject-matter and do not unreasonably prejudice the legitimate interests of the rightholder.[52]

This approach, inevitably, leads to a dilemma. If anything, a closed list of precisely defined exceptions has the advantage of enhanced legal certainty.[53] This potential advantage, however, is beyond reach under the current EC system. If national legislation adopts and further specifies exceptions from the EC catalogue, these specific national exceptions may still be challenged on the grounds that they are incompatible with the EC three-step test. In other words, national exceptions that are already embedded in an inflexible national framework may further be restricted by invoking the three-step test. On the one hand, national copyright exceptions are thus straitjacketed. Their validity is hanging by the thread of compliance with the abstract criteria of the EC three-step test. On the other hand, the test itself is deprived of the above-described enabling function which characterizes the international three-step test. The EC test may be invoked to further restrict national exceptions. However, it cannot be employed by the courts to create new, additional forms of permitted unauthorized use. Hence, it is impossible to realize the central advantage of flexibility that is inherent in open norms with abstract criteria.[54]

In consequence, the current EC system provides neither sufficient flexibility for copyright limitations nor sufficient legal certainty for users of

---

52 See Article 5(5) of the Copyright Directive 2001/29/EC.

53 Cf. Lucas, A. (2010), 'For a Reasonable Interpretation of the Three-Step Test', *EIPR*, pp. 277, 282. However, Lucas raises this argument with regard to the current regulation of copyright limitations in the EC. As argued here, the validity of the legal certainty argument is doubtful in this context. Cohen Jehoram, H. (1998), 'Fair Use – die ferne Geliebte', *AMI*, p. 174; 'Implementatie van de Auteursrechtrichtlijn – De stille strijd tegen een spookrijder', *Nederlands Juristenblad* 2002, p. 1690; 'Nu de gevolgen van trouw en ontrouw aan de Auteursrechtrichtlijn voor fair use, tijdelijke reproductie en driestappentoets', *AMI* 2005, p. 153; 'Wie is bang voor de driestappentoets in de Auteursrechtrichtlijn?', in van Eijk, N.A.N.M. and Hugenholtz, P.B. (eds), *Dommering-bundel*, Amsterdam: Otto Cramwinckel, 2008, p. 57.

54 Cf. Senftleben, M.R.F. (2009), 'Fair Use in the Netherlands – a Renaissance?', *AMI*, p. 1, available online at http://ssrn.com/abstract=1563986; Griffiths, *supra* note 35, p. 495; Geiger, *supra* note 35, p. 683; Koelman, K.J. (2003), 'De nationale driestappentoets', *AMI*, p. 6. The restrictive nature and freezing effect of the EC copyright three-step test has been confirmed by the ECJ, case C-5/08, [2009] *Infopaq v Danske Dagblades Forening*, para. 58. The Court pointed out that the precisely defined exception of Article 5(1) of the EC Copyright Directive, in addition, had to satisfy the criteria of the three-step test laid down in Article 5(5).

copyrighted material. It combines the disadvantage of the Anglo-American approach with the disadvantage of the continental-European approach. This dysfunctional concept has a corrosive effect on the national copyright systems in EC Member States.[55] Dutch courts, for instance, were already applying the three-step test prior to the Copyright Directive.[56] On the one hand, the adoption and implementation of the Directive led to more frequent references to the three-step test that are made to confirm and strengthen findings that equally follow from domestic rules.[57] This way of applying the three-step test has little impact on the Dutch catalogue of statutory exceptions. On the other hand, however, the Directive inspired a line of decisions that use the three-step test to override the closed Dutch system of precisely defined user privileges.[58]

In a decision of 25 June 2008, the District Court of The Hague, for

---

55 With regard to substantial differences in applying the three-step test, see Griffiths, *supra* note 35, pp. 493–9. For an overview of the implementation strategies followed by EC Member States with regard to copyright limitations, see Institute for Information Law, *Study on the Implementation and Effect in Member States' Laws of Directive 2001/29/EC on the Harmonization of Certain Aspects of Copyright and Related Rights in the Information Society*, Amsterdam: Institute for Information Law 2007, available online at www.ivir.nl.

56 In the case *Zienderogen Kunst*, dating back to the year 1990, the Dutch Supreme Court invoked the three-step test of Article 9(2) of the Berne Convention to support its holding that the quotation of a work may not substantially prejudice the right holder's interest in the exploitation of the work concerned. See Hoge Raad, 22 June 1990, no. 13933, NJ 1991, p. 268 with case comment by Spoor, J.H. (1990), *Informatierecht/AMI*, p. 202 with case comment by Dommering, E.J. (1991), *Ars Aequi* 40, p. 672 with case comment by Cohen Jehoram, H.

57 In 2003, the Amsterdam Court of Appeals found that a parody did not harm the normal exploitation of the parodied work because it concerned a different market. See Gerechtshof Amsterdam, 30 January 2003, *AMI* 2003, p. 94 with case comment by Koelman, K.J. In a 2006 decision concerning online advertisements reproducing the so-called 'TRIPP TRAPP chair', the Court of Zwolle-Lelystad referred to the three-step test of Article 5(5) of the Directive in the context of Article 23 of the Dutch Copyright Act – a limitation permitting the use of certain artistic works for the purpose of advertising their public exhibition or sale. The Court found that the use in question prejudiced the exploitation interest of the right holder. This was one of the reasons for denying compliance with Article 23. See Rechtbank Zwolle-Lelystad, 3 May 2006, case no. 106031, LJN: AW 6288, *AMI* 2006, p. 179 with case comment by Koelman, K.J., *Mediaforum* 2006/9 with case comment by Beuving, B.T.

58 Besides the following example, see also District Court of The Hague (Rechtbank Den Haag), 2 March 2005, case no. 192880, LJN: AS 8778, *Computerrecht* 2005, p. 143 with case comment by Koelman, K.J. For an overview of national case law using the three-step test to further restrict statutory exceptions, see Griffiths, *supra* note 35, p. 493; Geiger, *supra* note 35, p. 683; Geiger, C.

instance, invoked the three-step test in a case concerning the payment of equitable remuneration for private copying activities. In this context, the Court devoted attention to the question of use of an illegal source as a basis for private copying.[59] The detailed regulation of private copying in Article 16c of the Dutch Copyright Act does not contain any indication to the effect that private copying from an illegal source is to be deemed impermissible. The drafting history of the provision, by contrast, reflects the clear intention of the Dutch legislator to exempt private copying irrespective of whether a legal or illegal source is used.[60] Having recourse to the three-step test of Article 5(5) of the Copyright Directive, the District Court of The Hague, nonetheless, dismantled this seemingly robust edifice of legal certainty in one single sentence. Without offering a detailed analysis, the Court stated that private copying from an illegal source was 'in conflict with the three-step test'. Accordingly, it was held to fall outside the private copying exemption of Article 16c:

> In the parliamentary history, there are indications of a different interpretation. However, the interpretation advocated by the minister and supported by the government – assuming that private copying from an illegal source was legal – is in conflict with the three-step test of Article 5(5) of the Directive.[61]

The central point here is not the prohibition of private copying using illegal sources. It is the erosion of the central argument weighing in favour of precisely defined exceptions and against a fair use system. Regardless of detailed definitions given in the Dutch Copyright Act, the ruling of the Court minimizes the degree of legal certainty in the field of copyright limitations. Users of copyrighted material in the Netherlands can no longer rely on the wording of the applicable statutory exception. On the basis of the EC three-step test, a certain use may be held to amount to copyright infringement even though it is exempted from the authorization of the right holder in the Dutch Copyright Act.[62]

Hence, neither legal certainty nor sufficient flexibility can be attained. In EC copyright systems incorporating the three-step test into national law,

---

(2008), 'The Answer to the Machine Should not be the Machine: Safeguarding the Private Copy Exception in the Digital Environment', *EIPR*, p. 121.

59 See Rechtbank Den Haag, 25 June 2008, case 246698, LJN BD5690, *AMI* 2008, p. 146 with case comment by van der Net, C.B.

60 See the material quoted by the Rechtbank Den Haag, ibid., para. 4.4.1.

61 See Rechtbank Den Haag, 25 June 2008, case 246698, LJN BD5690, AMI 2008, p. 146 with case comment by C.B. van der Net, para. 4.4.3.

62 See Senftleben, M.R.F. (2008), 'Privé-kopiëren in het licht van de driestappentoets – opmerkingen naar aanleiding van het vonnis van de Haagse rechtbank inzake de thuiskopie', *Intellectuele eigendom en reclamerecht*, p. 265.

such as the French system, this dilemma is made obvious for users relying on copyright exceptions.[63] However, the problem as such remains. When it is considered that, in addition, law making in the EC is much slower than in individual countries, it becomes clear that current EC copyright law causes a high risk of frustrating opportunities for cultural, social and economic development that arise from the web 2.0. The process of updating EC copyright legislation requires not only lengthy negotiations at Community level, but also national implementation acts in all Member States. Without fair use provisions in the field of copyright limitations, this process will be far too slow to keep pace with the rapid development of the Internet or to maintain an appropriate balance between copyright protection and competing freedoms. The current situation in the EC is a worst case scenario.[64]

Not surprisingly, the inflexibility of the EC limitation infrastructure already prompted courts to bypass the dysfunctional system of copyright limitations altogether.[65] In a recent decision dealing with Google's image search service, for instance, the German Federal Court of Justice saw no possibility of broadening the statutory right of quotation in § 51 of the German Copyright Act to cover Google's display of picture thumbnails. To fulfil the traditional context requirement of 'criticism and review' that had not been abandoned during the implementation of the Copyright Directive in Germany, the user making the quotation had to establish an

---

63 See Article L. 122-5 of the French Intellectual Property Act (Code de la propriété intellectuelle). Lucas, A. and Sirinelli, P. (2006), 'Chronique: Droit d'auteur et droits voisins', *Propriétés intellectuelles*, pp. 297, 314–16; Benabou, V.L. (2006), 'Patatras! A propos de la décision du Conseil constitutionnel du 27 juillet 2006', *Propriétés intellectuelles*, p. 240; Geiger, C. (2008), 'The French Implementation of the Information Society Directive: A Disappointing Result of a Promising Debate', *AMI*, p. 1. Senftleben, M.R.F. (2007), 'L'application du triple test: vers un système de fair use européen?', *Propriétés intellectuelles*, p. 453. In the Netherlands, Cohen Jehoram, H., advocates the inclusion of the three-step test in the Dutch Copyright Act. See references *supra* note 53.

64 See Senftleben, *supra* note 54, pp. 2–4. To reduce the harm flowing from the Copyright Directive, the EC three-step test should at least be construed flexibly. For guidelines in this regard, see Geiger, C., Griffiths, J., and Hilty, R.M. (2008), 'Declaration on a Balanced Interpretation of the "Three-Step Test" in Copyright Law', *IIC* 39, p. 707. For a fair use approach to the EC three-step test, see Senftleben, *supra* note 44, p. 10.

65 Besides the following case of the German Federal Court of Justice, see the decision *Google–Caching* of the Barcelona Court of Appeals, which concerned acts of caching and proxy-caching necessary to run the Google search service. Applying the doctrine of *ius usus inoqui*, the Court finally arrived at the application of the US fair use doctrine instead of the Spanish copyright legislation. The case is reported by Kur, *supra* note 35, p. 34; Griffiths, *supra* note 35, p. 487.

inner connection between the quoted material and her own thoughts. This requirement was not satisfied in the case of picture thumbnails that were merely used to inform the public about content available on the Internet.[66]

Nonetheless, to create breathing space for the image search service, the Court held that Google's use of the pictures was not unlawful because the copyright owner had consented implicitly to use of her material in the image search service by making her works available online without employing technical means to block the automatic indexing and displaying of online content by search engines.[67] It is unclear whether this solution on the basis of implicit consent will yield satisfactory results in all cases of contested search engine use. When protected material is not made available by the copyright owner but by an unauthorized third party, implicit consent can hardly be assumed.[68] Referring to this situation, the German Federal Court of Justice indicated that the search engine provider could rely on the safe harbour for the hosting of third party content set forth in Article 14 of the E-Commerce Directive 2000/31/EC.[69] Accordingly, liability for copyright infringement could be avoided by providing for appropriate notice-and-take-down procedures.

The decision shows a further consequence of the EC worst-case scenario. As the hybrid concept of precisely defined exceptions and the three-step test does not offer sufficient room to manoeuvre, the courts choose alternative routes to arrive at satisfactory results. The assumption of implicit consent, for instance, is an attempt to supersede the entire inflexible copyright limitation infrastructure. It is questionable whether this solution is consistent. The German Federal Court of Justice has virtually introduced a flexible element through the back door of doubtful assumptions about the intentions of a copyright owner making her works available on the Internet.

The dilemma of dysfunctional EC legislation in the field of copyright limitations can hardly be solved convincingly in this way. The right place to strike a proper balance between freedom and protection in copyright law

---

[66] See Bundesgerichtshof, 29 April 2010, case I ZR 69/08, pp. 11–12, available online in German at www.bundesgerichtshof.de. Dreier, T. (2009), 'Thumbnails als Zitate? – Zur Reichweite von § 51 UrhG in der Informationsgesellschaft', in Blaurock, U., Bornkamm, J., and Kirchberg, C. (eds), *Festschrift für Achim Krämer zum 70. Geburtstag*, Berlin: De Gruyter, p. 225.

[67] See Bundesgerichtshof, ibid., pp. 15–19.

[68] With regard to this constellation, see Landgericht Hamburg, September 26, 2008, case no. 308 O 248/07, section B.I.6.d., available online at http://www.openjur.de/u/30461-308_o_248-07.html.

[69] See Bundesgerichtshof, ibid., 21–2, referring to ECJ, joined cases C-236/08 to C-238/08, [2009] *Google v Louis Vuitton* et al., available online at www.curia.eu.

is the appropriate regulation of copyright limitations. Instead of inducing courts to invent around an overly restrictive framework, EC copyright law should provide the courts with the legal instruments necessary to maintain copyright's delicate balance even in times of rapid technological developments that constantly require fast adaptations. Fair use legislation would make this possible. US courts relied on the US fair use doctrine, for example, to deal with enhanced search engine services[70] and user-created content.[71] In contrast to the reported German decision on Google's image search service, the US fair use doctrine allowed the Ninth Circuit Court of Appeals to stay within the copyright limitation system and conclude with regard to the unauthorized display of image thumbnails that

> the significantly transformative nature of Google's search engine, particularly in light of its public benefit, outweighs Google's superseding and commercial uses of the thumbnails in this case. In reaching this conclusion, we note the importance of analyzing fair use flexibly in light of new circumstances.[72]

5.4. Conclusion

In copyright law, broad exclusive rights and exposure to fast technological developments justify a fair use approach. International obligations do not preclude national fair use legislation. The international three-step test, by contrast, can serve as a model for the development of national fair use factors. Given the potential of the web 2.0 for social, cultural and economic development, it seems advisable to seize this opportunity for flexible law making. The example of the EC Copyright Directive testifies to the dilemma arising from a restrictive approach. If the three-step test is employed to further restrict precisely defined copyright exceptions, a copyright system is created that offers neither legal certainty nor sufficient flexibility.

6. PATENTS

While copyright law is characterized by a wide variety of limitations, patent law provides for a rather limited set of exceptions. In many national systems,

---

[70] See US Court of Appeals for the Ninth Circuit, 16 May 2007, *Perfect 10, Inc. v Amazon.com*, Fd 3d.

[71] See United States District Court Southern District of New York, 8 September 2008, *Warner Bros. and J.K. Rowling v RDR Books*, 07 Civ. 9667 (RPP). Cf. the case comment by Sanders, A.J. (2009), *EIPR*, p. 45.

[72] See US Court of Appeals for the Ninth Circuit, ibid., para. 12.

these exceptions concern private use, scientific experimentation and certain forms of compulsory licensing. A patent fair use provision would be a remarkable step towards enhanced flexibility.[73] Against this background, it seems advisable to ask first whether international patent law permits a fair use approach (6.1) before assessing the need for fair use (6.2), the scope of a potential patent fair use defence (6.3) and drawing conclusions (6.4).

6.1. Permissibility

In the course of the TRIPS negotiations, the copyright three-step test served as a model for a corresponding patent provision. Article 30 TRIPS offers WTO Members the freedom to

> . . . provide limited exceptions to the exclusive rights conferred by a patent, provided that such exceptions do not unreasonably conflict with a normal exploitation of the patent and do not unreasonably prejudice the legitimate interests of the patent owner, taking account of the legitimate interests of third parties.

This patent three-step test deviates from the copyright provision in several ways. Instead of 'certain special cases', Article 30 TRIPS requires 'limited exceptions'. A conflict with a normal exploitation is permissible as long as it is not unreasonable. When assessing prejudices to legitimate interests, the interests of third parties are to be taken into account besides those of the patent owner.

With regard to fair use legislation, use of the term 'limited exceptions' instead of 'certain special cases' seems particularly relevant. Arguments against copyright fair use systems have been based on alleged shortcomings in the field of legal certainty. As discussed above, the standard of legal certainty established by the WTO Panel dealing with the copyright three-step test, however, can hardly be understood to militate against fair use legislation. The WTO Panel report in 'Canada – Protection of Pharmaceutical Products'[74] is even more cautious in this regard.

---

[73] Nevertheless, copyright fair use is used as a reference point in the discussion on more flexibility for exceptions to patent rights. See de Larena, L.R. (2005), 'What Copyright Teaches Patent Law about "Fair Use" and Why Universities are Ignoring the Lesson', *Orlando Law Review* 84, p. 779; Mueller, J.M. (2004), 'The Evanescent Experimental Use Exemption from United States Patent Infringement Liability: Implications for University and Nonprofit Research and Development', *Baylor Law Review* 56, p. 917; O'Rourke, M.A. (2000), 'Toward a Doctrine of Fair Use in Patent Law', *Columbia Law Review* 100, pp. 1177, 1178.

[74] See WTO Document WT/DS114/R, available online at www.wto.org. For

Interpreting the patent three-step test, the Panel refrained from developing a separate requirement of legal certainty altogether. The report clarifies that the word 'limited' has to be given a meaning separate from the limitation implicit in the word 'exception' itself. It has to be read 'to connote a narrow exception – one which makes only a small diminution of the rights in question.'[75] The reference point for determining limited exceptions is the curtailment of exclusive rights.[76] A specific requirement of legal certainty, however, is sought in vain in the Panel's discussion of the 'limited exceptions' test.[77]

Instead, the Panel focused on quantitative and qualitative factors to determine whether the Canadian exceptions at issue fulfilled the test. The stockpiling exception of Section 55.2(2) of Canada's Patent Act was held not to constitute a 'limited exception'. The provision allowed competitors to manufacture a stock of goods six months prior to the expiry of the patent, thereby encroaching upon the rights of 'making' and 'using' the patent.[78] In this respect, the Panel emphasized that the exception contained 'no limitations at all upon the quantity of production'.[79] In the case of the Bolar-type regulatory review exception of Section 55.2(1) of Canada's Patent Act, the Panel focused on qualitative considerations instead. The exception was countenanced on the grounds that it was confined to conduct needed to comply with the requirements of a regulatory approval process for pharmaceutical products, and would not allow commercial use.[80]

The 'limited exceptions' test, thus, requires a weighing process that includes quantitative and qualitative considerations. While the large volume of exempted production tipped the scales against the stockpiling exception, the confinement to use during the regulatory approval process saved the regulatory review exception. Compliance with this standard could be ensured by national courts on the basis of a national patent fair use system. Like the 'certain special cases' test in copyright law, the 'limited exceptions' test does not preclude fair use legislation. Article 17 TRIPS – the trademark provision corresponding to Article 30 TRIPS – even refers to 'limited exceptions to the rights conferred by a trademark, such as fair use of descriptive terms . . .'. Therefore, an obligation to set

---

comments on the report, see Kur, *supra* note 35; Senftleben, *supra* note 46; Ficsor, *supra* note 46.

75 See WTO Panel – Patents, ibid., para. 7.30.
76 See WTO Panel – Patents, ibid., para. 7.31.
77 See Senftleben, *supra* note 46, p. 419.
78 See Article 28(1) TRIPS and WTO Panel – Patents, fn. 1, para. 7.35.
79 See WTO Panel – Patents, ibid., para. 7.34.
80 See WTO Panel – Patents, ibid., para. 7.45.

forth precisely defined exceptions can hardly be derived from the word 'exceptions' or the expression 'limited exceptions'. The TRIPS Agreement itself clarifies that fair use-type limitations may pass the test.

The remaining criteria of the patent three-step test are more flexible than their copyright counterparts. Article 30 requires that exceptions 'do not unreasonably conflict with a normal exploitation'. The word 'unreasonably' suggests that a conflict with a normal exploitation may be deemed reasonable under certain circumstances. The copyright three-step test, by contrast, prohibits conflicts with a normal exploitation in general. The last criterion of Article 30 – no unreasonable prejudice to legitimate interests – contains a reference to third party interests that is missing in copyright law. This additional reference clarifies that prejudices to the legitimate interests of patent owners may be acceptable, if they can be justified in the light of legitimate third party interests.

In sum, the criteria of Article 30 thus offer more room for national fair use approaches than the copyright three-step test. As to the scope of patent fair use legislation, however, it is to be considered that the TRIPS Agreement distinguishes between exceptions to the rights of patent owners falling under the flexible conditions of Article 30, and 'other use [. . .] without the authorization of the right holder' that is regulated in much more detail in Article 31. This detailed regulation concerns the grant of compulsory licences at the national level, including licences for the exploitation of dependent second patents. Given the rigidity of the rules set forth in Article 31, it is to be conceded that, in the area of compulsory licensing, international patent law does not leave room for flexible fair use elements.

It is noteworthy, however, that the inflexibility of Article 31 led to an amendment to the TRIPS Agreement. The strict conditions established in the provision, such as the requirement of domestic market supply in subparagraph (f), may prevent countries with insufficient manufacturing capacities in the pharmaceutical sector from availing themselves of compulsory licences to ensure sufficient access to medicines. Recognizing this problem, paragraph 6 of the Doha Declaration on the TRIPS Agreement and Public Health adopted on 14 November 2001, provides for certain derogations from the obligations laid down in Article 31.[81] This so-called

---

[81] Cf. Law, A. *Patents and Public Health: Legalising the Policy Thoughts in the Doha TRIPS Declarations of 14 November 2001*, Baden-Baden: Nomos, 2009; Gumbel, M. (2008), 'Is Article 31bis Enough? The Need to Promote Economies of Scale in the International Compulsory Licensing System', *Temple International and Comparative Law Journal* 22–1, p. 161; Abbott, F.M. and Reichman, J.H. (2007), 'The Doha Round's Public Health Legacy: Strategies for the Production and Diffusion of Patented Medicines under the Amended TRIPs Provisions', *Journal*

'paragraph 6 system' shows that the issue of compulsory licensing and its international regulation in Article 31 is particularly delicate. It may be seen as an indication that the international patent framework itself could be improved by replacing the rigid Article 31 with a more flexible standard, including fair use elements.[82] This question, however, concerns the need for international patent fair use provisions rather than the permissibility of national fair use approaches under the current set of international rules.

6.2. Need for Fair Use

As discussed above, factors weighing in favour of a fair use approach are broad exclusive rights that need to be counterbalanced, and exposure to rapid technological developments. In patent law, there can be little doubt about a broad grant of protection. The international minimum standard set forth in Article 28 TRIPS encompasses the rights of 'making, using, offering for sale, selling, or importing for these purposes . . .'. In case of processes, the right relates to 'using the process' and products directly obtained through such use. In contrast to copyright law, however, patent protection depends on registration. In examination systems, the invention is scrutinized as to novelty and inventiveness during the registration procedure. The factor 'broad grant of protection', therefore, seems to weigh less clearly in favour of fair use than in the case of copyright law. While exclusive rights are broad, access to these rights depends on a detailed examination. It may be argued that the filtering of subject matter as a result of the registration procedure keeps patent protection within pre-defined limits. Precisely defined exceptions may be sufficient to ensure an appropriate counterbalance within the protection system.

The registration requirement, however, is of a procedural nature. As clarified in Article 27 TRIPS, 'patents shall be available for any inventions, whether products or processes, in all fields of technology . . .'. As long as the threshold requirements of novelty, inventiveness and industrial

of International Economic Law 10–4, p. 921; Abbott, F.M. (2005), *Compulsory Licensing for Public Health: A Guide and Model Documents for Implementation of Doha Declaration Paragraph 6 Decision*, Washington: World Bank Publications.

[82] Cf. Matthews, D. (2006), 'From the August 30, 2003 WTO Decision to the December 6, 2005, Agreement on an Amendment to TRIPS: Improving Access to Medicines in Developing Countries?', *Intellectual Property Quarterly*, p. 91; Haag, T.A. (2002), 'TRIPS since Doha: How Far Will the WTO Go Toward Modifying the Terms for Compulsory Licensing?', *Journal of the Patent and Trademark Office Society*, p. 945; Gamharter, K. (2004), *Access to Affordable Medicines: Developing Responses under the TRIPS Agreement and EC Law*, Berlin and Heidelberg: Springer.

applicability are fulfilled, a patent is to be issued. Registration does not serve as a means to confine the system to a pre-defined circle of technologies. An unforeseen need for reconsidering and recalibrating the system may thus arise, just as in copyright law, from new technological developments. In patent law, software and biotechnological inventions are examples of subject matter that have created a need to reconsider the balance between freedom of use and protection of the right owner. Moreover, a need to recalibrate the balance in patent law can follow from external influence factors. Patented technology may be central to the provision of important public goods. The debate on patents and public health is currently supplemented by a debate on patents and measures against global warming.[83] In sum, a broad grant of protection and exposure to new technologies justify consideration of a fair use approach in patent law.

6.3. Scope of Fair Use

The central objective of patent fair use could be the facilitation of experimental use and follow-on innovation. Experiences in the field of copyright law show that fair use can serve as an engine of the productive reuse of existing material. So-called 'transformative use' is an important factor capable of justifying a finding of fair use, for instance, in the US copyright system.[84] With regard to patents, it is noteworthy that the WTO Panel applying Article 30 TRIPS referred to the patent policy of facilitating the dissemination and advancement of technical knowledge in the context of the 'legitimate interests' test. The Panel explained that the requirement in patent law, that the nature of the invention be disclosed to the public, would partly be frustrated if the patent owner could prevent experimental use during the term of the patent. Both society and the scientist had a

---

[83] See Derclaye, E. (2009), 'Should Patent Law Help Cool the Planet? An Inquiry from the Point of View of Environmental Law – Parts I & II', *EIPR*, pp. 168, 227.

[84] This line between transformative use in the field of copyright law and a potential patent fair use defence is also drawn by Mueller, *supra* note 73, p. 976. In *Campbell v Acuff-Rose*, 510 US 569 (1994), II A, the US Supreme Court described the notion of transformative use as follows: 'The central purpose of this investigation is to see [. . .] whether the new work merely supersedes the objects of the original creation [. . .] or instead adds something new, with a further purpose or different character, altering the first with new expression, meaning, or message; it asks, in other words, whether and to what extent the new work is "transformative".' Leval, P.N. (1990), 'Toward a Fair Use Standard', *Harvard Law Review* 103, pp. 1105, 1111; Netanel, N.W., (1996), 'Copyright and a Democratic Civil Society', *Yale Law Journal* 106, pp. 283, 381.

'legitimate interest' in using the patent disclosure to support the advance of science and technology.[85] This line of argument supports a flexible framework for experimental use.[86]

More flexibility in the field of experimental use may be required indeed. With courts refusing to apply the experimental use defence to research aimed at regulatory approval for marketing purposes, legislative action exempting this type of use had to be taken in many countries.[87] In the US, however, the experimental use defence is applied even more restrictively. Following the traditional distinction between unjustified commercial and exempted non-commercial use, the Federal Circuit held in *Madey v Duke* that the use of Madey's patents by Duke University went beyond the scope of the experimental use defence because it furthered Duke's overall business objectives, including educating and enlightening students and faculty, and benefited Duke's reputation. The Court concluded that

> regardless of whether a particular institution or entity is engaged in an endeavor for commercial gain, so long as the act is in furtherance of the alleged infringer's legitimate business and is not solely for amusement, to satisfy idle curiosity, or

---

[85] See WTO Panel – Patents, *supra* note 74, para. 7.69.

[86] More breathing space in the area of experimental use is particularly proposed in restrictive national systems, such as the US patent system. Cf. Cooper Dreyfuss, R. (2004), 'Protecting the Public Domain of Science: Has the Time for an Experimental Use Defense Arrived?', *Arizona Law Review* 46, p. 457; Strandburg, K.J. (2004), 'What Does the Public Get? Experimental Use and the Patent Bargain', *Wisconsin Law Review* 81; Mohr, J. (2004), 'Unshackle Academia and Allow it to Exemplify the Purpose of Patent Law: To Promote the Progress of Science and the Useful Arts', *Marquette Law Review* 88, p. 671; Mueller, J.M. (2001), 'No "Dilettante Affair": Rethinking the Experimental Use Exception to Patent Infringement for Biomedical Research Tools', *Washington Law Review* 76. A fair use solution resting on open-ended criteria is espoused in this context by O'Rourke, *supra* note 73; Mueller, *supra* note 73. Doubt is cast upon the need for more flexibility by Devlin, A. (2009), 'Restricting Experimental Use', *Harvard Journal of Law & Public Policy* 32, p. 599.

[87] See US Court of Appeals for the Federal Circuit, 733 F.2d 858 (Fed. Cir. 1984), *Roche Products v Bolar Pharmaceutical*; Dutch Supreme Court (Hoge Raad), 18 December 1992, *GRUR Int.* 1993, p. 887, ICI/Medicopharma ('Atenolol'). Schutjens, M.H.D.B., 'Arzneimittelversuche und Patentrecht – Anmerkungen zum Urteil des Hoge Raad vom 18. Dezember 1992 – "Atenolol"', *GRUR Int.* 1993, p. 827. In both countries, a specific exception for the use of patented material to obtain marketing approval has been introduced in the meantime. See § 271(e) of the US Patent Act and Article 53(4) of the Dutch Patent Act. With regard to this statutory solution, see Strandburg, K.J. (2006), 'The Research Exemption to Patent Infringement: The Delicate Balance between Current and Future Technical Progress', in Yu, P.K. (ed.), *Intellectual Property and Information Wealth*, Westport: Praeger Publishers, pp. 107, 112–15.

> for strictly philosophical inquiry, the act does not qualify for the very narrow and strictly limited experimental use defense. Moreover, the profit or non-profit status of the user is not determinative.[88]

Given the broad notion of commercial use applied in this case, and the increasing number of collaborative research involving universities and private companies, this approach renders the experimental use defence meaningless.[89]

Inspiration for reinstating the defence in the framework of fair use legislation can be found in the decisions *Clinical Trials I and II* of the German Federal Court of Justice. Section 11 No. 2 of the German Patent Act exempts 'acts done for experimental purposes relating to the subject matter of the patented invention'.[90] The decision *Clinical Trials I* concerned the use of patented material for the identification of new medical indications. In this context, the Court clarified that all kinds of experimental use were exempted to the extent to which the use served the purpose of obtaining knowledge and, therefore, concerned scientific research on the subject matter of the patented invention, including its application. In particular, it was not decisive whether the experiments were undertaken merely to review the particulars of the patent specification. Use for the purpose of obtaining new research results would also fall under the exception irrespective of whether the user had further intentions, such as use of the results for commercial purposes.[91] In *Clinical Trials II*, the Court confirmed that the defence applied to all experimental acts that relate to the subject matter of the invention, regardless of whether the tests produced

---

[88] See US Court of Appeals for the Federal Circuit, 307 F.3d 1351 (Fed. Cir. 2002), *Madey v Duke University*.

[89] Cf. Pulsinelli, G. (2006), 'Share and Share Alike: Increasing Access to Government-Funded Inventions Under the Bayh-Dole Act', *Minnisota Journal of Law, Science and Technology* 7, p. 393; Owens, J.L. (2005), '"Not Quite Dead Yet": The Near Fatal Wounding of the Experimental Use Exception and its Impact on Public Universities', *Journal of Telecommunication and High Tech Law* 3, p. 453; Sewell, D.G. (2005), 'Rescuing Science from the Courts: An Appeal for Amending the Patent Code to Protect Academic Research in the Wake of Madey vs. Duke University', *Georgetown Law Journal* 93, p. 759; Garde, T.V. (2004), 'The Effect of Disparate Treatment of the Experimental Use Exemption on the Balancing Act of 35 U.S.C. § 104', *IIC* 35, p. 241.

[90] Like corresponding provisions in many other European countries, this article has been modelled on Article 27(b) of the Community Patent Convention. Cornish, W.R. (1998), 'Experimental Use of Patented Inventions in European Community States', *IIC* 29, pp. 735, 735–6.

[91] See Federal Court of Justice (Bundesgerichtshof), 11 July 1995, case X ZR 99/92, *GRUR* 1996, 109 (113).

purely scientific or industrially exploitable results. The defence could be invoked as long as the research did not specifically aim at impeding or frustrating the sale of the original product.[92]

The conceptual contours of a patent fair use defence could be drawn along the lines of these German decisions. Fair use could particularly aim at providing more flexibility in the area of follow-on innovation by exempting research that is carried out to understand and improve the invention, explore new fields of application or design around it. In these cases, it should be possible to invoke the defence even when the experiments, ultimately, aim at the commercial exploitation of research results.[93] In consequence, the defence could be applied more broadly and support the advance of science and technology more efficiently than the current restrictive approach. Patent fair use factors would permit the courts to weigh the detriment to the patentee against the benefits accruing from enhanced technical knowledge. The more substantial the technical advance to be expected from research, the more clearly the factors should weigh in favour of fair use.[94] To facilitate the task of establishing a proportionate relation between the detriment to the patentee and the benefits for the researcher and the public, the courts should be entitled to provide, where necessary, for the payment of equitable remuneration. In this way, an additional balancing tool is provided that allows the courts to reduce the harm to the patentee to reasonable limits in cases where extensive experimental use needs to be justified under the fair use system.[95]

With a fair use doctrine of this type, the patent system would have less difficulty coping with current challenges, for instance, in the field of computer software. The decision to protect computer programs as literary works under international copyright standards indicates that, in line with the

---

92 See Bundesgerichtshof, 17 April 1997, case X ZR 68/94, *Neue Juristische Wochenschrift* 1997, p. 3092.

93 Cf. O'Rourke, *supra* note 73, p. 1199; Van der Merwe, A. (2000), 'Experimental Use and Submission of Data for Regulatory Approval', *IIC* 31, pp. 380, 388; Hieber, T. (1996), 'Die Zulässigkeit von Versuchen an patentierten Erfindungen nach § 11 Nr. 2 PatG 1981', *GRUR*, pp. 439, 447.

94 O'Rourke, *supra* note 73, p. 1203. For proposals of patent fair use factors to be applied in this context, see O'Rourke, ibid., pp. 1230–35; Mueller, *supra* note 73, pp. 973–9.

95 The copyright three-step test is traditionally understood to recognize the possibility of providing for the payment of equitable remuneration to enhance flexibility in the outlined sense. In the context of the third test, an unreasonable prejudice to legitimate interests can be reduced to a permissible, reasonable level by securing the payment of equitable remuneration. See Senftleben, *supra* note 13, pp. 127–33.

idea/expression dichotomy in copyright law, concepts, methods and processes underlying a computer program should remain free. In addition, copyright law provides for exceptions to enable the decompilation of the program for the purpose of achieving interoperability.[96] As innovation in the software sector is known to occur in small incremental steps, it is advisable to preserve this breathing space for follow-on innovation when software is additionally patented. Otherwise, patent protection may become too heavy a burden, in particular, for small- and medium-sized enterprises not involved in the patenting of software and, therefore, unable to pool patent portfolios to obtain use permissions for patented algorithms and interfaces.[97]

A restrictive approach to experimental use does not permit the reverse engineering of patented software with the aim of using knowledge about the deciphered interface to develop a new product that can be marketed.[98] A patent fair use defence that can be invoked irrespective of commercial motivations, by contrast, would enable this experimental use in line with applicable copyright standards. As shown by the analysis conducted by O'Rourke, patent fair use could prevent software patents from unduly impeding competition. The use of interfaces for achieving interoperability would remain possible. In this context, the payment of equitable remuneration could play an important role:

> . . . patent fair use would give the infringer a threat to use in negotiations, increasing the chances that the parties will reach a socially beneficial licensing agreement. By placing the compensation rate, if any, at something less than market value, the patentee is less likely to view competition through reverse engineering as an empty threat. [. . .] Yet, if the patentee refuses to license, the fair use doctrine could act as a safety valve, excusing the infringement when it would be socially beneficial.[99]

---

[96] For example, see Article 6 of the EC Computer Programs Directive 2009/24 and § 1201(a)(1) and (2) of the US Digital Millenium Copyright Act.

[97] Cf. Leistner, M. (2008), 'Computerimplementierte Erfindungen im System des "Geistigen Eigentums"', in Depenheuer, O. and Peifer, K.N. (eds), *Geistiges Eigentum: Schutzrecht oder Ausbeutungstitel?*, Berlin and Heidelberg: Springer, p. 188; Ghidini, G. and Arezzo, E. (2005), 'Patent and Copyright Paradigms vis-à-vis Derivative Innovation: The Case of Computer Programs', *IIC* 36, p. 166; Hilty, R.M. and Geiger, C. (2005), 'Patenting Software? A Judicial and Socio-Economic Analysis', *IIC* 36, p. 615; Weyand, J. and Haase, H. (2005), 'Patenting Computer Programs: New Challenges', *IIC* 36, p. 647; Cohen, J.E. and Lemley, M.A. (2001), 'Patent Scope and Innovation in the Software Industry', *California Law Review* 89, pp. 41–2; Caron, C. (2000), 'Réflexions sur la coexistence du droit d'auteur et du droit des brevets sur un même logiciel', *RIDA* 184, p. 3.

[98] Cf. O'Rourke, *supra* note 73, p. 1194.

[99] See O'Rourke, *supra* note 73, p. 1235.

Patent fair use could also have beneficial effects in areas of technology where the high number of patents creates an 'anti-commons': rights are held by so many different owners that the costs of accumulating all required licences for an envisaged production become prohibitively high. This problem has been identified, for instance, in the field of biotechnology.[100] With a fair use system extending the scope of the experimental use defence to commercially motivated activities, research use could be exempted that is undertaken to find ways of inventing around the patent for the purpose of enabling production for which the necessary licence cannot be obtained. In situations where a developer has already amassed the majority of the required licences to market a product, this freedom may serve as a catalyst inducing the patentee of the remaining technology to enter into a licensing agreement.[101]

A patent fair use system could also broaden the experimental use defence with regard to use that does not concern research 'on' but 'with' the patented invention.[102] This broader notion of research use is beyond the scope of systems that, like legislation in most European countries, exempt experiments only insofar as the use aims at enhancing knowledge

---

100 See O'Rourke, *supra* note 73, p. 1236–37; Heller, M.A. and Eisenberg, R.S. (1998), 'Can Patents Deter Innovation? The Anticommons in Biomedical Research', *Science* 280, p. 698. However, see also Hamme Ramirez, H. (2004), 'Defending the Privatization of Research Tools: An Examination of the "Tragedy of the Anticommons" in Biotechnology Research and Development', *Emory Law Journal* 53, p. 359; Epstein, R.A. and Kuhlik, B. (2004), 'Is There a Biomedical Anticommons?', *Regulation* 27, p. 54, casting doubt upon the assumption of an anti-commons in the field of biotechnology.

101 Cf. O'Rourke, *supra* note 73, p. 1238, who envisages a system in which a court 'might allow the infringement to proceed and award a royalty while the infringement continues'. This proposal goes beyond the solution developed here which focuses on designing around the patented technology. It would have to be clarified whether this broader approach complies with the restrictive Article 31 TRIPS.

102 Cf. Hoffman, D.C. (2004), 'A Modest Proposal: Toward Improved Access to Biotechnology Research Tools by Implementing a Broad Experimental Use Exception', *Cornell Law Review* 89, p. 993; Derzko, N.M. (2004), 'In Search of a Compromised Solution to the Problem Arising from Patenting Biomedical Research Tools', *Santa Clara Computer & High Tech Law Journal* 20, p. 347; Hantman, R.D. (1986), 'Experimental Use as an Exception to Patent Infringement', *Journal of the Patent and Trademark Office Society* 67, p. 617. However, see also Pfaff, E. (2007), '"Bolar" Exemptions – A Threat to the Research Tool Industry in the U.S. and the EU?', *IIC* 38, p. 258; Holzapfel, H. (2006), 'Die patentrechtliche Zulässigkeit der Benutzung von Forschungswerkzeugen', *GRUR*, p. 10; Pedrazzini, M.M. (1996), 'Zur patentrechtlichen Problematik von Versuchen, die ein fremdes Patentrecht benützen', *GRUR Int.*, p. 373.

on the used patented invention itself. As indicated above, German legislation, for instance, only covers 'acts done for experimental purposes relating to the subject matter of the patented invention.' As a result, use that employs a patented technology to examine the properties of something else falls outside the scope of the exemption. In particular, the confinement to research on the patented technology constitutes an obstacle to the unauthorized use of research tools. This restriction may be unjustified in the case of tools developed by non-profit inventors who are not primarily motivated by the prospect of commercial sales.[103] An even broader approach has been developed by Strandburg. She proposes to extend the exemption for experimental use to all kinds of research tools, including those developed by commercial inventors. With regard to the effect of this blanket exemption on the disclosure of technology, Strandburg's analysis indicates that the benefits of earlier availability of research tool inventions to researchers are likely to outweigh the social costs of later tool disclosure.[104] Considering the impact on commercial suppliers, she argues that

> [r]esearchers will buy many tools from suppliers whether or not the tools are patented, simply as a matter of efficiently allocating limited researcher time and resources. Because tool suppliers will already rationally focus on developing research tools and tool improvements that researchers will buy rather than make, a research use exemption may have little impact, simply bolstering that preference.[105]

A fair use framework would avoid disproportionate harm in this context. Given the unclear impact of a general experimental use exemption on research tool disclosure and commercial supply, a nuanced fair use weighing process seems more appropriate than the blanket solution proposed by Strandburg. With factors weighing in favour of follow-on innovation, but against use free of charge in standard research procedures, a fair use system could support the use of research tools for the advancement of technical knowledge without encroaching upon the market for non-inventive standard applications, such as standard trials in the medical sector. Article 30 TRIPS prohibits 'unreasonable' conflicts with a normal exploitation. The interests of third parties, such as researchers and the public at large, are to be factored into the equation when assessing 'unreasonable' prejudices to the legitimate interests of patent owners. These tests

---

[103] Strandburg, K.J. (2008), 'Users as Innovators: Implications for Patent Doctrine', *University of Colorado Law Review* 79, pp. 467, 508–18.

[104] See Strandburg, ibid., pp. 530–31.

[105] See Strandburg, ibid., pp. 526–7.

of reasonableness could be translated into national fair use legislation to ensure that the exemption of research use, covering experiments 'on' as well as 'with' patented technology, keeps within justifiable, reasonable limits.[106]

As indicated above, international patent law itself may also be considered a field of application for patent fair use legislation. The 'paragraph 6 system' following from the Doha Declaration testifies to the enormous difficulty of readjusting the detailed requirements laid down in Article 31 TRIPS. Against this background, the time seems ripe to consider a deliberate opening of the current system by introducing more flexible requirements. Factors to be considered could be an urgent need to provide certain public goods, such as public health and measures against global warming.[107] It is to be considered also that Article 31(l) governs compulsory licences in the area of dependent second patents. More flexibility in this field would be consistent with the proposed fair use defence. Given the small, incremental steps of follow-on innovation in the software industry, for instance, it is doubtful whether the requirement of 'an important technical advance of considerable economic significance' is an appropriate threshold for the grant of compulsory licences.

6.4. Conclusion

As in copyright law, broad exclusive rights and challenges arising from new technologies justify flexible fair use legislation in the area of patents. As the patent disclosure rationale, ultimately, aims at the use of disclosed know-how for the further advancement of science and technology, it is consistent to adopt a fair use standard that offers an open, flexible framework for experimental use and follow-on innovation. The application of fair use factors in this area can be expected to inhibit patent protection

---

106 However, see also the more nuanced 'double-edged sword' approach developed by Strandburg, *supra* note 103, pp. 534–9, which would exempt non-commercial research use of all patented inventions and all research use of inventions made by non-profit inventors.

107 See the references *supra* notes 81–3. Cf. Pogge, T., Rimmer, M., and Rubenstein, K. (eds) (2010), *Incentives for Global Public Health: Patent Law and Access to Essential Medicines*, Cambridge: Cambridge University Press; Cottier, T., Pauwelyn, J., and Bürgi, E. (eds) (2005), *Human Rights and International Trade*, Oxford: Oxford University Press; Maskus, K.E. and Reichman, J.H. (2005), 'The Globalization of Private Knowledge Goods and the Privatization of Global Public Goods', in Maskus, K.E. and Reichman, J.H. (eds), *International Public Goods and Transfer of Technology under a Globalized Intellectual Property Regime*, Cambridge: Cambridge University Press.

from impeding innovation without becoming an obstacle to investment in research and development and the disclosure of technology. The system will have beneficial effects in areas where innovation occurs in small, incremental steps, as in the software industry. It will also help to alleviate the problem of the anti-commons that has been identified, for instance, in the field of biotechnology.

7. TRADEMARKS

Trademarked identifiers of commercial source are reserved for one individual market participant as long as this trader continues to use the sign. The focus of trademark fair use, therefore, is likely to differ from the concepts discussed so far. While copyright and patent fair use systems may primarily aim to support transformative use and follow-on innovation, trademark fair use can be expected to be concerned predominantly with alleviating the rigours of a stable system of potentially indefinite protection. It will aim to keep certain signs available for use by all traders or the public at large.[108] It may also aim to reconcile trademark protection with competing interests, such as freedom of speech, that are not represented adequately in the trademark system that focuses on the relation between traders.[109] Again, the question of fair use permissibility will be raised (7.1) before assessing the need for fair use (7.2), analysing existing fair use approaches (7.3) and making concluding remarks (7.4).

---

[108] Cf. Phillips, J. (2005), 'Trade Mark Law and the Need to Keep Free – Intellectual Property Monopolies Have their Limits', *IIC* 36, p. 389; Sambuc, T. (1997), 'Das Freihaltebedürfnis an beschreibenden Angaben und der Ware selbst nach dem Markengesetz', *GRUR*, p. 403. For a general analysis of the evolution of limitations in trademark law, see Dinwoodie, G.B. (2009), 'Lewis & Clark Law School Ninth Distinguished IP Lecture: Developing Defenses in Trademark Law', *Lewis and Clark Law Review* 13/1, p. 99.

[109] Cf. Sakulin, W. (2010), *Trademark Protection and Freedom of Expression – An Analysis into the Conflict between Trademark Rights and Freedom of Expression under European, German and Dutch Law*, The Hague, London and New York: Kluwer Law International; Geiger, C. (2004), 'Fundamental Rights, a Safeguard for the Coherence of Intellectual Property?', *IIC* 35, p. 268; Timbers, L., and Huston, J. (2003), 'The "Artistic Relevance Test" Just Became Relevant: the Increasing Strength of the First Amendment as a Defense to Trademark Infringement and Dilution', *Trade Mark Reporter* 93, p. 1278; R. Cooper Dreyfuss (2008), 'Reconciling Trademark Rights and Expressive Values: How to Stop Worrying and Learn to Love Ambiguity', in Dinwoodie, G.B. and Janis, Mark D. (eds), *Trademark Law and Theory: A Handbook of Contemporary Research*, Cheltenham, UK and Northampton, MA, USA: Edward Elgar, p. 261.

7.1. Permissibility

Article 17 TRIPS allows WTO Members to

> . . . provide limited exceptions to the rights conferred by a trademark, such as fair use of descriptive terms, provided that such exceptions take account of the legitimate interests of the owner of the trademark and of third parties.

This trademark test deviates significantly from the three-step tests in copyright and patent law. However, it does not preclude national fair use legislation. As discussed above, the requirement of 'limited exceptions' does not preclude open-ended fair use legislation. In 'EC – Protection of Trademarks and Geographical Indications for Agricultural Products and Foodstuffs', the WTO Panel dealing with Article 17 followed the approach taken previously in the patent case concerning Article 30 TRIPS. It measured the extent to which a curtailment of exclusive trademark rights resulted from national limitations. The Panel did not require exceptions to be defined precisely in this context.[110] The remaining 'legitimate interests' test of Article 17 is much more flexible than the corresponding tests in Articles 13 and 30 TRIPS. It does not refer to an unreasonable prejudice. The WTO Panel inferred from this omission 'a lesser standard of regard for the legitimate interests of the owner of the trademark'.[111] Most importantly, however, Article 17 itself gives the example of 'fair use of descriptive terms'. As the words 'such as' indicate, this example may be supplemented with other forms of fair use. The provision can hardly be understood to preclude the identification of further types of fair use at the national level on the basis of open-ended factors.

7.2. Need for Fair Use

During recent decades, the realm of trademark law has been extended continuously. Several new types of marks, such as colour per se, shape marks, sound marks and multimedia signs, have been recognized and accepted for registration.[112] In addition, the exclusive rights of the trademark owner

---

110 See WTO Document WT/DS174/R, paras. 7.650–7.651, based on a complaint by the US and the twin report WTO Document WT/DS290/R dealing with a complaint by Australia. As to the interpretation of Article 17 TRIPs, the reports are identical in substance. For comments on the report, see Senftleben, *supra* note 46.

111 See WTO Document WT/DS174/R, ibid., para. 7.671.

112 Cf. Lewalter, I. and Schrader, P.T. (2005), 'Die Fühlmarke', *GRUR*, p. 476; Hauck, F. (2005), 'Aktuelle Entwicklungen bei der Eintragung von Farbmarken',

have been broadened constantly. This expansion may be less prominent in cases of similarity between the signs and the products involved. The current scope of protection in the area of similarity covers direct product confusion as well as indirect confusion with regard to affiliation and sponsorship. Highly distinctive marks enjoy broader protection. The showing of a likelihood of confusion, however, still constitutes the central requirement to be fulfilled before protection can be obtained.[113]

In the area of sign and product identity, however, there is a trend towards absolute protection that no longer depends on a likelihood of confusion. In *L'Oréal/Bellure*, the ECJ attached particular importance to the formula of absolute protection laid down in recital 11 of the EC Trademark Directive.[114] According to the Court, absolute protection implies that, in cases of sign and product identity, a likelihood of confusion does not constitute 'the specific condition for such protection'.[115] This holding goes beyond Article 16(1) TRIPS, which provides only for a presumption of a likelihood of confusion in double identity cases. The ECJ abandons the confusion requirement altogether and, instead, requires that

---

GRUR, p. 363; Kur, A. (2004), 'Alles oder Nichts im Formmarkenschutz?', *GRUR Int.*, p. 755; Bouvel, A. (2004), 'Qu'importe le flacon . . . Le droit des marques malmené par les emballages', *Propriétés Intellectuelles*, p. 863; Arnet, R. (2004), 'Markenschutz für Formen', *sic!*, p. 829, available at http://www.sic-online.ch/; sic! – zeitschift für Immaterialgüter, Informations- und Wettbewerbsrecht; Pagenberg, J. (2004), 'Trade Dress and the Three-Dimensional Marks – The Neglected Children of Trademark Law?', *IIC* 35, p. 831; Bölling, M. (2004), 'Der EuGH und die abstrakte Farbmarke – Von der bewussten Entwertung einer Markenform', *Markenrecht*, p. 384; Bingener, S. (2004), 'Das Wesen der Positionsmarke oder Wo die Positionsmarke hingehört', *Markenrecht*, p. 377; A. Firth, A., Gredley, E., and Maniatis, S.M. (2001), 'Shapes as Trade Marks: Public Policy, Functional Considerations and Consumer Perception', *EIPR*, p. 86.

113 See ECJ, case C-251/95, [1997], *Puma v Sabel*. The confusion requirement in similarity cases has been confirmed in ECJ, case C-487/07, [2009], *L'Oréal v Bellure*, para. 59. Cf. Würtenberger, G. (2001), 'Risk of Confusion and Criteria to Determine the Same in European Community Trade Mark Law', *EIPR*, p. 20. For a comparison with the approach taken in the US, see McCarthy, J.T. (2004), 'Dilution of a Trademark: European and United States Law Compared', *The Trademark Reporter* 94, p. 1163.

114 See Directive 2008/95/EC. Recital 11 reads as follows: 'The protection afforded by the registered trade mark, the function of which is in particular to guarantee the trade mark as an indication of origin, should be absolute in the case of identity between the mark and the sign and the goods or services. The protection should apply also in the case of similarity between the mark and the sign and the goods or services. It is indispensable to give an interpretation of the concept of similarity in relation to the likelihood of confusion . . .'.

115 See ECJ, case C-487/07, [2009], *L'Oréal v Bellure*, para. 59.

a third party's use of a trademark affect or be liable to affect the functions of the trademark. These functions, however, are understood to

> . . . include not only the essential function of the trade mark, which is to guarantee to consumers the origin of the goods or services, but also its other functions, in particular that of guaranteeing the quality of the goods or services in question and those of communication, investment or advertising.[116]

With protection ranging from source identification to investment in brand image, this broad definition offers various possibilities of establishing a conflict.[117] The only remaining hurdle seems to be the fact that the ECJ, so far, insists on some detriment to the trademark. The mere taking of unfair advantage without any detriment to a trademark's functions is insufficient to satisfy the function test.[118] Nevertheless, the mere showing of identity between signs and products will be decisive in many cases. As a result, EC trademark rights in the area of double identity come very close to the exclusive rights granted in copyright and patent law, where mere use of protected subject matter may amount to infringement.

Even more remarkable steps to broaden trademark protection, however, have been taken in the area of protection against dilution. Trademark rights in this field are becoming instruments for the exploitation of brand image.[119] Protection may be invoked against use of competing signs for

---

116 See ECJ, ibid., para. 58.

117 Cf. Hacker, F. (2009), 'Funktionenlehre und Benutzungsbegriff nach "L'Oréal"', *Markenrecht*, p. 333; Völker, S. and Elskamp, G. (2010), 'Die neuen Markenfunktionen des EuGH', *Wettbewerb in Recht und Praxis*, p. 64; Fezer, K.-H. (2010), 'Markenschutzfähigkeit der Kommunikationszeichen (§§ 3 und 8 MarkenG) und Kommunikationsschutz der Marken (§§ 14 und 23 MarkenG)', *Wettbewerb in Recht und Praxis*, p. 165. With regard to the earlier focus of the ECJ on the 'essential' function of source identification, see Simon, I. (2005), 'How Does "Essential Function" Doctrine Drive European Trade Mark Law', *IIC* 36, p. 401.

118 See the analysis concerning the advertising function in ECJ, cases C-236/08 to C-238/08, [2010], *Google v Louis Vuitton*, para. 92: '. . . in the case where that use adversely affects the proprietor's use of its mark as a factor in sales promotion or as an instrument of commercial strategy'. Other language versions, such as the Dutch ('afbreuk doen'), French ('porter atteinte') and German ('beeinträchtigen') versions, are clearer on that point. Cf. Ohly, A. (2009), comment on BGH, 22 January 2009, case I ZR 125/07, 'Bananabay', *Juristenzeitung*, pp. 856, 859.

119 See Senftleben, M.R.F. (2009), 'The Trademark Tower of Babel – Dilution Concepts in International, US and EC Law', *IIC* 40, p. 45; Bently, L., Davis, G., and Ginsburg, J. (eds) (2008), *Trade Marks and Brands – An Interdisciplinary Critique*, Cambridge: Cambridge University Press; Moskin, J. (2004), 'Victoria's Big Secret: Whither Dilution under the Federal Dilution Act?', *The Trademark*

similar and dissimilar products alike. To enter this area of protection, it is sufficient to show a mere risk of association – the establishment of a link between the mark and the competing sign in the minds of consumers.[120] In dilution cases, even decorative use of a sign that triggers associations with a protected mark may be qualified as relevant trademark use falling under the exclusive rights of the trademark owner.[121] In certain trademark systems, such as the EC system and those of its Member States, the threshold for eligibility for anti-dilution protection, moreover, is remarkably low. The ECJ accepts niche reputation. It is sufficient that a significant part of the target consumer group in a substantial part of an EC Member State knows the mark.[122] This low standard is in line with the approach taken at the international level in the WIPO Joint Recommendation Concerning the Protection of Well-Known Marks.[123]

Besides the broadening of trademark protection, exposure to technological developments justifies the consideration of a fair use approach in the field of trademark law. The trademark system is increasingly challenged by developments in the digital environment.[124] Difficult questions have

---

Reporter 93, p. 842; Fezer, K.-H. (2003), 'Entwicklungslinien und Prinzipien des Markenrechts in Europa – Auf dem Weg zur Marke als einem immaterialgüterrechtlichen Kommunikationszeichen', *GRUR*, p. 457; Pollaud-Dulian, F. (2001), 'Marques de renommée – Histoire de la dénaturation d'un concept', *Propriétés intellectuelles*, p. 43; Strasser, M. (2000), 'The Rational Basis of Trademark Protection Revisited: Putting the Dilution Doctrine into Context', *Fordham Intellectual Property, Media & Entertainment Law Journal* 10, p. 375; Brown, R.S. (1999), 'Advertising and the Public Interest: Legal Protection of Trade Symbols', *Yale Law Journal* 108, p. 1619. The broad approach to trademark functions in *L'Oréal v Bellure* seems to confirm this trend. With the inclusion of 'communication, investment or advertising', the ECJ recognizes that trademarks do not simply serve the objective to identify a given commercial source. They have become central instruments for the communication with consumers.

[120] See ECJ, case C-408/01, [2003], *Adidas v Fitnessworld Trading*.

[121] See Kur, A. (2008), 'Confusion Over Use? – Die Benutzung "als Marke" im Lichte der EuGH-Rechtsprechung', *GRUR Int.*, p. 1.

[122] See ECJ, case C-375/97, [1999], *General Motors v Yplon* ('Chevy'); ECJ, case C-301/07, [2009], *Pago v Tirolmilch*. Cf. Senftleben, *supra* note 119, pp. 54, 74–5.

[123] See WIPO Joint Recommendation Concerning Provisions on the Protection of Well-Known Marks, WIPO: Geneva 2000, available online at www.wipo.int/about-ip/en/development_iplaw/. Cf. Senftleben, *supra* note 119, pp. 51–3; Kur, A. (1999), 'Die WIPO-Vorschläge zum Schutz notorisch bekannter und berühmter Marken', *GRUR*, p. 866.

[124] See WIPO Joint Recommendation Concerning Provisions on the Protection of Marks, and Other Industrial Property Rights in Signs, on the Internet, WIPO: Geneva 2001, available online at www.wipo.int/about-ip/en/development_iplaw/.

already arisen, for instance, with regard to the use of trademarks for the purpose of keyword advertising.[125]

7.3. Existing Approaches

Law makers in several jurisdictions have been alert to the need for flexible limitations in the area of trademark protection against dilution. After the US Supreme Court had required 'a showing of actual dilution, rather than a likelihood of dilution' in *Moseley v V Secret Catalogue*,[126] the 2006 Trademark Dilution Revision Act amended the anti-dilution provisions in the US Lanham Act.[127] The adoption of new anti-dilution legislation was accompanied by the introduction of a statutory, open-ended fair use

---

Cf. Seichter, D. (2006), 'Markenrecht und Internet', *Markenrecht*, p. 375; Wichard, C. (2005), 'The Joint Recommendation Concerning Protection of Marks, and Other Industrial Property Rights in Signs, on the Internet', in Drexl, J., and Kur, A. (eds), *Intellectual Property and Private International Law,* IIC Studies 24, Oxford: Hart Publishing, p. 257; Kur, A. (2001), 'Die WIPO-Empfehlungen zur Benutzung von Marken im Internet', *GRUR Int.*, p. 961.

[125] See ECJ, cases C-236/08 to C-238/08, [2010], *Google v Louis Vuitton*. Cf. Ohly, A. (2009), 'Keyword-Advertising auf dem Weg von Karlsruhe nach Luxemburg', *GRUR*, p. 709; Knaak, R. (2009), 'Keyword Advertising – Das aktuelle Key-Thema des Europäischen Markenrechts', *GRUR Int.*, p. 551; Well-Szönyi, C. (2009), 'Adwords: Die Kontroverse um die Zulässigkeit der Verwendung fremder Marken als Schlüsselwort in der französischen Rechtsprechung', *GRUR Int.*, p. 557; Engels, G. (2009), 'Keyword Advertising – Zwischen beschreibender, unsichtbarer und missbräuchlicher Verwendung', *Markenrecht*, p. 289; Schubert, M. and Ott, S. (2009) 'AdWords – Schutz für die Werbefunktion einer Marke?', *Markenrecht*, p. 338; Sosnitza, O. (2009), 'Adwords = Metatags? Zur marken- und wettbewerbsrechtlichen Zulässigkeit des Keyword Advertising über Suchmaschinen', *Markenrecht*, p. 35; Gielen, Ch. (2008), 'Van adwords en metatags', in van Eijk N.A.N.M. et al. (eds), *Dommering-bundel*, Amsterdam: Cramwinckel, p. 101; van Daalen, O. and Groen, A. (2006), 'Beïnvloeding van zoekresultaten en gesponsorde koppelingen: De juridische kwalificatie van onzichtbaar merkgebruik', *BMM Bulletin*, p. 106.

[126] See Supreme Court of the United States of America, 4 March 2003, *Moseley v V Secret Catalogue, Inc.*, 537 US 418 (2003). Cf. Moskin, *supra* note 119, pp. 842–59.

[127] See Trademark Dilution Revision Act of 2006 (H.R. 683) amending the US Trademark Act of 1946 (15 USC 1125). With regard to the required proof of dilution, this new legislation clarifies that protection against dilution is to be granted 'regardless of the presence or absence of actual or likely confusion, of competition, or of actual economic injury'. Cf. Beebe, B. (2006), 'A Defense of the New Federal Trademark Antidilution Law', *Fordham Intellectual Property, Media & Entertainment Law Journal* 16, p. 1143.

provision focusing on breathing space for comparative advertising and freedom of speech without excluding other forms of fair use.[128]

EC legislation concerning dilution achieves similar results by providing for a defence of 'due cause'. Article 5(2) of the EC Trademark Directive 2008/95 offers EC Member States the freedom to provide for anti-dilution protection

> . . . where use of [a sign similar to a trademark having a reputation] without due cause takes unfair advantage of, or is detrimental to, the distinctive character or the repute of the trade mark.

This provision made its way into the national trademark legislation of all Member States. As a result, the flexible 'due cause' defence can be used by national courts to counterbalance the broad grant of protection. The 'Lila Postkarte' case of the German Federal Court of Justice, for instance, concerned the marketing of postcards that alluded ironically to trademarks and advertising campaigns of the chocolate producer Milka. On a purple background corresponding to Milka's abstract colour mark, the postcard sought to ridicule the nature idyll with cows and mountains that is evoked in Milka advertising. It showed the following poem attributed to 'Rainer Maria Milka':

---

128 Section 43(c)(3) of the US Lanham Act, as amended, reads as follows:

> (3) EXCLUSIONS – The following shall not be actionable as dilution by blurring or dilution by tarnishment under this subsection:
> (A) Any fair use, including a nominative or descriptive fair use, or facilitation of such fair use, of a famous mark by another person other than as a designation of source for the person's own goods or services, including use in connection with –
> (i) advertising or promotion that permits consumers to compare goods or services; or
> (ii) identifying and parodying, criticizing, or commenting upon the famous mark owner or the goods or services of the famous mark owner.
> (B) All forms of news reporting and news commentary.
> (C) Any noncommercial use of a mark.

For a description of the situation under the former US Federal Trademark Dilution Act, see Cantwell, M.K. (2004), 'Confusion, Dilution and Speech: First Amendment Limitations on the Trademark Estate: An Update', *The Trademark Reporter* 94, p. 549. With regard to common law fair use defences in the US, see Moskin, J. (2005), 'Frankenlaw: The Supreme Court's Fair and Balanced Look at Fair Use', *Trademark Reporter* 95, p. 848.

Über allen Wipfeln ist Ruh,
irgendwo blökt eine Kuh.
Muh![129]

In assessing this ironic play with Milka insignia, the Court first confirmed the broad scope of protection. It held that for the use of Milka trademarks to constitute trademark use in the sense of Article 5(2) of the Trademark Directive, it was sufficient that the postcard called to mind the well-known Milka signs.[130] Even though decorative, the use in question, thus, gave rise to the question of trademark infringement. Accordingly, the Court embarked on a scrutiny in the light of the infringement criteria of detriment to distinctive character or repute, and the taking of unfair advantage. At this stage, however, Milka could not succeed. In line with the EC Directive, the German Trademark Act offers the defence of 'due cause'. Weighing Milka's concerns about a disparagement of the trademarks against the fundamental guarantee of the freedom of art, the Court concluded that the freedom of art had to prevail in light of the ironic statement made by the postcard.[131] The use of Milka trademarks was found to have taken place with due cause.

These examples show that measures are taken in US and EC trademark legislation to counterbalance broad protection in the field of trademark dilution by adopting flexible fair use defences. However, comparable steps have not been taken to limit trademark protection in cases of sign and product identity. As explained above, recent developments in the EC have led to absolute protection in double identity cases irrespective of whether a likelihood of confusion can be presumed. The EC provision governing this area is Article 5(1)(a) of the Trademark Directive. It vests the trademark owner with the right to prevent third parties from using in trade

> . . . any sign which is identical with the trade mark in relation to goods or services which are identical with those for which the trade mark is registered.

---

[129] 'It is calm above the tree tops, somewhere a cow is bellowing. Moo!' See Federal Court of Justice (Bundesgerichtshof), 3 February 2005, case I ZR 159/02, *GRUR* 2005, p. 583, 'Lila Postkarte'. Cf. Born, C. (2006), 'Zur Zulässigkeit einer humorvollen Markenparodie – Anmerkungen zum Urteil des BGH "Lila Postkarte"', *GRUR*, p. 192.

[130] See Bundesgerichtshof, ibid., p. 584.

[131] See Bundesgerichtshof, ibid., pp. 584–5. For a further case in which freedom of speech prevailed over trademark protection, see German Federal Court of Justice, 11 March 2008, case VI ZR 7/07, *Neue Juristische Wochenschrift* 2008, p. 2110, 'Gen-Milch'. Cf. Sakulin, *supra* note 109; Geiger, *supra* note 109.

In this provision, it is not only the requirement of (presumed) confusion that is sought in vain. Article 5(1)(a) also fails to provide for the 'due cause' defence that applies in the area of EC protection against dilution. This lack of balancing tools may become problematic soon. In the case of a trademark parody falling under Article 5(1)(a), such as T-shirts or cartoons parodying the trademarked Mickey Mouse drawing,[132] it is unclear how the ECJ would provide sufficient breathing space for freedom of speech. In principle, the approach taken by the ECJ leaves room for a finding that the use in question is not actionable under Article 5(1)(a) because it does not affect any of the protected functions of a trademark. The room to manoeuvre created in this way, however, must not be overestimated. As pointed out above, the circle of relevant functions has been drawn broadly in *L'Oréal/Bellure*. It includes communication, investment and advertising. A biting parody, however, will inevitably impact on the way in which consumers perceive the target trademark. It may have a corrosive effect on a favourable trademark image that is the result of substantial investment in advertising and product control.[133]

The dilemma described has already arisen with regard to commercial speech. Harm to the investment and advertising function of a trademark can flow from comparative advertising that sheds new light on a trademark by informing consumers about better offers in the marketplace. The current, inflexible framework established by Article 5(1)(a) does not offer breathing space in this case. As the product comparison may interfere with the trademark communication initiated by the owner, affect prior investment in a favourable trademark image and reduce the trademark's advertising power, the verdict of infringement seems inevitable under Article 5(1)(a), even if the requirement of detriment to trademark functions is applied strictly.[134] In *L'Oréal/Bellure*, the ECJ nonetheless managed to escape the inflexible rules on sign and product identity by invoking the

---

132 See the international Madrid registration no. 296478 relating, among various other products, to printed matter (class 16) and clothing (class 25). The particulars of the registration can be consulted online at http://www.wipo.int/ipdl/en/madrid/search-struct.jsp.

133 In the copyright fair use case *Campbell v Acuff Rose*, the US Supreme Court solved this problem by stating that 'when a lethal parody, like a scathing theater review, kills demand for the original, it does not produce a harm cognizable under the Copyright Act'. See *Campbell v Acuff-Rose*, 510 US 569 (1994), II D. A similar ECJ finding of fair use would be necessary to safeguard parody under Article 5(1)(a) of the EC Trademark Directive.

134 The mere presumption of confusion in double identity cases would offer more flexibility. In cases of comparative advertising meeting the requirements stated in the EC Misleading and Comparative Advertisement Directive 2006/114/

EC Comparative Advertisement Directive.[135] Using the criteria for permissible comparative advertising as an external balancing tool, the Court arrived at the conclusion that a case of infringement would only arise where a trademark was used for the purpose of comparative advertising without all the requirements stated in the Comparative Advertisement Directive being satisfied.[136]

To add flexibility to the EC trademark system in double identity cases, the ECJ, thus, had to resort to the rules on comparative advertising. Against this background, the function analysis developed by the Court under Article 5(1)(a) of the Trademark Directive can hardly be deemed a sufficient safeguard of artistic and commercial freedom of speech.[137] Instead, EC trademark law seems incapable of providing the necessary room for manoeuvre. The constant broadening of protection has created a need for fair use provisions capable of counterbalancing EC trademark protection in the area of sign and product identity. The 'due cause' defence applied in dilution cases could serve as a model for satisfying this need.

7.4. Conclusion

International trademark law does not prevent national law makers from introducing fair use limitations. The international framework of protection is even more flexible than in the field of copyright and patents. Given the constant broadening of trademark protection during recent decades, and the increasing impact of Internet technology, it is advisable to use this flexibility at the national level. In this context, examples of current EC and US legislation show that fair use elements have already been introduced to counterbalance protection against dilution. In the area of sign and product identity, however, recent extensions of protection in the EC necessitate the adoption of similar fair use solutions.

EC of 12 December 2006, it could be concluded that the presumption has been rebutted.

135 The Court dealt with the Misleading Advertisement Directive 84/450 of 10 September 1984, as amended by the Comparative Advertisement Directive 97/55 of 6 October 1997. These two Directives are now consolidated in the Misleading and Comparative Advertisement Directive 2006/114/EC of 12 December 2006.

136 See ECJ, case C-487/07, [2009], *L'Oréal v Bellure*, paras. 54, 65.

137 It is doubtful whether the breathing space created in this way is sufficient to satisfy freedom of speech concerns. See Ohly, *supra* note 125, pp. 711–12; Kur, A., Bently, L., and Ohly, A., 'Sweet Smells and a Sour Taste – the ECJ's L'Oréal Decision', *Max Planck Institute for Intellectual Property, Competition and Tax Law Research Paper Series* No. 09-12, available online at http://ssrn.com/abstract=1492032.

8. CONCLUSION

Fair use has become a horizontal issue in intellectual property law. As the analysis has shown, there are important reasons for the adoption of flexible fair use defences in copyright, patent and trademark law. The constant expansion of protection in these systems, and constant exposure to technological challenges, necessitate the introduction of flexible counterbalances that safeguard user freedoms. In copyright law, an open-ended fair use defence offers the breathing space necessary for satisfying social, cultural and economic needs, particularly in the digital environment. Transformative user-generated content can be encouraged. New Internet industries are given room to flourish. In patent law, fair use provisions can be employed to enhance flexibility in the area of experimental use. Follow-on innovation in the fields of software and biotechnology can be fostered in this way. The use of research tools can be facilitated. In trademark law, fair use is required to counterbalance brand image protection against dilution, and the grant of absolute protection in cases of sign and product identity. A fair use defence would offer sufficient flexibility for freedom of speech, including commercial speech in cases of comparative advertising.

The continuous expansion of IP protection in recent decades, however, does not only create a need for fair use within individual IP domains. In addition, it is to be considered that the expansion of protection has broadened overlaps between the different branches of IP.[138] Software patents create an overlap with copyright protection of computer programs. The recognition of new types of marks, such as shape and sound marks, broadens the overlap between copyright and trademark protection.

Hence, there is not only a need for fair use counterbalances within individual IP protection regimes but also a growing need for flexible balancing tools that can be applied across these individual regimes. A network of corresponding fair use limitations in different IP domains can serve as a means to safeguard the inner consistency of the IP system when it comes to protection overlaps. On the basis of horizontal, open-ended fair use legislation, a form of unauthorized use that is permitted in one protection regime can be safeguarded in other, overlapping systems as

---

[138] For a description of this trend and an overview of current problems, see Derclaye and Leistner, *supra* note 8; Cruquenaire and Dussollier, *supra* note 8; Kur, A. (2001), 'Funktionswandel von Schutzrechten: Ursachen und Konsequenzen der inhaltlichen Annäherung und Überlappung von Schutzrechtstypen', in Schricker, G., Dreier, T., and Kur, A. (eds), *Geistiges Eigentum im Dienst der Innovation*, Baden-Baden: Nomos, p. 23; Hugenholtz, P.B. (2000), 'Over cumulatie gesproken', *Bijbald bij de intellectuele eigendom*, p. 240.

well. For instance, trademark fair use provisions, such as the EC defence of 'due cause', can ensure that a Mickey Mouse parody complying with copyright standards can also be declared permissible in the overlapping field of trademark protection. A patent fair use defence that supports follow-on innovation can help to ensure that copyright limitations allowing the decompilation of computer programs to achieve interoperability are not eroded when the program concerned also enjoys patent protection. The growth of protection overlaps is thus an additional argument for the introduction of fair use defences, and an additional confirmation that fair use has become a horizontal issue in IP law.

To safeguard the inner consistency of the IP system, fair use defences in different protection regimes must correspond to each other. They should function as a network allowing consistent decisions on forms of unauthorized use that are exempted in one protection system when it comes to overlaps with other systems. Common ground for such a fair use network became visible during the present analysis: all fair use defences in IP law should serve the overarching objective of fostering the use of pre-existing intellectual resources for the purpose of creating new material. This objective is central to cyclic innovation systems, such as copyright and patent law. Not surprisingly, the discussion on more flexible limitations in these systems focuses on transformative use and experimental use. Market transparency systems, such as trademark law, do not seek to encourage the reuse of existing material. Nonetheless, the transformative/experimental use rationale is equally applicable. Fair use ensures that the stable distribution of intellectual resources in these systems, like the indefinite protection of a trademark for one individual trader, does not frustrate cyclic innovation that is central to other systems. In case of a short melody enjoying cumulative copyright and trademark protection, a trademark fair use defence could be applied, for instance, to exempt use of the melody for cultural purposes after the expiry of copyright protection.[139]

---

[139] With regard to the problems raised by cumulative copyright and trademark protection, see Senftleben, M.R.F. (2010) 'Der kulturelle Imperativ des Urheberrechts', in Weller, M., Kemle, N.B., and Dreier, T. (eds), *Kunst im Markt – Kunst im Recht*, Baden-Baden: Nomos; Ohly, A. (2007) 'Areas of Overlap between Trade Mark Rights, Copyright and Design Rights in German Law', *GRUR Int.*, p. 704; Senftleben, M.R.F. (2007) 'De samenloop van auteurs – en merkenrecht – een internationaal perspectief', *AMI*, p. 67; Verkade, D.W.F. (1998) 'The Cumulative Effect of Copyright Law and Trademark Law: Which Takes Precedence?', in Kabel, J.J.C. and Mom, G.J.H.M. (eds), *Intellectual Property and Information Law – Essays in Honour of Herman Cohen Jehoram*, Den Haag, London and Boston: Kluwer, p. 69.

9. Intellectual property and technology – looking for the twelfth camel?

Maciej Barczewski* and Jerzy Zajadło**

1. INTRODUCTION

A well-known contemporary German law theoretician Günther Teubner very often invokes the following anecdote in his work:

> An old wealthy bedouin sheikh wrote his will and divided his fortune, a large herd of camels, among his three sons. Achmed, the eldest son, was to inherit the first half of the fortune, Ali, the second son, should get a fourth, Benjamin, the youngest son, a sixth. When the father died, unfortunately only eleven camels were remaining. Achmed, of course, demanded six of them and was at once contested by his brothers. Finally, when everything broke down, they turned to the khadi. He decided: 'I offer you one of my camels. Return it to me, Allah willing, as soon as possible'. Now, with 12 camels, the division was easy. Achmed got his half, 6 camels, Ali got a fourth, 3 camels, Benjamin a sixth, 2 camels. And indeed, the twelfth camel was left over which they kept and fed very well and happily returned to the khadi.[1]

In Teubner's concept, the anecdote is an element of a certain vision of law as an autopoietic system. For law and lawyers, however, other morals may also be drawn from this tale. One of these may be as follows: the work of every lawyer, both theoretician and practitioner, as a matter of fact consists in searching for the twelfth camel. The law in the meaning of the established law (*lex*) very often is not perfect and we face the need to finding a certain 'surplus' (*ius*) enabling us to take a rational and right decision. At times, when a problem and a legal norm applied to solving it are unambiguous and the actual state does not raise doubts, the process

* Head of Postgraduate Studies in Intellectual Property and High Technology Law, Faculty of Law and Administration at the University of Gdansk.

** Head of the Chair of Theory and Philosophy of State and Law, Faculty of Law and Administration at the University of Gdansk.

[1] Teubner, G. (2004), 'Alienating Justice: On the Surplus Value of the Twelfth Camel', *Ius et Lex*, 1, p. 109 f.

of searching for the twelfth camel is comparatively simple. In practice, especially in cases when law meets other normative systems (e.g. ethics, economy, politics), we may encounter a hard case. The clash between *lex* and *ius* may happen not only in the process of applying law and its interpretation, but also with reference to its formation, binding and observing. The 'khadi' who lends us the twelfth camel (*ius*) in order to solve a legal equation (*lex*) which then will have to be returned is simply the widely understood idea of law expressed as a harmony of its three elements: security, usefulness and justice. The author of this three-element concept of law, German law philosopher Gustav Radbruch, however, indicated possible conflicts between these values. In principle, he resolved them in favour of safety and in extreme cases – in favour of justice.[2] Hard cases show that there is an immanent connection between *ius* and *lex* – *ius* without *lex* seems to be helpless; *lex* without *ius* in turn is often heartless. So what is in fact the relation between law and the humanities as widely understood?[3] What actually is law: is it a part of humanistic culture or just a tool of social engineering?[4] Are the problems underlying hard cases just a taboo which may be broken or an archetype which we do not want to challenge? And, finally, do hard cases in fact make bad law or may the opposite be true – hard cases make good lawyers? The opinion of a well-known Australian judge Michael Kirby that 'judging means learning' may be hard to undermine and consequently formalism and a purely mechanical approach to performing the function of judge makes real fulfilment of the judicial role impossible.[5] In this context, however, the words of Aaron Barak, the President of the High Court of Israel, are noteworthy. He claims that although not much can be achieved with good philosophy alone, without it nothing can be achieved.[6]

According to Radbruch, the conflict between *ius* and *lex* was mainly of a moral character and therefore was connected with justice. From the point of view of the subject of this chapter, namely, the technical protection of intellectual property, another interpretation of Teubner's tale is possible.

---

2 Alexy, R. (2002), *The Argument from Injustice: A Reply to Legal Positivism*, Oxford: Oxford University Press.

3 Balkin, J.M. and Levinson S. (2006), 'Law and Humanities: An Uneasy Relationship', *Yale Journal of Law & Humanities*, 18, pp. 155–87.

4 Howarth, D. (2004), 'Is Law a Humanity (or is it more like Engineering)?', *Arts & Humanities in Higher Education,* 3 (1), pp. 9–28.

5 Kirby, M. (2007), 'To Judge is to Learn', *Harvard International Law Journal*, 48, p. 36.

6 Barak, A. (2006), *The Judge in a Democracy*, Princeton and Oxford: Oxford University Press, p. 116.

Law should be not only secure and just but also intentional, ergo – effective. If the discussion is transferred to economic analysis of the law, it turns out that the value of effectiveness may, in certain spheres, be the most significant.[7] In our opinion, the area of protection of intellectual property is in fact such a sphere. Granting authors their rights (*lex*) is not enough, the system must be complemented with a certain surplus of the twelfth camel (*ius*). Paradoxically *ius*, semantically associated with justice (*iustitia*), in this case may be connected with effectiveness (*efficientia*). In intellectual property law, the role of the twelfth camel as the complement of the system is played by technological measures. The relationship between *ius* and *lex* is treated here *à rebours*. Copyright (*lex*) without technical measures of protection (*ius*) is frequently of no help; and vice versa – technical measures of protection (*ius*) deprived of legal protection may appear pointless. Contrary to appearances, intellectual property law is not free of philosophical-legal dilemmas, on the contrary – the above-mentioned antinomies between security, usefulness and justice acquire in this sphere new, previously not unknown dimensions.[8] In recent years, the use of technical measures in order to enhance the effectiveness of protection for artistic work and plant breeding has been its most illustrative example.

2. DIGITAL RIGHTS MANAGEMENT (DRM)

With the evolution of technology, the simplicity of copying digital works exposed their authors to infringement of different types of vested rights in their content. As a remedy enabling secure distribution of the data in the digital environment, certain technological solutions were proposed that would protect files by encryption so that they could be accessed only after the entity desiring access had had its identity authenticated and its rights to that specific type of access verified.[9] These solutions – generally referred to as Digital Rights Management ('DRM') systems – evolved from technological protection measures impeding unauthorized access or copying to sophisticated systems that would allow not only the distributing of content

---

7 Mathis, K. (2009), *Effizienz statt Gerechtigkeit? Auf der Suche nach den philosophischen Grundlagen der Ökonomischen Analyse des Rechts,* Berlin: Duncker & Humblot Verlag.

8 Gosseries, A., Marciano, A., and Strowel, A. (eds) (2008), *Intellectual Property and Theories of Justice*, New York: Palgrave-Macmillan.

9 Rosenblatt, B. and Dykstra, G., 'Integrating Content Management with Digital Rights Management: Imperatives and Opportunities for Digital Content Lifecycles', www.giantstepsmts.com.

in a controlled way, but also the definition and management of the particular actions an authorized recipient might take in regard to that content.[10]

Assuming that copyright statutes and related case law constitute the fundamental layer of protection, it can also be assumed that technical protection measures, along with rights management information, represent the second, technological layer of protection of copyright holders.[11] But although DRM systems are meant to provide a high level of technological security, they have been and will be hacked into. As a consequence, it was necessary to create a third layer of protection – so-called anti-circumvention laws. For that reason, in the early 1990s, both in the United States of America and in the European Union right holders began to look at laws that would safeguard technical measures of protection for their works.[12] These activities resulted in numerous regulations passed at universal,[13] regional[14] and national[15] levels which forbid circumventing and deleting technical measures of protection of work and accompanying data concerning management of copyright.

Application of DRM technology has been the subject of much controversy resulting from the different nature of protection granted by traditional norms of copyright law and by technological protection measures. First, it concerns different subject and time of protection – copyright law defines what content it protects, whereas technical measures may protect any content which is made available digitally, regardless of its copyright protection status. Moreover, there is a time limit for copyright, whereas when using technological measures protected by anti-circumvention laws the content may be locked up for a theoretically unlimited amount of time. Secondly, it is pointed out that although, according to exhaustion doctrine,

---

[10] Barczewski, M. (2005), 'International Framework for Legal Protection Digital Rights Management Systems', *EIPR*, 5, p. 165.

[11] See de Werra, J. (2001), 'The Legal System of Technological Protection Measures under the WIPO Treaties, the Digital Millennium Copyright Act, the European Union Directives and other National Legislations (Australia, Japan)', *RIDA*, 189, pp. 66–213.

[12] Barczewski, M. (2008), 'The Twilight of Digital Rights Management? – Towards a New Model of Content Distribution Control', in M. Barczewski, M. Miłosz, and R. Warner (eds), *When Worlds Collide: Intellectual Property, High Technology and the Law*, Warsaw: Oficyna, 26.

[13] E.g. WIPO Copyright Treaty ('WCT'), WIPO Performances and Phonograms Treaty ('WPPT'), Convention on Cybercrime of 2001.

[14] E.g. The EU Directive 2001/29/EC on the harmonisation of certain aspects of copyright and related rights in the information society, as well as numerous Free Trade Agreements concluded by the United States.

[15] E.g. The Digital Millennium Copyright Act of 1998 in the United States.

a right holder can no longer control distribution if a copy of the work has been lawfully put into circulation in a given territory, DRM systems don't allow the reselling of the acquired content, thereby providing right holders with the means to control commercial and non-commercial transactions of the acquired product, even if copyright law dictates otherwise.[16] A further significant drawback for Digital Rights Management is the lack of interoperability, understood as the ability to access content via different delivery platforms. Common interoperability is not available since most DRM implementations are based on 'island solutions' from a particular vendor, rather than widely adopted standards[17] – there is no doubt that the lack thereof is one of the reasons why DRM systems are circumvented by users. Finally, the biggest challenge connected with the different nature of protection granted by Digital Rights Management solutions seems to be the necessity to adapt copyright exemptions within the realm of the technology.[18] As a consequence, such technological override of copyright exemptions may lead to the technical prevention of access to content for people for whom former regulations made such access possible, in particular in developing countries – DRM and anti-circumvention laws could have a significant negative effect on the innovation agendas of developing nations, because they depend on a technological and legal environment that fosters innovation.[19]

Prima facie the problem of recognizing and preserving copyright exemptions by DRM systems seems to be technical in character – it amounts to creation of a rights management code that would approximate both the results of and the dynamism of fair use jurisprudence.[20] However, according to the prevailing view, at the present moment it seems impossible for technical devices to effectively substitute for human decision-making in administering the limitations and exceptions to copyright.[21] In recent

---

16 See Deirdre, Mulligan, Urban, Jennifer M., et al., 'Letter to CEN/ISSS (February 2003)', www.law.berkeley.edu/clinics/samuelson/projects_papers/CENISSS_Letter_022103.pdf.

17 Cunard, J.P., Hill, K. and Barlas, C., 'Current Developments in the Field of Digital Rights Management' (WIPO doc. SCCR/10/2 Rev. of 4 May 2004), p. 105.

18 Barczewski, *supra* note 12, p. 33.

19 'CIPPIC Comments regarding DRM and Developing Nations', www.cippic.ca/en/news/documents/Letter_to_Mark_Jeffrey_Feb_26_2005.pdf.

20 Burk, D.L. and Cohen, J.E. (2001), 'Fair Use Infrastructure for Rights Management Systems', *Harvard Journal of Law and Technology,* 15, 56.

21 See Armstrong, T.K. (2006), 'Digital Rights Management and the Process of Fair Use', *Harvard Journal of Law and Technology,* 20, 54; Akester, P. and Akester, R. (2006), 'Digital Rights Management in the 21st Century', *EIPR*, 3, p. 161.

years, representatives of doctrine of law have put forward several proposals aimed at enabling the exercise of copyright exemptions within DRM systems. The most discussed was a scheme suggested by professors Dan L. Burk and Julie E. Cohen which hinged upon management of rights management keys by a trusted third party, who would release them to users applying for access to make fair use (key-escrow system).[22]

According to another proposal – put forward by Professor Timothy K. Armstrong – upon approval of the user's request, the licensing authority would issue the digital keys necessary to effectuate the requested use – either automatically (with respect to common and narrow exceptions to rights) or with an element of human decision-making (with respect to more vague or not yet foreseen cases of fair use). Nevertheless, if the licensing authority denied the request, or if the user judged that the burden of applying to the licence authority was too great, he should still be able to assert a right to engage in a fair use of the protected content, provided that such an activity was recorded in an audit trail.[23] It must be noted, however, that on the one hand such a model raises some privacy concerns, and on the other hand, creating a network system which would deal both with queries concerning possibilities of exercising exceptions and limitations and recording activities beyond authorization procedures, while ensuring a proper level of anonymity, would require considerable financial and organizational efforts.[24]

Notwithstanding such proposals, numerous concerns relating to technologically managed content affect the behaviour of consumers, so that they are suspicious of technological protection measures and prefer purchasing content free of DRM, even if it is more expensive.[25] Therefore a change in the hitherto prevailing paradigm of legal protection of such technologies, as well as the change of business model of digital content distribution, seems to be unavoidable.

3. GENETIC USE RESTRICTION TECHNOLOGIES (GURTS)

Global crop production shifts, transgenic and hybrid seed technologies and changes in targeted plant populations helped increase the value of

---

22 Burk and Cohen, *supra* note 20, p. 63.

23 Armstrong, *supra* note 21, pp. 101–108.

24 Barczewski, *supra* note 12, p. 33.

25 See 'The 2007 Digital Music Survey', www.olswang.com/dms/digital_music_survey2007.pdf.

the global proprietary seed market to more than $17 billion in 2005.[26] As noted by Jeremy P. Oczek, advancements in the genetic engineering of plants important to agriculture and the proliferation of the sale of genetically engineered seeds have created unique problems for seed developers interested in protecting their biological innovations. Seed developers have been concerned that they spend enormous amounts of time and financial resources on developing genetically engineered crop varieties, yet farmers are allowed to use the seeds harvested from these crops in future seasons without paying for them.[27]

Traditionally, seed researchers have relied on intellectual property (IP) laws that make it illegal for farmers to re-use or sell harvested seed.[28] Companies can protect IP rights in genetically modified (GM) plants through patents or licensing agreements (so called Technology Use Agreements) with their customers that prohibit the saving or sale of patented seed. It needs to be noted, however, that these mechanisms have a number of shortcomings and have thus presented enforcement limitations for seed developers. First, given the vast pool of potential infringers, monitoring for cases of patent infringement or breaches of a licensing agreement is difficult and expensive, especially in developing countries. Additionally, when a case of infringement is found, the litigation that follows is expensive, time-consuming and unpredictable.[29] Undoubtedly, protection of GM plants is effective only if infringers can be identified, monitored and successfully sued for damages and/or enjoined from further infringement.[30] What is more, appropriate legal protection in some countries is either non-existent or insufficient. And without efficient protection of intellectual property, the innovator of the genetically engineered seed loses ownership and control over its intellectual investment in the seed.[31]

To address the challenge of inadequacies and limitations of existing

---

26 *The Corn and Soybean Digest*, 13 June 2006, cornandsoybeandigest.com/news/Global-Seed-Market-Valued-At-17-Billion/.

27 Oczek, J.P. (2000), 'In the Aftermath of the "Terminator" Technology Controversy: Intellectual Property Protections for Genetically Engineered Seeds and the Right to Save and Replant Seed', *Boston College Law Review*, 41, p. 627.

28 Muscati, S. (2005), 'Terminator Technology: Protection of Patents or a Threat to the Patent System?', *IDEA: The Journal of Law and Technology*, 45, p. 481.

29 Ibid., 482.

30 Pendleton C.N. (2004), 'The Peculiar Case of "Terminator" Technology: Agricultural Biotechnology and Intellectual Property Protection at the Crossroads of the Third Green Revolution', *Biotechnology Law Report*, 23(1), p. 9.

31 Oczek, *supra* note 27, p. 644.

intellectual property rights in the 1990s it was decided to use technological measures and as a result the so-called Genetic Use Restriction Technologies (GURTs) that insert new genetic material into the genome of plants, animals or microbes were drawn up. In relation to development of seeds, in March 1998 the United States Patent and Trademark Office granted the first patent jointly to the United States Department of Agriculture and the Delta and Pine Land Co. for a technology that blocks genetically altered seeds from germinating after one season, thereby preventing farmers from saving and replanting seeds. Since then, it is estimated that more than 50 GURTs patents have now been issued worldwide.[32]

There are two basic types of GURTs: Variety-level Genetic Use Restriction Technologies (V-GURTs) and Trait-specific Genetic Use Restriction Technologies (T-GURTs). V-GURTs restrict and allow control of the seed's capacity to germinate under specific conditions – such control is usually exercised by the application of an external chemical inducer. In relation to T-GURTs, on the other hand, application of the stimulus merely activates expression of some value-added trait (e.g. color, ripening) but does not affect seed viability.

As rightly noted by Cullen N. Pendleton, such technologies can address both the needs of companies to protect their investments in IP and the investment distortions produced by weak IP protection. For a company, Genetic Use Restriction Technologies might have value as a surrogate for or supplement to traditional IP protection, while avoiding its inadequacies.[33] GURTs may also limit the ability of a commercial competitor to appropriate know-how and free-ride on the innovator's labor, potentially improving incentives for innovation.[34] They could also be useful as a bargaining chip when a company could use the prospect of the commercial use of GURTs in negotiations with governments or customers as leverage to achieve greater legal protections, better enforcement, or contractual concessions.[35]

On the other hand, although Genetic Use Restriction Technologies are deemed to be more efficient and enforceable than intellectual property protection, a huge public backlash followed their introduction. Various groups levelled criticism at GURTs, ranging from advocates of farmers' rights who feared that they threatened to destroy a millennia-old culture

---

32 Ojanji, W. (2000), 'Suspend GM crops for 5 Years – Scientists', *The East African*, quoted in Pendleton, *supra* note 30, p. 6.

33 Pendleton, *supra* note 30, p. 10.

34 Ibid., 11.

35 Ibid., 13.

of seed-saving among farmers, to environmentalists threatened by the environmental risks posed by yet another form of genetic engineering.[36]

First, it has been argued that genetic material engineered into a crop grown in an open field may travel by wind, insects, or animals into adjacent fields, causing genetically engineered material to transfer and create new transgenic organisms (genetic pollution).[37] Another ecological concern posed by the introduction of genetically engineered seeds is that contamination can also occur in the food chain – it is unclear how the sterility gene, or the chemical triggers associated with it, will affect birds, insects, fungi and bacteria that eat or infect genetically modified seeds. Nor is it clear how such seeds, left in the field, will affect the ecology of soil organisms.[38] Genetically modified plants may not be edible by both humans and animals because of their increased toxicity – there are potential changes to the nutritional content and value of the seeds that have had several proteins in them destroyed by artificially induced toxic agents. And although the toxins in question may not be directly poisonous, it is possible that they may cause allergenic reactions in humans, particularly, if they are mixed up in the general food supply chain without adequate warning or notice to the public.[39]

Another hazard of GM seeds is the possibility that the sterility genes could be attached randomly, again producing unpredictable behaviour and possibly decreasing the reproductive ability of natural species. This could ultimately lead to increases in the rate of extinction of native plant species or famine – the very problem many advances in seed technology have sought to alleviate.[40]

Genetic Use Restriction Technologies also raise extremely complex issues and policy concerns for developing countries, where many farmers depend on farm-saved seed and seeds exchanged with neighbours as their primary seed source. As Graham Dutfield remarks, maintaining the freedom to do this is important for two reasons. First, if it turns out that the benefits of genetically modified seeds are insufficient to compensate for

---

[36] Muscati, *supra* note 28, p. 477.

[37] Caplan, R. (2007), 'The Ongoing Debate over Terminator Technology', *Georgetown International Environmental Law Review,* 19, p. 763.

[38] Muscati, *supra* note 28, p. 501.

[39] Mgbeoji, I. (2004), 'The "Terminator" Patent and its Discontents: Rethinking the Normative Deficit in Utility Test of Modern Patent Law', *Saint Thomas Law Review*, 17, p. 119.

[40] Barron, J.A. (2008), 'Genetic Use Restriction Technologies: Do the Potential Environmental Harms Outweigh the Economic Benefits?', *Georgetown International Environmental Law Review*, 20, p. 288.

their higher price, farming may become even more risky for small-scale farmers. Secondly, many of them do much more than simply grow seed produced elsewhere. Indeed, local varieties are themselves the result of generations of improvement through on-farm selection and experimentation. Turning such farmers into mere customers of companies selling GM seeds will halt such practices. And this could weaken plant breeding efforts worldwide by reducing the variety of germplasm available.[41]

It can easily be seen that Genetic Use Restriction Technologies also raise many of the same legal and policy issues that have been identified with DRM. In both cases, the substitution of technological protection for legal protection allows private parties to displace the public policy balance of ownership and control that is inherent in intellectual property law.[42] First, GURTs may be applied to any seed, irrespective of whether they are themselves subject to the requirements of intellectual property. Hence, they offer a significantly broader ambit of protection than is provided by the existing IP law framework. Furthermore, patents create monopolies limited to 20 years that are restricted to specific claims, while GURTs can in principle provide an indefinite duration of protection, allowing the maximization of profits which can be extracted from the technology,[43] which in consequence could lead to the establishment by the seed company of a concentrated, dominant market position that could then be abused.[44] Yet, assuming that the patent applies to the chemical key to the trait, any user could activate the trait after the patent has expired.

It also needs to be added that, just as a skilful software pirate can circumvent technological protection measures used to protect digital content delivered via DRM, a dedicated seed pirate could use advanced molecular biology techniques to isolate the DNA sequences encoding the value-added trait in a GM plant, separate it and then introduce it into 'generic' GM seeds that he sells. However, it needs to be noted that here infringers will face higher costs and have to commit more time to be successful.[45]

---

41 Dutfield, G. (2003), 'Should We Terminate Terminator Technology', *EIPR*, 25 (11), p. 494.

42 Burk, D.L. (2004), 'DNA Rules: Legal and Conceptual Implications of Biological "Lock-Out" Systems', *California Law Review*, 92, p. 1553.

43 Kariyawasam, K. (2009), 'Terminator Technology as a Technological Means of Forcing Intellectual Property Rights in Plant Germplasm: Its Implications for World Agriculture', *EIPR*, 31 (1), p. 40.

44 Muscati, *supra* note 28, p. 494.

45 Pendleton, *supra* note 30, pp. 11–12.

4. CONCLUDING REMARKS

The exemplification presented here confirms that in intellectual property protection law, technological measures may play the role of the twelfth camel as complementation of the system. The above-discussed examples indicate, however, that the paradigm of protection reinforced by the means of technology creates many important problems which make recognition of such technologies as a commonly accepted tool difficult. Economy-based reasoning shows that reflection of the needs of the recipients of technologically managed goods in the design of technical protection measures is of pivotal importance in terms of their market success.

As Dan L. Burk points out, the proliferation of restrictive technologies such as DRM and GURTs poses a challenge not only to the traditional balance of control over intellectual property, but also to our understanding of legal doctrines related to ownership and control. As restrictive technologies blur the distinctions between property, contract, and physical products, these categories may be redefined in light of the interplay between law and the values that restrictive technologies embed in the design of physical products.[46]

---

46 Burk, *supra* note 42, pp. 1553–4.

PART III

IP rights as objects of property

10. Individual, multiple and collective ownership of intellectual property rights – which impact on exclusivity?

Alexander Peukert*

1. INTRODUCTION

The TRIPS Agreement covers no fewer than seven categories of intellectual property (IP) rights.[1] National IP law may comprise even more types of IP rights. In German law, for example, plant varieties and utility models are also governed by specific acts.[2] In addition, there are IP-related statutes on employee inventions, copyright collecting societies, etc.[3] All these issues are regulated on a national, regional[4] and international level.

* Dr. iur., Professor of Law, Chair for Civil Law, Commercial Law and Intellectual Property Law, Goethe University Frankfurt am Main, Cluster of Excellence Normative Orders, http://www.jura.uni-frankfurt.de/peukert/.

[1] See Art. 1(2) Agreement on Trade-Related Aspects of Intellectual Property Rights (TRIPS), available at http://www.wto.org/english/docs_e/legal_e/27-trips.pdf (accessed 2 February 2010): Copyright and Related Rights, Trademarks, Geographical Indications, Industrial Designs, Patents, Layout-Designs (Topographies) of Integrated Circuits, and the Protection of Undisclosed Information.

[2] German Plant Variety Protection Act (*Sortenschutzgesetz*), available at http://www.gesetze-im-internet.de/sortschg_1985/index.html (accessed 19 January 2010); German Utility Models Act (*Gebrauchsmustergesetz*), available at http://www.gesetze-im-internet.de/gebrmg/ (accessed 19 January 2010).

[3] German Employee Inventions Act (*Gesetz über Arbeitnehmererfindungen*), available at http://www.gesetze-im-internet.de/arbnerfg/ (accessed 19 January 2010); German Law on the Administration of Copyright and Neighboring Rights (*Urheberrechtswahrnehmungsgesetz*), available at http://www.gesetze-im-internet.de/ urhwahrng/index.html (accessed 19 January 2010).

[4] See the EU rights in trademarks (Council Regulation (EC) No. 207/2009 of 26 February 2009 on the Community trade mark (codified version), OJ L 78, 24 March 2009, p. 1), designs (Council Regulation (EC) No. 6/2002 of 12 December 2001 on Community designs, OJ L 3, 5 January 2002, p. 1) and plant varieties (Council Regulation (EC) No. 2100/94 of 27 July 1994 on Community plant

No wonder that a textbook on German, European and international intellectual property law sources contains 35 statutes, directives, regulations and international treaties.[5]

A legal field of such size and fragmentation is not only hard to handle, the fact that closely related questions are governed by distinct legal sources of different provenance also increases the danger of conflicting rules. The many cases of overlapping protection schemes are one prominent example.[6] In order to reveal these conflicts and to identify general principles of IP law that may guide possible solutions, one has to take a 'horizontal' approach. This means that one has to cut across the traditionally segmented areas of patent, copyright, trademark law, etc. The task is to explore whether a certain issue is specific to just one area of IP law or whether it is a structural feature that emerges in the context of several IP rights. This systematic approach[7] is not only of help in addressing contradictions in the field of IP law, but may also be useful for teaching purposes.

This chapter applies such 'horizontal' thinking to different ownership structures and their impact on exclusivity. This rather abstract theme needs a little explanation: much of the current debate about IP is in one sense or another related to the famous *balance* between exclusive rights in inventions, works, signs, etc. and the larger public interest in access to knowledge, functioning competition and so on.[8] However, most state-

---

variety rights, OJ L 227, 1 September 1994, p. 1), with equal effect throughout the European Union. See further the Agreement Revising the Bangui Agreement of 2 March 1977 on the Creation of an African Intellectual Property Organization (OAPI) of 24 February 1999, creating uniform IP protection for 16 West African countries, available at http://www.oapi.wipo.net/doc/en/bangui_agreement.pdf (accessed 19 January 2010).

[5] Mächtel, Uhrig and Förster (eds) (2009), *Geistiges Eigentum: Vorschriftensammlung*. 2nd ed.

[6] On these overlaps, see Derclaye and Leistner (2010), *Intellectual Property Overlaps: a European Perspective*.

[7] This approach follows the German legal tradition of thinking in *Allgemeiner Teil* (general part, see German Civil Code, book one) and *Besonderer Teil* (special part, see German Civil Code, books two to five; all available in English at http://bundesrecht.juris.de/englisch_bgb/index.html (accessed 19 January 2010)). See also Ahrens (2006), 'Brauchen wir einen Allgemeinen Teil der Rechte des Geistigen Eigentums?', *GRUR*, pp. 617 et seq.

[8] See, e.g., Declaration on the TRIPS Agreement and Public Health, adopted on 14 November 2001, WT/MIN(01)/DEC/W/2, available at http://www.wto.org/english/theWTO_e/minist_e/min01_e/mindecl_trips _e.htm (accessed 19 January 2010); WIPO, 'Striking a Balance, The Patent System and Access to Drugs and Health Care', available at http://www.wipo.int/freepublications/en/patents/491/wipo_pub_491.pdf (accessed 19 January 2010); Hilty and Peukert (2004), *Interessenausgleich im Urheberrecht*; Geiger (2004), *Droit d'auteur et droit*

ments deal with exclusivity as a kind of monolithic block. No distinction is made depending on whether one or several owners are involved.

In the following, I will consider to what extent the general balance of protection is modified due to different ownership structures. For this purpose, I will define and distinguish individual, multiple and collective ownership. With regard to each category, I will ask whether one can identify repercussions on the scope of exclusivity, which bear again on these different ownership structures. In doing so, I will stick to the horizontal approach, meaning that I will consider all areas of IP law. Obviously, this is an ambitious scheme. On a comparative level, the chapter is based first on international conventions, secondly on European Union law and thirdly on additional references to German, US, French and some other selected national laws.

2. INDIVIDUAL OWNERSHIP

The starting point of the analysis is individual ownership. *One person holding one exclusive IP right* is the paradigm case of the classical, Western idea of the right to property.[9]

The preamble of TRIPS[10] refers to this notion by recognizing that intellectual property rights are 'private rights'. These are considered to be the basis of economic individual freedom and a market economy.[11] IP rights in particular are meant to stimulate[12] and at the same time

---

du public á l'information; Depenheuer and Peifer (2008), *Geistiges Eigentum: Schutzrecht oder Ausbeutungstitel?*; Götting and Lunze (2009), *Überprotektion durch Geistiges Eigentum?*.

[9] See Peukert (forthcoming 2011), 'Intellectual Property', in Basedow, Hopt and Zimmermann (eds), *Encyclopaedia of European Private Law*, http://www.ssrn.com/abstract=1550103; Hilty (2009), 'Rationales for the Legal Protection of Intangible Goods and Cultural Heritage', *IIC*, pp. 883, 887 et seq.

[10] See preamble TRIPS, *supra* note 1.

[11] Posner (2007), *Economic Analysis of Law*, 7th ed., pp. 9, 33 ('necessary rather than a sufficient condition for the efficient use of resources'); Shavell (2004), *Foundations of Economic Analysis of Law*, pp. 18 et seq.; Cooter and Ulen (2008), *Law and Economics*, 5th ed., pp. 78 et seq.; Anderson and McChesney (2003), 'The Economic Approach to Property Rights', in Anderson and McChesney (eds), *Property Rights, Cooperation, Conflict, and Law*, 6; Merges (2005), 'A Transactional View of Property Rights', *Berkeley Technology Law Journal* 20, 1477 et seq.

[12] See Art. I, Sec. 8, Cl. 8 US Constitution: 'The Congress shall have power . . . to promote the Progress of Science and useful Arts, by securing for limited Times to Authors and Inventors the exclusive Right to their respective Writings and Discoveries.'; Recital 1, 2 Directive 2004/48/EC of the European Parliament

reward[13] individual innovation, creativity and investment. The persons vested with the original right or the entitlement to it are thus either the individual inventor,[14] designer,[15] breeder,[16] creator of a topography of an integrated circuit,[17] etc. or the responsible investor, such as the producer of a phonogram or a broadcasting organization.[18] In a comparative perspective, the terms 'author' and 'rightholder' in copyright law cover both categories, i.e. the creator (authors' rights systems) as well as the producer (copyright systems).[19] Since trademarks have a different purpose, namely

---

and of the Council of 29 April 2004 on the enforcement of intellectual property rights (OJ L 157, 30 April 2004), corr. OJ L 195, 2 June 2004, p. 16 (the protection of IP is an essential element for the success of the internal market; it is important not only for promoting innovation and creativity, but also for developing employment and improving competitiveness, that it should allow the inventor or creator to derive a legitimate profit from his/her invention or creation, and that it should also allow the widest possible dissemination of works, ideas and new know-how without hampering freedom of expression, the free movement of information, or the protection of personal data, including on the Internet).

[13] See, e.g., Schack (2007), *Urheber- und Urhebervertragsrecht*, 4th ed., note 1228; Kraßer (2009), *Patentrecht*, 6th ed., pp. 38 et seq.

[14] Art. 60(1) s. 1 European Patent Convention (EPC), available at http://www.epo.org/patents/law/legal-texts/html/epc/2000/e/contents.html (accessed 19 January 2010) ('The right to a European patent shall belong to the inventor or his successor in title.'); Art. L611-6 Code de la Propriété Intellectuelle (CPI), available at http://www.celog.fr/cpi/ (accessed 20 January 2010); 35 United States Code (USC) §§ 101 (whoever invents. . .), 261 (personal property), available at http://www.law.cornell.edu/uscode/ (accessed 2 February 2010).

[15] Art. 14(1) Reg. (EC) No. 6/2002 (*supra* note 4); Art. L511-9 CPI (*supra* note 14); 17 USC § 1320(a) (*supra* note 14).

[16] Art. 2 International Convention for the Protection of New Varieties of Plants of 2 December 1961, as Revised at Geneva on 10 November 1972, on 23 October 1978, and on 19 March 1991 (UPOV); Art. 11(1), 13 Council Reg. (EC) No. 2100/94 (*supra* note 4).

[17] Art. 3(1) Council Directive 87/54/EEC of 16 December 1986 on the legal protection of topographies of semiconductor products, OJ L 024, 27 January 1987, p. 36; 17 USC § 901(a)(6) (*supra* note 14) ('person who created the mask work').

[18] See Art. 2(d) WIPO Performances and Phonograms Treaty (WPPT), available at http://www.wipo.int/treaties/ en/ip/wppt/ (accessed 2 February 2010); Art. 14(2), (3) TRIPS (*supra* note 1).

[19] See Art. 14bis(2) Berne Convention (BC), available at http://www.wipo.int/treaties/en/ip/berne/ (accessed 2 February 2010); Art. 2(1) Council Directive 2009/24/EC of 23 April 2009 on the legal protection of computer programs (codified version), OJ L 111/16, 5 May 2009 ('The author of a computer program shall be the natural person or group of natural persons who has created the program or, where the legislation of the Member State permits, the legal person designated as the rightholder by that legislation. Where collective works are recognized by the legislation of a Member State, the person considered by the legislation of the

to distinguish products and companies to reduce search costs and to guarantee to consumers the origin of the goods or services, they are not allocated to the 'creator' of the sign, but to the person who registers or uses the sign in order to identify herself or her goods or services.[20]

All these rights have a pre-defined scope. Within that scope, they negatively exclude the world and positively grant the owner an exclusive right to use the subject matter.[21] The reach of exclusivity and the requirements

---

Member State to have created the work shall be deemed to be its author.'), Article 3 (Beneficiaries of protection: Protection shall be granted to all natural or legal persons eligible under national copyright legislation as applied to literary works.); ditto Art. 4(1) Council Directive 96/9/EC of 11 March 1996 on the legal protection of databases, OJ L 077, 27 March 1996, p. 20; see also 17 USC § 201(b) (*supra* note 14) (works made for hire).

[20] See Art. 16(1) TRIPS (*supra* note 1); Art. 5(1) Directive 2008/95/EC of the European Parliament and of the Council of 22 October 2008 to approximate the laws of the Member States relating to trade marks (Codified version), OJ L 299, 8 November 2008, p. 25; Art. 9(1) Reg. (EC) No. 207/2009 (*supra* note 4). On the function of a trademark see, on the one hand, *Ty Inc. v Perryman*, 306 F.3d 509 (7th Cir. 2002, Posner, J.) ('The fundamental purpose of a trademark is to reduce consumer search costs by providing a concise and unequivocal identifier of the particular source of particular goods') and on the other, ECJ Case C-487/07, [2009] ECR 0000, *L'Oréal v Bellure*, para. 58 ('These functions include not only the essential function of the trade mark, which is to guarantee to consumers the origin of the goods or services, but also its other functions, in particular that of guaranteeing the quality of the goods or services in question and those of communication, investment or advertising').

[21] See Peukert (2008), *Güterzuordnung als Rechtsprinzip*, 54, 884 et seq.; WIPO Intergovernmental Committee on Intellectual Property and Genetic Resources, Traditional Knowledge and Folklore, 'Composite Study on the Protection of Traditional Knowledge', WIPO/GRTKF/IC/5/8, 28 April 2003, para. 119 ('Regardless of the answer to be given to this question, it should be stressed that a common denominator links all IP rights: the right to exclude others from making certain usage of the protected subject matter (e.g. acts such as reproducing, fixing, making, or using in the course of trade)'). This assumption is disputed with regard to patent law; see Recital 14, Directive 98/44/EC of the European Parliament and of the Council of 6 July 1998 on the legal protection of biotechnological inventions, OJ L 213, 30 July 1998, p. 13 ('Whereas a patent for invention does not authorise the holder to implement that invention, but merely entitles him to prohibit third parties from exploiting it for industrial and commercial purposes; whereas, consequently, substantive patent law cannot serve to replace or render superfluous national, European or international law which may impose restrictions or prohibitions or which concerns the monitoring of research and of the use or commercialisation of its results, notably from the point of view of the requirements of public health, safety, environmental protection, animal welfare, the preservation of genetic diversity and compliance with certain ethical standards . . .'); Art. 27(2) TRIPS (*supra* note 1).

of protection reflect the general balance vis-à-vis the public interest. In current patent, copyright, design and trademark law, this kind of *individual exclusivity is conceived as the 'normal' case*. Legislators may depart from it only according to the famous three- or two-step test under TRIPS and other international conventions.[22]

Since they have a positive, pre-defined scope, IP rights are in principle transferrable.[23] Thereby, markets for innovations and for products embodying protected information are established. If the right is not fully assigned but only licensed, the licensor as well as the potentially numerous licensees may at the same time be entitled to use the subject matter. Thus, individual licensing could already be qualified as a case of multiple ownership. To what extent licensing contracts limit the exclusive right of the licensor and establish a limited exclusive right with the licensee, is a matter of party autonomy. In any event, these reciprocal limitations are of a 'relative' nature – they only concern the parties to the contract. As far as the world at large is concerned, the trade-off between exclusivity and access remains intact. Who has not acquired a license still has to observe the statutory prohibitions. Since this chapter is concerned with *general* implications of ownership structures on that balance, licensing as a way to multiply the number of 'rightholders' will not be addressed in detail here.[24]

3. MULTIPLE RIGHTS OR OWNERS

The first variation from individual ownership is the case of multiple rights or owners respectively. It is characterized by the fact that *not only one, but a plurality of IP rights is relevant for a certain product*. The rights are independent of each other and have to be observed cumulatively. They do not necessarily come into existence with the same owners. How do these exclusive rights relate to each other? Does the law limit the rights concerned to still allow access without prior authorization? At least five subcategories of multiple rights or owners can be identified. In each case, the answers to the questions raised are different.

---

22 See Art. 9(2) BC (*supra* note 19), Art. 10 WIPO Copyright Treaty (WCT), available at http://www.wipo.int/treaties/en/ip/wct/ (accessed 20 January 2010); Art. 16 WPPT (*supra* note 18); Art. 13, 17, 26(2), 30 TRIPS (*supra* note 1).

23 For an exception, see Sec. 29 German Copyright Act (German CA, *Gesetz über Urheberrecht und verwandte Schutzrechte*) ('*Das Urheberrecht ist nicht übertragbar. . .*'), available at http://www.gesetze-im-internet.de/urhg/ (accessed 20 January 2010).

24 See Enchelmaier (Chapter 11) in this volume.

3.1. Double Innovation/creativity and Parallel Trademarks

First, several persons may develop identical or very similar IP subject matter independently from each other, for example, in the case of double inventions. According to the principles of individual ownership, a third party would have to ask both rightholders for authorization to use the respective subject matter. Moreover, the two may block each other so that the subject matter cannot be used at all.

In order to avoid this result, registered industrial property rights will be granted only to the one who first files for registration[25] or who first made the innovation.[26] However, the winner of the race does not necessarily take all. The second-comer may have a right of prior use if she can establish that, before the date of priority of the other IP right, she has in good faith commenced use or has made serious and effective preparations to that end. This right of prior use entitles the second-comer to continue the internal exploitation of the independently created subject matter.[27]

The solution is different with regard to IP rights that come into existence without registration. If the holder of a copyright,[28] a non-registered right in a topography[29] or design,[30] is able to show that the defendant simply copied the work, etc., she will be granted protection. If, however, the work, topography or design was independently created, the plaintiff

---

25 Art. 60(2) EPC (*supra* note 14), Sec. 6 s. 3 German Patent Act (*Patentgesetz*), available at http://www.gesetze-im-internet.de/patg/ (accessed 20 January 2010); Art. L611-6(2) CPI (*supra* note 14).

26 See 35 USC § 101 (*supra* note 14).

27 For patent law, see, e.g., Sec. 12(1) German Patent Act (*supra* note 25); 35 USC § 273(b) (*supra* note 14). For design protection, see, e.g., Sec. 41 German Design Protection Act (*Gesetz über den rechtlichen Schutz von Mustern und Modellen*), available at http://www.gesetze-im-internet.de/geschmmg_2004/ (accessed 20 January 2010); Art. 22 Reg. (EC) 6/2002 (*supra* note 4); Art. 12(2) Directive 98/71/EC of the European Parliament and of the Council of 13 October 1998 on the legal protection of designs, OJ L 289, 28 October 1998, p. 28. For a similar bona fide concept with regard to semiconductor chip protection see 37(1) TRIPS (*supra* note 1), Art. 5(6) Dir. 87/54/EEC (*supra* note 17).

28 See Art. 5(2) BC (*supra* note 19); 20 WPPT (*supra* note 18).

29 Topographies may be protected even before registration; see Art. 7(1) Washington Treaty on Intellectual Property in respect of Integrated Circuits (IPIC), available at http://www.wipo.int/treaties/en/ip/washington/ (accessed 20 January 2010), Art. 4(1) Dir. 87/54/EEC (*supra* note 17), Sec. 5(1) German Topographies Protection Act (*Gesetz über den Schutz der Topographien von mikroelektronischen Halbleitererzeugnissen*), available at http://www.gesetze-im-internet.de/halblschg/index.html (accessed 19 January 2010).

30 Art. 1(2)(a) Reg. (EC) 6/2002 (*supra* note 4).

may not exercise her rights vis-à-vis the other one. The rights exist and can be exploited independently of each other.[31] Double protection is accepted in these areas because it occurs rarely and no public register informs a second-comer as to the state of the art. Copyright, moreover, is not about novelty and innovation, but about individuality/originality.[32]

Due to its different functions, trademark law applies other instruments to solve this conflict. Whoever first files a trademark registration or uses the sign in commerce and thereby acquires protection, prevails against identical or confusingly similar younger signs.[33] Rights of prior use are generally not known in trademark law. The reason is that the parallel existence of confusing signs on the market would run contrary to the very purpose of trademark law. In two situations, however, trademark law accepts such coexistence. First, anyone may continue to use in the course of trade his own name or address if this is done in accordance with honest practices and confusion is avoided as far as possible.[34] Secondly, under certain conditions the protection of geographical indications (GIs) cannot be exercised against identical or similar older names, trademarks and other GIs.[35] This kind of prior use right reflects that signs indicating geographical origin are of high competitive significance. Without the sign,

---

[31] For copyrights, see Court of Appeals Berlin (*Kammergericht*) *ZUM* 2001, pp. 503, 505; Schack, *supra* note 13, pp. 63, 161. For the protection of topographies, see Art. 6(2)(c) IPIC (*supra* note 29), Art. 35 TRIPS (*supra* note 1) ('The holder of the right may not exercise his right in respect of an identical original layout-design (topography) that was independently created by a third party'). For design rights, see Art. 19(2) Reg. (EC) 6/2002 (*supra* note 4) ('An unregistered Community design shall, however, confer on its holder the right to prevent the acts referred to in paragraph 1 only if the contested use results from copying the protected design. The contested use shall not be deemed to result from copying the protected design if it results from an independent work of creation by a designer who may be reasonably thought not to be familiar with the design made available to the public by the holder').

[32] See *Feist Publications, Inc. v Rural Telephone Service Co., Inc.*, 499 US 340 (1991); ECJ, case C-5/08, [2010] ECR 0000, *Infopaq v Danske Dagblades Forening*, para. 37; Canadian Supreme Court *CCH Canadian Ltd. v Law Society of Upper Canada*, 2004 SCC 13, [2004] 1 SCR 339, paras. 14 et seq.

[33] See Art. 16(1) s. 2 TRIPS (*supra* note 1); Art. 4 Dir. 2008/95/EC (*supra* note 20), Art. 8(1) Reg. (EC) 207/2009 (*supra* note 4), Art. 14(1) Council Regulation (EC) No. 510/2006 of 20 March 2006 on the protection of geographical indications and designations of origin for agricultural products and foodstuffs, OJ L 093, 31 March 2006, p. 12.

[34] Art. 12(a) Reg. (EC) 207/2009 (*supra* note 4), Art. 6(1)(a) Dir. 2008/95/EC (*supra* note 20).

[35] See Art. 24(4), (5) TRIPS (*supra* note 1), Art. 13(3), (4), 14(2) Reg. (EC) 510/2006 (*supra* note 33).

it may be impossible to market the respective product at all. Such an effect on the product market is characteristic of patents and other rights in innovations, which also know prior use rights.

3.2. Unilateral Combination/adaptation of Protected Subject Matter

The second subcategory of multiple rights or owners concerns the unilateral combination or adaptation of pre-existing subject matter. For example, a mobile phone is covered by hundreds, if not thousands, of patents, some of them derivative ones.[36] Broadcasts and databases contain large numbers of protected writings, music and films, some of them again adaptations of other works. As in the first subcategory, the subject matters and rights concerned are independent of each other. They leave intact and in no way prejudice other IP rights. Thus, someone who wants to market a mobile phone, who wants to retransmit a broadcast or exploit a modified musical composition, needs the authorization of all holders of pre-existing rights.[37]

---

[36] For other examples in the field of biotechnology, see Van Overwalle (2009), 'Of Thickets, Blocks and Gaps: Designing Tools to Resolve Obstacles in the Gene Patents Landscape', in Van Overwalle (ed.), *Gene Patents and Collaborative Licensing Models*, pp. 383 et seq.

[37] On related rights, see Art. 1 Rome Convention for the Protection of Performers, Producers of Phonograms and Broadcasting Organizations (RC), available at http://www.wipo.int/treaties/en/ip/rome/ (accessed 2 February 2010) ('Protection granted under this Convention shall leave intact and shall in no way affect the protection of copyright in literary and artistic works . . .'), available at http://www.wipo.int/treaties/en/ip/rome/ (accessed 20 January 2010); Art. 1(2) WPPT and Agreed Statement concerning Art. 1(2) WPPT (*supra* note 18) ('. . . In cases where authorization is needed from both the author of a work embodied in the phonogram and a performer or producer owning rights in the phonogram, the need for the authorization of the author does not cease to exist because the authorization of the performer or producer is also required, and vice versa'); Art. 12 Directive 2006/115/EC of the European Parliament and of the Council of 12 December 2006 on rental right and lending right and on certain rights related to copyright in the field of intellectual property (codified version), OJ L 376, 27 December 2006, p. 28; Art. 5 Council Directive 93/83/EEC of 27 September 1993 on the coordination of certain rules concerning copyright and rights related to copyright applicable to satellite broadcasting and cable retransmission, OJ L 248, 6 October 1993, p. 15; Art. 7(4) Dir. 96/9/EC (*supra* note 19). On database protection, see Art. 3(2) Dir. 96/6/EC (*supra* note 19) ('The copyright protection of databases provided for by this Directive shall not extend to their contents and shall be without prejudice to any rights subsisting in those contents themselves'). See also 17 USC § 201(c) (*supra* note 14) ('Copyright in each separate contribution to a collective work is distinct from copyright in the collective work as a whole, and vests

Neo-classical property-rights theory argues that owners in situations like these will privately contract into liability rules.[38] Here, one might mention collecting societies, patent pools and industry standards. However, this solution does not work if some rightholders veto for strategic or other reasons or if it is too burdensome or virtually impossible to identify them in the first place. The result is a tragedy of the anti-commons: too many rights and owners cause transaction costs that prevent commercially viable uses in the public interest.[39]

One possible reaction is to *generally limit exclusivity*.[40] Examples are limitations of copyright for the purpose of caricature or parody under European law[41] and for transformative uses under US law.[42] The scope of design protection with regard to similar designs[43] and of patents beyond

---

initially in the author of the contribution'). On adaptations, see Art. 2(3) BC (*supra* note 19) ('Translations, adaptations, arrangements of music and other alterations of a literary or artistic work shall be protected as original works without prejudice to the copyright in the original work'); Sec. 3 s. 1 German CA (*supra* note 23); Art. L113-3 CPI (*supra* note 14); 17 USC § 103(b) (*supra* note 14). On derivative patents, see Melullis (2002), in Benkard (ed.) *EPÜ*, Art. 52 no. 143 et seq.

38 Merges (*supra* note 11); Merges (2004), 'Compulsory Licensing vs. the Three "Golden Oldies" Property, Contract Rights and Markets', *CATO Institute Policy Analysis* No. 508, available at http://www.cato.org/pubs /pas/pa508.pdf (accessed 6 January 2010).

39 Heller (1998), 'The Tragedy of the Anticommons: Property in the Transition from Marx to Markets', *Harvard Law Review* 111, pp. 621–88; Buchanan and Yoon (2000), 'Symmetric Tragedies: Commons and Anticommons Property', *Journal of Law & Economics* 43, pp. 1–13; Vanneste, van Hiel, Parisi and Depoorter (2006), 'From "Tragedy" to "Disaster": Welfare Effects of Commons and Anticommons Dilemmas', *International Review of Law and Economics* 26, pp. 104–22; Parisi, Schulz and Depoorter (2006), 'Duality in Property: Commons and Anticommons', *International Review of Law and Economics* 25, pp. 578–91.

40 For an economic analysis of copyright limitations, see Dowell (1998), 'Bytes and Pieces: Fragmented Copies, Licensing, and Fair Use in a Digital World', *California Law Review* 86, pp. 843, 849 et seq.; Cohen (1998), 'Lochner in Cyberspace: The New Economic Orthodoxy of "Rights Management"', *Michigan Law Review* 97, pp. 462, 547 et seq.

41 Art. 5(3)(k) Directive 2001/29/EC of the European Parliament and of the Council of 22 May 2001 on the harmonisation of certain aspects of copyright and related rights in the information society, OJ L 167, 22 June 2001, p. 10; Sec. 24(1) German CA (*supra* note 23) ('An independent work created by free use of the work of another person may be published and exploited without the consent of the author of the used work.').

42 *Campbell v Acuff-Rose Music, Inc.*, 510 US 569 (1994).

43 See Art. 10(2) Reg. (EC) 6/2002 (*supra* note 4) ('In assessing the scope of protection, the degree of freedom of the designer in developing his design shall be taken into consideration').

the literal meaning of the claim under a doctrine of equivalence[44] also takes the needs of incremental innovation into account. Usages that do not modify, but simply combine and concern, a large amount of protected subject matter are sometimes also subject to a liability rule. This is true of so-called 'secondary uses', for example, the broadcasting of performances and phonograms.[45] To grant performers and producers of phonograms not an exclusive right, but only a right to remuneration, benefits broadcasting organizations and authors of pre-existing works who do not have to fear a veto by these other rightholders. Effectively the same result is achieved by compulsory collective licensing. This approach has been adopted with regard to the cable retransmission of works and other subject matter as part of television and other programs in EU law[46] and recently with regard to 'orphan works' in Swiss copyright law.[47]

An alternative approach to dealing with access problems in the case of multiple rights is to limit the *exercise* of exclusivity in *individual cases*. Thereby, the strategic behavior of outsiders can be overcome. For the

---

44 See, e.g., Art. 69 and protocol of the EPC (*supra* note 14); 35 USC § 112(6) (*supra* note 14) and *Festo Corp. v Shoketsu Kinzoku Kogyo Kabushiki Co.*, 535 US 722 (2002).

45 See Art. 12 RC (*supra* note 37) ('If a phonogram published for commercial purposes, or a reproduction of such phonogram, is used directly for broadcasting or for any communication to the public, [only] a single equitable remuneration shall be paid by the user to the performers, or to the producers of the phonograms, or to both. Domestic law may, in the absence of agreement between these parties, lay down the conditions as to the sharing of this remuneration.'); Art. 15(1) WPPT (*supra* note 18) ('Performers and producers of phonograms shall enjoy [only] the right to a single equitable remuneration for the direct or indirect use of phonograms published for commercial purposes for broadcasting or for any communication to the public.').

46 See Art. 9, 10 Dir. 93/83/EEC (*supra* note 37) (Recital 28: 'Whereas, in order to ensure that the smooth operation of contractual arrangements is not called into question by the intervention of outsiders holding rights in individual parts of the programme, provision should be made, through the obligation to have recourse to a collecting society, for the exclusive collective exercise of the authorization right to the extent that this is required by the special features of cable retransmission; whereas the authorization right as such remains intact and only the exercise of this right is regulated to some extent, so that the right to authorize a cable retransmission can still be assigned; whereas this Directive does not affect the exercise of moral rights.'); Art. 9(1) Dir. 93/83 (*supra* note 37) ('Member States shall ensure that the right of copyright owners and holders or related rights to grant or refuse authorization to a cable operator for a cable retransmission may be exercised only through a collecting society.').

47 See Art. 22(a)–(c) Swiss Copyright Act (*Bundesgesetz über das Urheberrecht und verwandte Schutzrechte*), available at http://www.admin.ch/ch/d/as/2008/2421.pdf (accessed 6 January 2010).

rest, individual licensing is still required. In this respect, one can refer to Canadian copyright law, where a copyright board upon application grants a non-exclusive license to use certain orphan works.[48] Another example is compulsory cross-licensing of patents according to Art. 31(l) TRIPS if the second patent involves 'an important technical advance of considerable economic significance in relation to the invention claimed in the first patent'.[49] Under EU competition law, a refusal to license an IP right may also establish a misuse of a dominant position if the refusal relates to an essential facility, excludes any effective competition on a neighboring market and prevents the appearance of a new product for which there is potential consumer demand.[50] The US Supreme Court decision in *eBay v MercExchange*, which allows permanent patent injunctions only according to the general principles of equity, including a consideration of the public interest, can also be qualified as an instrument to avoid the misuse of exclusive IP rights in exceptional cases – here with regard to patent trolls blocking the manufacture of complex products involving a plurality of patents.[51] Finally, the *Google Book* class action settlement reacts to the

---

[48] Copyright Act (R.S., 1985, c. C-42), Sec. 77 ('77. (1) Where, on application to the Board by a person who wishes to obtain a licence to use (a) a published work, (b) a fixation of a performer's performance, (c) a published sound recording, or (d) a fixation of a communication signal in which copyright subsists, the Board is satisfied that the applicant has made reasonable efforts to locate the owner of the copyright and that the owner cannot be located, the Board may issue to the applicant a licence to do an act mentioned in section 3, 15, 18 or 21, as the case may be. (2) A licence issued under subsection (1) is non-exclusive and is subject to such terms and conditions as the Board may establish. (3) The owner of a copyright may, not later than five years after the expiration of a licence issued pursuant to subsection (1) in respect of the copyright, collect the royalties fixed in the licence or, in default of their payment, commence an action to recover them in a court of competent jurisdiction.'). For a list of cases see http://www.cb-cda.gc.ca/unlocatable-introuvables/licences-e.html (accessed 6 January 2010).

[49] See also Art. 12 Dir. 98/44/EC (*supra* note 21); Art. 29(5), (5a) Reg. (EC) 2100/94 (*supra* note 4).

[50] See ECJ, joined cases C-241/91 and C-242/91, [1995] ECR I-743, *RTE and ITP v Commission* ('Magill'); ECJ, case C-418/01 [2004] ECR I-5039, *IMS Health v NDC Health*, para. 52; Court of First Instance, case T-201/04, [2004] ECR II-4463, *Microsoft v Commission*, paras. 319, 331 et seq.; see also German Federal Supreme Court, Case KZR 39/06, 6 May 2009, BGHZ 180, 312 – *Orange Book Standard*.

[51] *eBay Inc v MercExchange*, 547 US 388 (2006) (Kennedy, J., concurring: 'When the patented invention is but a small component of the product the companies seek to produce and the threat of an injunction is employed simply for undue leverage in negotiations, legal damages may well be sufficient to compensate for the infringement and an injunction may not serve the public interest.'). On the difficulties of applying this common law solution to European law under Dir.

impossibility of licensing all books under copyright in the US by turning the principles of exclusivity upside down: the rightholder who does not accept the licensing scheme has to opt out. Only then may she try to stop Google in an individual lawsuit.[52]

3.3. Group Innovation/creativity Concerning Several Rights

The third subcategory of multiple rights pertains to *group innovation, combining or resulting in several independent IP rights*. The paradigm case is a movie that is subject to a number of possibly pre-existing copyrights (screenwriter, director, etc.), as well as related rights of performers and the producer.[53]

By definition, this type of multiple rights or owners does not cause access concerns like the previous category of unilateral usage of pre-existing knowledge. The reason is that the rightholders involved have agreed to collaborate and if necessary license their rights to that end. However, in case of internal disputes, such an agreement may come to an end. One collaborator – for example a film director – may then block the whole teamwork on the basis of her individual right. Access problems thus arise from within the group and have to be addressed there.

Several legal instruments aim at avoiding this risk. Copyright law may define that only the principal director of a film is considered the author, so that the number of potential areas of conflict is limited upfront.[54] A functional equivalent with regard to group performances, such as an orchestra, is a rule specifying an agent who represents the others.[55] German law even

---

2004/48/EC (*supra* note 12), see: Ohly (2008), '"Patenttrolle" oder: Der patentrechtliche Unterlassungsanspruch unter Verhältnismäßigkeitsvorbehalt? – Aktuelle Entwicklungen im US-Patentrecht und ihre Bedeutung für das deutsche und europäische Patentsystem', *GRUR Int.*, pp. 787 et seq.

[52] See *The Authors Guild, Inc. et al. v Google Inc.* SDNY Case No. 05 CV 8136-DC, Amended Settlement Agreement, Art. 1.134, 17.33.

[53] On this terminology, see Peukert (forthcoming 2011), 'Related Rights', in Basedow, Hopt and Zimmermann (eds), *Encyclopaedia of European Private Law*, http://www.ssrn.com/abstract=1550084.

[54] See Art. 2(2) Dir. 2006/115/EC (*supra* note 37) ('The principal director of a cinematographic or audiovisual work shall be considered as its author or one of its authors. Member States may provide for others to be considered as its co-authors.'); regarding the term of protection, see Art. 2(1) Dir. 2006/115/EC.

[55] See Art. 8 RC (*supra* note 37) ('Any Contracting State may, by its domestic laws and regulations, specify the manner in which performers will be represented in connection with the exercise of their rights if several of them participate in the same performance'); Sec. 80 German CA (*supra* note 23) regarding economic rights in joint performances: these rights are held jointly ('*zur gesamten Hand*'); contrary to

limits the moral rights of group performers to ease the exploitation of such performances.[56] The rules regarding works made for hire under US law and *oeuvre collective* under French copyright law consolidate the rights with the employer, commissioner or other investor.[57] The same effect is achieved with a statutory transfer or an assumption of such a transfer in favor of the (film) producer.[58] A similar effect is achieved by provisions vesting the employer of inventors, authors, etc. in one way or another with the exclusive rights to market the respective product.[59]

3.4. Cumulation of Different IP Rights

The fourth type of multiple rights relates to a *cumulation of different IP rights in one product*. The typical case is a bottle, which is protected by copyright as applied art, by design law and possibly as a three-dimensional trademark.[60]

This situation entails unique difficulties. First, the rules benefitting employers may differ. Whereas the creator may still hold the copyright, her design rights may be allocated to the employer.[61] I am not aware of rules addressing this particular conflict. Neither is the problem resolved as to which balance *erga omnes* applies if the cumulative rights have a

---

good faith ('*Treu und Glauben*'), none of the performing artists involved may refuse his approval for an exploitation.

[56] Sec. 74(2) German CA (*supra* note 23): limitation of the right to be identified in the case of joint performances; if it is an unreasonable burden to mention each performer, only the group name has to be mentioned (s. 1); only an elected board, director or agent is entitled to speak for the group (ss. 2, 3).

[57] See 17 USC § 201(b) (*supra* note 14); Art. 113-2, L113-5 CPI (*supra* note 14) ('*L'oeuvre collective est, sauf preuve contraire, la propriété de la personne physique ou morale sous le nom de laquelle elle est divulguée. Cette personne est investie des droits de l'auteur.*').

[58] See Art. 19 RC (*supra* note 37) ('Notwithstanding anything in this Convention, once a performer has consented to the incorporation of his performance in a visual or audio–visual fixation, Article 7 shall have no further application.') and Sec. 92 German CA (*supra* note 23) regarding performers; regarding authors of pre-existing works and film authors, see, in the same vein, Secs. 88, 89 German CA.

[59] See Secs. 5 et seq. German Employee Inventions Act (*supra* note 3); Sec. 2(2) German Topographies Protection Act (*supra* note 29); Sec. 7(2) German Design Protection Act (*supra* note 27), Art. 14(3) Reg. (EC) 6/2002 (*supra* note 4).

[60] On the possible cumulation of copyright and design protection, see Art. 96 Reg. (EC) 6/2002 (*supra* note 4); Art. 16, 17 Dir. 98/71/EC (*supra* note 27); 17 USC § 113(b) (*supra* note 14).

[61] This may be the case under German law; compare Sec. 43 German CA (*supra* note 23) and Sec. 7(2) German Design Protection Act (*supra* note 27).

divergent scope of exclusivity. The landmark case in EU law is the 1997 ECJ decision *Dior/Evora*, which had to cope with different reaches of exhaustion of trademarks and copyrights.[62] Without going into the details of this matter, such protection overlaps can only be resolved by applying a 'horizontal' approach in search of overarching, general principles that form the basis of all IP rights.

3.5. Parallel Territorial Rights

The final subcategory of multiple rights concerns the territorially limited reach of IP rights. No subject matter is uniformly protected by one global right. Instead, inventions, works, signs, etc. are subject to a bundle of up to 150[63] and more territorial rights of national or regional provenance. This territoriality principle[64] has consequences for the international jurisdiction of courts – especially in proceedings concerned with the registration or validity of registered rights[65] – and on the applicable law, which for many IP-related aspects like the scope and duration of rights is each

---

62 ECJ, case C-337/95, [1997] ECR I 6013, *Dior v Evora,* paras. 37, 38; German Federal Supreme Court, Case I ZR 256/97, 4 May 2000, paras. 21 et seq., BGHZ 144, 232 – *Parfumflakon*; Kur (1999), 'Händlerwerbung für Markenartikel aus urheberrechtlicher Sicht – Präsentationsrecht als neue Schutzschranke? – Bemerkungen zu i. S. Dior ./. Evora', *GRUR Int.*, pp. 24 et seq.; Hoffmann (2008), *Mehrfachschutz geistigen Eigentums im deutschen Rechtssystem*, pp. 104 et seq.; Ineichen (2002), *Das urheberrechtlich geschützte Werk als Zeichen für Waren und Dienstleistungen*.

63 As of 6 January 2010, the WTO had 153 members (see http://www.wto.org/english/theWTO_e/whatis_e/ tif_e/org6 _e.htm (accessed 6 January 2010)), 164 contracting parties signed the Berne Convention (see http://wipo.int/treaties/en/ShowResults.jsp?lang=en&treaty_id=15 (accessed 6 January 2010)), and 173 the Paris Convention (PC) (see http://www.wipo.int/treaties/en/ShowResults.jsp?lang=en&treaty_id=2 (accessed 6 January 2010)).

64 See Art. 5(2) BC (*supra* note 19); Art. 4bis Paris Convention for the Protection of Industrial Property, available at http://www.wipo.int/treaties/en/ip/paris/ (accessed 2 February 2010); Supreme Court of the German Reich, Case II 409/26, 20 September 1927, RGZ 118, 76, 80 et seq.; German Federal Supreme Court, Case Ib ZR 92/62, 22 January 1964, BGHZ 41, 84; ECJ, case C-192/04, [2005] ECR I-7199, *Lagardère v SPRE*; Supreme Court of Japan *IIC* (1998), 331.

65 See Art. 22(4) Council Regulation (EC) No. 44/2001 of 22 December 2000 on jurisdiction and the recognition and enforcement of judgments in civil and commercial matters, OJ L 012, 16 January 2001, p. 1; ECJ, case C-4/03, [2007] ECR I-6509, *Gesellschaft für Antriebstechnik mbH & Co. KG v Lamellen und Kupplungsbau Beteiligungs KG (GAT/LuK)*, paras. 14 et seq.; ECJ, case C-539/03, [2006] ECR I-6535, *Roche Nederland BV and Others v Frederick Primus and Milton Goldenberg*, paras. 18 et seq.; *Voda v Cordis Corp.*, 476 F.3d 887 (Fed. Cir. 2007).

country for which protection is sought.[66] This mosaic of rights, court competences and applicable laws must not be set aside by extending the scope of national/regional IP law to activities occurring outside the respective territory.[67]

From a strictly territorial point of view, this concept does not lead to a multiplicity of rights because each right originates from a distinct legislature and is in principle independent of other rights in force in another territory. Only *within* a national/regional IP framework can one reasonably discuss different ownership structures and their impact on exclusivity.

Such a hermetical separation of parallel territorial protection, however, has never been accepted. First, the difficulties of exploiting and enforcing over 150 rights have led to proposals to consolidate international jurisdiction with one court that may apply one IP law only, particularly in 'ubiquitous', internet-related infringement cases.[68] The problems of identifying a universally competent court and an IP law with the closest connection to an inherently global dispute are somewhat similar to the as yet unresolved case of overlaps of IP rights.[69] In both situations, one protection scheme shall take precedence over others that are, however, in principle equally applicable.

Secondly, and even more importantly, activities of the rightholder and other users outside a country of protection are not completely irrelevant for the internal scope of exclusivity. The most important example[70] for

---

66 See Art. 8 Regulation (EC) No. 864/2007 of the European Parliament and of the Council of 11 July 2007 on the law applicable to non-contractual obligations (Rome II), OJ L 199, 31 July 2007, p. 40.

67 See *Microsoft v AT&T*, 127 S.Ct. 1746 (2007); see also Canadian Supreme Court *Society of Composers, Authors and Music Publishers of Canada v Canadian Assn. of Internet Providers* 2004 SCC 45, [2004] 2 SCR 427.

68 See American Law Institute (2008), *Intellectual Property Principles Governing Jurisdiction, Choice of Law, and Judgments in Transnational Disputes*, §§ 204, 321; European Max-Planck-Group for Conflict of Laws in Intellectual Property (CLIP), 'Principles for Conflict of Laws in Intellectual Property', 2d preliminary draft (6 June 2009), Art. 2.203, 3.603, available at http://www.ip.mpg.de/ww/de/pub/forschung/forschungsarbeit/cl_ip_eu/home.cfm (accessed 6 January 2010).

69 See *supra*, section 3.4.

70 There are other, more specific situations where the multiplicity of parallel territorial rights does have an impact on exclusivity. Here one can mention the need to streamline the relationship between national and regional protection for the same territory (see Art. 92 Reg. (EC) 2100/94 (*supra* note 4): no cumulative protection by a community plant variety right and a national plant variety right or any patent for a specific variety) and rare cases of conflict between different owners of parallel rights in identical subject matter due to political developments

the significance of extraterritorial behavior is the principle of exhaustion of rights (implied license/first sale doctrine). If the rightholder puts copies of copyrighted works or products under a trademark or embodying a protected invention, design, etc. on the market, she cannot control the subsequent circulation of these copies/products. Instead, the owners of the tangible property in the copy/product are entitled, without the authority of the holder of the IP right concerned, to sell or otherwise dispose of it. This limitation of exclusivity is not only triggered by local sales, etc. of the rightholder (national exhaustion), but in many jurisdictions also by placing the copy/product on a regional or even any international market.[71] Such regional or international exhaustion can also be conceived of as a way to streamline the multiplicity of parallel territorial IP rights. The limitation of the right to distribute copies/products fosters the free movement of goods and at the same time respects the rights of owners of tangible property.

3.6. Summary

In summary, the impact of multiple rights or owners on exclusivity is thus twofold. Either exclusivity is limited vis-à-vis third parties to allow access, incremental innovation and the free circulation of goods – this is the case for unilateral combination or adaptation of protected subject matter, for cumulation of different rights and for parallel territorial rights. Or exclusivity is limited only with regard to certain other affected rightholders to prevent internal logjams – this kind of relative limitation concerns independent creations and group innovation.

---

like German unification (see German Law on the Extension of Industrial Property Rights (*Gesetz über die Erstreckung von gewerblichen Schutzrechten*), available at http://bundesrecht.juris.de/erstrg/ index.html (accessed 20 January 2010)) or an expropriation (see ECJ, case C-192/73, [1974] ECR 731, *Van Zuylen frère v Hag* ('Hag I'); ECJ, case C-10/89, [1990] ECR I-3711, *Van Zuylen frères v Hag* ('Hag II')).

[71] All three solutions can be found for different categories of protected inventions in Art. 9(a) Swiss Patent Act (*Patentgesetz*), available at http://www.admin.ch/ch/d/sr/2/232.14.de.pdf (accessed 20 January 2010). See also 17 USC § 109 (*supra* note 14); *Quanta Computer, Inc. v LG Electronics, Inc.*, 128 S.Ct. 2109 (2008) (first sale doctrine in US patent law); Art. 13 Reg. (EC) 207/2009 (*supra* note 4); Art. 21 Reg. (EC) 6/2002 (*supra* note 4); Art. 16 Reg. (EC) 2100/94 (*supra* note 4); ECJ, case C-51/75, [1976] ECR 811, *EMI v CBS*, paras. 8 et seq.; ECJ, case C-479/04, [2006] ECR I-8089, *Laserdisken v Kulturministeriet*, paras. 57, 75 (principle of regional exhaustion in the EU). There is no international consensus or harmonization in this respect; see Art. 6 TRIPS (*supra* note 1).

Table 10.1 Multiple rights/owners and the impact on exclusivity

Ownership structure: multiple rights/owners	Impact on exclusivity
Unilateral combination/ adaptation	General limitation of exclusivity (e.g. transformative use/compulsory licensing)
Cumulation of different rights	General limitation of exclusivity (problem: which scope of protection is applicable?)
Parallel territorial rights	General limitation of exclusivity (e.g. exhaustion)
Double innovation/parallel trademarks	Relative limitation of exclusivity (e.g. prior use rights)
Group innovation/creativity	Relative limitation of exclusivity (e.g. works made for hire/*oeuvre collective*)

4. COLLECTIVE OWNERSHIP

The second major variation from individual ownership is *collective ownership*. Collective ownership is characterized by the fact that – as in the case of individual ownership – only *one IP right* is at stake. However, this IP right is *held by a plurality of persons*. Two subcategories with different repercussions on exclusivity can be distinguished: joint or co-ownership on the one hand and, in the field of trademark law, collective marks and geographical indications on the other.

4.1. Joint Ownership

Joint ownership is again a case of group innovation. It occurs, for example, if two inventors jointly develop a new technology, two authors write a detective story, etc. In contrast to a film or an orchestra performance, the collaboration does not result in multiple subject matters and rights, independently held by different owners. Instead, joint ownership concerns one subject matter of protection only. Since there is only one object – the technology, the detective story – there is also only one IP right.

As regards the ownership of this IP right, European and US law speak of joint or co-ownership or *propriété commune*.[72] In spite of this termino-

[72] See Art. 2(2) Dir. 2009/24/EC (*supra* note 19) ('In respect of a computer program created by a group of natural persons jointly, the exclusive rights shall be owned jointly.'); ditto Art. 4(3) Dir. 96/9/EC for copyrights in databases (*supra*

logical coherence, it seems that there are diverse views on what this means exactly. Neither international IP conventions nor EU law regulate the internal structure of such groups.[73] Instead, the applicable general contract or company law governs the relationship of joint owners among themselves and vis-à-vis third parties. Even at national level, a horizontal approach to IP law reveals little consistency. German law, for example, treats joint ownership of copyright differently from joint ownership of industrial property rights. Due to the fact that a German *Urheberrecht* cannot be assigned at gross,[74] a joint creation of a work leads to a so-called *Gesamthandsgemeinschaft*. Thus, there are no distinct assets in the copyright as such, but only one rightholder composed of several partners.[75] In contrast, an industrial property right filed jointly is held by a so-called *Bruchteilsgemeinschaft*. In this case, the joint inventors, designers etc. control distinct shares in the right, which can also be transferred separately.[76] If it is true that joint innovation and creativity become ever more frequent, it seems vital to have legal security at the level of the applicable

---

note 19); Art. 11(2) Reg. (EC) 2100/94 (*supra* note 4) ('If two or more persons bred, or discovered and developed the variety jointly, entitlement shall be vested jointly in them or their respective successors in title.'); Art. 14(2) Reg. (EC) 6/2002 (*supra* note 4) ('if two or more persons have jointly developed a design, the right to the Community design shall vest in them jointly'); Art. L113-3 CPI (*supra* note 14) ('*L'oeuvre de collaboration est la propriété commune des coauteurs.*'); 17 USC § 201(a) s. 2 (*supra* note 14) ('authors of a joint work are coowners of copyright in the work'); 35 USC §§ 116, 262 (*supra* note 14) (joint owners of a patent based on a joint application).

73 Regarding Art. 59 EPC (*supra* note 14), see Melullis (*supra* note 37), Art. 60 no. 20; apparently also Kühnen (2008), in Schulte (ed.), *Patentgesetz mit EPÜ*, 8th ed., § 6 no. 19 et seq.; regarding Reg. (EC) 6/2002 on community designs (*supra* note 4), see Ruhl (2007), *Gemeinschaftsgeschmacksmuster*, Art. 14 no. 10–12; but see Art. 11(5), 28 Reg. (EC) 2100/94 (*supra* note 4) (shares of jointly held community plant variety rights).

74 See *supra*, section 2.

75 See Sec. 8(1) s. 1 German CA (*supra* note 23) ('*Das Recht zur Veröffentlichung und zur Verwertung des Werkes steht den Miturhebern zur gesamten Hand zu . . .*') and Secs. 705 et seq., 718, 719 (partnership), 2032, 2033 (community of heirs) German Civil Code (*supra* note 7); Düsseldorf Court of Appeals, Case I-20 U 72/06, 25 November 2008, *Zeitschrift für Urheber- und Medienrecht Rechtsprechungs-Dienst (ZUM-RD)* 2009, 182.

76 See Secs. 7 s. 2 German Design Protection Act (*supra* note 27), Sec. 6 s. 2 German Patent Act (*supra* note 25), Sec. 2(1) s. 2 German Topographies Protection Act (*supra* note 29), Sec. 13(3) Utility Models Act (*supra* note 2) and Secs. 741 et seq. German Civil Code (*supra* note 7) (*Bruchteilsgemeinschaft* – Co-ownership); German Federal Supreme Court, Case X ZR 223/98, 17 October 2000, *GRUR* 2001, 227 – *Rollenantriebseinheit*.

law as well as in substantive law. Topics like this, cutting across IP laws and general private law, are therefore important fields for future comparative research.[77]

Returning to our general question: What is the impact of such ownership structures on exclusivity? First of all, the general limits of exclusivity apply unmodified. The reason is that there is only one IP right in one subject matter held by one group of people – as in the paradigm case of individual exclusivity.[78] As in the case of group innovation resulting in multiple rights (e.g. a movie),[79] the specific problem posed by joint ownership pertains to *internal* disputes. The necessity to agree on a mode of exploitation increases transaction costs and can even prevent desirable uses. Therefore, the law should help to coordinate the internal operations of the group.

Irrespective of the applicable contract or company law, I have come across some specific IP provisions addressing this issue. Absent an agreement to the contrary, US and French patent law authorize each of the joint owners of a patent to exploit the invention without the consent of and without accounting to the other owners.[80] German copyright law is a little more restrictive. Alterations to the jointly created work shall be permissible only with the consent of all authors; however, a joint author may not unreasonably refuse her consent to the publication, exploitation or alteration of the work. In addition, each one is entitled to assert claims arising from infringements of the joint copyright, but payments may only be demanded on behalf of all the joint authors.[81]

4.2. Collective Marks/geographical Indications

The previous analysis concerned group innovation and creativity resulting in a patent, copyright, design right, etc. Again, trademark law has to be considered separately.

First of all, I did not encounter specific rules on joint ownership in trademarks. For example, the EU regulation on Community trademarks

---

77 See Henke et al. (2009), Internationale Vereinigung für den Schutz des Geistigen Eigentums (AIPPI), 'Der Einfluss der Mitinhaberschaft an Rechten des geistigen Eigentums auf deren Verwertung (Q194)', *GRUR Int.*, pp. 818 et seq.

78 See *supra*, section 2.

79 See *supra*, section 3.3.

80 35 USC § 262 (*supra* note 14); Art. L613-29 CPI (*supra* note 14); see also Art. L113-3 CPI concerning jointly created works.

81 Sec. 8(2) German CA (*supra* note 23); Waldenberger (1991), *Die Miturheberschaft im Rechtsvergleich*.

provides that any natural or legal person may become a proprietor. Companies or firms and other legal bodies shall be regarded as legal persons if they have the capacity in their own name to have rights and obligations of all kinds. Thus, the owner of a trademark has to be a single person in legal terms. The reason is that trademarks are not allocated to the person or group that has created the sign but to the natural or legal person using it in commerce to identify *itself* or *its* product. A plurality of independent, lawful users of a sign would thwart the purpose of trademark law to prevent confusion.

Formally, collective marks also constitute a case of individual ownership to which the general rules on trademarks apply *mutatis mutandis*.[82] Collective marks distinguish the goods or services of the members of an association from those of other undertakings. These marks are not owned by individual market participants, but by an association of manufacturers, producers or – under US law – even a nation or a state.[83] The members entitled to use the collective mark may bring an action for infringement only if the association as the proprietor agrees.[84] Thus, collective marks are owned by one person, but they may be lawfully used and enforced by a plurality of persons.

Geographical indications thus present the only example where several independent persons are entitled to protection. According to Art. 22(1) TRIPS, GIs identify a good as originating in a territory, region or locality, where a given characteristic of the good is essentially attributable to its geographical origin. In the EU, they may be protected either as a collective mark or under a specific regime.[85] According to the latter EU regulation, only a 'group' shall be entitled to apply for registration of a GI or a 'designation of origin'. Such a group may be any association, irrespective of its legal form or composition, of producers working with the same agricultural product or foodstuff.[86] A single natural or legal person may exceptionally be treated as a 'group' where that person is the only producer

---

[82] See Art. 64(3) Reg. (EC) 207/2009 (*supra* note 4); 15 USC Ch 22 § 1054 (*supra* note 14).

[83] See Art. 66 et seq. Reg. (EC) 207/2009 (*supra* note 4); Sec. 98 German Trademark Act (German TA; *Markengesetz*), available at http://www.gesetze-im-internet.de/markeng/ (accessed 20 January 2010); Art. L715-1 CPI (*supra* note 14) (*marque collective*); 15 USC Ch 22 § 1054 (*supra* note 14).

[84] Art. 72 Reg. (EC) 207/2009 (*supra* note 4); Sec. 101 German TA (*supra* note 83).

[85] See Art. 66(2) Reg. (EC) 207/2009 (*supra* note 4); Art. 15(2) Dir. 2008/95/EC (*supra* note 20) on the one hand and Reg. (EC) 510/2006 (*supra* note 33); Secs. 126–9 German TA (*supra* note 83) on the other hand.

[86] Art. 5(1), (2) Reg. (EC) 510/2006 (*supra* note 33).

in the geographical area, she engages in authentic and unvarying local methods, and the geographical area or product possesses characteristics which differ appreciably from those of neighboring areas or products.[87] Thus, individual entitlement to the protection of geographical indications is the exception, not the rule.

Collective marks and geographical indications have particular implications for exclusivity. As in the case of joint ownership of patents or copyrights, the balance *erga omnes* is not modified since only one association or group is entitled to protection. Internal transaction costs are also of lesser importance because each member may use the sign for her own purposes. Moreover, geographical indications are not transferable to groups or persons outside the respective geographical area.[88] Instead, the relevant implication for exclusivity is how one may become a member to lawfully use the collective mark or GI. In other words, the question is whether outsiders have a right to access the association or group.

Collective marks may be used only by members of the association subject to its regulations.[89] The freedom to restrict membership is, however, limited by a number of safeguards. The Paris Convention allows a refusal of protection if the collective mark is contrary to the public interest.[90] To this end, EU and German trademark law require that the regulation of the association including the conditions of membership be submitted in the course of application. If these are contrary to public policy or to accepted principles of morality, the application shall be refused.[91] Even if registered, a collective mark is subject to additional limitations compared to regular trademarks. In particular, it cannot be invoked against third parties using the sign in accordance with honest practices in industrial or commercial matters.[92] These rules are motivated by competition concerns. The ability

---

87 Art. 5(1) s. 4 Reg. (EC) 510/2006 (*supra* note 33), Art. 1 Commission Regulation (EEC) No. 2037/93 of 27 July 1993 laying down detailed rules of application of Council Regulation (EEC) No. 2081/92 on the protection of geographical indications and designations of origin for agricultural products and foodstuffs (OJ L 185, 28 July 1993, p. 5).

88 See for entitlement to apply Art. 5(2) Reg. (EC) 510/2006 (*supra* note 33); for entitlement to enforce protection, see Sec. 128 German TA (*supra* note 83).

89 See Art. 70 Reg. (EC) 207/2009 (*supra* note 4); Art. L715-1 CPI (*supra* note 14).

90 Art. 7bis(2) PC (*supra* note 63).

91 Art. 67, 68 Reg. (EC) 207/2009 (*supra* note 4); Sec. 102(1), 103 German TA (*supra* note 83).

92 Art. 66(2) s. 2 Reg. (EC) 207/2009 (*supra* note 4); Art. 15(2) s. 2 Dir. 2008/95/EC (*supra* note 20); Sec. 100(1) German TA (*supra* note 83) ('in addition to the limits of protection according to Sec. 23. . .').

to use a collective mark can be a tool of market power. Nevertheless, EU and German trademark law do not expressly provide a right to access the association. A refusal of membership application can thus only be set aside on the basis of general competition law.

Collective guarantee or certification marks (*Gütezeichen, marque collective de certification*) do not only signal that the user is a member of a certain association of producers, but also that her product complies with a specific quality standard set by this association. Correspondingly, it can be decisive to be able to use this sign in order to enter or stay in a market. To account for this additional competitive significance, the German Act against Restraints of Competition expressly prohibits objectively unjustified refusals to become a member of such an association.[93] The French CPI likewise states that the usage of a certification mark is open to any person who meets the quality standards.[94]

Geographical indications can imply even more market power. Consider how difficult it is to sell 'hard cheese' if you may not use the term 'Parmesan' or anything similar because it is reserved for members of the local consortium 'Parmigiano Reggiano'. Nevertheless, the ECJ has held that 'Parmesan' has to be produced in the Parma region of Italy according to the respective product specifications.[95] If the consortium were a closed group, it would effectively hold an exclusive right to market this kind of cheese. In order to mitigate the negative consequences of such a scenario, EU law declares that any person whose goods or services originate in a geographical area may lawfully use and claim protection for the respective GI.[96] Thus, producers of hard cheese are still able to market 'Parmesan'. They only have to move their facilities to the Parma region.

To sum up, there is a correlation between the competitive impact of collective marks and geographical indications and the right of third parties to access the associations and groups that are exclusively entitled to protection and use. The purpose of this access right is to prevent a situation where trademark law supports the formation of cartels.

---

93 Sec. 20(6) German Act against Restraints of Competition (*Gesetz gegen Wettbewerbsbeschränkungen*); available in English at http://www.bundeskartellamt.de/wEnglisch/download/pdf/GWB/0911_GWB_7_Novelle_E.pdf (accessed 6 January 2010).

94 Art. L715-2(3) CPI (*supra* note 14).

95 See ECJ, case C-132/05, [2008] ECR I-957 *Commission v Germany*, paras. 46 et seq.; Heath (2008), 'Parmigiano Reggiano by Another Name – The ECJ's Parmesan Decision', *IIC*, pp. 951 et seq.

96 See Art. 10(2), 9 (3) PC (*supra* note 63); Art. 5(1) s. 3 Reg. (EC) 510/2006 (*supra* note 33). Regarding collective marks depicting a GI, see Art. 67(2) s. 2 Reg. (EC) 207/2009 (*supra* note 4); Sec. 102(3) German TA (*supra* note 83).

5. TRADITIONAL KNOWLEDGE

The ownership structures discussed up to now form part of the classical, Western IP system. At first glance, the protection of *traditional knowledge* (TK) can also be described along those lines. The common feature of all types of traditional knowledge – ranging from technical know-how to cultural forms of expressions, signs, and genetic resources[97] – is an association with a cultural tradition as exercised by a certain community.[98] If this community is entitled to the protection of its traditional knowledge, such protection seems to be just another case of collective ownership like joint ownership and collective marks/GIs.[99]

However, such a characterization of TK is ill conceived.[100] First, the respective rules are extremely heterogeneous. There is as yet no international consensus as to why, what, how and who should be protected. Proposals and national legislations vary widely with regard to each of these fundamental questions.[101] Moreover, TK covers manifold factual situations: individual creativity resulting in individual ownership under local customary law; simultaneous group innovation; as well as the combination and adaptation of pre-existing knowledge, again by individuals or groups.[102]

---

[97] See Art. 1(a) WIPO Intergovernmental Committee on Intellectual Property and Genetic Resources, Traditional Knowledge and Folklore, 'The Protection of Traditional Cultural Expressions/Expressions of Folklore: Revised Objectives and Principles', WIPO/GRTKF/IC/9/4, 9 January 2006; Art. 2(2) WIPO Intergovernmental Committee on Intellectual Property and Genetic Resources, Traditional Knowledge and Folklore, 'The Protection of Traditional Knowledge: Policy Objectives and Core Principles', WIPO/GRTKF/IC/9/5, 9 January 2006; Lucas-Schloetter (2008), in von Lewinski (ed.), *Indigenous Heritage and Intellectual Property*, 2nd ed., pp. 339 et seq.

[98] Composite Study on Traditional Knowledge, WIPO/GRTKF/IC/5/8 (*supra* note 21), para. 71(e).

[99] See *supra* section 4.

[100] See Composite Study on Traditional Knowledge, WIPO/GRTKF/IC/5/8 (*supra* note 21), para. 24 ('However, many participants in the Committee have highlighted that these conventional IP mechanisms may not be fully consistent or adequate for the protection of TK, given the distinctive characteristics of TK as subject matter for IP protection'); Munzer, Raustiala (2009), 'The Uneasy Case for Intellectual Property Rights in Traditional Knowledge', *Cardozo Arts & Entertainment Law Journal* 27, 37.

[101] See, e.g., WIPO Intergovernmental Committee on Intellectual Property and Genetic Resources, Traditional Knowledge and Folklore, 'Final Report on National Experiences with the Legal Protection of Expressions of Folklore', WIPO/GRTKF/IC/3/10, 25 March 2002.

[102] See Art. 1(a)(cc) Protection of Folklore, Revised Principles, WIPO/

And even if one subsumes all these cases under the heading of 'community TK' because none of the original innovators or creators can any longer be identified, international model laws and national legislations do not necessarily vest the indigenous peoples or communities with exclusive rights. A WIPO report on national experiences of 2002 summarizes its findings as follows:

> . . . the vast majority of States regard expressions of folklore as the 'property' of the country as a whole (as part of the national cultural heritage). The remaining responses are more or less evenly divided between those States treating expressions as belonging to indigenous and local communities, and as the 'property' of individual artists.[103]

Indeed, a tentative survey on entitlement to the protection of TK also reveals that *state authorities* – not the indigenous communities – are the most important party involved: first of all, international treaties like the Convention on Biological Diversity and the International Treaty on Plant Genetic Resources address nation states rather than local communities. It is the *signatory states* that shall, 'subject to their national legislation, respect, preserve and maintain knowledge, innovations and practices of indigenous and local communities . . ., promote their wider application with the approval and involvement of the holders of such knowledge . . . and encourage the equitable sharing of the benefits'.[104] With *them* rests the responsibility for realizing Farmers' Rights.[105] As regards traditional

---

GRTKF/IC/9/4 (*supra* note 97) ('maintained, used or developed by such community, or by individuals'); Composite Study on Traditional Knowledge, WIPO/GRTKF/IC/5/8 (*supra* note 21), para. 130; Brahy (2008), *The Property Regime of Biodiversity and Traditional Knowledge*, pp. 296 et seq.; Art. 6 Pacific Model Law for the Protection of Traditional Knowledge and Expressions of Culture, 2002 ('traditional owners of traditional knowledge or expressions of culture means: (a) the group, clan or community of people; or (b) the individual who is recognized by a group, clan or community of people as the individual; in whom the custody or protection of the traditional knowledge or expressions of culture are entrusted in accordance with the customary law and practices of that group, clan or community'), available at http://www.wipo.int/export/sites/www/tk/en/laws/pdf/spc_framework.pdf (accessed 20 January 2010).

103 Final Report on the Legal Protection of Folklore, WIPO/GRTKF/IC/3/10 (*supra* note 101), para. 102.

104 Art. 8(j) Convention on Biological Diversity, Rio de Janeiro, 5 June 1992, available at http://www.cbd.int/convention/convention.shtml (accessed 20 January 2010); see, e.g., Stoll and von Hahn (2008), in von Lewinski, *supra* note 97, pp. 31 et seq.; Brahy, *supra* note 102, pp. 223 et seq.

105 See Art. 9(2) International Treaty on Plant Genetic Resources for Food and Agriculture, available at http://www.planttreaty.org/ (accessed 6 January

cultural expressions, many national and regional legislations equally provide that the respective rights are held or exercised solely by a government agency. The local communities may hold the knowledge, but they are not entitled to the protection.[106] Ultimately, the currently pending South African bill on traditional intellectual property also follows this approach. Although the indigenous community from which a 'traditional work' originated is declared to be the 'author', the ownership of 'any' copyright in a traditional work shall vest in a newly established 'National trust fund for traditional intellectual property'. Any payment made in respect of traditional IP shall be paid into this fund. Only indirectly shall it be applied 'for the benefit of indigenous communities'.[107]

An alternative solution more favorable to indigenous communities is to grant them a *veto right* regarding the exploitation of traditional knowledge. For example, the African and Pacific model laws of 2000 and 2002 respectively, as well as the Panama *sui generis* protection of collective rights of indigenous communities of 2000, require authorization by both a state agency and the local community. The latter may furthermore be entitled to a share of the earnings.[108]

2010); McManis (ed.) (2007), *Biodiversity and the Law: Intellectual Property, Biotechnology and Traditional Knowledge*; Brahy, *supra* note 102, pp. 246 et seq.

[106] See, e.g., Art. 6, 18 UNESCO/WIPO Tunis Model Law on Copyright for Developing Countries, 1976, available at http://portal.unesco.org/culture/en/files/31318/11866635053tunis_model_law_en-web.pdf/tunis_model_law_en-web.pdf (accessed 20 January 2010); Annex VII, Art. 73(2) OAPI Bangui Agreement (*supra* note 4); Art. 4(2) Ghanaian Copyright Act ('The rights of folklore are vested in the President for the people of the Republic'), Art. 59 et seq. (National Folklore Board), available at http://www.wipo.int/export/sites/www/tk/en/laws/pdf/ghana_copyright.pdf (accessed 6 January 2010); Art. 28, 29 Nigerian Copyright Act (Nigerian Copyright Commission), available at http://www.wipo.int/export/sites/www/tk/en/laws/pdf/nigeria_copyright.pdf (accessed 6 January 2010); Art. 24 et seq. Tanzanian Copyright Act (National Arts Council; funds for 'national culture'), available at http://www.wipo.int/export/sites/www/tk/en/laws/pdf/tanzania_copyright.pdf (accessed 6 January 2010); Art. 10 Indonesian Copyright Act, available at http://www.wipo.int/export/sites/www/tk/en/laws/pdf/indonesia_copyright.pdf (accessed 6 January 2010) ('. . . The State shall hold the Copyright for folklores and works of popular culture that are commonly owned . . .').

[107] See Sec. 10 (new Sec. 19(C)(3) South African Copyright Act (ZA Copyright Act)), 11 (new Sec. 21(f) ZA Copyright Act), 16 (new Sec. 40(D)(4) ZA Copyright Act) Intellectual Property Laws Amendment Bill 2007, Notice 552 of 2008, Department of Trade and Industry, Staatskoerant, 5 May 2008, No. 31026; Department of Trade and Industry, 'The Protection of Indigenous Knowledge through the Intellectual Property System, A Policy Framework', available at http://www.dti.gov.za/ccrd/ip/policy.pdf (accessed 6 January 2010).

[108] See Art. 5(1), 12(2) African Model Legislation for the Protection of the

In contrast, many indigenous peoples strive for full autonomy to decide, which would mean *sole ownership*.[109] The 2007 UN Declaration and the 2008 draft American Declaration on the Rights of Indigenous Peoples acknowledge this point of view at a human rights level.[110] The 2006 draft provisions of the WIPO Intergovernmental Committee apparently follow this line of thinking too.[111] Protection shall directly benefit individual or collective holders of TK, taking into account local laws and customs. Finally, some national acts on *sui generis* TK protection grant the communities the right to apply for registered exclusive rights.[112]

If no formal registration is required, it is, however, extremely difficult to identify the community entitled to protection and the agents who may act for it.[113] The South African bill on traditional IP, for example, defines 'indigenous community' as 'any community of people currently living

---

Rights of Local Communities, Farmers and Breeders, and for the Regulation of Access to Biological Resources, 2000, available at http://www.cbd.int/doc/measures/abs/msr-abs-oau-en.pdf (accessed 20 January 2010); Art. 20 Panama Law No. 20, 26 June 2000 on the special intellectual property regime upon collective rights of indigenous communities, for the protection of their cultural identities and traditional knowledge, and whereby set forth other provisions; available at http://www.wipo.int/export/sites/www/tk/en/laws/pdf/panama_indigenous.pdf (accessed 6 January 2010); Art. 15(1) Pacific Model Law (*supra* note 102).

109 See Mataatua Declaration on Cultural and Intellectual Property Rights of Indigenous Peoples, June 1993, available at http://www.wipo.int/export/sites/www/tk/en/folklore/creative_heritage/docs/mataatua.pdf (accessed 6 January 2010).

110 See *infra* notes 125, 126.

111 See Art. 2, 4(a) Protection of Folklore, Revised Principles, WIPO/GRTKF/IC/9/4 (*supra* note 97); Art. 1(5) Protection of Traditional Knowledge, WIPO/GRTKF/IC/9/5 (*supra* note 97).

112 See WIPO, 'Comparative Summary of Existing National Sui generis Measures and Laws for the Protection of Traditional Knowledge', available at http://www.wipo.int/export/sites/www/tk/en/laws/pdf/grtkf_ic_5_inf_4_annex.pdf (accessed 6 January 2010), pp. 18–20.

113 Gupta (2004), *WIPO-UNEP Study on the Role of Intellectual Property Rights in the Sharing of Benefits Arising from the Use of Biological Resources and Associated Traditional Knowledge*, p. 27 ('Some participants in the current debates on IP and benefit-sharing over TK assume a uniform homogeneity between all members of a local community; that is, an assumption that there is a convergence between the interests of local community leaders and those of local experts and TK holders. However, this is often very far from reality. The asymmetry in knowledge systems and related power differentials are apparent in global discourses on incentives and consultations. Such global discourses have often been dominated by the so-called representatives of indigenous communities, often themselves of Western origin, and both in identity and in their ways of approaching an issue.'); Abeyesekere (2007), 'The Protection of Expressions of Folklore in Sri Lanka', *IIC*, pp. 187 et seq.

within the borders of the Republic, or which historically lived in the geographic area currently located within the borders of the Republic'.[114] The problems of designating an owner of TK and delineating the communities are certainly one important practical reason for the still eminent role of state authorities.

The exceptional character of TK protection also proves true at the level of exclusivity. In particular, classical IP on the one hand and TK protection on the other have different attitudes towards the public domain.[115] The latter is not a secondary feature of the IP system. In fact, the public domain is the fundamental principle from which IP rights depart. These are 'islands of exclusivity in an ocean of freedom'.[116] Therefore, they are limited in scope and time.[117] Any knowledge must at some point in time become part of the public domain to fuel a free public discourse and competition. A kind of cultural conservation via IP is incompatible with this thinking.[118]

These fundamental principles, in turn, do not apply to traditional knowledge. Some proposals and existing national legislation provide for an unlimited term of protection.[119] Others apply retroactively. The South African bill, for example, confers copyright on a traditional work if the

---

114 See Sec. 1 (new Sec. 1(c) Performers' Protection Act 1967) 2007 ZA IP Amendments Bill (*supra* note 107).

115 See also Hilty, *supra* note 9, p. 899 with further references; Godt (2007), *Eigentum an Information*, p. 379.

116 See Geiger (2004), 'Fundamental Rights, a Safeguard for the Coherence of Intellectual Property Law?', *IIC*, pp. 268, 272; Peukert, *supra* note 21, pp. 784 et seq., 891 et seq. with further references.

117 See US Constitution, Patent and Copyright Clause (*supra* note 12); House of Lords *Donaldson v Beckett* 2 Bro.P.C. 129 (1774); German Constitutional Court, Case 1 BvR 766/66, 8 July 1971, BVerfGE 31, pp. 275, 286 et seq. (no eternal copyright); for patent law, German Constitutional Court, Case 1 BvR 1864/95, 10 May 2000, *NJW* 2001, pp. 1783, 1784; draft bill for the German Copyright Act 1965, Bundestags-Drucksache IV/270, 33; Dietz (2006), in Schricker (ed.), *Urheberrecht*, 3rd ed., before §§ 12 et seq. no. 33 et seq. with further references.

118 See Dietz, in Schricker, *supra* note 117, before §§ 12 et seq. German CA no. 34 with further references. With regard to traditional knowledge, see also von Hahn (2004), *Traditionelles Wissen indigener und lokaler Gemeinschaften zwischen geistigen Eigentumsrechten und der public domain*, pp. 324, 349.

119 Sec. 6 Tunis Model Law (*supra* note 106), (exclusive rights without time limit exercised by competent authority); Art. 9(1) Protection of Traditional Knowledge, WIPO/GRTKF/IC/9/5 (*supra* note 97) ('Protection of traditional knowledge against misappropriation should last as long as the traditional knowledge fulfills the criteria of eligibility for protection according to Article 4. . .'). On existing national legislation see Final Report on the Legal Protection of Folklore, WIPO/GRTKF/IC/3/10 (*supra* note 101), Annex I, p. 24 (11 countries that provide

work was created within a period of fifty years preceding the coming into force of the act.[120] In terms of classical IP, this would be considered a very problematic, retroactive encroachment upon the public domain.[121]

It is true that indigenous communities reject such a concept of the public domain. Since traditional knowledge was never protected under classical IP, it could not be said to have entered the 'public domain'. They claim instead that this knowledge has been, is, and will be regulated by customary law to be recognized by governments.[122] The problem with that attitude is that one cannot claim exclusive protection akin to classical IP without respecting the public domain, which is the other side of the coin.

It should have become clear that neither the ownership structures nor the exclusive protection of traditional knowledge can be conceived in terms of classical, Western IP. This is equally true regarding the underlying human rights. It is not the right to property[123] which is concerned, but the right of all peoples to self-determination.[124] By virtue of that right we freely pursue our economic, social and cultural development.[125] The right

---

specific protection for expressions of folklore answered the question of a limited time of protection with 'no').

[120] See Sec. 7 (new Sec. 3(1A) Copyright Act 1978), 2007 ZA IP Laws Amendment Bill (*supra* note 107).

[121] See Art. 18(1) BC (*supra* note 19), Art. 70(3) TRIPS (*supra* note 1) ('There shall be no obligation to restore protection to subject matter which on the date of application of this Agreement for the Member in question has fallen into the public domain.'); *Golan v Gonzales*, 501 F.3d 1179 (10th Cir. 2007) with further references.

[122] See Protection of Folklore, Revised Principles, WIPO/GRTKF/IC/9/4 (*supra* note 97), Annex, p. 40.

[123] Art. 27(2) Universal Declaration of Human Rights ('Everyone has the right to the protection of the moral and material interests resulting from any scientific, literary or artistic production of which he is the author').

[124] Hilty, *supra* note 9, p. 910; Godt (2009), 'Enforcement of Benefit-Sharing Duties in User Countries', in Kamau and Winter (eds), *Genetic Resources, Traditional Knowledge and the Law*, pp. 419, 429.

[125] See Art. 1(1) International Covenant on Economic, Social and Cultural Rights (1966), available at http://www2.ohchr.org/english/law/cescr.htm (accessed 20 January 2010); Art. 1, 27 International Covenant on Civil and Political Rights (1966), available at http://www2.ohchr.org/english/law/ccpr.htm (accessed 20 January 2010); Art. 20(1) 1981 African Charter on Human and Peoples' Rights, available at http://www.africa-union.org/official_documents/Treaties_%20Conventions_%20Protocols/Banjul%20Charter.pdf (accessed 20 January 2010); Art. 2 Vienna Declaration on Human Rights (1993), available at http://www2.ohchr.org/english/law/vienna.htm (accessed 20 January 2010); UNESCO (2005), Convention on the Protection and Promotion of the Diversity of Cultural Expressions ('The protection and promotion of the diversity of cultural expressions presuppose the recognition of equal dignity of and respect for all cultures, including

to cultural self-determination forms the basis of the more specific right of indigenous peoples under Art. 31 of the 2007 UN Declaration on the Rights of Indigenous Peoples to 'maintain, control, protect and develop their intellectual property over their cultural heritage, traditional knowledge, and traditional cultural expressions'.[126] A protection scheme for TK relying on this foundation would have to look different from most of the former and current IP-style proposals.[127] Nevertheless, such an effort seems worthwhile in light of the misconceptions and failed attempts of the past.

6. CONCLUSION

Unfortunately, it is difficult to put the subject of this chapter in a nutshell. Starting from individual ownership, different cases of multiple and collective ownership, as well as TK protection, each have different repercussions on exclusivity. Nevertheless, one can classify these implications into two groups.

In some situations, the balance *erga omnes* is no different than in the 'normal' case of individual ownership. Third parties may use the respective knowledge only according to the general limitations and exceptions. This concerns independent double innovations, group innovation concerning several rights (film), and joint ownership. The specific problem here is that more than one person is entitled to use and decide about a subject matter. This, in turn, leads to increased transaction costs and possible internal logjams. IP law reacts by limiting the exclusivity of individual owners vis-à-vis the other owners involved. Examples are prior use rights, the consolidation of all rights with the employer or investor, and rules to allow each partner of a jointly held right to independently exploit the subject matter. Collective marks and geographical indications also fall into this category. Depending upon their competitive significance, the associations or groups entitled to their protection may be compelled to

---

the cultures of persons belonging to minorities and indigenous peoples.'), available at http://portal.unesco.org/en/ev.php-URL_ID=31038&URL_DO=DO_TOPIC&URL_SECTION=201.html (accessed 20 January 2010); Art. 3 United Nations Declaration on the Rights of Indigenous Peoples (2007), available at http://www.un.org/esa/socdev/ unpfii/en/drip.html (accessed 20 January 2010).

[126] See also Article XXVIII Draft American Declaration Rights of Indigenous Peoples (2008), GT/DADIN/doc.334/08, available at http://www.oas.org/consejo/CAJP/Indigenous%20documents.asp#Record (accessed 20 January 2010).

[127] Brahy, *supra* note 102, p. 364.

Table 10.2 Ownership structures and their impact on exclusivity

Ownership structure	General implications for exclusivity	Only relative (internal) implications for exclusivity
Double innovation/creativity and parallel trademarks		X
Group innovation/creativity concerning several rights		X
Joint ownership		X
Collective marks/ geographical indications		X
Unilateral combination/ adaptation of protected subject matter	X	
Cumulation of different IP rights	X	
Parallel territorial rights	X	

admit outsiders. The scope of protection in general, however, is not modified due to this particular ownership structure.

Other situations do imply modifications of the general balance. This holds true of unilateral combinations or adaptations of pre-existing subject matter, which are facilitated by limitations like free or transformative use or via compulsory licensing. The cumulative protection of products by different IP rights raises the question of how to streamline overlapping rights and limitations. Similar problems are posed by parallel territorial IP protection whose negative effects on the free circulation of goods are reduced by regional or international exhaustion of rights.

Finally, traditional knowledge should not be conceived in terms of IP ownership and exclusive rights at all because these concepts necessarily imply a tribute to the public domain. No one owns knowledge in the public domain. And that status, to be clear, is not the exception, but the rule.

11. Proprietary transactions in intellectual property in England and Germany: transfer of ownership, licensing, and charging

Stefan Enchelmaier*

1. INTRODUCTION

In the following, we shall consider proprietary transactions in intellectual property: transfer of ownership, licensing, and charging. The legal regime governing these transactions in England and Germany,[1] respectively, will be analysed with regard to patents, trade marks, and copyright. As it turns out, there are many similarities between the two legal systems, many of which these days are due to the harmonisation of intellectual property law through European Union law. Nevertheless, some fundamental differences in approach remain, in particular with regard to copyright. Leaving

---

* Dr. iur. (Bonn), LL.M. (Edinburgh), MA (Oxon), Professor of European and Comparative Commercial Law, York Law School, University of York. Many thanks are due to Professor Bill Cornish for his very helpful comments on a draft of this chapter. None of my opinions or errors should, however, be imputed to him. Thanks also to Professor Willem Grosheide for his suggestions.

[1] 'England' or, in legal terms, 'England and Wales' means that part of the United Kingdom which is neither Scotland (which has been in political and partial legal union with England since 1707) nor Northern Ireland (which came into existence in 1921 on the formation in the southern part of the island of Ireland of the Republic of Ireland or *Eire*). The substantive provisions on intellectual property discussed in the following apply identically to all parts of the United Kingdom. Occasionally, there are separate procedural rules for Scotland (see, e.g., s. 114B Copyright, Designs and Patent Act (CDPA) 1988), and adaptations of expressions for Scotland (as in, for instance, s.177 CDPA 1988). Without putting too fine a point on it, it is fair to say that England as the biggest, most populous, and historically the most powerful part of the United Kingdom has had a dominant influence on those provisions that apply throughout the realm. For this reason, the text above focuses on England rather than on the other constituent parts of the United Kingdom.

aside the detailed rules for each type of intellectual property, there are also marked differences in legal technique. While English intellectual property law is now mostly governed by statute, the (judge-made) common law both complements the provisions in the various acts, and influences their interpretation. Conversely, English legislation is typically piecemeal yet very detailed in the rules that it does establish; the legislature leaves the rest to the common law. German law, by contrast, seeks to develop specific rules from overarching principles. These principles are at times expressly articulated in the statute; copyright law offers an example of this technique. Apart from this, however, German intellectual property law cannot be fully understood without the interpretation given to it by the courts (and by legal academics, whose role is much more integral to the shaping of German intellectual property law than that of their English colleagues in relation to English law).

It is trite law to state that intellectual property rights are property and as such at the disposition of their owner; they are his to hold and to employ for his own purposes, or, against remuneration, to let others have them or share in them in one form or another. The differences between intellectual property on the one hand, and tangible property (land or chattels) on the other, are less marked in this respect than when it comes to defining and defending intellectual property, given its non-exclusionary, non-possessory nature. If there are differences between the modes of transferring tangible and intellectual property, respectively, they stem from the fact that the law was generally slower in recognising as property intangibles of any kind, and in devising rules for proprietary transactions in such assets. Financing techniques since the industrial age, with its huge and permanent demand for working capital, depend heavily on the use of contractual claims as collateral. Lately, intellectual property has emerged as a store of wealth, too. The value of a good number of companies, not only in the software industry, lies primarily in their intellectual assets. Nevertheless, it was only in the nineteenth century that the law in this area took the shape still recognisable today. Much intellectual property legislation is of even more recent vintage. Land law, by contrast, developed much earlier and has been stable for much longer.

England and Germany are paradigm cases of two very different patterns of legal development. English politics and English law enjoyed a continuous development, free from any violent external interference, since the last successful invasion into the country, by the Normans in 1066. Germany, by contrast, was the battlefield of most major European conflicts, saw several profound upheavals in her political and legal system, had weak central authorities for most of her history, and only in the late nineteenth century achieved modern statehood and the unified legal system that goes with it. On the positive side, the late adoption of the Civil Code (*Bürgerliches Gesetzbuch* or BGB) meant that the code's provisions on the transfer of intangibles were adapted to modern needs. The code specifically encompasses intellectual property rights as 'other rights' and makes the legal regime for the assignment of contract claims applicable to them, §413 BGB.

The book (sub-set of rules) of the BGB on property law also makes provision for the use of intangibles as security. As with regard to chattels, these proved less geared towards the needs of business practice. This is because they require the transfer of possession (if constructive) for chattels, and notification of the third party debtor in the case of contract debts. Intellectual property rights, however, do not suffer from this drawback: they do not involve a bi-partite relationship in which a third party (the secured creditor) becomes involved. Their use as security for debts is instead hampered by the fact that the typical financier has no need for, and little experience in dealing with, intellectual property rights. Such lenders instead prefer security that can be more easily realised, such as book debts, shares, or stock-in-trade.

English law, by comparison, has to this day retained many of the institutions that developed over its long history. Its pragmatism has, however, largely ensured that they did not become a hindrance for trade and industry. For a meaningful discussion of proprietary transactions involving intellectual property rights in English law, the distinction between law and equity (with medieval roots) has to be borne in mind. *At law,* an assignment of choses in action (as opposed to choses in possession or 'tangibles') was in principle not possible.[2] It was permissible only *in equity.* This changed only with the Victorian reforms (Supreme Court of Judicature Acts) of 1873/75. A further distinction that was necessary before then was that between legal and equitable choses in action. To put it simply, in the context of intellectual property there is a legal chose in action if a statute recognises an interest in an invention, creation, etc., as enforceable. If there is no statutory recognition, such as when the parties have failed to comply with all the statute's conditions for such recognition, there can still be an equitable chose in action. The distinction between legal and equitable assignments thus refers to the way the assignee acquires rights in an intangible, and to the nature of these rights; the distinction between

2 For a short overview, see *Holt v Heatherfield Trust,* [1942] 2 KB 1 (KBD), 3 f. (Atkinson J); *Colonial Bank v Whinney,* (1885) LR 30 Ch D 261 (CA), 276 f. (Cotton LJ), 284 (Lindley LJ), 286 f. (Fry LJ).

legal and equitable choses in action, by contrast, focuses on the object of the transaction and of the resulting rights.

Vis-à-vis debtors of the assignor, the position of the acquirer of an interest in the intangible has also changed as a consequence of the 1873/75 reform. Previously, the assignee could sue in his name only on an equitable chose in action. By contrast, if he wanted to enforce a legal chose in action he required the assignor's consent. The assignor was bound in equity to allow the assignee to use his (the assignor's) name to bring the action.[3] In order to obtain this consent if it was not volunteered, the assignee had to turn to the court of equity, which would compel the assignor to allow the action in the court of law to go ahead.[4] This clumsy necessity of proceedings in two different courts for the realisation of a single claim[5] is today dispensable under s.136 of the Law of Property Act (LPA) 1925 which replaced the provision of s.25 No. 6 of the Judicature Act 1873.[6] It enables the assignee to realise his rights without having to involve the assignor as either co-plaintiff or defendant.[7]

---

3 *Glegg v Bromley* [1912] 3 KB 474 (CA), 489 (Parker J).

4 *Holt v Heatherfield Trust* [1942] 2 KB 1 (KBD), 3 (Atkinson J).

5 *Torkington v Magee* [1902] 2 KB 427 (Divisional Court), 430.

6 S.136 reads:

Legal assignments of things in action – (1) Any absolute assignment by writing under the hand of the assignor (not purporting to be by way of charge only) of any debt or other legal thing in action, of which express notice in writing has been given to the debtor, trustee or other person from whom the assignor would have been entitled to claim such debt or thing in action, is effectual in law (subject to equities having priority over the right of the assignee) to pass and transfer from the date of such notice –
(a) the legal right to such debt or thing in action;
(b) all legal and other remedies for the same; and
(c) the power to give a good discharge for the same without the concurrence of the assignor:
Provided that, if the debtor, trustee or other person liable in respect of such debt or thing in action has notice –
(a) that the assignment is disputed by the assignor or any person claiming under him;
or
(b) of any other opposing or conflicting claims to such debt or thing in action;
he may, if he thinks fit, either call upon the persons making claim thereto to interplead concerning the same, or pay the debt or other thing in action into court under the provisions of the Trustee Act 1925.
(2) . . . (3) . . . .

For a transfer of equitable interests as opposed to debts or legal things in action, s.53(1)(c) LPA 1925 requires only writing.

7 *Tolhurst v The Associated Portland Cement Manufacturers (1900), Ltd.* [1903] AC 414 (HL), 424 (Lord Lindley); *Holt v Heatherfield Trust* [1942] 2 KB 1 (KBD), 4 (Atkinson J).

Most laws on intellectual property now contain specific provisions for the assignment of items of the type of intellectual property governed by the respective statute. These provisions apply with precedence over the general rule in s.136 LPA 1925. The latter provision comes to apply only in the absence of specific rules on assignment in the individual statutes. For present purposes, two limitations apply: first, s.136 applies only to presently existing choses in action; the provision does not allow for the assignment of future intangibles. Secondly, s.136 allows only for an assignment of the chose in action as a whole. The assignment of parts of an intangible is not possible under that provision[8] – £500 out of £1000, say, or of a trade mark for footwear only, not also for spectacle frames and other goods it is registered for.

An assignment that complies with the requirements of the various statutes on intellectual property is known as a 'legal assignment' or, more precisely, an assignment *at law*. If the assignment fails to comply with these requirements, it may still be valid *in equity*. For this to be the case, however, the conscience of the proprietor must be bound by the interest of the would-be assignee. To this end, it is necessary that the acquirer of the interest has given valuable consideration, typically by paying the agreed price. Otherwise, there is a mere *nudum pactum,* whose breach will give rise to a claim in damages, but not to any interest in the intellectual property right that was the intended object of the transaction. Furthermore, if the acquirer is not on notice of any older or stronger competing rights ('equities') held by third parties in the same item of intellectual property, he takes his interest free from these higher-ranking interests. If the acquirer has notice, he takes the interest 'subject to equities'.

Lastly, some intangibles do not permit any transfer because they are personal in nature. This can be said in two respects: first, the relationship between the parties to a contract can be so close, economically or personally, that the debtor would not have contracted with any person but his present creditor. Also (under the same heading), the nature or extent of the obligation might change significantly with the different needs of the assignee.[9] Secondly, some intellectual property rights (or aspects thereof)

---

8 *In Re Steel Wing Company, Ltd.* [1921] 1 Ch 349 (ChD), 354 (PO Lawrence J).

9 For an example, see *Tolhurst v The Associated Portland Cement Manufacturers (1900), Ltd.* [1902] 2 KB 660 (CA), 668 f. (Collins MR): duty of the owner of a quarry to supply the demand in chalk of a cement factory whose former owners had assigned their rights to their successor, who now wanted to expand the facilities. See also *Kemp and Others v Baerselman* [1906] 2 KB 604 (CA), where the benefit was held unassignable of a contract between a food trader and a cake manufacturer for the supply by the trader of the manufacturer with all

are so intimately linked to the personality of the owner, and to his creativity, that an assignment to a third party is not conceivable, at least not if it purports to encompass these aspects.

From these premises follow five theses that will be explained in turn: first, intellectual property is transferable in principle; secondly, inchoate and future intellectual property can be the subject of proprietary rights (interests); thirdly, however, moral rights of the creators of intellectual property cannot be transferred; fourthly, proprietors may limit the (further) transferability of their (former) intellectual property and rights therein; fifthly, security interests can be taken over intellectual property.

2. INTELLECTUAL PROPERTY IS TRANSFERABLE IN PRINCIPLE

2.1. Patents and Patent Licences

2.1.1. Patents

2.1.1.1. Germany Pursuant to §15(1), 2nd sentence PatG (German Patents Act 1980, as subsequently amended),[10] the patent right (that is, the legal position as defined in §23(1)) can be transferred to an unlimited or to a limited extent. By contrast with the provision of §15(2) on licences, subs. 1 does not define the differences between limited and unlimited transfers. Usufruct (§§1068 ff. BGB) and pledge (§1273 BGB) certainly count as limited transfers;[11] an assignment by way of security, on the other hand, is an unlimited transfer although it imposes on the secured creditor obligations as defined in the credit agreement.[12] When in doubt it will be assumed that the patent proprietor ceded only as few of his rights as necessary,[13] a general principle of German intellectual property law that has found legislative expression in §31(5) UrhG (Copyright Act).

---

the eggs of a specified quality 'that he shall require for manufacturing purposes for one year'.

[10] For the consolidated German text, see http://bundesrecht.juris.de/bundesrecht/patg/gesamt.pdf.

[11] Kraßer, *Patentrecht,* 5th ed., §40 III 1 (p. 951); Benkard and Ullmann, *PatG,* 10th ed., §15 no. 42; Götting, *Gewerblicher Rechtsschutz*, 8th ed., §25 no. 19.

[12] *Contra,* but without reasons, Mes, *PatG*, 2nd ed., §15 no. 10.

[13] BGH of 11.4.2000, X ZR 185/97, II 1 c = *GRUR* 2000, pp. 788, 789 – '*Gleichstromsteuerschaltung*' – applies to the transfer of a patent application.

2.1.1.2. England S.30(1), (2) PA 1977 declares the patent personal property. This means that it can be transferred by way of sale or of security (mortgage). A co-owner needs the other co-owners' consent to the sale of his share in the patent (s.36(3)(b)); in every other respect, the proprietor of a patent is free to deal with it as he sees fit.[14] The object of the transfer is the patent as a whole. A partitioning of patents is not provided for in the Act. Every patent application must describe one invention (only), or several that are so closely connected as to form a single inventive concept, s.14(5)(d). This is meant to prevent the inventor from obtaining, as it were, 'two patents for the price of one'.[15] These rules, however, only exclude a partial assignment *at law*. The Act, in ss.8(8) and 37(6), recognises equitable interests in patents. In the same vein, the Court of Appeal has held that while according to s.32(3), trusts may not be entered in the register, equitable assignments may be so entered as 'transactions . . . affecting rights in . . . patents', s.32(2)(a),[16] even if the transaction creates a trust in favour of the assignee.[17]

The transition of the right takes place outside the register as s.30 does not make the transfer dependent on an entry in the register.[18] The provisions on the proprietor's rights against infringers (ss.60, 61) do not refer to the 'registered proprietor' but to the proprietor *simpliciter*. These rights may therefore be exercised by whoever is legitimated as the proprietor by an unbroken chain of assignments, regardless of whether the same person appears as proprietor in the register.[19] Nevertheless, as the register is *prima facie* evidence of ownership, s.32(9), *bona fide* acquisition from a non-owner is possible, but vulnerable to a rectification of the register at the behest of the true owner, either before (s.8(2)(a)) or after the granting of the patent (s.37).

---

[14] *National Carbonising Co., Ltd., v British Coal Distilation Ltd.* [1936] 2 All ER 1012 (CA), 1015 f. (Slesser LJ), 1020 (Romer LJ) [LexisNexis].

[15] Cornish and Llewelyn, *Intellectual property*, 6th ed., no. 4-15.

[16] *In Re Casey's Patents, Stewart v Casey* [1892] 1 Ch 104 (CA), 110 f. (Lindley LJ), 113, 116 (Bowen LJ): '[i]f it is an equitable assignment, it is a document which affects the proprietorship of the patent. It does not alter the proprietorship, but it affects it because it gives a man a right in equity to have it altered at law'; 119 (Fry LJ).

[17] *Performing Rights Society, Ltd., v London Theatre of Varieties* [1922] 2 KB 433 (CA), 454 f. (Younger LJ), on copyright.

[18] Clark and Cornish, *Encyclopedia of UK and European Patent Law*, no. 8-104 by and in note 10.

[19] *Xtralite (Rooflights) Ltd. v Hartington Conway Ltd.* [2004] RPC 7 (ChD) = [2003] EWHC 1872 (Ch), para. 25 (Pumfrey J).

2.1.2. Patent licences

2.1.2.1. Germany Licences under §15(2), 1st sentence PatG, are temporary transfers of some of the rights of the patentee except for the right to dispose of the patent altogether.[20] They are a subdivision of transfers under sub-1[21] and, hence, limited transfers of the patent.[22]

The *Bundesgerichtshof* (Federal Court – Germany's highest court in civil matters) has left open the question whether licences are mere 'negative' licences, whereby the licensor only promises not to invoke his rights as against the manufacture and marketing by the licensee of products embodying the protected invention; or whether the licensor has 'positive' duties to allow the licensee to use of the invention, and to support him against infractions by third parties.[23] The latter view appears preferable,[24] not least because the former cannot explain why the licensor should not be allowed to turn against the customers of the licensee, against whom he has not undertaken any obligation to let them exploit his invention undisturbed.[25] Nevertheless, licences are transferable according to either view.[26] Despite the silence of the law, licences may in principle be transferred or made the subject of further (i.e. sub-) licences.

2.1.2.2. England A patent licence constitutes a limited transfer of a patent, that is, of the exclusive right to put the protected invention to commercial application. In the literature, one finds commentators who espouse the theory of 'negative' licence as explained above in the context of German law.[27] For the reasons there given, the 'positive' view should prevail in English law, too. The parties are largely at liberty to define their mutual rights and obligations,[28] the Act offering pointers rather

20 Lindenmaier, Weiss, *PatG*, 6th ed., §9 no. 28, 1st para.
21 Benkard, Ullmann, *PatG*, 10th ed., §15 no. 57.
22 Götting, *Gewerblicher Rechtsschutz*, 8th ed., §26 no. 1.
23 BGHZ 83, 251 (256) = KZR 5/81 of 23.3.1982, 2 a – '*Verankerungsteil*'.
24 Kraßer and Schmid (1982), GRUR Int., pp. 324 (328 f. at II 1 a).
25 Kraßer (1983), *GRUR Int.*, pp. 537 (542 f. at 4–6, 547 at 5–7); *idem*, *GRUR Int.* 2002, pp. 381 (383 at b).
26 Bartenbach (2002), *Mitt.*, pp. 503 (514 at i aa, bb).
27 Demetriades, Kelly, and Vivis (2008), 'Assignment', in Demetriades, (ed.), *Intellectual Property Issues in Commercial Transactions,* para. 2-02: 'a licence of intellectual property is in essence a grant of permission by the licensor to the licensee to undertake certain otherwise prohibited acts'.
28 Cornish and Llewelyn, *Intellectual property*, 6th ed., no. 7-19.

than compulsory provisions.[29] The Act does, however, draw a distinction as to the rights of exclusive and non-exclusive licensees, respectively, see ss.38(3), 46(4), 67. The exclusive licensee has the same right as the proprietor of the patent to bring proceedings in respect of any infringements of the patent (s.67). He prevails even as against the proprietor himself (ss.67(3), 130).

2.1.3. Comparative conclusion

Despite differences in the technical details, patents and patent licences are fully marketable property rights in both jurisdictions.

2.2. Copyright as a partial exception

2.2.1. Germany: The Non-transferability of Copyright

Since its reform in 1965,[30] copyright in German law is subdivided in several respects. At its core is the author's personality right *(Urheberpersönlichkeitsrecht)* which manifests itself in three rights: the right to make the work known to the public (*Veröffentlichungsrecht,* §12 UrhG), to be recognised as the author (§13), and to turn against distortions (*Entstellung;* 'derogatory treatment' in English parlance) of the work, §14.[31] As a consequence, the author may at any time and under any circumstances renounce his earlier works and revoke any rights over them that he has granted to third parties, §42(1), (2) UrhG. In another category are the author's rights to derive economic benefit from his works *(Verwertungsrechte),* with several subdivisions, such as the right to make copies, to distribute, to exhibit, and to perform and broadcast the work.[32] In an innominate category *(sonstige Rechte)* are the right to have access to the physical original of the work, to be remunerated for the renting and leasing of the work, and the *droit de suite*.[33] Juxtaposed to the author's economic rights *(Verwertungsrechte)* are the rights to exploit the work which the author can grant to third parties (*Nutzungsrechte,* §29(2) UrhG)

---

[29] Clark and Cornish, *Encyclopedia of UK and European Patent Law*, no. 8-406.

[30] Gesetz über Urheberrecht und verwandte Schutzrechte (Urheberrechtsgesetz – UrhG) of 9.9.1965, as subsequently amended; consolidated German version under http://bundesrecht.juris.de/bundesrecht/markeng/gesamt.pdf.

[31] §§12–14 UrhG.

[32] §15 Abs. 1, §§16–18 UrhG; §15 Abs. 2, §§19–22 UrhG. The enumeration of *Verwertungsrechte* in §15 is, however, not exhaustive: Schricker and von Ungern-Sternberg, *UrhR*, 3rd ed., §15 nos. 18, 22, 23.

[33] §§25–27 UrhG.

and which allow these third parties to copy, distribute, exhibit, broadcast etc. the work.[34] The provision of §31(1), 2nd sentence (*Nutzungsrechte* may be granted on an exclusive or non-exclusive basis; they may be restricted as to their territory, duration, and content) reveals them to be akin to licences over other types of intellectual property.[35]

The foundation of this conceptual edifice is the idea that the work is an expression of the author's personality (*persönliche geistige Schöpfung*, §2(2) UrhG). From this follows the goal of the law, as expressed in §11, namely to protect the tie between the author's personality and his work, and to ensure that the author receives adequate remuneration for his creativity. As a consequence, the author's personality rights and his economic rights are inalienable, §29(1). This is known as 'monism': the author's idealistic and economic interests are inseparably intertwined.[36] In this sense, the recognition by the law of *Urheberpersönlichkeitsrecht* is not purely idealistically motivated, nor is the motivation of the *Verwertungsrechte* exclusively economic.[37] Instead, these two strands are integrated into one another.[38]

The *Nutzungsrechte,* by contrast, are not subject to the same restrictions. Nevertheless, they too always retain a link with the author's personality rights. This is despite the fact that according to §97, an exclusive 'licensee' (for want of a more proximate English translation of *Nutzungsberechtigter*) may prohibit even the author from making such uses of the work as are allowed to the licensee and not expressly retained

---

[34] Wandtke, Bullinger, Wandtke and Grunert, *UrhG*, introduction before §§31 nos. 19, 20; Dreier, Schulze and Schulze, *UrhG*, 2nd ed., §15 no. 6; Schricker and Schricker, *UrhR,* 3rd ed., introduction before §§28 ff. no. 20, according to whom the various designations mark a functional difference (funktionalen Unterschied).

[35] Schricker and Schricker, *UrhR*, 3rd ed., introduction before §§28 ff. no. 21, who prefer to use the term 'licences' for those rights that are derived from *Nutzungsrechte;* likewise Dreier, Schulze and Schulze, *UrhG*, 2nd ed., §31 no. 4. The differences in terminology do not result in different outcomes.

[36] The literature on this point abounds; see, e.g., Schricker and Schricker, *UrhR*, 3rd ed., Introduction no. 21; *idem*, §11 no. 2; Schricker and Dietz, *UrhR*, 3rd ed., introduction before §§12 ff., no. 6; Dreier, Schulze and Schulze, *UrhG*, 2nd ed., §11 no. 2; Möhring, Nicolini and Ahlberg, *UrhG*, 2nd ed., Introduction, no. 12; Wandtke, Bullinger and Bullinger, *UrhG*, §11 no. 1; Dreier, Schulze and Schulze, *UrhG*, 2nd ed., introduction before §28 no. 1; Schricker and Dietz, *UrhR*, 3rd ed., introduction before §§12 ff., no. 11; Ulmer, *UrhR*, 3rd ed., pp. 113, 114; Rehbinder, *UrhR*, 14th ed., no. 92. On the development of this doctrine, see Rehbinder, *UrhR*, 14th ed., no. 31; Ann (2004), *GRUR Int*., pp. 597, 598–600; Hilty (2002), *Festschrift für Rehbinder*, pp. 259, 261–7.

[37] Götting (1995), *Festgabe für Schricker*, pp. 53, 65.

[38] Dietz (2002), *Festschrift für Erdmann*, pp. 63, 65.

by the author. The granting of the *Nutzungsrechte* must be conceived of as a 'constitutive' act that creates these rights from scratch, rather than a 'derivative' or 'translative' grant by which the author assigns some of his rights to another person, as the latter would go against the inalienable nature of the author's rights.[39]

These distinctions, motivated by the concern to maintain the intimate link between the author and his work,[40] may appear obscure enough already.[41] What is more, they create a paradox: on the one hand, the author and his creative personality is exalted and given far-reaching control over any dealings involving the work. On the other hand, monism is meant to protect the author against unforeseen consequences of his own ill-considered transactions concerning the work.[42] No other group of persons is afforded such protection, although it is not obvious that authors are more vulnerable than other adults of full capacity.

This is not to say that authors' creativity does not deserve special protection. This protection should, however, be tailored to this specific goal, that is, the link between the author's personality and its manifestation in the work. To this end, *Dietz* has suggested a distinction between the author's personality rights in the narrow and in the wide sense.[43] The former, as laid down in §11 UrhG, gives the author the right to respect of said link, and is inalienable;[44] the latter comprises the author's *Verwertungsrechte* which should be assignable[45] as long as the conditions of the assignment

---

[39] Again, there is ample literature on this; see, e.g., Rehbinder, *UrhR,* 14th ed., no. 559; v. Gamm, *UrhG*, §31 no. 6; similarly Loewenheim, Loewenheim and Jan Bernd Nordemann, §26 no. 1: a disposition that does split off part of the author's right but that gives rise to a new right in the person of the authorised to exploit the work ('. . . Verfügung über das Urheberrecht, die nicht nur das Mutterrecht belastet, indem sie einen Teil von ihm abspaltet, sondern auch in der Person des Nutzungsrechtsinhabers ein neues Recht (das Nutzungsrecht) entstehen läßt'); Schricker and Schricker, *UrhR*, 3rd ed., introduction before §§28 ff. no. 18, 43; §29 no. 7, 8, each with further references.; Dreier, Schulze and Schulze, *UrhG*, 2nd ed., §29 no. 3, 15; Möhring, Nicolini and Spautz, *UrhG*, 2nd ed., §29 no. 5.

[40] Schack, *UrhR*, 4th ed., no. 531, calls this an elaborate dogmatic construction ('aufwendige dogmatische Konstruktion').

[41] Rehbinder, *UrhR*, 14th ed., no. 598 even calls this a single big obscurity ('eine einzige große Unklarheit').

[42] Schricker and Schricker, *UrhR*, 3rd ed., §29 no. 4.

[43] Schricker and Dietz, *UrhR*, 3rd ed., introduction before §§12 ff. no. 6 ff.; concurring, Dreier, Schulze and Schulze, *UrhG*, 2nd ed., introduction before §12 no. 2, 3.

[44] Schricker and Dietz, *UrhR*, 3rd ed., introduction before §§12 ff. no. 26.

[45] Likewise Schricker and Schricker, *UrhR*, 3rd ed., §29 no. 4.

ensure this respect.[46] This purpose is served by those provisions in the law which protect the author and which are not at the disposition of the parties *(ius cogens)*. In particular, authors are protected against rash decisions by the requirement of writing, in conjunction with a guaranteed right to rescind for the author (§40(1), (2) UrhG), for any transactions concerning future works. In the same vein are provisions which ensure authors' adequate remuneration (§§ 26, 27, 32, 32a, 54, 54a). Another example is the requirement of consent by the author to any creditor's execution into the copyright or into unpublished originals of work protected by copyright, §§113, 114 UrhG

2.2.2. The transferability in German law of third parties' rights to exploit works protected by copyright

As we have seen, the author cannot, according to the dominant monistic interpretation of German copyright law, transfer his economic rights, but he may grant third parties the right to exploit works that are protected by his copyright, so-called *Nutzungsrechte.* These rights, in their turn, are transferable, but any assignment requires the author's consent (which may also be given to future assignments on the right's first grant), §34(1), (5). The grantee of an exclusive *Nutzungsrecht* requires the author's consent for the granting of further (that is, non-exclusive) licences, §35(1), 1st sentence. Consent is unnecessary only if the right has been granted not in the interest of the licensee, but exclusively in the interest of the author (2nd sentence), as is the case with (not-for-profit) collecting societies as licensees.[47] Again, the parties may agree otherwise, §§35(2), 34(5), 2nd sentence.

2.3. England: Copyright and Copyright Licences

2.3.1. Copyright

The English law of copyright originates in the right of publishers ('stationers' in old usage) to prevent third parties from producing reprints ('copies')

---

45 BGHZ 126, 245 (249) = I ZR 3/92 of 16.4.1994, II 2 a, second-to-last para. – 'Namensnennungsrecht des Architekten': 'general clause'; similarly Schricker and Schricker, *UrhR*, 3rd ed., §11 no. 4, who argues that the provision gives orientation and guidelines ('Normzweckbestimmung mit Leitbildfunktion'); Schricker and Dietz, *UrhR*, 3rd ed., introduction before §§12 ff. no. 8: to be drawn on whenever required for the protection of the intellectual and personal concerns of the author ('immer dann heranzuziehen, wen es der Schutz der geistigen und persönlichen Interessen des Urhebers erfordert').

47 Schricker and Schricker, *UrhR*, 3rd ed., §35 no. 3, 10.

of works in which they had acquired the rights from authors.[48] Copyright is, in this sense, 'the right to make copies'.[49] From the perspective of the author, it is the right to determine whether and how to derive economic benefit from the publishing of the work. The starting point is, hence, the gainful exploitation of the work, not the creative process. In this, *Cornish* and *Llewelyn* identify an 'old strain of common law thought which sees no difference of kind between true creators and investors in the creation of others; and which is inclined to prefer the latter to the former'.[50]

The categories of protected works as the subject-matter of copyright are, in ss.1–8 CDPA 1988, defined largely in similar terms to German copyright law. Nevertheless, s1(1) expressly classifies copyright as a property right in the types of work subsequently listed. As a consequence, copyright can be transferred by assignment, s.90(1), either in whole and for its entire duration or, by virtue of sub-s.(2), as to individual acts reserved to the author in accordance with s.16, or for a shorter duration; a subdivision by place of exercise, however, is not possible.[51] These are all instances of legal assignments:[52] the partial right becomes the assignee's without any residual interest in the assignor.[53] The assignee is henceforth capable of enforcing the copyright independently of the assignor.[54]

The (self-employed) author is, hence, only the first owner of the copy-

---

48 Cornish and Llewelyn, *Intellectual Property*, 6th ed., no. 10-01 ff.; for details, see *Copinger and Scone James on Copyright*, no. 2-09–2-39; Davies, *Copyright and the Public Interest*, 2nd ed., no. 4-001–4-023.

49 Bainbridge, *Intellectual Property*, 6th ed., p. 30.

50 Cornish and Llewelyn, *Intellectual property*, 6th ed., no. 11-01; less critical are *Copinger and Scone James on Copyright*, no. 2-05 and Bently and Sherman, *Intellectual Property Law*, 2nd ed., p. 30: 'The common law copyright model is said to be primarily concerned with the production of new works. This is reflected in copyright law's emphasis on economic rights, such as the right to reproduce copies.'

51 *Copinger and Scone James on Copyright*, no. 5-99; Mathys, Mitchell, and Demetriades, (2008), 'Assignment', in Demetriades, (ed.), *Intellectual Property Issues in Commercial Transactions*, para. 1-12, contend that '[i]t is also possible to limit the assignment to specific territories', but the following examples are all of substantive divisions of the copyright assigned.

52 *Chaplin v Leslie Frewin (Publishers), Ltd., & anor.* [1966] Ch 71 (CA), 93 (Danckwerts LJ): 'The statutory method of assignment of copyright is by writing signed by the copyright owner, and so *that form of transfer is fully effective at law*' (emphasis added).

53 *Performing Rights Society, Ltd., v London Theatre of Varieties* [1924] AC 1 (HL), 28 f., 37 (Lord Sumner): 'partial assignments do not mean incomplete assignments but assignments of part . . .'.

54 *Jonathan Cape Ld. v Consolidated Press Ld.* [1954] 1 WLR 1313 (QBD), 1317 (Danckwerts J).

right (s.11(1) CDPA 1988);[55] ownership and authorship can subsequently become separated.[56] Nevertheless, the author always retains his right to an equitable remuneration from the rental right.[57] He may assign this right only to a collecting society (s.93B(2), 1st para.). Once any of the author's rights are assigned, they can no longer be acquired from the author by a third party acting in good faith.[58]

The author's moral rights, by contrast, are not assignable (s.94). Among these are the right to be identified as the author ('paternity right')[59] (s.77), which must, however, be asserted (s.78). Conversely, it is a moral right of the author not to have someone else's work attributed to himself (s.84).[60] Another moral right is the right to object to derogatory treatment of the work (s.80, 'integrity right').[61] The legal position is, thus, what German law might look like, were it not for its monistic approach to copyright. In practice, however, and in accordance with the code of conduct of the British publishers' association,[62] exclusive licences occur more often than

---

55 See already *University of London Press, Ltd., v University Tutorial Press, Ltd.* [1916] 2 Ch 601 (ChD), 612 (Peterson J).

56 Bainbridge, *Intellectual Property*, 6th ed., p. 78.

57 This default position instead of an exclusive right in the author is based on the exception in Art. 6(1) of Directive 2006/115/EC of the European Parliament and of the Council of 12 December 2006 on rental right and lending right and on certain rights related to copyright in the field of intellectual property (codified version), [2006] OJ L376, p. 28.

58 *Ward, Lock & Co., Ltd., v Long* [1906] 2 Ch 550 (ChD), 559 (Kekewich J) – this remains valid despite the criticism of the judgment in *Performing Rights Society, Ltd., v London Theatre of Varieties* [1922] 2 KB 433 (CA), 457 f. (Younger LJ).

59 Thus Laddie, Prescott and Vitoria, *Copyright and Designs*, 3rd ed., para. 13.1, 13.6 ff.; Bently and Sherman, *Intellectual Property Law*, 2nd ed., p. 234; Bainbridge, *Intellectual Property*, 6th ed., p. 111.

60 Bently and Sherman, *Intellectual Property Law*, 2nd ed., p. 239: '. . . this right is effectively the flip side of the attribution right'.

61 Laddie, Prescott and Vitoria, *Copyright and Designs*, 3rd ed., para. 13.1, 13.17 ff.; Bently and Sherman, *Intellectual Property Law*, 2nd ed., p. 242; Bainbridge, *Intellectual Property*, 6th ed., p. 117.

62 English law has no rules specifically on publishing contracts, such as the German *Gesetz über das Verlagsrecht* of 1901 (subsequently amended). Instead, general contract law applies; Bently and Sherman, *Intellectual Property Law*, 2nd ed., p. 272. In this context, the principle is recognised that 'if there is one thing which more than another public policy requires it is that men of full age and competent understanding shall have the utmost liberty of contracting, and that their contracts when entered into freely and voluntarily shall be held sacred and shall be enforced by courts of justice'; *Printing and Numerical Registering Co. v Sampson* (1874–75) LR 19 Eq. 462 (Ct of Chancery), 465 (Sir George Jessel MR) on the assignment of a patent; virtually identical for copyright Bently and Sherman, ibid.

assignments.[63] The opposite might have been expected in light of the weaker position of a licensee compared to that of an assignee.[64]

2.3.2. Copyright licences

S.90(4) CDPA 1988 does not itself give, but presupposes, the proprietor's right to grant licences in the copyright. Remarkably, although the licence confers a legal right (because the Act in principle attributes it binding force against successor in title of the licensor's), a licence can be overcome by a purchaser in good faith and for valuable consideration, as if the licence were a mere equity. The Act is silent on whether licences may be transferred. This will be for the licensing agreement to stipulate. If the parties have not made any provision in this respect, the nature of the respective rights and duties will determine whether the bond between the parties is so close that it must not be severed by substituting another person for the licensee without the licensor's consent. Nevertheless, if the licence is assignable, the assignment will, in the absence of specific provisions in the CDPA, be governed by s.136 LPA 1925.

2.3.3. Comparative conclusion

Copyright displays most differences between the two jurisdictions. The deviation arises from the German copyright reform of 1965 which remodelled the Copyright Act along monistic lines. Nevertheless, much as German lawyers (and on this occasion, law makers, too) revel in sophisticated conceptual constructs, the practical results are not too far apart.

2.4. Trade Marks and Licences thereof

2.4.1. Trade marks

2.4.1.1. Germany § 27(1) MarkenG (Trade Marks Act 1994, as subsequently amended)[65] allows the proprietor to assign his rights in the trade mark to third parties; the mark can also be transmitted by, for instance,

---

63 Bently and Sherman, *Intellectual Property Law*, 2nd ed., p. 255, fn. 35.

64 See on this question *Frisby v British Broadcasting Corporation* [1967] Ch 932 (ChD), 948 (Goff J); *Copinger and Scone James on Copyright*, no. 5-201; Bently and Sherman, *Intellectual Property Law*, 2nd ed., p. 255; on the distinction between partial assignment and licence, see *In Re Jude's Musical Compositions* [1907] 1 Ch 651 (CA), 661 (Fletcher Moulton LJ), 662 f. (Buckley LJ).

65 For the consolidated German text, see http://bundesrecht.juris.de/bundesrecht/markeng/gesamt.pdf.

succession.[66] Assignment is governed by the provision in the Civil Code on the transfer of claims, §398 BGB, which is applicable to 'other' (that is, debtor- and creditor-less, i.e. 'absolute') rights by virtue of §413 BGB.[67] Trade marks are, thus, fully merchantable. Before the partial reform of 1992,[68] under the old §8 WarenzeichenG (Designation of Goods Act), trade marks were inseparable from the place where the proprietor manufactured the goods that bore the mark. The mark could not be transferred independently of the production plant.[69] Still of such accessory nature are business designations *(Unternehmenskennzeichen),* which German law protects specifically (§5 MarkenG),[70] whereas in English law, these would be subject only to the law on passing-off. The owner may transfer the mark for any or all goods or services for which it is registered. Partial assignments are according to classes of goods or services, whereas the graphic representation of the mark as such is indivisible.[71]

Transfer of ownership through assignment takes place outside the register,[72] which subsequently only records the change (§27(3)).[73] For this reason, there can be no *bona fide* acquisition of a trade mark from a registered non-owner: the register has no substantive effect on the ownership of the mark.[74] There is only the presumption for the purpose of any proceedings, before the patents office or in court, that the person on the register is entitled to the mark; third parties are not bound by this, but they bear the burden of proving that they are the true proprietor.[75]

---

66 'Transmission' refers to a transfer by operation of law, such as by succession, BGH *GRUR* 2004, p. 868 = I ZR 31/02 of 9.6.2004, II 1 a (p. *8) – '*Dorf Münsterland II*'; Starck (1994), *WRP*, pp. 698, 700 at 5.

67 OLG Stuttgart *NJWE-WettbR* 1999, 260 (261 at b).

68 Gesetz über die Erstreckung von gewerblichen Schutzrechten of 23.4.1992, BGBl. I p. 398, §47; on the background, see Götting, *Gewerblicher Rechtsschutz*, 8th ed., §50 no. 4.

69 The situation under English law was similar, which additionally allowed a partial assignment if the production plant to which the mark referred was equally divided among products or categories of products, *Sunbeam Motor Co's Application* (1916) 33 RPC 389.

70 OLG Stuttgart *NJWE-WettbR* (1998), p. 183, headnote 3; Götting, *Gewerblicher Rechtsschutz*, 8th ed., §50 no. 2; critical remarks at §55 no. 26, 28.

71 Starck (1994), *WRP*, pp. 698 (699 at 2 b); Klaka (1995), *GRUR*, pp. 713 (716 at 3 b).

72 Rauch (2001), *GRUR*, pp. 588 (589, second-to-last para.).

73 Fezer, *MarkenG*, 3rd ed., §27 no. 20, 35 reaches the same conclusion; likewise Ingerl and Rohnke, *MarkenG,* 2nd ed., §27 no. 11.

74 BGH *GRUR* 1998, 699 (701) – '*SAM*'; HK-MarkenR/Pahlow, §28 no. 2.

75 BGH *GRUR* 1999, 498 (499) = I ZR 176/96 of 5.11.1998, II 1 a – '*Achterdiek*'; BGH *GRUR* 1998, 699 (701) = I ZR 113/95 of 22.1.1998, III 2 b – '*SAM*'; Fezer,

2.4.1.2. England According to 22 TMA 1994, a registered trade mark is personal property. Accordingly, it may be assigned, either with or without the business's goodwill (s.24(1)). This has been possible since the Trade Marks Act 1938.[76] By contrast, non-registered marks to this day cannot be transferred independently of the goodwill of the business that uses the mark.[77] As the statute expressly allows the assignment of registered trade marks, the assignment is a legal one. With regard to unregistered marks, the Act expressly abstains from making any rules on their assignment (s.24(6)), so that their transfer is possible only in equity. In view of the limited economic significance of unregistered trademarks,[78] no further attention appeared warranted.[79] What is more, because the Act has no other rules on unregistered marks, either, but makes them subject to the law of passing off only (s2(2)), such marks merely exist in equity. Their assignment is, hence, governed by the provision of s.53(1)(c) LPA 1925, which requires writing and signing by both parties and, like s.136, does not allow partial assignment.

Registered trade marks may also be assigned by way of security (that is, mortgaged) or encumbered with a charge (s.24(4), (5)). The mortgage gives rise to an equity of redemption in the assignor (s.26(2)). This equity allows the assignor, as long as he (or the debtor if these are two different persons) fulfils his side of the bargain, i.e. repays his debt as provided, to prevent in particular a surrender of the mark (s.45(1)) by the assignee. The equity does not, however, affect a purchaser in good faith and for valuable consideration[80] who acquires the mark before the mortgage is entered in the register. The assignor-debtor can protect himself against this by means of a forfeiture clause in the security agreement. According to such a clause, the trade mark reverts to the assignor as soon as the assignee-creditor purports to assign it free from the equity of redemption to a third party; alternatively, payment of the loan to be secured can be made conditional

---

MarkenG, 3rd ed., §28 no. 7; Rauch (2001), *GRUR*, pp. 588 (593 at 6). The situation is different with regard to Community Trade Marks: according to Art. 17(6) Reg. 207/2009, as long as the transfer has not been registered, the successor in title may not invoke the rights arising from the registration of the Community trade mark, unless the third party had knowledge of the transfer, Art. 23(2).

[76] On the development of English trade mark law in this respect and regarding licences, see *Scandecor Development AB v Scandecor Marketing AB & ors.* [2001] ETMR 74 (HL), para. 20–35 (Lord Nicholls); Kerly's Law of Trade Marks, 14th ed., no. 13-004–13-008.

[77] Bently and Sherman, *Intellectual Property Law*, 2nd ed., p. 949.

[78] Mathys et al., above note 51, para. 1-59.

[79] Morcom, Roughton and Graham, *Trade Marks,* 2nd ed., para. 11.4.

[80] Morcom, Roughton and Graham, ibid., para. 11.6.

on the mortgage becoming evident from the register. Moreover, as the assignment transfers the right to use the mark, too, the assignor needs a licence to carry on using the mark.[81]

By derogation from s.136 LPA 1925, s.24(2) TMA 1994 allows a partial assignment of the trade mark by way of legal assignment. The partition can take place along the classes of goods or services for which the mark is registered, as well as according to the manner or place of its use. Such a partition is possible also in case the assignment is by way of security (s.24(4).)

Any change of proprietor takes place outside the register;[82] the register only records the transaction that led to the change (s.25(1), (2)). The trade mark cannot be acquired *bona fide* from a registered non-owner, as the registration is *prima facie* evidence of his ownership only 'in all legal proceedings relating to a registered trade mark' (s.72). That is, this rule of evidence does not apply to the situation in which a third party purports to acquire the property from a non-owner by virtue of a contractual stipulation.

2.5. Trade Mark Licences and their In rem-Nature

2.5.1. Germany

A trade mark's proprietor is not restricted to transfer the mark definitively, be it in whole or in part. §30(1) MarkenG allows him to grant licences in the mark, that is, temporarily to transfer all or some of his rights.[83] This provision is inspired by Art. 17 of the Community Trade Mark Regulation,[84] whereas the German Trade Marks Act otherwise transposes the Trade Marks Directive,[85] which does not contain any provisions on licensing. Licences, too, may refer to any or all goods or services for which the mark is registered, and they may be limited to designated territories.

There is a controversy (and some confusion, too) about the *in rem* nature *(Dinglichkeit)* of trade mark licences. Under the previous trade mark legislation, as we have seen, the trade mark was bound to the physical organisation of its proprietor for the production or provision of the goods or services for which the trade mark was registered. This was meant

---

81 *Kerly's Law of Trade Marks*, 14th ed., no. 13-018.

82 *Kerly's Law of Trade Marks*, 14th ed., no. 13-021.

83 Ingerl and Rohnke, *MarkenG*, 2nd ed., §30 no. 27.

84 Reg. (EC) no. 207/2009, [2009] OJ L78/1, replacing and repealing Reg. (EC) no. 40/94.

85 Directive 2008/95/EC, [2008] OJ L299/25, codifying the amendments to Dir. 89/104/EEC.

to ensure that the trade mark truthfully indicated the origin of goods and services from that particular source.[86] For the same reason, the trade mark could only be transferred as a whole and in permanence.[87] Licences were inconceivable: they would have entailed the appearance on the market of goods that bore the same mark but did not originate in the same production facility.[88]

From an economic point of view, this was awkward in case the proprietor wanted to penetrate new markets but lacked the means to extend his own production plant, and could not obtain credit or did not want to incur debt to this end. It also restricted the possibilities of establishing franchising systems. Nevertheless, a contractual way around these limitations was found: the proprietor would grant third parties a 'permission to use the trade mark' *(Gebrauchsüberlassung),* carefully distinguished from an outright licence. This meant that the proprietor would still take action against those who used the mark without authorisation. At the same time, the proprietor promised the grantees of the permission that he would tolerate their use of the mark – even if as a consequence, several independent operators used the same mark for the same type of product.[89] The grantees, in turn, had no rights of their own vis-à-vis third parties using the mark without the proprietor's permission. Since the entry into force of the present *Markengesetz*, the parties may stipulate that the licensee shall have such powers;[90] in practice, however, they are unlikely to be granted to non-exclusive licensees.

Seen in this light, it is a mere question of taste whether one wants to refer to a licence as *dinglich* if it grants the licensee powers as against third party violators of the mark. This label alone, not least because it is not used in the Act, is of no consequence. What is alone relevant is whether the

---

86 von Gamm, *WZG*, § 1 no. 2, §8 no. 23, 25, with further references.

87 von Gamm, *WZG*, §8 no. 4.

88 English law before the Trade Marks Act 1994 shared this fear that assignments and licensing of trade marks might muddy the origin function of the mark. Nevertheless, in both England and Germany commercial practice and its perceived necessities eventually prevailed over what public interest there arguably is in trade marks' fulfilling their origin function. Regarding trade between Member States, the jurisprudence of the European Court of Justice has added further nuances.

89 von Gamm, *WZG*, §8 no. 14, 19, 20.

90 Lange, *Marken- und Kennzeichenrecht*, no. 1414, emphasises that the law does not determine the character of a licence but that this depends on the agreement of the parties, who are free to mould the licence as they see fit ('Das Gesetz enthält . . . keine Vorgabe für den Charakter einer Lizenz. Da im Rahmen von § 30 MarkenG Vertragsfreiheit gilt, kommt es auf die Regelung der Rechtsnatur der Lizenz im jeweiligen Lizenzvertrag an').

licensee is to be allowed of his own volition to enforce, against violators, the rights that the trade mark confers in accordance with the provisions of §§14, 17–19, 146, 147 MarkenG (prohibition of use, damages, delivery-up etc.).[91] The *Bundesgerichtshof* recognises the possibility of granting such a licence, and cites with apparent approval the prevailing opinion to the effect that exclusive licences are *dinglich* in that sense.[92] This may well be usual practice. Nevertheless, it is not inconceivable that a sole licensee (i.e. the only one at present, but who has not been promised by the proprietor that no further licences will be granted) is expressly granted any or all of these rights.[93] This would depend on the economic importance of that licensee for the business strategy of the licensor.[94]

2.5.2. England

The Trade Marks Act 1994 does not expressly allow the proprietor to grant licences, but recognises such a right by listing the grant of a licence as a registrable transaction (s.25(2)(b)), and by making provisions about licences in s.28 ff. In particular, the Act distinguishes between general licences, allowing the licensee to use the mark for all goods or services covered, and for all manners and localities of use, and limited licences, which do not (s.28(1)). Exclusive (and by implication, non-exclusive) licences are defined in s.29 similarly to a patent licence. Any combination of licences is possible, including a limited exclusive[95] and a non-exclusive general licence.

The Act contains no provisions on the assignment of licences. It does, however, allow the licensee to grant sub-licences (only) where the licence agreement so provides (s.28(4)). This must apply in equal measure to an assignment of the licence: here, too, the proprietor must be allowed to retain the right to assess for himself the suitability of anyone who is to use the mark. The same would follow from s.31(1) according to which the licence 'may' provide that the licensee shall have all the rights of the assignor, including the right to assign the respective interest in the trade

---

91 Götting, *Gewerblicher Rechtsschutz*, 8th ed., §25 no. 17 at 3 on patents, §41 no. 8 on designs, §51 no. 9 on trade marks.

92 BGH, I ZR 93/04 of 19 July 2007, para. 29 = BGHZ 173, 269 – '*Windsor Estate*'; strictly speaking, however, this was an *obiter dictum* not relevant to the outcome of the case, and para. 34 might be read to call into question whether anybody other than the proprietor may claim damages for violations of the trade mark.

93 Schanda (1994), *GRUR*, pp. 275 (286 before d).

94 Rosenberger (1983), *GRUR*, pp. 203 (203 f. at 2 b).

95 Thus expressly s.29(1): 'In this Act an "exclusive licence" means a licence *(whether general or limited)* . . .' (emphasis added).

mark. The assignment of a licence, if permitted, is governed by s.136 LPA 1925.

S.31(1) also holds the key to the question whether a trade mark licence has effects *in rem,* that is, whether the licensee can turn against any third party's infringement of the trade mark. The Act leaves this to the parties to determine. According to sub-s.(7), the licensee may in the agreement (sub-s.(8)) be granted the right to take action against infringements of the mark. In taking such action, the licensee acts in his own name (s.31(1), 2nd para). Nevertheless, the licensee's powers are limited in that he cannot go after infringements of the licensee's rights by the proprietor himself (ibid.) and, by implication, by those who act by authority of the proprietor. This is because the licensee's and the proprietor's rights are, according to s.31(2), 'concurrent'. Regardless of the rights of the licensee, the licensor may therefore continue to exercise his rights as before. Just as the licensor cannot violate his own rights, neither can he violate those of the licensee. Conversely, as both licensee and licensor act in the same sphere (and the legality of their actions can only be assessed uniformly),[96] an action by the licensee against the licensor would be an action against himself. Such an action is inadmissible: the licensee is 'not entitled to bring infringement proceedings against . . . the proprietor', (s.31(1), 2nd para. *in fine*).

2.5.3. Comparative conclusion

Trade marks and licences therein are largely freely marketable in both jurisdictions, with some limitations as to the transferability of exclusive licences.

3. INCHOATE AND FUTURE INTELLECTUAL PROPERTY CAN BE THE SUBJECT OF PROPRIETARY RIGHTS

Patents and trade marks undergo an application and examination procedure before they are entered on a public register and thus become fully enforceable against third parties. Copyright, by contrast, is not registered but arises out of the very creation of a protected work. With copyright, only future rights can be the object of proprietary transactions; with patents and trade marks, the rights flowing from the application – as distinct from the future (registered) rights – can also be transferred or encumbered.

---

[96] Similarly, *Copinger and Scone James on Copyright*, no. 5-205.

3.1. Patents

3.1.1. Germany

The German Patents Act distinguishes three rights: the inventor's right to be awarded a patent (*Recht auf das Patent*, §6); the applicant's right against the Patent Office to conclude the procedure for the award of a patent (*Anspruch auf Erteilung des Patents*, §8); and the patentee's exclusive right as flowing from the (granted) patent (*Recht aus dem Patent*, §9). §15 PatG declares all of these rights transferable. The right pursuant to §6 arises as soon as the invention is complete, i.e. when no further trials are required to solve the technical problem that is the subject-matter of the invention, and when the invention is capable of commercial or industrial application ('gewerbliche Anwendung', §1(1)).[97] The right to a patent is transferable,[98] even before completion of the invention, if it can be unambiguously determined to which future patent the invention is to relate.[99] On the same condition, the patent can be assigned;[100] even its belonging to a clearly defined technical field may be sufficient to this end.[101] The inventor may see the application process through; as soon as the patent is entered in the register, it belongs to the assignee,[102] who can have the register rectified in accordance with §30(3) PatG. Alternatively, the inventor can allow the assignee to apply for the patent in his own name or to take over an application already lodged with the patent office.

3.1.2. England

S.18(4) PA 1977 provides that the comptroller shall grant the applicant a patent if the application meets all relevant conditions (sub-ss.(1), (2), (4)). This right is akin to that granted by §8 PatG. S.30(1), (2) PA 1977 declares the application personal property (but, for no apparent reason, 'without [it] being a thing in action'). The application is, hence, assignable and capable of being mortgaged. In light of the length of the patent

---

97 Benkard and Melullis, *PatG*, 10th ed., §6 no. 7.

98 BGH of 20.2.1979, X ZR 63/77, III 1 = *GRUR* 1979, 540 (541) – '*Biedermeiermanschetten*'; OLG Frankfurt am. Main, *GRUR* 1987, pp. 886, 890 – '*Gasanalysator*'.

99 Kraßer, *Patentrecht*, 5th ed., §19 II 6 (p. 337).

100 Ibid., §40 III 2 (p. 951); Busse and Keukenschrijver, *PatG*, 6th ed., § 6 no. 28.

101 Benkard and Ullmann, *PatG*, 10th ed., §15 no. 13.

102 RGZ 139, 52 (56) – '*Kunstdarm*'; BGH of 24.3.1994, X ZR 108/91, III 2 c = *GRUR* 1994, 602 (604) – '*Rotationsbürstenwerkzeug*'; Busse and Keukenschrijver, *PatG*, 6th ed., §6 no. 28; Götting, *Gewerblicher Rechtsschutz*, 8th ed., §25 no. 5.

examination, which often takes years, this is a sensible rule,[103] enabling the inventor to derive income from the invention even before patent protection becomes fully effective. Licences and sub-licences in an application are also possible, as is their assignment and mortgaging (s.30(4)). Licences in the application may continue in existence as know-how licences if the application is withdrawn or refused before it is published (see s.16(1)). Licences granted in the patent lapse if the court orders the transfer of a patent that was granted to a person that was not entitled to it (s.38(2)). In that case, however, the licensees are entitled as against the new proprietor of the patent to a non-exclusive licence if they had, at the time of the transfer order, already worked the patent *bona fide* or had made serious preparations to do so (s.38(3)).

These are rules for the *legal* assignment and licensing of patents, patent applications, and licences therein. Even before the lodging of a patent application, assignments and licences are possible, but as transactions in future property, these will take effect in equity only.[104]

3.2. Trade marks and licences thereof

3.2.1. Germany

Future trade marks may be assigned even before an application for their registration is lodged if they are described with sufficient detail in the agreement to assign.[105] Sufficient determinants are the time or period at which an application is to be lodged, the goods or services that are to bear the mark, or particular words or sequences of signs. On registration, the right arises in the assignee,[106] who can have the register rectified (§27(3) MarkenG).

Even before then, the applicant for registration of a trade mark has a right to have the mark entered on the register *(Anspruch auf Eintragung)* against the Patents and Trade Marks Office *(Deutsches Patent- und Markenamt)* as soon as he has lodged a formally correct application and there are no absolute grounds for refusing registration of the mark (§33(2) MarkenG). This point in time also determines the priority of the mark over one whose registration is applied for later but that is entered on the register earlier (§§47(1), 6(1), (2) MarkenG). The right against the Office can also be assigned (§§31, 27(1)). The assignee will prefer this option over

103 Bainbridge, *Intellectual Property*, 6th ed., p. 429.
104 *Terrell on Patents*, no. 9.15.
105 Ingerl and Rohnke, *MarkenG*, 2nd ed., §27 no. 9.
106 BGH NJW-RR 1998, 1057 (1058).

an assignment of the future mark after registration. This is because the assignee of the rights from the application will appear on the register as soon as the mark is entered therein.

Nevertheless, the assignee of the rights that flow from the application for registration would not be protected where the assignor had already assigned his rights in the future mark (rather than in the application). Entry on the register is a condition for the protection of the mark, but it does not determine the ownership of the mark. The property in the mark arises in the first assignee (that is, the assignee of the future mark) as soon as the mark is registered. The assignor has by the first assignment used up his rights in regard to the mark, including the rights in the subsequent application for registration of the mark. He has nothing left to transfer to subsequent assignees. Should the second assignee be entered on the register, the first has a claim in unjust enrichment (§812 BGB) for the consent of the second assignee to a rectification of the register. Should the second assignee, once entered on the register, surrender the mark, such impairments of the first assignment would be void in accordance with §161(1), 1st sentence BGB. If the rights in the application were first assigned, it is the other way round. While both assignments were meant to transfer the mark to the assignee, only the first is in the power of the assignor.

§31 MarkenG declares not only the provision on assignment applicable to the rights flowing from an application for registration, but also that on licensing (§30 MarkenG). There is no provision on the licensing of purely future marks (i.e. those whose registration has not even been applied for). Nevertheless, it is a fundamental principle of German civil law that future rights can be assigned (§§398, 413 BGB),[107] and as a *minus*, that partial assignments and encumbrances of such rights are also possible (§1273 BGB).[108] Licences in future rights can, hence, also be granted. These are more common than licences in applications for registration of a trade mark: the examination period for trade marks is usually shorter than that for a patent, so that not much time would be gained.

Just as the proprietor can grant licences in his future mark, so can a licensee in principle transfer those licences to third parties. There is, however, no effective acquisition of licences in a mark that is subsequently denied registration. The same is true if the licensee grants sub-licences in a future mark. This also applies if the purported exclusive licensee of a future mark only acquires a non-exclusive or no licence at all, because the proprietor had previously granted someone else an exclusive licence. On

---

107 Palandt and Grüneberg, *BGB*, 68th ed., §398 no. 11.
108 Paland and Bassenge, *BGB*, 68th ed., §1273 no. 1.

registration of the mark, the first exclusive licensee acquires an exclusive licence, and there can be only one such licence in respect of the same goods (or services) and of the same territory. The would-be 'second exclusive licensee' acquires nothing if the proprietor, under the terms of the (first) exclusive licence, must not grant even non-exclusive licences any more.

3.2.2. England

According to s.27(1) TMA 1994, the Act's provisions on trade marks as objects of property (ss.22–6) apply likewise to applications for the registration of trade marks. Trade mark applications may, hence, be assigned absolutely or by way of security, and be encumbered by charges, ss.27(1), 24(1), (4), (5). These transactions become effective against all third parties on registration, s.25(2), (3). Because of the reference to s.24(2) in s.27, partial assignments of applications and licences in parts of an application are possible *at law*. Such assignment will result in several identical marks of different scope being entered on the register for different proprietors pursuant to s.40. An alternative to the partial assignment of the undivided application is the division of the application into several independent applications in accordance with s.41(1)(a) TMA 1994, r19(1) Trade Mark Rules 2000,[109] and the assignment of these new applications.

Apart from assigning or licensing the trade mark application, the future proprietor can do the same with the future trade mark. Because this is not, however, provided for in the Act, these transactions will be effective in equity only. As said transactions are, like trusts (s.26), not registrable, the assignment etc. of the future trade mark can be superseded by the assignment of the application to a purchaser without notice and for valuable consideration. This risk will not be present, of course, where the assignor is a subsidiary of the assignee company. Nevertheless, the assignment and licensing of the application remains the more secure and hence more attractive variant when the parties want to grant (sub-)licences to third parties.

3.3. Copyright

3.3.1. Germany

For want of an examination or entry in a register, copyright subsists in a work as soon as the work is created. §40 UrhG allows the author to

---

[109] Statutory Instruments 2000 no. 136, http://www.opsi.gov.uk/si/si2000/20000136.htm.

grant third parties rights to exploit *(Nutzungsrechte)* future works. These rights, too, can be transferred if the author consents, §34(1), and if they are exclusive rights, allow their holder to grant further rights to third parties, again with the author's consent, §35(1). Authors can grant *Nutzungsrechte* in future works (§40), but no further rights accrue in regard to such works if the agreement is terminated. The assignee of these rights (§34) can in that case have no more permanent rights than his assignor.[110] The same is true of sub-'licensees' (§35). After termination of the original agreement conferring *Nutzungsrechte* in future works on their licensor, they do not on creation of further works become sub-licensees of those who have in the meantime acquired rights in these works. In relation to these new 'licensees', there is no contractual stipulation to that effect.[111]

3.3.2. England

S.91(1) CDPA 1988 governs the transfer of future copyright. The expression 'purports to assign' encompasses both the case that the parties want the present transfer of a future right, which is to become effective as soon as the right arises; and the case that the parties want a future assignment of the right once it has arisen (agreement to assign).[112] As we have seen, future rights can not be assigned *at law* under s.136(1) LPA 1925. On a cursory reading, s.91(1) CDPA 1988 allows just this because it provides that copyright shall automatically vest in the assignee. In equity, the right would vest in the assignor, who would, however, be bound to transfer it to the assignee.[113] S.91(1) saves the assignee having to enforce his equity.[114] Nevertheless, the Act stops halfway. The automatic vesting occurs only 'if . . . the assignee . . . would be entitled as against all other persons' to the copyright. This he will not be if a third person has a better equity, such as a prior assignee, or if he is the author's employer (see s.11(2) CDPA 1988). If he holds a crystallised floating charge, he even has the legal right to sell

110 Schricker and Schricker, *UrhR*, 3rd ed., § 34 no. 22, § 35 no. 11 with references to the opposite view.

111 Similarly Schricker and Schricker, *UrhR*, 3rd ed., § 35 no. 11, with further references, who points to the limitations of a licence in accordance with its purpose ('Zweckbindung der Übertragung', § 31(5), see above), which an isolated sub-right must not exceed.

112 Laddie, Prescott and Vitoria, *Copyright and Designs*, 3rd ed., para. 23.6; *Copinger and Scone James on Copyright*, no. 5-73, 5-179.

113 *Performing Rights Society, Ltd., v London Theatre of Varieties* [1922] 1 KB 539 (KBD), 549 (Branson J); [1922] 2 KB 433 (CA), 454 (Younger LJ); *Wah Sang Industrial Co. v Takmay Industrial Co. Ltd.* [1980] FSR 303 (CA of Hong Kong), 309 (Roberts CJ).

114 Laddie, Prescott and Vitoria, *Copyright and Designs*, 3rd ed., para. 23.5.

the copyright under s.101(1)(i), (iii), (4) LPA 1925.[115] S.91(1) CDPA 1988 is, thus, a peculiar hybrid of law and equity.

S.91(3) allows the proprietor of future copyright or his assignee (see the definition in (2)) to grant licences in that copyright. As in the case of assignments just discussed, these licences are vulnerable because a *bona fide* purchaser for valuable consideration can acquire the copyright unencumbered. Once the licences have lapsed in this way, they are not revived on the transfer of the right to a subsequent purchaser who had notice of them.[116] Although the Act does not say so, it follows from general equitable principles, not abrogated by the Act, that an assignee of a licence in future copyright can, on the same conditions, acquire the licence without any sub-licences granted previously by the assignor.

3.3.3. Comparative conclusion

Inchoate intellectual property rights are well-integrated into both jurisdictions' system of rules for proprietary transactions in those rights. Nevertheless, German law again displays some peculiarities involving copyright, and English law has moved (only) one step further away from its traditional unease regarding future intangibles.

4. MORAL RIGHTS OF THE CREATORS OF INTELLECTUAL PROPERTY CANNOT BE TRANSFERRED

4.1. Moral Rights of Inventors

4.1.1. Germany

The right of the inventor to the patent (§6 PatG) has a dual nature.[117] On the one hand, it is a transferable property right. On the other hand, the invention is also a manifestation of the inventor's personality,[118] so that it has been dubbed 'technical copyright'.[119] For this reason, the inventor has

---

115 Ibid., para. 23.59.

116 Bainbridge, *Intellectual Property*, 6th ed., p. 99.

117 Busse and Keukenschrijver, *PatG*, 6th ed., § 6 no. 11.

118 Benkard and Melullis, *PatG*, 10th ed., § 6 no. 16; Kraßer, *Patentrecht*, 5th ed., §19 I 1 (p. 333); Götting, *Gewerblicher Rechtsschutz*, 8th ed., §17 no. 3, 8; Schulte (1985), *GRUR*, pp. 772 (775 at 6.): an act of creative creativity ('Akt schöpferischer Kreativität') (*sic* – to be fair, the pleonasm is less obvious in German).

119 BVerfG of 10.5.2000, 1 BvR 1864/95, II 1 = *GRUR* 2001, pp. 43 (43) – '*Klinische Versuche*'; likewise already BVerfGE 36, 281 (298 f.).

to be identified in the patent application (§37), and the application will be refused if he is not (§48). The inventor must also be identified in the patent (§63), unless he specifically wishes to remain anonymous (§63(1), 3rd and 5th sentences). This right to be identified is inseverable from the inventor and cannot, therefore, be assigned.[120]

4.1.2. England

S.13(1) PA 1977 gives the inventor the right to be mentioned as such in any patent granted for the invention, and already the application must contain this identification (sub-s.(2)). These provisions mark the right to be identified as the inventor as a subjective right of the person concerned. At the same time, however, any person alleging that somebody has been wrongly mentioned as the inventor (or one of several) can turn to the comptroller for rectification of the register (sub-s.(3)). Respect for the truth about who is the inventor is thus not only a subjective right but an objective principle; the inventor's right is merely a means to the end of helping the truth to be established. From this it follows that the right to be mentioned as the inventor cannot be assigned: in the hands of the assignee, it would lead to a falsehood appearing on the register.

4.2. Authors' Moral Rights (Urheberpersönlichkeitsrecht)

4.2.1 Germany

As we have seen, the author's personality rights comprise the rights to make the work known to the public (§12 UrhG), to be identified as the author (§13), and to prohibit derogatory treatment of the work (§14).

The right pursuant to §12 is not assignable. It enables the author to determine how he is perceived by the public; his reputation rests on the content and quality of the works that appear under his name. The definition of his own identity as a writer, composer, architect, academic, etc., depends on ultimate control over the first release into the public of his work. The same is true of the other two rights under §12, namely to communicate the contents of the work and to describe it.[121] The right under §14 complements that under §12. It enables the author to protect the creative uniqueness of his work,[122] rather than the physical integrity of its

---

120 BGH of 20.6.1978, X ZR 49/75, III 2 = *GRUR* 1978, pp. 583 (585), with a concurring annotation by Harmsen – 'Motorkettensäge'; Kraßer, *Patentrecht*, 5th ed., §19 II 5 (p. 336); Benkard and Melullis, *PatG*, 10th ed., §6 no. 17a, with further references.

121 Schricker and Dietz, *UrhR*, 3rd ed., §12 no. 28.

122 Dreier, Schulze and Schulze, *UrhG*, 2nd ed., §2 no. 11.

embodiments. The creator's renown with the audience and his peers rests on his works as put out to the public. If the decision about the initial publication cannot be left to someone else, neither can the creator leave the decision about which alterations to his works to tolerate and which not. Third persons cannot by assignment acquire the right to be identified as the author, and neither can they become the authoritative interpreters and guardians of his works' character. The right to be identified as the author (§13), finally, cannot be assigned for the simple reason that someone else would not thereby become the author of the work; to claim to be identified as such would be to insist on a lie.

4.2.2. England

Authors' moral rights – that is, the right to be identified as the author, and the right to prohibit derogatory treatment of his works (ss.77, 80 CDPA 1988) – are not assignable (s.94). As these rights are meant to offer protection to authors, rather than furnish them with a tradable asset, they may arguably not be licensed, either.[123]

4.3. Trade Marks and Licences Thereof

4.3.1. Germany

A trade mark is supposed to make the goods and services for which it is registered recognisable. It is meant to allow the consumer to distinguish these goods or services from competing offers, and to give assurance that the goods or services are of a tried and tested quality because they originate from the same source or are made under unitary control.[124] Trade marks thus identify things, not persons; in principle, therefore, personality rights do not come into play.

Nevertheless, an overlap can occur in that names of persons and their images can also serve as trade marks, §§3(1), 13(2) nos. 1, 2 MarkenG. There may also subsist copyright in the mark or some of its aspects, no. 3. The personality rights thus implicated must be respected in the

---

[123] Concurring, Demetriades et al. (above note 27), para. 2–10.

[124] BGH *GRUR* 2002, 1070 (1071 at 1, 1st para.) = I ZB 1/00 of 13.6.2002, III 1 – 'Bar jeder Vernunft'; for details on the functions of trade marks, see Fezer, *MarkenG*, 3rd ed., Introduction, nos. 30–34a, and on the MarkenG especially at nos. 39–41: product-identifying distinguishing mark ('produktidentifizierendes Unterscheidungszeichen'); Ingerl and Rohnke, *MarkenG*, 2nd ed., Introduction, no. 66; introduction before §§ 27–31 no. 1; Götting, *Gewerblicher Rechtsschutz*, 8th ed., §47 nos. 1–6, 17; Cornish and Llewelyn, *Intellectual Property*, 6th ed., no. 16-28; Wilkof and Burkitt, *Trade Mark Licensing*, 2nd ed., nos. 2-04–2-41.

course of assignment or licensing of such trade marks. At the same time, however, the holder of these rights has voluntarily employed them for commercial purposes and in the expectation of some gain from such employment; trade marks originated in industrialists using their 'good name' to warrant for the quality of their wares ('nominative mark').[125] For this reason, personality rights will only rarely hinder proprietary transactions in those trade marks. On the contrary, the person concerned, by commercialising aspects of his personality, has placed the marketability of the goods and services offered under the mark above other concerns.[126]

The *Bundesgerichtshof* initially took a different stance. On the question whether a liquidator could sell a firm (the name under which a partnership trades) containing the family name of the person controlling the insolvent company, it held in *Vogeler* that the person by the use of that firm had 'not released his name from the sphere of his personality'. His personal interest in hindering others from using his name was, therefore, not subordinate to the interests of those who might wish to acquire the mark; the mark was accordingly unassignable.[127]

This seems unconvincing: there are too many goods and services and their respective trade marks, and the legal and economic relations between their producers and/or distributors too little transparent for the public to associate any specific person with a name that might occur in a trade mark. On the contrary, the more famous the name becomes as a trade mark, the more it subsumes the real person that might have (or might once have had) that name. 'Dr. Oetker', to use a famous example, has assumed a meaning against which the historic person whom the mark originally conjured up has almost completely paled. The invocation of personality rights in this context misses the reality of an increasingly indifferent, even cynical public.[128] More realistically, the House of Lords held as early as 1863 that

---

125 Götting, *Festgabe für Beier*, pp. 233 (234 f.); Fezer, *MarkenG*, 3rd ed., Einl. no. 2; HK-MarkenR/Klippel, Einl. 1 no. 3. In England, the firm's name was one of the few marks that were at all registrable according to s.10 Trade Marks Registration Act 1875.

126 Similarly, HK-MarkenR/Pahlow, §29 no. 3 on attachment.

127 BGHZ 32, 103 (111, 113) = I ZR 159/58 of 26.2.1960, I 1 d, II – '*Vogeler*'.

128 Friedrich, annotation to *Vogeler, GRUR* 1960, pp. 490, 495, calls this false romanticism ('falsche Romantik'); this jurisprudence may be a belated echo of the view that the trade mark was an emanation of the personality of its owner ('Ausfluß der Persönlichkeit'), which prevailed until the 1920s and which was only overcome by RGZ 118, 76 (81) – '*Springendes Pferd*'; see also von Gamm, *WZG*, Introduction, no. 45, and Götting, *Festgabe für Beier*, pp. 233, 234, with further references.

a mark or a trade name can be protected even though the producer is not known to the public, provided that the public understands the mark as an indication of a trade source and hence as a quality seal.[129]

The legal context of the BGH's judgment has also changed: German law no longer requires sole traders or partnerships to indicate the names of one or more natural persons involved in the business. Pure 'fantasy firms' have been permissible since 1994,[130] which renders the use of one's real name entirely voluntary. Remarkably, the BGH acknowledged as much in a later judgment involving a German private limited company's (GmbH's) name containing a personal name, which also served as the trade mark for the company's products.[131]

The same principles apply to the licensing of a mark that contains a person's name, and to assignments of such a mark.

4.3.2. England

S.1(1), 2nd para. TMA 1994 allows the use of personal names as trade marks. The Act does not make special provisions for the assignment or licensing of marks of that kind. Such rules are dispensable when it comes to fantasy names that do not designate a real living or dead person. Arguably, none is required either for names that do. Someone who has commodified his name by using it as a trade mark cannot complain if others continue to do so after an assignment. The granting of mere licences allows him to retain control over who uses his name and how; this is of no help, however, in liquidation or administration of a company, when the liquidator or administrator seeks to realise the economic value of the mark in the interest of a company's creditors.

4.3.3. Comparative conclusion

Predictably, after the above discussion of copyright law, German law places strong emphasis on personality rights. English law, nevertheless, is not entirely averse to this concept. Not so much with the idea as with the treatment of authors' moral rights, it offers a viable compromise that takes it close to the German solution but avoids the latter's conceptual rigour in the area of copyright.

---

129 *Hall v Barrows* (1863) 4 De G.J. & S. 150 (HL), 157 (Lord Westbury LC).

130 Baumbach and Hopt, *HGB*, 32nd ed., §17 nos 2, 3, §19 no. 8.

131 BGHZ 109, 364 (367 f.) = I ZR 17/88 of 14.12.1989, three last paras. – '*Benner*'.

5. PROPRIETORS MAY LIMIT THE (FURTHER) TRANSFERABILITY OF INTELLECTUAL PROPERTY AND RIGHTS THEREIN

5.1. Patents and Patent Licences

5.1.1. Patents

5.1.1.1. Germany The limitations of a transfer under §15(1), 2nd sentence, 1st alternative PatG can refer not only to the right transferred, but to the result of the transfer, namely the power of the assignee to enter into further transactions involving the patent. There is a limited transfer if the new owner is not given the power to assign the patent, or is bound to seek the assignor's consent when purporting to do so. According to §30(3), only changes in the person of the proprietor are registrable. Later assignees cannot, hence, acquire the patent free from the restriction. The content of the register (and the absence of any notice of the restriction) is immaterial for the substantive relations between the first proprietor and his assignee,[132] and likewise between the parties to later transactions involving the patent.[133] The transfer is brought about solely by the assignment,[134] which falls outside, and is independent, of the register.[135] Entry in the register merely confers on the person entered therein procedural legitimation in accordance with §30(3), 2nd and 3rd sentences.[136]

The *Reichsgericht* (Imperial Court, the predecessor of the *Bundesgerichtshof*, 1871–1945), by contrast, argued that such restrictions were effective in contract only, i.e. between assignor and assignee, not between the assignee and third parties. This was because the provision in the Civil Code allowing restrictions of assignability (§399 BGB) did not apply to absolute rights without a debtor.[137] It is certainly true that the provisions of the code that protect the debtor against having to perform

132 Busse and Keukenschrijver, *PatG*, 6th ed., §15 no. 29, 37; Benkard and Schäfers, *PatG*, 10th ed., §30 no. 8a.

133 RGZ 139, 52 (57) – '*Kunstdarm*', adding that the acquisition of the patent is equally independent of the handing over of the patent instrument.

134 RGZ 126, 280 (284 *in fine*) – '*Lampenschirm*'.

135 BGHZ 82, 13 (17) = X ZR 57/80 of 6.10.1981, II 2, 2nd para. – '*Pneumatische Einrichtung*'; Busse and Schwendy, *PatG*, 6th ed., §30 no. 32; no. 88: the patents and trade marks office only checks the legal plausibility *(rechtliche Evidenzprüfung)* of the transfer as evident from the documents submitted.

136 Rauch (2001), *GRUR*, pp. 588, 590.

137 RGZ 127, 197 (205 at c) – '*Hakenschraubenmuttern*'; concurring, Benkard and Ullmann, *PatG*, 10th ed., §15 no. 12.

twice over in case of an assignment (§§407 ff. BGB) are not applicable to intellectual property rights.[138] Nevertheless, §413 BGB on the assignability of rights other than those resulting from a debtor/creditor relationship declares all provisions on assignment applicable to such rights *mutatis mutandis* ('entsprechend'). The Court fails to explain what these necessary adaptations might be.[139] Today, with the applicability of §§413, 399 BGB to intellectual property rights accepted, §137 BGB poses no problem either. That provision prohibits restrictions of assignments of transferable rights. Nevertheless, a right is not transferable in the first place if its proprietor is only willing to assign it stripped of the right to transfer it further.[140] At any rate, §15(1) PatG, allowing for 'limited transfers', would take precedence as the more specific provision *(lex specialis)* over the general rules of the Civil Code.[141]

5.1.1.2. England S.30(2) PA 1977 ordains the assignability of patents without adding 'to the extent that the [contract] so provides' as in the provision on licences, sub-s.(4)(a). This difference is no editorial fluke. S.30(2) governs a case of legal assignment: the Act says that the assignment is permissible, and that it must be in writing to be effective. This does not render any restrictions on further assignments illegal, merely ineffective at law. In equity, they are possible,[142] but vulnerable under the usual conditions. If the assignor wants to prevent the disappearance of the equity on acquisition by a *bona fide* purchaser for valuable consideration, there are two ways open to him.

The first way to ring-fence the non-assignability clause would be to convey not the outright title, but to grant the assignee a mere mortgage whose equity of redemption would be triggered by an acquisition apt to extinguish the equity. Such a mortgage would appear on the register (s.32(2)(a)), so that any later purchaser would be put on enquiry as to the existing equities. Alternatively, the assignor could insist on a fixed charge over the patent. As a consequence, the assignee would be unable further to assign the patent or licence without the consent of the assignor. Such a charge and mortgage would be vulnerable only in the time between when the agreement is made and its recording on the register. To guard against any risks

---

138 BGH *GRUR* 1993, 822 (823) = I ZR 194/90 of 12.11.1992, II 1, 2nd para. – 'Katalogbild'.

139 Rosenberger (1983), *GRUR*, pp. 203 (208 at c).

140 Palandt-Ellenberger, *BGB*, 68th ed., §137 no. 2.

141 Bühling (1998), *GRUR*, pp. 196 (198 f. at IV 2); Rosenberger (1983), *GRUR*, pp. 203 (208 at c); Palandt and Grüneberg, *BGB*, 68th ed., §413 no. 2.

142 *Terrell on Patents*, no. 9.15.

of an acquisition in good faith in the meantime, the transfer of the patent can be made conditional on the publication of the charge or mortgage in the register. The absence of the property in the hands of the assignee purporting further to assign the patent cannot be overcome, as this is no mere equity.

5.2. Patent Licences

5.2.1. Germany

The Patents Act leaves the contents of patent licences largely to the parties to the transaction. This is why restrictions on the transferability of licences are permissible.[143] The courts have held that an exclusive licence is transferable and allows the licensee to grant sub-licences,[144] whereas a non-exclusive licence, being a mere contractual permission, is inseparable from the person or enterprise to which it is granted, and does not allow the licensee to grant sub-licences.[145] This may or may not be stipulated from case to case. The proposition regarding non-exclusive licences, however, is counter-intuitive because contractual claims are generally assignable (§§398, 413 BGB),[146] and there is little by way of explanation for why patent licences should be treated differently in this respect. What is more, an exclusive licence is often granted in order to allow the patented invention to penetrate new markets,[147] or to ensure a permanent local presence, allowing for a swift reaction to market trends. Granting a licence with this aim would entail a very close mutual dependence between licensor and licensee, and thus militate against the general assumption that exclusive licences are assignable.

5.2.2. England

S.30(4)(a) PA 1977 provides as the default rule that licences allow for sub-licences, and that any licence and sub-licence granted may be assigned or mortgaged. The assigning or mortgaging of licences or sub-licences may,

---

143 Same result in Benkard and Ullmann, *PatG*, 10th ed., §15 no. 103, but it is doubtful whether this follows from RGZ 134, 91 (96) – '*Drahtgewebeziegel*'; similarly, Benkard and Ullmann, Busse and Keukenschrijver, *PatG*, 6th ed., §15 no. 71.

144 RGZ 142, 168 (170) – '*Loseblätterbuch*'; BGH *GRUR* 1955, pp. 338 (340 at 2), concurring Götting, *Gewerblicher Rechtsschutz*, 8th ed., §25 no. 18; Benkard and Ullmann, *PatG*, 10th ed., §15 no. 105.

145 BGHZ 62, 272 (276 f.) = X ZR 4/71 of 23.4.1974, 3 b – '*Anlagengeschäft*'; concurring Benkard and Ullmann, *PatG*, 10th ed., §15 nos. 70, 103.

146 Kraßer, *Patentrecht*, 5th ed., §40 V d 1 (p. 958).

147 Cornish and Llewelyn, *Intellectual Property*, 6th ed., no. 7-23; for examples, see the ECJ's judgments in joined cases C-56/64 and 58/64, [1966] ECR 321, *Consten und Grundig v Commission*, and in case C-56/65, [1966] ECR 282 *La Technique Minière v Maschinenbau Ulm*.

however, be prohibited in the licensing agreement. If the parties have agreed that the licence shall not be assignable, this exclusion has effect vis-à-vis third parties[148] as the licence or sub-licence, unlike the patent it is derived from, is a mere contractual relationship, to which the rule to that effect in *Linden Gardens*[149] applies. Despite the fact that such a limitation on further assignments is not a registrable transaction (by contrast with the grant of the licence itself; s.33(3)(c)), it would appear not to allow the *bona fide* acquisition without the limitation. S.30(4)(a) PA 1977, by expressly allowing limitations on further assignments, puts would-be acquirers of licences on enquiry whether any such restrictions apply. Leaving the possibility of outright fraud aside, few economic operators would anyway be so gullible as to buy a licence, like a cat in the sack, without first perusing the instrument that establishes it.

5.3. Copyright (Authors' Economic Rights)

5.3.1. Germany

We have seen above that the monistic approach taken by German law renders the author's personality rights and his economic rights *(Verwertungsrechte)* unassignable, but that third parties' rights to exploit the work *(Nutzungsrechte),* granted by the author, are akin to licences in all but name. In the hands of the 'licensees', these rights are ordinary property rights and as such assignable. Nevertheless, any transfer requires the author's consent. This requirement can, however, be abrogated by the parties (§§34(5), 2nd sentence, 35(2) UrhG). Alternatively, certain conditions for an assignment to be permissible may be stipulated in the licensing agreement.

5.3.2. England

Copyright, too, can be assigned in whole or in part (s.90 CDPA 1988). The courts have accepted limitations on further assignment, such as the permission to assign only to the successor in the running of a particular business.[150] It has been held, however, that such negative covenants are binding only on the parties involved.[151] This need not give rise to any

---

148 Clark and Cornish, *Encyclopedia of UK and European Patent Law*, no. 8-406.

149 *Linden Gardens Trust Ltd. v Lenesta Sludge Disposal Ltd.* [1994] 1 AC 85 (HL).

150 *Barker v Stickney* [1919] 1 KB 121 (CA), 122 at 6.

151 *Barker v Stickney* [1919] 1 KB 121 (CA), 132 (Scrutton LJ); positive duties such as the payment of royalties to the author are even less valid against the successors, at 128 (Warrington LJ); such obligations may only be imposed by agreement, if need be under the Contracts (Rights of Third Parties) Act 1999, s.1(1)–(3).

problems, as observance of this stipulation can be ensured by a forfeiture clause. Such a clause deprives the assignee of the right altogether as soon as he attempts to breach the covenant. Copyright licences follow the same principles as patent and trade mark licences.

5.4. Trade Marks and Licences thereof

5.4.1. Trade marks

5.4.1.1. Germany As far as restrictions of the assignment of a trade mark are concerned, §27(1) MarkenG speaks only of limitations referring to categories of goods or services. Nevertheless, this does not rule out restrictions of the mark's further assignment, be it through a prohibition or through a consent requirement. A *bona fide* acquisition by subsequent assignees is not possible as the register does not entertain a belief in the absence of restrictions in this respect.[152] Only the transfer of the mark is registrable, if necessary according to different classes of goods or services (§27(3), (4), 46 MarkenG, §32 MarkenV (Trade Mark Rules)). Whoever wants to acquire a fully marketable trade mark must make enquiries and decline the offer of a shackled mark. This can be left to the market: trade marks do not represent scientific or cultural achievements in whose dissemination there is a public interest; on the contrary, there is no shortage of trade marks, or of goods or services.

5.4.1.2. England S.24(2) TMA 1994 allows the partial assignment of a trade mark. An assignment that does not give the assignee the power to make further assignments could be seen as a partial assignment. Nevertheless, such a partition is not one mentioned in letters (a) and (b) of that provision. There is no indication that this list is not meant to be exhaustive; thus, it is not preceded by 'in particular' as in the otherwise identical list in s.28(1) on licences. This, however, merely means that such a restriction is ineffective at law. In equity, it can be stipulated in the agreement between the parties. The assignor can protect himself by means of a forfeiture clause (see above on patents) against any attempts by the assignee at transferring the mark to a purchaser in good faith and for valuable consideration.[153] If the assignment is merely by way of

[152] Ingerl and Rohnke, *MarkenG*, 2nd ed., §27 no. 14; HK-MarkenR/Pahlow, §27 no. 8.

[153] For an example of such a clause in copyright law, see *Python (Monty) Pictures Ltd. v Paragon Entertainment Co. & anor.* [1998] EMLR 640 (ChD), 685 (Rattee J); such clauses are valid, 686 f.

security (s.20(4)) for a loan, and the assignor wants to continue using the trade mark, he will need licence to do so. As long as he repays the debt, the mortgagee-creditor must not foreclose him with his equity of redemption (see ss.103, 109 LPA 1925). This equity cannot be overcome by an acquisition in good faith and for valuable consideration, as the entry of the security interest on the register (s.25(2)(c)) gives notice to would-be assignees.

5.5. Trade Mark Licences

5.5.1. Germany

§30(1), (2) MarkenG allows for substantive, temporal, and territorial limitations of trade mark licences, and distinguishes between exclusive and non-exclusive licences. Again, however, this does not rule out other restrictions, particularly limitations of transfers of the licence. The question is thus left to the parties to the licensing agreement, and if not expressly stipulated, will depend on whether their mutual obligations require personal trust and co-operation on such a scale as to rule out an unfettered substitution of one licensee for another.

5.5.2. England

A trade mark licence is a mere contractual relationship, as is a patent licence. What has above been said in regard to patent licences, therefore, applies also to trade mark licences.

5.5.3. Comparative conclusion

Both jurisdictions allow holders of intellectual property rights to limit (further) assignments of those rights or licences therein. The German idea that the proprietor retains, from among the bundle of rights that together constitute the intellectual property right, the power to assign it (further) has a convincing simplicity to it. English law manages to achieve similar results but in more complicated ways.

6. SECURITY INTERESTS OVER INTELLECTUAL PROPERTY

As has been mentioned above, intellectual property rights are increasingly understood as valuable assets. It is natural, therefore, that companies should seek to use their intellectual property as security for the credit they require for the financing of their economic operations.[154] As security interests are an area of property law in general, not only of intellectual property law, which has been subject to little harmonisation as between legal systems, there are some marked divergences between English and German law.

6.1. Germany: The Pledging of Intellectual Property

While in English law, pledge is a purely possessory security and can thus not apply to intangibles, German law allows the pledging of incorporeal things, too. Those intellectual property rights that are assignable in German law are also capable of being pledged: patent (§15(1), 2nd sentence PatG);[155] trade mark (§29 MarkenG);[156] but not copyright. As the latter is not assignable (§29(1) UrhG), it is not pledgeable, either. The author can, however, pledge his claims under any rights to exploit his work which he has granted third parties in accordance with §31 UrhG (*Nutzungsrechte*). This follows from §113, 1st sentence UrhG, which allows for his copyright to be levied in execution (*gepfändet*) to the extent that he can grant *Nutzungsrechte.* As these rights are amenable to execution, they may also be pledged (§§1274(2), 400 BGB).[157] Because intellectual property rights, being absolute rights against everybody, have no specific debtor, the rule in §1280 BGB does not apply. According to that provision, the pledgor (the creditor) must inform his debtor that he has pledged his claim against the debtor to a creditor of his. In particular, the patent office is not a debtor in this sense. (Optional)[158] publication in the register (§§30(2) PatG, 29(1) DPMAV,[159] § 29(2) MarkenG) acts as a substitute for this mechanism, informing third parties of the pledging.

The pledgee (creditor) is only allowed to use the intellectual property

---

[154] For lack of space, it can only be noted here that UNCITRAL (the United Nations Commission on International Trade Law) is currently working on a Legislative Guide on Secured Transactions dealing with security rights in intellectual property. This will complement the 2006 Legislative Guide on Secured Transactions. Comprehensive documentation of the progress of this work can be found under http://www.uncitral.org/uncitral/en/commission/working_groups/6Security_Interests.html#1.

[155] Benkard and Ullmann, *PatG*, §15 no. 42.

[156] Ingerl and Rohnke, *MarkenG*, §29 no. 6.

[157] Dreier, Schulze and Schulze, *UrhG*, §113 no. 7.

[158] Fezer, *MarkenG*, §29 no. 6; Lange, *Marken- u. Kennzeichenrecht*, no. 1384.

[159] Benkard and Schäfers, *PatG,* §30 no. 7; the opposite view seemingly espoused by Benkard and Ullmann, *PatG*, §15 no. 42 *in fine,* is in reality a printer's error, as is clear from Ullmann's approving reference to Schäfers.

right that he took as a pledge if this is stipulated in the pledging agreement, (§§ 1273(2), 1st sentence, 1213(2) BGB).[160] If it is, the pledgee would, by virtue of §§100, 99(3) BGB, be allowed to grant licences in the right. At this point, however, the provisions of intellectual property law supersede those of the general civil law. The object of the pledge is the intellectual property right (or right therein) subject to any limitations on the pledgor's permission to deal with it; his creditor's (the pledgee's) rights cannot extend further. If, thus, the pledgor is the proprietor, and he has not granted any exclusive licences, the pledgee is allowed to grant licences to the extent that this is necessary to satisfy him for the secured debt. If the pledgor is a mere licensee, he may pledge the licence only if it is assignable, and the pledgee may only grant sub-licences if this, too, is within the gift of the pledgor.[161] If the pledgee is not allowed to seek satisfaction in this way, or to the extent that it is insufficient, he may sell the pledge as soon as the debt is payable (which, in the case of a credit repayable in instalments, requires default by the debtor; §§1273(2), 1228(1), (2) BGB). Sale normally takes place by public auction (§§1273(2), 1235(1) BGB).

6.2. England: Charges over Companies' Intellectual Property

English law allows the taking of two forms of security rights over intangibles: mortgage and charge. The other two security rights recognised in English law (pledge and lien) are possessory, but there can be no possession of an intangible.

A mortgage entails an assignment of the intellectual property right to the proprietor's creditor (the mortgagee), coupled with the right (so-called equity of redemption) for the proprietor (the mortgagor, who is usually but not necessarily the same person as the debtor) to redeem the right by paying the debt, and to have it re-transferred once the secured debt is discharged. Once the mortgagor has transferred the intellectual property right, he loses his right to use it: he has to cease working the patent, exploiting the copyright, affixing the trade mark to his goods, etc., unless the mortgagor expressly permits him to continue these uses.[162]

A charge leaves the legal title to the intellectual property right with the proprietor, and gives the creditor a right in equity to seek satisfaction out of the right should the proprietor default on the secured debt. Charges

---

160 *Münchner Kommentar BGB*/Damrau, §1274 no. 80.

161 *Münchner Kommentar BGB*/Damrau, §1274 no. 85.

162 Freed, Tang, and Tostivin (2008), 'Security over Intellectual Property', in C. Demetriades, (ed.), *Intellectual Property Issues in Commercial Transactions,* para. 6-08.

come as fixed or floating charges. The former binds any disposition by the debtor over the charged right to the creditor's consent. The latter allows him to dispose over the charged right in the normal course of his business without such consent. Only when he makes default on the secured debt (other conditions can also be stipulated) will the charge crystallise. The charged right then becomes assigned to the creditor, who may seek satisfaction out of it for his claim against the proprietor. Apart from this, fixed and floating charges differ in that creditors holding floating charges are subordinated, in the lender company's insolvency, to several other groups of creditors (ss.175, 176ZA, 176A Insolvency Act 1986).[163]

Charges (and mortgages) granted over intellectual property rights are registrable if granted by a company formed under the Companies Act 2006, s.860(7) lit. (i) CA 2006. In this context, two questions arise. The first concerns the relationship between the register of company securities under the Companies Act 2006 and the patent, trade mark, and other specialist registers for intellectual property rights (if such rights are registered at all). The second question is which type of security right (mortgage, fixed charge, floating charge) is best suited to a given type of intellectual property right. This depends on whether the right is registrable (patents, trade marks, registered design) or not (copyright, unregistered design right).

6.2.1. The relationship between the register of company charges and the registers of rights pertaining to Intellectual Property

The answer to the first question follows from the different functions of the register of company securities on the one hand, and of the specialist registers on the other. The register of company charges is meant to determine the order of priority among registrable securities in case the company becomes insolvent (see s.874(1)(a), (b) CA 2006) or if two or more creditors otherwise compete for the company's assets (lit. (c)). For this reason, there is only a short period of 21 days allowed for registration (s.870(1)(a)), after which the charge is void (s.874(1), (2)), and the secured debt becomes instantly repayable (sub-s.(3)). Such deadlines are alien to the specialist registers. They are meant to make evident which intellectual property rights exist, lest competitors infringe them. They also publicise who owns these rights so that actual or potential competitors can seek licences; such persons may also challenge the person on the register as to the validity of the right or to the ownership in the right. Finally, entry

---

163 For more details, see Enchelmaier (2008), 'Something Intangible to Hold on to – the Spectrum of Security over receivables in England and Germany', 10 *Cambridge Yearbook of European Legal Studies*, pp. 99–132.

in the register allows the public to know with whom to reckon in case of infringements.

From this it follows that an intellectual property right cannot come into existence and enjoy protection simply by virtue of its appearance on the register of company securities. Conversely, a security right entered in one of the specialist registers does not confer priority in the event of the company's insolvency or individual execution into its assets.[164] Moreover, each set of provisions is exhaustive within its scope of application. Entries on either register do not, therefore, depend for their validity on compliance with the rules for the other register.[165] There is one aspect, however, in which the neat separation breaks down. An assignor of a registered intellectual property right cannot take the right free from a security interest that does not appear on the specialist register but of whose existence he knows from the register or company securities.[166]

Nevertheless, there is no obligation to consult the register of securities before an ordinary purchase of an intellectual property right, and hence no constructive notice.[167] As a consequence, the creditor cannot enforce his security right against the new proprietor. In practice, however, this will not matter much: if the creditor has a mortgage over the intellectual property right, the debtor cannot sell more than his equity of redemption, no matter what the registers say; if a fixed charge, the sale is void without the chargee's consent; and if a floating charge, the chargor is free to sell within the ordinary course of his business anyway, although if he squanders his assets, the charge will crystallise.

By contrast with the situation under the specialist registers, the question of good faith is irrelevant to the order of priority pursuant to the register of company charges. An earlier chargee who registers his charge after a later one, but still within the registration period of 21 days, takes precedence because in substance, his equity is better since older. Despite his ignorance of the earlier incumbrance, the later chargee does not gain priority.

---

164 On the last point, see Davies, (2006), 26 *OJLS* 559 (568); Law Commission, Consultation Paper no. 296, *Company Security Interests,* Cm. 6654 (London, TSO 2005), no. 3.231; the Commission proposed to retain this rule, nos. 3.233, 3.234.

165 The Law Commission, Consultation Paper no. 164, *Registration of Security Interests: Company Charges and Property other than Land: A Consultation Paper* (London, TSO 2002), no. 2.50.

166 Likewise, Law Commission, Consultation Paper no. 164, *Registration of Security Interests: Company Charges and Property other than Land: A Consultation Paper* (London, TSO 2002), no. 2.55.

167 Ferran, *Company Law and Corporate Finance*, p. 543; Calnan (2004), *JIBFL* pp. 88, 90.

6.2.2. Types of security interests in Intellectual Property

The vulnerability of rights that exist in equity only, such as a charge, has repeatedly been discussed above. It is compounded if there is no register to notify would-be acquirers of the right's existence, so that the right perishes. For this reason, creditors will insist on a mortgage if the security on offer is copyright or a licence thereof.[168] The absence of a register for copyright, on the other hand, makes it cheap to acquire a mortgage and to maintain the right (there are no renewal costs).[169] At the same time, however, the mortgagor loses his right to use and to defend the intellectual property right. For this reason, he needs a licence from the mortgagee, and the security agreement must oblige him to defend the right,[170] as he will know his market better than the creditor, and will better be able to assess where infringers may lurk.

With registered rights, the problems associated with the equitable nature of charges are less acute. This raises the question whether a creditor should insist on a fixed or on a floating charge. Fixed charges are a suitable form of security for intellectual property rights which are indispensable to the debtor's business or which are turned over only at long intervals, such as the basic patents employed in his manufacturing process, or the franchise (licence) which provides him with his business model. Floating charges will only be taken over such rights, typically end-user licences, which are turned over in the debtor's business regularly and in some number.[171] The fact that there is no case law on these can be taken as an indication that this is not often a viable proposition.

Know-how, finally, is an unsuitable security. This is not because it does not come within the definition of 'intellectual property' in s.861(4) CA 2006 (patents, trade marks, registered design copyright, unregistered design right); it still falls within the wide concept of 'the company's property or undertaking' in s.860(7)(g). It is, rather, because mere knowledge cannot be properly transferred (the giver of the security retains the securing object) but can only be shared. It can, hence, not be mortgaged ('charge' includes 'mortgage', s.861(5)). What is more, for it to serve any security purpose, it would have to be sufficiently identified in the instrument that

---

[168] Copinger and Scone James, *Copyright*, no. 5-191; Drew and Starmer (2007), *JIBFL* pp. 320, 322; Bromfield (2006), *JIBFL* pp. 182 (183 by fn. 18); Lovells (2001), *JIBFL* pp. 267 (267 *in fine*, 268).

[169] Bromfield (2006), *JIBFL* pp. 182 (183 by fn. 8, 184).

[170] Lovells (2001), *JIBFL* pp. 310 (314 by and following fn. 29); Lipton (2001), 9 *IJLIT* pp. 65, 76; Smith, *Trade marks as Collateral*, p. 250.

[171] Bromfield (2006), *JIBFL* pp. 182 (183 by fn. 13); Lovells (2001), *JIBFL* pp. 310 (313 *in fine*).

creates the security right. These instruments, however, must be kept by the company for inspection by the public (ss.875(1), 876(1)(b), (2), 877(4)(b)). Such publicity would destroy the very subject-matter of the security.

6.2.3. Comparative conclusion

The German Civil Code and the individual statutes governing intellectual property rights manage well to integrate those rights into the general system of property law. The difficulties of using intellectual property as security for credit are of a factual and economic rather than of a legal nature. The latter point is true of English law, too. Nevertheless, its piecemeal approach has created some problems of coordination between the regime for intellectual property rights, and that for certain types of security granted by companies. There is also a rich historic legacy of different types of security, whose workings are reasonably predictable in practice, but which make the system somewhat obscure to the outsider.

7. OVERALL CONCLUSIONS

England and Germany approach the question of proprietary transactions in intellectual property from very different starting points, and many of the detailed solutions discussed above mirror the different historic paths that both countries' laws have taken. Nevertheless, the overall picture is one of broad convergence. German law's peculiarities lie in a strong emphasis on personality rights, particularly as regards copyright, but also in other areas. This emphasis has practical consequences, if only in creating the need for pragmatic compromises in order to accommodate the economic needs of creators, investors, and users of intellectual property. English law shows only traces of this. The most striking of its features is the omnipresence of the concept of equity, which has a long pedigree but has proven adaptable enough in its application to intellectual property rights.

12. Control of museum art images: the reach and limits of copyright and licensing*

Kenneth D. Crews and Melissa A. Brown*****

1. INTRODUCTION

Many museums and art libraries have undertaken major initiatives in recent years to digitize their collections of artworks. Digital imaging capabilities represent a significant development in the academic study of art, and they enhance the availability of art images to the public at large. The number of art images available online has expanded rapidly, and these images are increasingly integral to the creation, study, and teaching of art and art history.[1] The possible uses of these images are likewise broad. While many digitization efforts are geared primarily towards making art images available for study – reflecting the centrality of art images for scholarly work and the need to preserve and safeguard original works – digital art images can also serve as sources of enjoyment and creative inspiration.[2] Many of these uses, however, are potentially defined by

* Prepared for the Proceedings of the Annual Congress of the International Association for the Advancement of Teaching and Research in Intellectual Property Vilnius, Lithuania, 13–16 September 2009. This chapter is a preliminary study as part of a larger project funded by The Samuel H. Kress Foundation.

** Director, Copyright Advisory Office, Columbia University Lecturer in Law, Columbia Law School. Contact: Columbia University, 535 West 114th Street New York, NY 10027, USA. Email: kcrews@columbia.edu, Telephone: + (212) 851-0757.

*** Scholarly Communications Librarian, New York University (previously, Copyright Research Associate, Copyright Advisory Office, Columbia University).

1 Simor, Suzanna (2003), 'Visual Art Resources Online: Issues, Trends and Challenges', 22 *Art Documentation*, pp. 33–40 (discussing the increased availability of digital art images and their impact on the creation, study, and teaching of art and art history).

2 Ibid. at 33.

copyright law or by license agreements imposed by some museums and libraries that attempt to define allowable uses.

Museums and libraries often allow free online access to digital images of their art collections, or supply individual images upon request, but at the same time limit how these images can be used by, for example, prohibiting their reproduction or alteration. The terms and conditions of a museum's website may further restrict the ability of users to 'distribute, modify, transmit, reuse, download, repost, copy, or use the contents of the Site for public or commercial purposes, or for personal gain, without the [museum's] express prior written permission'.[3] Similarly, terms and conditions commonly limit the accessibility of web images by specifying that they are made available 'for the sole purpose of viewing'[4] or 'for personal, informational, and non-commercial use only'.[5] Whether or not they explicitly claim copyright over art images, museum site terms and conditions thus operate as a means of controlling whether and how online images can be used. Often, these terms and conditions will mean that an online image is not truly available for many purposes, including publication in the context of research or simple enjoyment. Not only do these terms and conditions restrict uses, they also have dubious legal standing. This chapter examines the legal premises behind claiming copyright in art images and the ability to impose license restrictions on their use.

Typically, the terms and conditions governing image usage are set forth in a standardized license agreement developed by the museum. Permission seekers consent to these terms and conditions in order to obtain the image and receive the museum's permission to publish it. For some museums, a single agreement is used for granting permission. Other museums, however, have developed multiple license agreements according to the medium involved – for example, distinct agreements may apply to print versus electronic publication – or the type of use, with separate agreements for private study, educational uses, or commercial uses.[6] Permission seekers wanting to use multiple images, or wanting to publish a single

---

[3] The Art Institute of Chicago, Terms and Conditions (2004), http://www.artic.edu/aic/copyright.html.

[4] Cincinnati Art Museum, Cincinnati Art Museum Collection Database: Terms and Conditions of Use/Copyright Policy (2010), http://72.249.182.183/collection/terms.page.do?request=/results.do%3Fhighlight%3D2.

[5] The Andy Warhol Museum, the warhol: Legal & Credits (2006), http://www.warhol.org/credits.html.

[6] *See, e.g.*, The Frick Collection, Copyright Information (2010), http://www.frick.org/copyright/rights.htm; The Getty, Ordering and Reproducing Images from the J. Paul Getty Museum's Collection (2010), http://www.getty.edu/legal/image_request/index.html.

image in a variety of media, may be confronted with understanding and negotiating numerous license agreements. The terms and durations of these agreements can differ or conflict, complicating the process of obtaining permission.

As the creators and possessors of art images, museums are typically the entities in the position of developing the license agreements and determining what restrictions to place on the use of the images they make available. In doing so, many museums have struggled with whether and how to impose copyright or analogous licensing terms over art images. On the one hand, exercising control over the publication and reproduction of art images may be compelling, because it can translate into a source of badly needed revenue for museums and libraries[7] and strengthen the ability of museums and libraries to be stewards of their collections.[8] License terms and conditions are sometimes also viewed as necessary tools to avoid potential liability of museums and libraries, where the underlying works reproduced in the images involve intellectual property rights of third parties, particularly artists or their representatives or heirs.[9] Even where the use of an image would not implicate the legal rights of third parties, museums are motivated to maintain good relationships with artists and their estates, and so want to prevent uses of an image that would be objectionable to the artist.

On the other hand, the assertion of copyright and imposition of restrictive licensing terms by museums and libraries have been criticized as inconsistent with the mission of these institutions to disseminate their collections as broadly as possible and to allow for the public to meaningfully engage with art, particularly when the digital images in question involve works of art in the public domain.[10] Beyond substantively restricting how

---

[7] Cameron, Colin T. (2006), 'In Defiance of Bridgeman: Claiming Copyright in Photographic Reproductions of Public Domain Works', 15 *Tex. Intell. Prop. L.J.* 31, pp. 59–60 ('An assumption implied in construing the motivation to claim copyright in photographic reproductions of public domain paintings is that the additional control creates an opportunity to generate more revenue.').

[8] American Association of Museums, AAM Member Museums Rights & Reproductions Survey 2004 30 (2004), http://www.panix.com/~squigle/rarin/RCAAMSurvey2003-4.pdf.

[9] Ibid. at 30.

[10] *See* Hamma, Kenneth, 'Public Domain Art in an Age of Easier Mechanical Reproducibility', *D-LIB Magazine*, November 2005, http://www.dlib.org/dlib/november05/hamma/11hamma.html (arguing that placing art reproductions in the public domain and clearly removing all questions about their availability for use and reuse would likely cause no harm to the finances or reputation of museums, and would contribute to the public good); Wojcik, Mary Campell, 'The Antithesis

images can be used, license agreements also make the process of obtaining and using art images more complicated, time consuming, and costly for permission seekers. Restricting uses of images sometimes contradicts larger principles of art and law. Most art is to some extent derivative, and new creativity is commonly based on existing works.[11] To prohibit cropping, distortion, and other experimentation with an image may actually hinder the development of art. Further, license terms that assert rights can undercut the public domain of copyright law. Copyright law has a limited reach, and materials enter the public domain for the public benefit. License restrictions can undermine the policy of copyright law by asserting limitations over the use of public domain materials.

This chapter is one outcome of a study of museum licensing practices funded by The Samuel H. Kress Foundation. This chapter is principally an introduction to the relevant law in the United States and a survey of examples of museum licenses. The project is in its early stages, with the expectation that later studies will expand on this introduction and provide greater analysis of the legal complications of copyright, the public domain, and the reach of license agreements as a means for controlling the use of artwork and potentially any other works, whether or not they fall within the scope of copyright protection.

2. COPYRIGHT AND LICENSING RESTRICTIONS: THEIR SCOPE AND CONTENT

2.1. Assertions of Copyright in Digital Art Images

An image of a work of art, whether the image is produced digitally or in any other medium, may comprise two copyrights. One copyright is in the underlying artwork. If this copyright is still in effect, it may be held by the artist, heirs, or sometimes the museum or other transferee. Those rights

---

of Originality: Bridgeman, Image Licensors, and the Public Domain', 30 *Hastings Comm. & Ent. L.J.* pp. 257–88 (arguing that the art history and legal communities need to address image licensing in order to preserve meaningful access to public domain artworks).

[11] *See generally* Greenberg, Lynne A. (1992), 'The Art of Appropriation: Puppies, Piracy, and Post-Modernism', 11 *Cardozo Arts & Ent. L.J.* 1, pp. 1–33 (discussing how post-modernist art critiques the concepts of artistic creativity and originality used within copyright law to define art); Landes, William M. (2000), 'Copyright, Borrowed Images, and Appropriation Art: An Economic Approach', 9 *Geo. Mason L. Rev.* 1, pp. 1–24 (discussing the sometimes conflicting interests between appropriation artists and copyright holders).

must be taken into consideration by any users of the image, leading the user to secure permission or to determine whether the activity may be within fair use or other copyright exception.[12] A second possible copyright is in the digitized reproduction of the artwork, separate and distinct from whatever rights may exist in the original work.[13] This copyright would belong to the museum or library undertaking the digitization effort and thus arguably creating whatever copyrightable aspects may be part of the reproduction. Additionally, any rights of the copyright holder may be further defined by contractual terms and conditions governing the use of the digitized image.[14] Under the law of the United States and likely other countries, however, the existence of such a separate copyright in digital reproductions of art is subject to serious doubt.

For copyright to vest in any work under American law, it must be an 'original work of authorship'.[15] That requirement has been interpreted to mean that a copyrightable work must include some minimum amount of creativity.[16] A photographic or digital reproduction of an existing work could be sufficiently creative, particularly if the composition of the image includes more than just the work of art, or includes some original angles, lighting, or other features. However, a direct reproduction of artwork, simply reproducing the original and not adding more, may not possess any originality and as a result may not be copyrightable. Any claim of copyright in such images, under US law, by museums, libraries, photographers, or anyone else was drawn into question by a 1999 federal court ruling in the case of *Bridgeman Art Library, Ltd. v Corel Corp.*[17] The Bridgeman Art Library, a British company, alleged that Corel Corporation had copied its digital art images onto Corel's commercially sold CDs, in violation of US copyright law.[18] The images in question were of early artworks that were, at the time of litigation, in the public domain. With no copyright in the underlying artwork, the only possible claimant was Bridgeman, the creator of the reproduction. Faced with whether Bridgeman had grounds to restrict use of its images, the court ruled that no new copyright was

---

12 Pessach, Guy (2007), 'Museums, Digitization and Copyright Law – Taking Stock and Looking Ahead', 1 *J. Int'L Media & Ent. L.*, pp. 253, 276–7.

13 Ibid.

14 Ibid.

15 Copyright Act of 1976 § 101, 17 USC § 102(a) (2010).

16 *Feist Publ'ns, Inc. v. Rural Tel. Serv. Co.*, 499 US 340, 355 (1991).

17 *Bridgeman Art Library, Ltd. v Corel Corp.*, 36 F. Supp. 2d 191 (SDNY 1999); *see also Bridgeman Art Library, Ltd. v Corel Corp.*, 25 F. Supp. 2d 421 (SDNY 1998).

18 *Bridgeman*, 36 F. Supp. 2d at 192.

created when Bridgeman made an exact photographic replication of an artwork in the public domain.[19]

The court reasoned that the reproductions lacked originality; the entire point of Bridgeman's efforts was to replicate as closely as possible the original works of art. The court recognized that quality reproductions demand substantial technical skill and labor, but hard work does not qualify for copyright protection. Copyright law protects originality.[20] The court also concluded that a change in the medium of a work – from, for example, an original oil painting to a photographic image – did not constitute originality for purposes of copyright protection. In broad language, the court made this determination about copyrightability of the reproductions:

> In this case, plaintiff by its own admission has labored to create 'slavish copies' of public domain works of art. While it may be assumed that this required both skill and effort, there was no spark of originality – indeed, the point of the exercise was to reproduce the underlying works with absolute fidelity. Copyright is not available in these circumstances.[21]

The legal analysis in *Bridgeman* has generally been greeted with applause, while photographers and some museums have lamented that the images they create, and often market to publishers and others, evidently lack copyright protection.[22] Nevertheless, principles of *Bridgeman* have been reinforced in later rulings. While *Bridgeman* was a ruling from one district court with jurisdiction in only part of New York State, its principles were adopted in 2008 by an appellate court with much greater legal jurisdiction. The Court of Appeals for the Tenth Circuit ruled in *Meshwerks, Inc. v Toyota Motor Sales U.S.A., Inc.*[23] that digital images

---

19 *Bridgeman*, 36 F. Supp. 2d at 199–200.

20 *Bridgeman*, 36 F. Supp. 2d at 196–97.

21 *Bridgeman*, 36 F. Supp. 2d at 197.

22 *See* Conferences/Copyrights: Lawyers, Art Professionals Revisit Bridgeman Case on Protection of Photo Art, 76 *BNA Patent, Trademark & Copyright J.* 18 (2008). The *Bridgeman* decision addresses only the copyrightability of reproductions of two-dimensional images and therefore does not undercut all legal claims of photographers. For example, a photographer of a sculptural work or other three-dimensional object is probably introducing choices about angles and lighting and background, likely making the photograph 'original' under copyright law. Further, the photographer can probably allow uses of the uncopyrighted image under the terms of a license, thus creating contract rights against the other party. The variety and appropriateness of such agreements, as advanced by museums, is an important component of this study.

23 *Meshwerks, Inc. v Toyota Motor Sales U.S.A., Inc.*, 528 F.3d 1258 (10th Cir. 2008).

of the basic design of existing automobiles did not have copyright protection. Again, the court noted that the creators of the images were striving to depict precisely an existing shape – converting a three-dimensional original to a two-dimensional image.[24] The court emphasized that the plaintiff's purpose was to capture as accurately as possible the shapes of the vehicles. The court also looked for any original contributions and found none:

> [T]he facts in this case unambiguously show that Meshwerks did not make any decisions regarding lighting, shading, the background in front of which a vehicle would be posed, the angle at which to pose it, or the like – in short, its models reflect none of the decisions that can make depictions of things or facts in the world, whether Oscar Wilde or a Toyota Camry, new expressions subject to copyright protection.[25]

The reference to Oscar Wilde was the court's reminder that these recent cases are not a diversion from past law, but instead are built squarely upon it. The United States Supreme Court ruled in 1884 that photographs – then a newly invented technology – were protectable under copyright law.[26] The Court found creativity and originality in exactly some of the same features that the *Bridgeman* and *Meshwerks* courts looked for: posing, angles, lighting, shading, and background. These are the features that the Supreme Court long ago found in a photograph of Oscar Wilde, qualifying it for copyright protection. The rulings are also consistent with a more recent foundational decision from the US Supreme Court. In 1991, the Court ruled in *Feist Publications, Inc. v Rural Telephone Service Co.* that copyright protects creativity, not hard work or the 'sweat of the brow'.[27] In accord with *Feist*, the judges in *Bridgeman* and in *Meshwerks* were looking for evidence of creativity and were not persuaded by the investment of time, money, and expertise to create the images.

Although the *Bridgeman* case is consistent with other legal developments, and has been regarded by many commentators as a sound interpretation of the originality requirement,[28] many museums, libraries, and commercial art databases continue to claim copyright in digital images

---

24 *Meshwerks*, 528 F.3d at 1264–5. This imaging of a three-dimensional work may bring into question the copyrightability of a photograph of a sculpture or other solid work. However, in *Meshwerks*, the images were merely digitally created wire-frame images and lacked original shadowing, angles, and background.

25 *Meshwerks*, 528 F.3d at 1265.

26 *Burrow-Giles Lithographic Co. v Sarony,* 111 US 53 (1884).

27 *Feist*, 499 US at 359–60.

28 Cameron, *supra* note 7, at 47–8; Wojcik, *supra* note 10, at 266–7.

of artworks that are in the public domain.[29] Some images have copyright notices superimposed, and are provided only subject to payment and adherence to license terms and conditions.[30] Similarly, many museum websites include broad statements that all content, including images, contained therein are copyrighted, without regard to whether or not the underlying artworks are in the public domain.[31] Other museums assert more directly that all images 'are protected by United States and International Copyright law and do not constitute material in the public domain',[32] or that 'none of the materials published here within may be reused within the public domain'.[33] Museums have also taken care to distinguish their art images from those that were at issue in *Bridgeman* by claiming that 'the Images depict objects from the [museum's] collection in a manner expressing the scholarly and aesthetic view of the [museum]. The images are not simple reproductions of the works depicted and are protected by copyright.'[34] Thus, despite *Bridgeman*, users often face widespread assertions from some libraries and museums that digital art images are subject to copyright, constraining activities such as downloading, copying, publication, the creation of derivative works, and many other uses of art images that may in fact be legally unprotected.

2.2. Contractual Terms and Conditions

Whether or not the copyright in the reproduction is ultimately found to be legally valid, license terms and conditions of use are also often imposed through contract law. These terms may appear as statements connected with online art databases, or they may be licensing contracts that must be negotiated and accepted as a condition of an institution's release of an image to a user. While the terms and conditions of individual museums and libraries vary significantly, they are often more restrictive than copyright.[35] For example, though copyright protections are subject to a

---

[29] Allan, Robin J. (2007), 'After Bridgeman: Copyright, Museums, and Public Domain Works of Art', 155 *U. Pa. L.R.*, pp. 961–2; Cameron, *supra* note 7, at 47–52.

[30] Ibid. at 961.

[31] *See* Hamma, *supra* note 10, at 1–2.

[32] The Asia Society, Asia Society Terms & Conditions (2009), http://www.asiasociety.org/util/terms-conditions.

[33] Minneapolis Institute of Arts, About the Museum/Contact Us: Rights and Reproductions (2010), http://www.artsmia.org/index.php?section_id=39.

[34] Museum of Fine Arts Boston, Terms and Conditions of Image Usage (2009), http://www.mfa.org//master/sub. asp?key=45?key=2179.

[35] Allan, *supra* note 29, at pp. 964, 980–81.

number of exceptions, such as the exceptions for libraries and fair use, contractual terms and conditions have no such limitations. Accordingly, contract terms and conditions can operate to prevent many uses of images that would be lawful under copyright law.[36]

In addition, many museum and library licensing terms are often drafted so as to prevent *any* use of the image beyond that specifically requested by the applicant and granted by the museum. In that respect, the terms may not only overreach the language of copyright, they may also define specific uses that are not explicitly a part of copyright law. For example, the ability to reproduce, display, publish, or share the image may be prohibited by the licensing terms even when this would fall under 'fair use' or another exception to the Copyright Act.[37] Such terms and conditions take a variety of forms. One common approach is for license agreements to grant permission only for the exact use of the image detailed in the application. License terms may specify that 'permission is granted for ONE usage in ONE publication, ONE edition and ONE language only', with any further reproduction requiring 'an additional fee and written permission'.[38] Terms may also go beyond this 'one time use' provision to expressly prohibit the reproduction, conversion, transmission, and distribution of images, as well as the creation of derivative works.[39] Image reproduction is also controlled through provisions that permit reproduction 'only from materials originally supplied by the [museum]' and prohibit the reuse, transfer, assignment, or sale of images and the permission to reproduce them.[40]

Significantly, licensing terms and conditions also control the appearance of art images. They commonly prohibit any modification, preventing both the creation of derivative works and any alteration of the art image such as cropping, bleeding, change of color composition, or the use of detail. Some examples of these types of provisions are as follows:

- 'Composition may not be masked out, cut down, superimposed with type matter, or in any way defaced or altered.'[41]

---

[36] Ibid.

[37] Allan, *supra* note 29, at pp. 980–81.

[38] Detroit Institute of Arts, Rights & Reproduction – Print Media (2007), http://www.dia.org/the_collection /rights_and_reproductions/print.asp.

[39] Museum of Fine Arts Boston, Terms and Conditions of Image Usage (2009), http://www.mfa.org//master/sub .asp?key=45?key=2179.

[40] Peabody Essex Museum, Application for Permission to Reproduce Images (2009), http://www.pem.org/ museum/photo_permission_application.pdf.

[41] The Carnegie Museum of Art, Conditions for Print Reproduction (2010), http://www.cmoa.org/collections /RRprintconditions.pdf.

- 'Any reproduction which deviates from the original photograph or transparency, including but not limited to computer manipulation, renders this permission void.'[42]
- The image may only be reproduced with the strict understanding that it will not be cropped or altered in any way, bled to the edges, guttered, wrapped around the outside cover if allowed, nor superimposed with any printing. The image must also be surrounded by a white border of appropriate size.'[43]

The substantive scope of licensing terms and conditions is broad. In order to attempt to control the use of art images – particularly where the museum may in fact not hold any copyright to the image – license agreements must address a range of situations and legal issues. The following examples, culled from publicly available licensing agreements currently in use at a number of museums, provide a sense of this scope. While not comprehensive, this sampling is an overview of terms and conditions that users commonly face when seeking permission to publish or otherwise reproduce art images.

2.2.1. Media and format

- '[P]ermission and license granted herein is for reproduction and publication of the Image(s) in analog formats only. Applicant may only make digital copies as absolutely necessary in intermediate process steps to the creation of a book or periodical published exclusively in analog format.'[44]
- 'Electronic reproduction can be used in the following applications: LAN or stand alone systems including Kiosks, WAN including the Internet, Television, Broadcast and Cable Portable Disks and Tapes.'[45]
- '[The museum] will not grant rights for "all media now known or hereafter devised."'[46]

---

42 Fine Arts Museums of San Francisco, Policy on Rights and Reproductions of Electronic Images (2006), http://www.famsf.org/fam/about/imagebase/subpage.asp?subpagekey=75.

43 Georgia O'Keeffe Museum, Rights & Reproductions (2008), http://www.okeeffemuseum.org/media-press-room/rights-reproductions.aspx.

44 The J. Paul Getty Trust, Terms of Use for Print Publication for the J. Paul Getty Trust (2010), http://www.getty.edu/legal/image_request/terms_print.html.

45 Detroit Institute of Arts, Rights and Reproduction: Electronic Media (2007), http://www.dia.org/the_collection/rights_and_reproductions/electronic.asp.

46 Carnegie Museum of Art, Carnegie Museum of Art Fee Schedule (2008), http://www.cmoa.org/collections /FeeSchedule2008.pdf.

2.2.2. Copyright notification

- 'The following documentation: artist, title, medium and dimensions, object date and copyright notification, must accompany the reproduction, either directly under it, on the page facing, on the reverse, or elsewhere in the book, such as in the index or list of illustrations.'[47]
- 'Your product must be copyrighted and contain a general notice of copyright which includes the following language: "Warning: All rights reserved. Unauthorized public performance, broadcasting, transmission, or copying, mechanical or electronic, is a violation of applicable laws. This product and the individual images contained within are protected under the Laws of the U.S. and other countries. Unauthorized duplication, distribution, transmission, or exhibition of the whole or of any part therein may result in civil liability and criminal prosecution. The downloading of images is not permitted."'[48]

2.2.3. License term

- 'License is granted for one time, non-exclusive use in one medium and one product. Licenses will be granted for terms of the following duration: LAN – 3 years, WAN – 1 year, Television, broadcast, and cable – 5 years, Portable Disks & Tapes – lifespan of edition.'[49]
- 'Permission is granted as stated on the Application for use for a period of 8 years (or other agreed time).'[50]
- 'Web site rights are granted for a period of twelve (12) months at a time only unless otherwise negotiated.'[51]

---

47 Detroit Institute of Art, Rights and Reproduction: Print Media (2007), http://www.dia.org/the_collection/ rights_and_reproductions/print.asp.

48 Fine Arts Museums of San Francisco, Policy on Rights and Reproductions of Electronic Images (2006), http://www.famsf.org/fam/about/imagebase/subpage.asp?subpagekey=75.

49 Detroit Institute of Arts, Rights and Reproduction: Electronic Media (2007), http://www.dia.org/the_collection/rights_and_reproductions/electronic.asp.

50 Fine Arts Museums of San Francisco, Policy on Rights and Reproductions of Electronic Images (2006), http://www.famsf.org/fam/about/imagebase/subpage.asp?subpagekey=75.

51 Peabody Essex Museum, Application for Permission to Reproduce Images (2009), http://www.pem.org/aux/pdf/library/2009_Permission_to_reproduce_form.pdf.

2.2.4. Third party rights

- 'Material under copyright owned by a third party may not be used in any form and may not be copied or downloaded without permission from the holder of the underlying copyright.'[52]
- 'If the work is not in the public domain, requestors will be asked to provide written confirmation indicating that permission has been obtained, and from whom, or that due diligence has been conducted.'[53]

2.2.5. Museum's discretion and approval

- Permission is granted 'on a case-by-case basis at the sole discretion of the Institute or the appropriate rights holder.'[54]
- 'Special permission is required if the reproduction is to appear as frontispiece, chapter divider, book cover/dust jacket, calendar, poster, individual reproduction, or if it is not referred to directly in the text. In such cases, an additional fee is payable. The final layout must be submitted before production for approval.'[55]
- '[The museum] may refuse to approve any request for reproductions for any reason. Among the factors the [museum] will consider when deciding whether to permit reproduction are: the condition of the archival materials whose reproduction is sought; the length and number of the materials requested; the purpose of the reproduction; the sensitivity of the material's contents; whether the materials have been published previously; and whether the materials are protected by copyright and whether the copyright is owned by or licensed to the [museum].'[56]

---

[52] Art Institute of Chicago, Terms and Conditions (2004), http://www.artic.edu/aic/copyright.html.

[53] The J. Paul Getty Trust (2010), Contact Library Rights and Reproductions: Request for Images and/or Permission to Publish or Quote, http://www.getty.edu/research/conducting_research/library/rights_repro/index.html.

[54] Art Institute of Chicago, Terms and Conditions (2004), http://www.artic.edu/aic/copyright.html.

[55] Fine Arts Museums of San Francisco, The ImageBase: Photo Services, Conditions for Permission (2006), http://www.famsf.org/fam/about/imagebase/subpage.asp?subpagekey=75.

[56] The Frick Collection, Application for Reproduction of Archival Materials for Publication (2004), http://www.frick.org/assets/PDFs/library/archives_pub_app_2004.pdf.

3. RATIONALES AND ARGUMENTS FOR AND AGAINST COPYRIGHT AND LICENSING RESTRICTIONS

The arguments in favor of and against imposition of copyright and licensing restrictions on digital art images are primarily related to two concerns. First, museums and libraries have seen licensing as a method to ensure that the images of works in their collections are not 'misused' or 'misrepresented', in keeping with the view that collecting institutions should function as stewards guarding the works within their holdings.[57] Consistent with this view, some institutions have developed licensing conditions that tightly proscribe the dissemination of their images, even though the artwork in question may have been in the public domain for centuries, or in fact may have been created before the development of copyright law. This position, however, has been criticized as a 'notion deriv[ing] from something of a paternalistic stance by museums that has existed for more than a century, that they alone can properly interpret the works in their collections. By attempting to hold works of art within an institutional voice, the single interpretation has often effectively isolated those works from a more engaged public experience.'[58] Perhaps at a more basic level, this position on the part of museums 'assert[s] rights that the law seems to indicate they simply do not have'.[59]

The second commonly cited motivating factor behind image licensing is revenue.[60] It is argued that art museums and libraries rely on the validity of their copyrights and abilities to dictate licensing terms in order to generate income through the use of the images within their collections.[61] Without a means to limit the unfettered dissemination and reproduction of these images, museums would be deprived of revenue and would lack any means of recouping their economic investments in undertaking digitization efforts. While the licensing of images for commercial purposes – particularly with regard to well-known, 'greatest hits' works of art – can undoubtedly result in significant income, little evidence suggests that the licensing of non-commercial uses of art images results in

---

57 Allan, *supra* note 29, at pp. 982–3.

58 Hamma, *supra* note 10, at p. 4.

59 Wojcik, *supra* note 10, at p. 273.

60 *See* Tanner, Simon (2004), 'Reproduction Charging Models and Rights Policy for Digital Images in American Art Museums: A Mellon Foundation Study', 40, *available at* http://www.kdcs.kcl.ac.uk/fileadmin/documents/USMuseum_SimonTanner.pdf.

61 Allan, *supra* note 29, at pp. 962, 982.

significant revenue.[62] Even assuming that it does, profiting from educational and other non-commercial uses of images may be inconsistent with the missions of museums and libraries. The choice to do so is ultimately a business decision that can be evaluated by weighing an institution's economic success or sustainability against its mission, but this process should involve an examination of 'how much income justifies the diminution of the institution's mission driven goals?'[63]

4. CONCLUSION: CURRENT TRENDS AND CONTROVERSIES RELATING TO ART IMAGE LICENSING

In recent years, the use of licensing terms and conditions to control access to and use of art images has been subject to increasing criticism, primarily when considering restrictions imposed on works that are in the public domain. While digitization and internet technologies provide the capability of developing extensive, broadly accessible online art image databases at relatively low cost, copyright and licensing restrictions operate as a significant hindrance on the development of an art 'commons' that could do much to engage the public with its artistic and cultural heritage.[64] The overall missions of libraries and museums would seem undoubtedly to support placing high quality images of public domain art 'back into the public domain, unfettered and unrestricted for all'.[65]

This recognition has sparked something of a trend toward reducing or eliminating the use of copyright and licensing restrictions and allowing for more liberal use of art images. For example, a number of institutions, including the Library of Congress, the New York Public Library, the Getty Research Institute, and the Smithsonian, have contributed their public domain photograph collections to The Commons on Flickr.com, a project launched in 2008.[66] These and other participating institutions contribute images of their collections with the usage rights attribution 'No Known Copyright Restrictions', in order to promote their free access and use.[67] Similarly, the Brooklyn Museum's online copyright policy

---

62 Hamma, *supra* note 10, at p. 4; Tanner, *supra* note 60, at p. 40.

63 Hamma, *supra* note 10, at p. 4.

64 *See* Hamma, *supra* note 10, at pp. 5–6; Simor, *supra* note 1, at pp. 34–5; Wojcik, *supra* note 10, at pp. 285–6.

65 Hamma, *supra* note 10, at p. 5.

66 Flickr (2010), The Commons, http://www.flickr.com/commons/.

67 Ibid.

allows for non-commercial sharing of the images on its website through a Creative Commons license.[68] Additionally, some museums have adopted policies to encourage educational uses of their digital image collections. The Guggenheim's Terms and Conditions of Use contain a section entitled 'Beyond Fair Use', allowing for certain educational uses of its images beyond what may qualify as fair use under the Copyright Act.[69] In 2007, the Metropolitan Museum of Art launched its Images for Academic Publishing initiative, to provide scholars with high-quality images from its collection free of charge for educational publication purposes.[70]

Despite these developments, however, many libraries and museums continue to impose restrictive terms and conditions on their digital art collections, as well as assert their ability to control the use of digital reproductions of public domain artwork through copyright. Recently, the issue of whether reproductions of art in the public domain can be copyrighted was debated anew, owing to a controversy between Wikipedia and the London National Portrait Gallery. The Portrait Gallery undertook a program of digitization of its collection, and subsequent to making the results of that effort available on its website, high-resolution images were uploaded onto Wikipedia by one of its volunteers.[71] The Portrait Gallery threatened litigation, arguing that the images are copyrighted and that Wikipedia's appropriation of the images undermines its ability to recoup the cost of its digitization program.[72] In turn, Wikipedia argued that because the works of art are in the public domain, its use of the images is legal, and that the Portrait Gallery is 'betraying its public service mission' in seeking to prevent the dissemination of the images.[73] As this episode illustrates, copyright and licensing terms continue to assert restrictions over public domain artworks, as well as to generate significant controversy within the art library and museum community.

This introductory examination of the issues is an indication of the diversity of conditions imposed by museums on the use of images from

---

[68] Brooklyn Museum, About: Copyright (2009), http://www.brooklynmuseum.org/copyright.php.

[69] The Solomon R. Guggenheim Foundation (2009), Terms and Conditions of Use, http://www.guggenheim.org/terms-conditions/.

[70] Press Release, The Metropolitan Museum of Art, Metropolitan Museum and ARTstor Announce Pioneering Initiative to Provide Digital Images to Scholar at No Charge (March 12 2007), *available at* http://www.metmuseum.org/press_room/full_release.asp?prid={A113E0AD-AA4E-471B-8F04-736A21F1A70A}.

[71] Cellan-Jones, Rory, 'Wikipedia Painting Row Escalates', *BBC News*, 17 July 2009, http://news.bbc.co.uk/2/hi/ technology/8156268.stm.

[72] Ibid.

[73] Ibid. As of this writing, the controversy remains unresolved.

their collections. More important, this study demonstrates that many museums are in fact imposing license terms in an effort to control uses beyond the limits of copyright law. One might infer that such museums are not content with the exact parameters of copyright protection, or that they perceive a need for more detailed standards. One might also infer that such museums – at least in the United States – are simply not deterred by the ruling in *Bridgeman*. They may be distinguishing the case, or they may conclude that it does not apply outside the New York jurisdiction, or they may simply be giving it little regard. They may simply be pursuing the familiar technique of employing contract law to override the limits of copyright. Whatever the motivations, license terms continue to be an important part of the accessibility and usability of art images, setting up conflicts with the law and with the public interest. Future studies as part of this project may explore some of these issues.

PART IV

International IP law: one size does not fit all

13. Exploring the flexibilities of the TRIPS Agreement's provisions on limitations and exceptions

Christophe Geiger*

1. INTRODUCTION

Important concerns have been expressed in recent times about the Agreement on Trade-Related Aspects of Intellectual Property Rights (TRIPS) and it has become obvious that many scholars seem not to be satisfied with its provisions.[1] More then ten years have passed since the adoption of this international convention and one can presume that it is unlikely that this agreement would be signed if it were presented today to the member states of the WTO. Anyhow, this agreement has been adopted and member states are now bound by it. However, the TRIPS Agreement, despite having many unsatisfying provisions, has one major advantage: some provisions are vague, unclear, and their exact scope is often hard to understand. This can be an advantage because when legal provisions are unclear, judges or scholars have to give them a meaning, to propose interpretations. This allows the IP community to have a certain influence where provisions of the TRIPS Agreement offer some flexibility,[2] by 'rethink-

* Associate Professor and Director of the Centre for International Intellectual Property Studies (CEIPI), University of Strasbourg; Senior Researcher, Max Planck Institute for Intellectual Property and Competition Law, Munich.

[1] Critical literature on the TRIPS Agreement is too abundant to be quoted extensively. *See e.g.* Vaver, D. and Basheer, S. (2006), 'Popping Patented Pills: Europe and A Decade's Dose of TRIPs', *EIPR*, p. 282; Malbon, J. and Lawson, C. (eds) (2008), *Interpreting and Implementing the Trips Agreement: Is It Fair?*, Cheltenham, UK and Northampton, MA, USA: Edward Elgar; Remiche, B. and Kors, J. (eds) (2007), *L'accord ADPIC, 10 ans après: regards croisés, Europe-Amérique Latine*, Brussels: Larcier; Correa, C. (2007), *Trade Related Aspects of Intellectual Property Rights: A Commentary on the TRIPS Agreement*, Oxford: Oxford University Press; Yu, P.K. (2006), 'TRIPs and its Discontents', 10 *Marquette Intellectual Property Law Review*, p. 369.

[2] *See* the chapters by Drexl, J., Geiger, C., Kors, J., Trometter, M., Lengyel,

ing' them in a balanced manner when they present a risk of leading to unbalanced solutions. Therefore, I would like to use the little (admittedly limited) power that we – legal scholars – have left, to 'rethink', not the entire TRIPS Agreement, but one very important provision related to limitations and exceptions to exclusive rights, commonly known as the 'Three-Step Test' (Articles 13, 17, 26.2 and 30 TRIPS).[3] I will first start with a few observations of a general nature, then take a critical look at how the three-step test has been interpreted so far by the World Trade Organization (WTO) Panel, explore some new ways of interpretation, including a declaration on the three-step test commonly elaborated by a group of scholars in a research project co-ordinated jointly by the Max Planck Institute in Munich and the School of Law at Queen Mary, University of London, and finally propose the implementation of an instrument in international law safeguarding and clarifying a balanced interpretation of the limitations and exceptions provisions.

2. INTERPRETING THE TRIPS AGREEMENT: GENERAL OBSERVATIONS

As with any other legal provisions, the TRIPS Agreement is submitted to general principles of interpretation, such as the need to understand a rule in the light of its function and in the context of the entire legal order.

2.1. Any Legal Provision has to be Interpreted According to its Objectives

This is true of every legal provision, and so is true also of the TRIPS Agreement. In the context of international public law, this is clearly

---

M.F. and Bottino, G. in Remiche, B. and Kors, J. (eds), (2007), *L'accord ADPIC, 10 ans après: regards croisés, Europe-Amérique Latine*, Brussels: Larcier.

3 Analysing the flexibilities left by international law regarding limitations and exceptions and the three-step test *see also* Hugenholtz, P.B. and Okediji, R., 'Conceiving an International Instrument on Limitations and Exceptions to Copyright, Final Report', March 2008, 11 *et seq.*; Kur, A. 'Of Oceans, Islands, and Inland Water – How much Room for Exceptions and Limitations under the Three-step Test?', *Max Planck Institute for Intellectual Property Research Paper Series* No. 08-04 (also available in Kur, A. (ed.), *Intellectual Property Rights in a Fair World Trade System – Proposals for Reform of TRIPS*, Cheltenham, UK and Northampton, MA, USA: Edward Elgar, 2011); Geiger, C. (2008), 'Flexibilising Copyright – Remedies to the Privatisation of Information by Copyright Law', 39 *IIC*, p. 196.

confirmed by Article 31 (1) of the Vienna Convention on the Law of Treaties, stating that 'a treaty shall be interpreted in good faith in accordance with the ordinary meaning to be given to the terms of the treaty in their context and in the light of its *object and purpose*' (emphasis added).[4] Article 7 of the TRIPS Agreement lays down a principle of balance between rights and obligations and emphasizes that the Agreement has the goal of fostering not only economic development, but also social welfare. This means that while interpreting the provisions of TRIPS, the single economic perspective cannot be followed exclusively.[5] Article 8 TRIPS goes in the same direction, as it allows the member states to adopt measures for the promotion of 'the public interest in sectors of vital importance to their socio-economic and technological development'. Furthermore, the preamble of the TRIPS Agreement refers to the objective of promoting effective IP but also to adequate protection mechanisms, recognizing the 'underlying public policy objectives of national systems' and even for

---

[4] *See* for a more detailed exposition, Frankel, S. 'WTO Application of "the Customary Rules of Interpretation of Public International Law" to Intellectual Property', 46 *Virginia Journal of International Law* 365 (2006). *See* also the Doha Declaration on the TRIPS Agreement and Public Health adopted by the Ministerial conference (WT/Min (01)/DEC/2, 20 November 2001), where it is explicitly stated that 'in applying the customary rules of interpretation of international law, each provision of the TRIPS Agreement shall be read in the light of the object and purpose of the Agreement as expressed, in particular, in its objectives and principles' (Article 5 a).

[5] *See* for more detail Grosse Ruse-Khan, H., 'A Comparative Analysis of Policy Space in WTO Law' (26 November 2008), *Max Planck Institute for Intellectual Property, Competition & Tax Law Research Paper Series* No. 08-02 (also available in Kur, A. (ed.), *Intellectual Property Rights in a Fair World Trade System – Proposals for Reform of TRIPS*, Cheltenham, UK and Northampton, MA, USA: Edward Elgar, 2011). Yu, P.K. (2009), 'The Objectives and Principles of the TRIPS Agreement', 46 *Houston Law Review*, p. 979 sq., stating that the TRIPS Agreement 'includes a number of flexibilities to facilitate development and to protect the public interest. To safeguard these flexibilities, Article 7 and 8 provide explicit and important objectives and principles that play important roles in the interpretation and the implementation of the Agreement'. He also points out, following other commentators, that Article 7 is a 'should' provision and is contained in the text of the Agreement and not in the Preamble, which gives it a higher weight in the process of interpretation (*see also* in this sense UNCTAD-ICTDS, *Resource Book on TRIPS and Development*, Cambridge: Cambridge University Press, 2005, at p. 123). *See also* the WTO Panel Report of 17 March 2000, Canada – Patent Protection of Pharmaceutical Products, WT/DS114/R, § 7.26, where the Panel declares that 'both the goals and the limitations stated in Articles 7 and 8.1 must obviously be borne in mind when (examining the wording of the limitation provision) as well as those of other provisions in the TRIPS Agreement which indicate its object and purposes'.

least developed countries, the needs 'in respect of maximum flexibility in the domestic implementation'.[6] As has been very eloquently argued by Henning Grosse Ruse-Khan in a recent article, there is a principle of proportionality in international trade law that has to be respected while interpreting its provision.[7] 'Proportionality' is actually a notion that is used mostly in the context of issues of fundamental rights, especially as a method to solve conflicts between different values at stake.[8] This leads to my second remark.

2.2. Any Agreement has to be Placed in the Context of the Entire Legal Order

No provision of any text can be read bearing in mind only the context of the provision *within* the Agreement.[9] A larger perspective has to be taken. This means that even if the TRIPS Agreement is part of trade law, international obligations resulting from treaties protecting human rights and fundamental rights which member states are party to, have to be taken into account while interpreting its provisions.[10] Such international obliga-

---

[6] For more detail on the Preamble and its impact on the interpretation of the Agreement, *see* Gervais, D. (2003), *The TRIPS Agreement – Drafting History and Analysis*, 2nd ed., London: Sweet and Maxwell, § 2.08.

[7] Grosse Ruse-Khan, H. (2008), 'Proportionality and Balancing within the Objectives for Intellectual Property Protection', in Torremans, P. (ed.), *Intellectual Property and Human Rights*, Austin, Boston, Chicago, New York and The Netherlands: Kluwer law International, p. 161. *See also* Andenas, M. and Zleptnig, S. (2007), 'Proportionality and Balancing in WTO Law: A Comparative perspective', 20(1) *Cambridge Review of International Affairs*, pp. 71 *seq*, discussing the concepts of proportionality, necessity and balancing in the WTO legal framework; Kur, A., *supra* note 3, at p. 39, stating with reference to Article. XX GATT that 'the need to interpret the three-step test in the light of proportionality considerations cannot be emphasized enough'.

[8] Geiger, C. (2006), '"Constitutionalizing" Intellectual Property Law: The Influence of Fundamental Rights on Intellectual Property in Europe', 37 *IIC* pp. 371, 386; 'Copyright's Fundamental Rights Dimension at EU Level', in Derclaye, E. (ed.), *Research Handbook on the Future of EU Copyright*, Cheltenham, UK and Northampton, MA, USA: Edward Elgar, 2009, p. 27.

[9] *See* in this sense Remiche, B. (2007), 'L'accord ADPIC, dix ans après: un accord de libre-échange ou d'intégration force', in Remiche, B. and Kors, J. (eds), *L'accord ADPIC, 10 ans après: regards croisés, Europe-Amérique Latine*, Brussels: Larcier, p. 533.

[10] On the interaction between IP and international human rights provisions, *see* Helfer, L.R. (2008), 'Three Approaches for Reconciling Human Rights and Intellectual Property Rights', in ALADDA (ed.), *Copyright and Freedom of Expression: ALAI Study Days 2006*, Barcelona: ALADDA, p. 116. According to

tions can result, for example, from the Universal Declaration of Human Rights (UDHR) of 1948 and the International Covenant on Economic, Social and Cultural Rights (ICESCR) of 19 December 1966 that both have to be used as a guideline for the interpretation of the TRIPS Agreement, and therefore also of the three-step test. Such an interpretation of TRIPS in the light of the international fundamental rights provisions could result from the general rule of interpretation of treaties to be found in Article 31 of the Vienna Convention on the Law of Treaties of 23 May 1969, which entered into force on 27 January 1980.[11] According to Article 31 (3) (c), for the interpretation of a treaty, 'any relevant rules of international law applicable in the relations between the parties' should be taken into account.[12] Given the numerous ethical questions involved, it is hard to deny that the UDHR, for example, can be just such a relevant rule in the context of the TRIPS Agreement. It is true that the exact interaction of the TRIPS Agreement and the UDHR is unclear from a legal point of view. However, it cannot be ignored that many scholars argue that there is actually primacy of international human rights acts over trade liberalization rules that makes it mandatory that these rules be interpreted in the light of the UDHR.[13] Furthermore, the UN Sub-Commission on Human

---

this author, it is certain 'that the rules, institutions, and discourse of international human rights are now increasingly relevant to intellectual property law and policy and that the two fields, once isolated from each other, are becoming ever more closely intertwined'. *See* also in this sense from the same author: 'Towards A Human Rights Framework for Intellectual Property', 40, *UC Davis Law Review* (2007), p. 971 and Yu, P.K. (2007), 'Reconceptualizing Intellectual Property Interests in a Human Rights Framework', 40, *UC Davis Law Review*, p. 1039; 'Ten Common Questions about Intellectual Property and Human Rights', 23 (4), *Georgia State University Law Review* (2007), p. 709; Bronzo, N. (2007), *Propriété intellectuelle et droits fondamentaux*', Paris: L'Harmattan.

[11] United Nations, Treaty Series, Vol. 1155, 331. However, it is true that some important WTO members such as the USA have not ratified the Vienna Convention.

[12] *See* Frankel, S., *supra* note 4, p. 420, underlining that 'Art. 31 (3)(c) is not limited to rules in relation to intellectual property law, but all rules of international law' and that therefore the 'open-textured nature of some TRIPS Agreement carve-outs may call for other areas of international law to be treated as part of the context for interpretation'.

[13] *See e.g.* the article of Marceau, G. (2002) (Counsellor for the Legal Affairs Division of the WTO Secretariat), 'WTO Dispute Settlement and Human Rights', 13 *European Journal of International Law*, pp. 753 *et seq.*, and from the same author: 'The WTO Dispute Settlement and Human Rights', in Abbott, F.M., Breining-Kaufmann, C. and Cottier, T. (eds), *International Trade and Human Rights: Foundations and Conceptual Issues*, World Trade Forum, Vol. 5 (Ann Arbor: University of Michigan Press, 2005), chapter 10; Howse, R. and Mutua,

Rights in its resolutions has, on several occasions, urged the World Trade Organization in general, and the Council on TRIPS during its ongoing review of the TRIPS Agreement in particular, '*to take fully into account the existing State obligations under international human rights instruments*' (emphasis added).[14] Of course, these resolutions have no binding character for the member states, but their political significance is not to be neglected. Furthermore, it is absolutely not excluded that these soft-law principles may evolve into customary international law.[15] Anyhow, to erase any doubts in this regard, an explicit reference to the UDHR in the TRIPS Agreement should be included during a future review.[16] This would guarantee that the enforcement of rules with prevailing economic considerations would not leave aside ethical considerations. Such a correction could be incorporated without substantial changes and could even achieve a consensus at international level, thus helping to 'constitutionalize' the Agreement and thus its acceptance. In fact, international trade law is complementary to human rights concerns and vice versa. As Robert Anderson and Hannu Wager have rightly stated, 'it remains that efficiently functioning markets, backed up by appropriate laws and institutions, are central to any realistic programme for development and hence to the fulfilment of human rights'.[17]

M. (2000), 'Protecting Human Rights in a Global Economy: Challenges for the World Trade Organization', Executive summary (Montreal, Rights & Democracy, International Centre for Human Rights and Democratic Development), arguing 'that trade and human rights regimes need not be in conflict, so long as the trade regime is interpreted and applied in a manner consistent with the human rights obligations of states. This interpretation respects the hierarchy of norms in international law, where human rights, to the extent that they have the status of custom in international law, and certainly where they have the status of preemptory norms, will normally prevail over specific, conflicting provisions of any treaties including trade agreements'.

[14] Resolution 2000/7 of the UN Sub-Commission on Human Rights, 17 August 2000, on 'Intellectual Property Rights and Human Rights' (E/CN.4/SUB.2/RES/2000/7). *See also* in this sense Resolution 2001/21 of the UN Sub-Commission on Human Rights, 16 August 2001 (E/CN.4/SUB.2/RES/2001/21).

[15] *See e.g.* Chinkin, C.M. (1989), 'The Challenge of Soft Law: Development and Change in International Law', 38 *International & Comparative Law Quarterly*, pp. 856 *et seq.*

[16] Geiger, C. (2008), 'The Constitutional Dimension of Intellectual Property', in Torremans, P. (ed), *Intellectual Property and Human Rights*, Austin, Boston, Chicago and New York and The Netherlands: Kluwer Law International, p. 118. Favouring a link between the TRIPS Agreement and human rights treaties, *see also* Helfer, L. (2003), 'Human Rights and Intellectual Property: Conflict or Coexistence?', 5 *Minnesota Intellectual Property Review*, p. 61.

[17] Anderson, R.D. and Wager, H. (2006), 'Human Rights, Development,

3. JUDICIAL INTERPRETATIONS OF THE THREE-STEP TEST IN THE TRIPS AGREEMENT (ESPECIALLY BY THE WTO PANEL)[18]

At first, scholars did not give the three-step test much attention and for a long time very few studied it. Things radically changed, however, when the WTO Panel convicted the United States for having adopted a law in violation of Article 13 of TRIPS, thus indicating to the world that the three-step test was to be taken very seriously and that the United States (or any other state) was not free to do as it pleased in the field of limitations and exceptions. In fact, the interpretation proposed by the Panel allows very limited latitude for legislators when adopting copyright limitations and for judges when applying a three-step test in a particular case. Let me recall briefly this WTO Panel ruling.

In a decision dated 25 June 2000,[19] the WTO Panel, referred to by the European Union, stated that the exception adopted by the American legislature, which exonerated all commercial establishments that broadcast music (such as bars or restaurants) from copyright royalty payments,[20] violated the three-step test of Article 13 TRIPS.[21] For the first time, the

---

and the WTO: The Cases of Intellectual Property and Competition Policy', 9 (3) *Journal of International Economic Law*, p. 715.

[18] Some parts of Section 3 are drawn from the article, 'The Role of the Three-Step Test in the Adaptation of Copyright Law to the Information Society', *e-Copyright Bulletin* (January–March 2007).

[19] Panel Report of 15 June 2000, United States – Article 110 (5) of the US Copyright Act, WT/DS160/R.

[20] 17 USC § 100 (5), as modified by an act of 1998 (Fairness in Music Licensing Act).

[21] Concerning this decision, *see e.g.* Ginsburg, J.C. (2001), 'Towards Supranational Copyright Law? The WTO Panel Decision and the 'Three-Step Test' for Copyright Exceptions', 187 *RIDA* p. 2; Lucas, A. (2001), 'Le "triple test" de l'article 13 de l'Accord ADPIC à la lumière du rapport du Groupe spécial de l'OMC "Etats-Unis Article 110 5) de la Loi sur le droit d'auteur"', in Ganea, P., Heath, C. and Schricker, G. (eds), *Urheberrecht, Gestern – Heute – Morgen: Mélanges A. Dietz*, Munich: C.H. Beck, p. 423; Goldmann, B.C. (2001), 'Victory for Songwriters in WTO Music-Royalties Dispute between US and EU – Background of the Conflict over the Extension of Copyright Homestyle Exemption', 32 *IIC*, p. 412; Brennan, D.J. (2002), 'The Three-Step Test Frenzy – Why the TRIPS Panel Decision might be considered Per Incuriam', 2 *IPQ*, p. 212; Hugenholtz, P.B., (2000), 'De wettelijke beperkingen beperkt: De WTO geeft de driestappentoets tanden', 2000 *AMI* 10; Oliver, J. (2002), 'Copyright in the WTO: The Panel Decision on the Three-Step Test', 25 *Columbia Journal of Law & the Arts*, p. 119; Ficsor, M. (2002), 'How Much of What? The 'Three-Step Test' and its Application in Two Recent WTO Dispute Settlement Cases', 192 *RIDA*,

Panel offered a definition of the conditions set by the test, whose content had until then been very unclear. It is not my purpose to examine the Panel's decision in detail. I will merely attempt to expose the way in which the national legislature's freedom could be restricted and then show how this could be prevented by a 'rethinking' or a 're-reading' of the requirements laid down in TRIPS.

According to the Panel, the first condition of the test, the requirement of a 'certain special case', implies that 'an exception or limitation in national legislation must be clearly defined' (which corresponds to the requirement of a 'certain' case) and then that it has 'an individual or limited application or purpose' (which corresponds to the requirement of a 'special' case). Whereas the Panel adopts a quantitative approach, asking for a quantitative restriction of allowed uses,[22] other commentators have proposed a qualitative appreciation, taking into account the justification of the exception and the underlying public interest.[23] According to the general principles of interpretation previously exposed, it seems that the function of the exception, which can be derived from fundamental and human rights provisions to which signatory states are also bound, should always be taken into account.[24] Anyhow, it is not my purpose to elaborate on this debate, but simply to note that the first criterion requires that the use covered by the text of the exception be generally determinable. As underlined by Séverine Dusollier, 'an overly vague provision whose scope of application could not be foreseen would not be admissible'.[25] In countries of the continental tradition, where legislation includes a limited list of exceptions, the question is not really relevant. To a certain extent, the enumerated cases

p. 111; Gaubiac, Y. (2001) 'Les exceptions au droit d'auteur: un nouvel avenir?', *Comm. com. électr.*, June p. 12. More recently, *see* Senftleben, M. (2006), 'Towards a Horizontal Standard for Limiting Intellectual Property Rights? WTO Panel Reports Shed Light on the Three-Step Test in Copyright Law and Related Tests in Patent and Trademark Law', 37 *IIC*, p. 407; Kur, A. *supra* note 3, p. 20.

22 § 6.108 *et seq.* of the Panel Report.

23 *See e.g.* Senftleben, M. (2004), *Copyright, Limitations and the Three-Step Test*, The Hague. Kluwer, pp. 138 *et seq.*; Ficsor, M., *supra* note 21, p. 132; Ricketson, S. (1987), *The Berne Convention for the Protection of Literary and Artistic Works: 1886–1986*, London: Kluwer, p. 482, according to whom the term 'special' means that 'the exception must be justified by some clear reason of public policy or some other exceptional circumstance'.

24 *See*, for a more detailed exposition, Geiger, C. (2004), *Droit d'auteur et droit du public à l'information, approche de droit compare*, Paris: Litec, p. 200; 'Fundamental Rights, a Safeguard for the Coherence of Intellectual Property Law?', 35 *IIC* (2004), p. 268.

25 Dusollier, S (2005), 'L'encadrement des exceptions au droit d'auteur par le test des trois étapes', *IRDI* p. 218.

generally indicate the scope of the exception, and this first condition is met without much difficulty. In common-law countries, however, which use an 'open' system of exceptions with a fair use or fair dealing-type clause, the condition could cause some problems.

In this sense, a few authors have wondered if the fair use exception was really compatible with the 'special case' requirement, some even answering (often with serious arguments) in the negative.[26] In my opinion, however, the history of the three-step test allows us to reject this analysis. One should not forget that the three-step test appeared for the first time in 1967 during the revision of the Berne Convention in Stockholm. At this conference, the definitive formulation of the test was proposed by the United Kingdom, which has a fair dealing exception. Similarly, the United States did not need to modify their legislation when they joined the Berne Convention in 1989. The argument according to which the fair use exception would violate the first step of the test thus appears to be refuted by the diplomatic context of the adoption of this legal instrument,[27] which one can also find in Articles 1705 (5) and 1706 (3) of the North American Free Trade Agreement (NAFTA) of 1994. Similarly, it is noteworthy that the United States was the main promoter of the TRIPS Agreement. It is very improbable that it intended to adopt (on many occasions, since the solution was

---

[26] *See e.g.* Cohen-Jehoram, H. (2005), 'Restrictions on Copyright and their Abuse', *EIPR*, p. 359 and from the same author: 'Is there a Hidden Agenda Behind the General Non-implementation of the EU Three-Step Test', *EIPR* (2009), p. 408; Bornkamm, J. (2002), 'Der Dreistufentest als urheberrechtliche Schrankenbestimmung- Karriere eines Begriffs', in Ahrens, H.J., Bornkamm, J., Gloy, W., Starck, J. and von Ungern-Sternberg, J. (eds), *Festschrift für Willi Erdman zum 65. Geburtstag*, Cologne, Berlin, Bonn and Munich: Carl Heymanns, p. 45; Lucas, A. (2009), 'Pour une interpretation raisonnable du triple test, ou pourquoi il faut éviter d'ajouter le flou au flou', 3 *Auteurs & Media*, p. 227; Ricketson, S. (2003), 'WIPO Study on Limitations and Exceptions of Copyright and Related Rights in the Digital Environment', *SCCR* 9/7, Geneva: WIPO, April, pp. 68 *et seq.*

[27] *See* in this sense Senftleben, M., *supra* note 23, pp. 163, 168, as well as from the same author: 'Die Bedeutung der Schranken des Urheberrechts in der Informationsgesellschaft und ihre Begrenzung durch den Dreistufentest', in Hilty, M.R. and Peukert, A. (eds), *Interessenausgleich im Urheberrecht*, Baden-Baden: Nomos, 2004, p. 177; Geiger, C. (2007), 'From Berne to National Law, via the Copyright Directive: The Dangerous Mutations of the Three-Step Test', *EIPR*, p. 486; Griffiths, J., 'The "Three-Step Test" – its Relationship with the Common Law concepts of "Fairness" and "Public Interest"', paper presented at a workshop on: 'Rethinking the Three-Step Test', jointly organized by the Max Planck Institute for Intellectual Property, Competition and Tax Law and Queen Mary, University of London, Paris, ULIP, 16 February 2007.

afterwards used in 1996 in the WIPO treaties[28]) a provision that would have been radically contrary to its legal tradition. However, one cannot deny that to this day the question is not entirely settled. If, in the future, a state having a limited list of exceptions decided to introduce more flexibility into its system in order to better adapt to technical and social changes, it might risk being accused of violating its international commitments. For example, Israel recently introduced a fair use-type provision into its copyright legislation.[29] Could Israel be condemned by the WTO Panel for having done so? This uncertainty should be clarified for the future by clear guidelines of interpretation. We will come back to that later.

The condition that really presents a problem, since it has the potential to considerably restrict the freedom of national legislatures, is that of non-conflict with the normal exploitation of the work. Indeed, how is 'normal exploitation' to be understood? The TRIPS Agreement does not shed any light on this point and interpretation of the notion is far from clear. In the WTO Panel's decision on copyright, the criterion of normal exploitation was deemed to involve consideration of the forms of exploitation that currently generate an income for the author as well as those which, in all probability, were likely to be of importance in the future.[30] This interpretation includes a certain number of dangerous potentialities. On the one hand, it could impose a *status quo* and prevent any extension of exceptions to new situations unforeseen by the letter of the text, but which could derive from

---

[28] *See* the Minutes of the Main Committee I of the 1996 WIPO conference (WIPO Doc. CRNR/DC/102, para. 488), where it is obvious that the general exception of fair use, although very broad in its application, was not prohibited.

[29] Section 19 of the Israeli Copyright Law 2007. *See* on this issue, Afori, O.F. (2008) 'An Open Standard "Fair Use" Doctrine: A Welcome Israeli Initiative', *EIPR* 85; Pessach, G. (2010) 'The New Israeli Copyright Act – A Case Study in Reverse Comparative Law', 41 *IIC* 187. A version of the fair use doctrine was also adopted in Singapore (*see* Loon, N. (2009), 'Exploring Flexibilities within the global IP Standards', *IPQ*, p. 162) and Japan is currently seriously considering implementing a fair use provision in its copyright legislation. *See* Tamura, Y., 'Current Trends and the Future of Copyright in Japan', Paper presented at the International Symposium 'Intellectual Property and Global Justice', Hokkaido University, Sapporo, Japan, 19 August 2009. In the European context, introducing some more flexibility into the closed system of limitations has been advocated; *see e.g.* Geiger, C. (2010) 'The Future of Copyright in Europe: Striking a Fair Balance between Protection and Access to Information', *I.P.Q.* at 8. For an argument in favour of the introduction of horizontal fair use provisions in order to maintain a proper balance between protection and competing freedoms, *see also* Chapter 8 by M. Senftleben, 'Overprotection and Protection Overlaps in Intellectual Property Law – The Need for Horizontal Fair Use Defences', in this book.

[30] WTO Panel Report of 15 June 2000, *supra* note 19, § 6.180.

its spirit. On the other hand, reference to future exploitations runs the risk of paralysing exceptions every time a technical evolution allows control of previously uncontrollable uses, and thus creates new possibilities for exploitation.[31] Bearing in mind the new possibilities for right holders to control uses of their works through technical measures, this could even lead, in the long run, to the disappearance of limitations in the digital environment.[32]

In any case, it is not at all certain that this interpretation is correct or takes sufficiently into account the fundamental rights obligations resulting from international law. Indeed, the Panel's interpretation of Article 13 TRIPS Agreement follows a predominantly economic logic.[33] The sociocultural dimension of copyright law, predominant in Article 27 UDHR and Article 15 ICESCR, should lead to a more normative approach to the second step, taking into account member states' cultural policy objective.[34] A more normative reading could also follow from the objectives of the agreement laid down in Article 7, as this article is 'crucial for interpreting broad and open legal concepts within TRIPS treaty language which are likely to have significant influence on the ability of WTO member states to balance different interests addressed in or affected by IP protection'.[35] In the opposite case, it would leave almost no discretion to national legislatures regarding the implementation of new limitations in the future, especially to adapt the system to technical or social evolutions. The WTO

---

[31] In this sense, *see also* Buydens, M. and Dusollier, S., (2001) 'Les exceptions au droit d'auteur: évolutions dangereuses', *Comm. com. électr.*, September, p. 13; Ginsburg, J.C., *supra* note 21, p. 48, underlining the risk that 'the traditionally free uses, such as for training purposes or parody, be considered as normal exploitations, supposing that right holders manage to implement a profitable collecting system'.

[32] *See also* Buydens, M. and Dusollier, S., *supra* note 31, p. 12. For further developments, *see* Geiger, C., *supra* note 24, p. 357.

[33] *See* Geiger, C., Griffiths, J. and Hilty, R.M. (2008), 'Towards a Balanced Interpretation of the "Three-Step Test" in Copyright Law', *EIPR*, p. 489, stating that under the interpretation of the WTO Panel, 'the second step of the "test" becomes a form of "show-stopper", precluding law-makers from taking into account any interests other than the private economic interests of right-holders'.

[34] For a normative approach to the second step, *see also* Ginsburg J.C., *supra* note 21, p. 23. Ricketson, S. and Ginsburg, J.C. (2006), *International Copyright and Neighbouring Rights – The Berne Convention and Beyond*, 2nd ed., Oxford: Oxford University Press, § 13.21, stating that the second step requires the taking into account of 'non-economic as well as economic normative considerations'.

[35] Grosse Ruse-Khan, H., 'Proportionality and Balancing within the Objectives for Intellectual Property Protection', *supra* note 7, p. 162. This author lists the concept of 'normal exploitation' among the open provisions to be interpreted in the light of the TRIPS objectives specified in Articles 7 and 8 of the Agreement. *See also* Yu, P.K., 'The Objectives and Principles of the TRIPS Agreement', *supra* note 5.

Panel has incidentally expressly admitted this normative approach in the framework of interpretation of Article 30 TRIPS Agreement, which also provides a three-step test in patent law.[36] According to this report, to which reference is rarely made in the debate regarding the three-test step, exploitation must be considered normal when it is 'essential to the achievement of the goals of patent policy'.[37] It is true that the formulation remains somewhat vague, but it seems to provide the legislature with the option to take normative elements into account and thus not limit its analysis to a strictly economic approach.[38] Admittedly, the wording of the second step in Article 30 is slightly different than in Article 13 TRIPS and seems to imply that a conflict with a normal exploitation can be justified under a normative approach. In fact, 'exceptions must not *unreasonably* conflict with normal exploitation of the patent'. Similarly, according to Article 26.2 TRIPS, 'members may provide limited exceptions to the protection of industrial designs, provided that such exceptions do not *unreasonably* conflict with the normal exploitation of protected industrial designs' (emphasis added). The reference to a notion such as the 'reasonableness' of the restriction to the exclusive right allows taking into account other interests than those of the right holder. Article 30 and Article 26.2 TRIPS thus seem to allow a more flexible application of the test. However, there is no objective reason why restrictions to the right of the owner of a patent or of an industrial design should be treated differently from those of the owner of a copyright.[39]

Anyhow, it would be advisable to go a little further and adopt, in addi-

---

[36] Article 30 TRIPS: 'Members may provide limited exceptions to the exclusive rights conferred by a patent, provided that such exceptions do not unreasonably conflict with a normal exploitation of the patent and do not unreasonably prejudice the legitimate interests of the patent owner, taking account of the legitimate interests of third parties'.

[37] WTO Panel Report of 17 March 2000 (WT/DS114/R), *supra* note 5, § 7.58. On this report, *see* Senftleben, M., 'Towards a Horizontal Standard for Limiting Intellectual Property Rights? WTO Panel Reports Shed Light on the Three-Step Test in Copyright Law and Related Tests in Patent and Trademark Law', *supra* note 21. *See also* the paper presented by this author on the different reports of the WTO Panel at the workshop 'Rethinking the Three-Step Test', jointly organized by the Max Planck Institute for Intellectual Property, Competition and Tax Law and Queen Mary, University of London, Paris, ULIP, 16 February 2007.

[38] More generally, for an analysis of exclusions and exceptions to Patent Law provisions in TRIPS from an international Human Rights perspective, *see* Haugen, H.M. (2009), 'Human Rights and TRIPS Exclusion and Exception Provisions', 5 (6) *Journal of World Intellectual Property*, p. 345.

[39] As Annette Kur, *supra* note 3, p. 19, interestingly points out, the drafting history of the TRIPS Agreement also does not offer an explanation as to why these

tion to a normative approach, an extremely restrictive approach to the notion of normal exploitation of a work in order to avoid the legislature and judges losing all their powers. In fact, such interpretations have been put forward. According to Martin Senftleben, conflict with normal exploitation should occur only if 'the author is deprived from a current or potential market of considerable economic and practical importance'.[40] The notion of normal exploitation would then cover, as justly underlined by Séverine Dusollier, only 'the main avenues of the exploitation of the work, i.e. those which constitute the author's major sources of income'.[41] That being said, the problem is that even when adopting a restrictive approach and when integrating a normative dimension, the approach remains above all economic and the viewpoint that of the right holder.

Such a restrictive reading of the second step is necessary to allow the third step to be taken into account, which is by far the most important one, since it allows an examination of the justification that underlies the limitations. In fact, under the third step, the copyright limitations cannot cause an 'unjustified' prejudice to the right holder. In fact, the right holder cannot have the power to control *all* uses of his works, as some prejudices may be justified in light of values deemed superior to the interests of the right holder.[42] This formulation allows the carrying out of a proportionality test, which recalls the method used to settle conflicts between fundamental rights.[43] The legislature and the judge applying the test must then

---

differences in wording occurred and whether they were intended to have a special meaning.

40 Senftleben, M., *supra* note 23, p. 193.

41 Dusollier, S., *supra* note 25, p. 220. This author adds that 'to reason otherwise would make the exceptions lose their meaning and gradually disappear'. *See also* in this sense, Lucas, A. 'For a Reasonable Interpretation of the Three-Step Test", *supra* note 26, stating that the definition of normal exploitation should take into account 'the potential effect of the exception only if these effects are suited to deprive the right owners *substantial* gains' (emphasis added); Griffiths, J. (2009), 'The "Three-Step test" in European Copyright Law – Problems and Solutions', IPQ at 457, according to whom 'there is strong argument that a conflict with a normal exploitation of the work should only be regarded as arising where an author or copyright owner is deprived of an extensive share of his or her potential market'. He concludes that the test should not be considered 'as a form of long-stop, a loose constraint prohibiting only exceptions that would generally be acknowledged to be unjustifiable'.

42 Reasoning on the basis of conflicting fundamental rights, the German Constitutional Court specified this very clearly in its '*School Book*' decisions of 7 July 1971, *GRUR* 1972, p. 481.

43 Senftleben, M., *supra* note 23, p. 226; Dusollier, S., *supra* note 25, p. 221. *See* also Gervais, D. (2005), 'Towards a New Core International Copyright Norm: The

consider the justification behind the limitation and come to a differentiated analysis in light of the many interests and fundamental rights at stake.[44]

4. FOR A NEW INTERPRETATION OF THE THREE-STEP TEST

In order to allow taking all interests involved into account, it seems necessary to 'rethink' the three-step test and to adopt a new reading of it.[45] Indeed, to reach balanced solutions, it could be useful to begin with the third step and to use the second step afterwards as a corrective measure to eliminate the most abusive conflicts with the exploitation of the work.[46] The TRIPS Agreement does not seem to forbid such a reading. In fact, if you compare the wording of Article 13 with other provisions

---

Reverse Three-Step Test', 9 *Marquette Intellectual Property Law Review*, pp. 1 *et seq.*, stating 'that the inclusion of a reasonableness/justifiability criterion is a key that allows legislators to establish a balance between on the one hand, the rights of authors and copyright holders, and the needs and interests of users, on the other hand'.

44 Geiger, C. (2006), 'The Three-Step Test, A Threat to a Balanced Copyright Law?', 37 *IIC*, pp. 683, 696. *See also* Hugenholtz, P.B., 'Free Speech and the Three Step-Test: A Tongue Twister', paper presented at the workshop 'Rethinking the Three-Step Test', jointly organized by the Max Planck Institute for Intellectual Property, Competition and Tax Law and Queen Mary, University of London, Paris, ULIP, 16 February 2007.

45 It has to be noted that, in the meantime, national courts have started to read the three-step test in a different way from the Panel decision, in a much more liberal manner. *See e.g.* the decision of the Swiss Supreme Court, 1st Civil Division, 26 June 2007, 39 *IIC* 990 (2008). For a comment *see* Geiger, C. (2008), 'Rethinking Copyright Limitations in the Information Society: The Swiss Supreme Court Leads the Way', 39 *IIC*, p. 943; Court of Appeal of Barcelona (SAP), 17 September 2008. Commenting on recent cases in Spain related to the test, one scholar even notes that 'Spanish case law proves that the test can be used by courts not to further "restrict" the scope of a statutory exception but to provide for some well-needed room to "manoeuvre" in applying the exceptions to specific cases and scenarios' (Xalabarder, R. (2008), 'Fair Use in Spain: The EUCD Aftermath', in Ghidini, G. and Genovesi, L.M. (eds), *Intellectual Property and Market Power*, Buenos Aires: EUDEBA, p. 811). For a discussion of many national court decisions on the three-step test, *see* Griffiths, J. *supra* note 41, part. 428.

46 *See* Geiger, C. (2005), 'Right to Copy v. Three-Step Test, The Future of the Private Copy Exception in the Digital Environment', *Computer Law Review International* (*CRi*), p. 12; 'The Three-Step Test, a Threat to a Balanced Copyright Law?', *supra* note 44. Approving such a reading, Vivant, M., 'Rethinking the Three-Step Test: What are the Possibilities Left by Interpretation of the Conditions?', paper presented at the workshop 'Rethinking the Three-Step Test', jointly organ-

in TRIPS modelled on the three-step test, some of them, like Article 17 (trademarks), even provide for only one main criterion for member states, namely to 'take account of the legitimate interests of the owner of the trademark and of third parties'.[47] This seems to indicate that the 'third step' is to be considered as the most important one. As we have already underlined, it is therefore appropriate to adopt an extremely restrictive approach to the notion of normal exploitation of the work, in order to place the third step – which allows a balancing of the different interests at stake – at the center. However, this is not enough and it must be ensured that the legislature and judges examine the third step. In order to do so, the test should be examined in reverse. The psychological effect would not be negligible: after having balanced the different interests involved, they would certainly be less inclined to censor the use by adopting a purely economic approach and would therefore use the second step as a mere correcting tool.

Another solution would be to read the test as stating a number of factors that need to be considered by the judge, on the model of the American doctrine of fair use.[48] In fact the second step of the test is strongly reminiscent of the fourth factor of Article 107 of the American Copyright Act of 1976, according to which the effect of the use upon the

---

ized by the Max Planck Institute for Intellectual Property, Competition and Tax Law and Queen Mary, University of London, Paris, ULIP, 16 February 2007.

[47] The full wording of Article 17 TRIPS is: 'Members may provide limited exceptions to the rights conferred by a trademark, such as fair use of descriptive terms, provided that such exceptions take account of the legitimate interests of the owner of the trademark and of third parties'. The first 'step' is therefore still present through the reference to the need to provide only 'limited' exceptions. Anyhow, it has to be noted that no reference to the normal exploitation can be found.

[48] Koelman, K.J. (2006), 'Fixing the Three-Step Test', *EIPR*, p. 407; 'The Room for Interpretation of the Three-Step-Test', Paper presented at the workshop 'Rethinking the Three-Step Test', jointly organized by the Max Planck Institute for Intellectual Property, Competition and Tax Law and Queen Mary, University of London, Paris, ULIP, 16 February 2007. Senftleben, M. (2007), 'L'application du triple test: vers un système de fair use européen', *Propriété Intellectuelle* 453, and from the same author: 'Fair Use in the Netherlands – A Renaissance?' *AMI* (2009), 1: 'The adoption of a fair use system that rests on the flexible, open criteria of a conflict with a normal exploitation and an unreasonable prejudice to the legitimate interests would pave the way for this more flexible and balanced application of the test' (at 7). Such an interpretation has been strongly contested as being contrary to the wording of the test (see Lucas, A. *supra* note 26, 281: 'It is sufficient to recall that the order of conditions (of the two last conditions) was discussed at Stockholm and that the drafters have explicitly indicated that one must not examine the third condition if the second one is not fulfilled').

potential market for or value of the copyrighted work must be taken into account. However, it is only one factor among others. The second step of the impact on normal use of the work would thus constitute *one of the criteria* to implement, one of the parameters to take into account during the analysis of the application of a limitation. However, it would not be the only one. Under this approach, the three-step test would probably have to be renamed the 'three-factor test'.

In any case, whatever interpretation is followed, it is crucial that the three-step test is interpreted in a new way in order to ensure a just balance of the different interests involved. In fact, the scope of this legal instrument has steadily extended and understanding of it in the course of time has radically changed its legal impact.[49] Today, the test affects all debates concerning the future of exceptions and limitations to copyright.[50] Against that background, in a joint project by the Max Planck Institute for Intellectual Property, Competition and Tax Law and Queen Mary, University of London, a group of experts has jointly elaborated a declaration aiming at securing a balanced interpretation of the 'Three-Step Test' in copyright law[51]. The aim of this declaration was clearly 'to restore the 'three-step

---

[49] Geiger, C., 'From Berne to National Law, via the Copyright Directive: The Dangerous Mutations of the Three-Step Test', *supra* note 27; 'The Role of the Three-Step Test in the Adaptation of Copyright Law to the Information Society', *supra* note 18.

[50] *See* the Green Paper 'Copyright in the Knowledge Economy' of the Commission of the European Communities, COM(2008) 466/3, p. 5, stating that the three-step test 'has become a benchmark for all copyright limitations'. On this document, *see* Geiger, C., Macrez, F., Bouvel, A., Carre, S., Hassler, T. and Schmidt-Szalewski, J. (2009), 'What Limitations to Copyright in the Information Society? A Comment on the European Commission's Green Paper "Copyright in the Knowledge Economy"', *IIC*, p. 412; Hilty, R.M., Krujatz, S., Bajon, B., Früh, A., Kur, A., Drexl, J., Geiger, C. and Klass, N. (2009), 'European Commission – Green Paper: Copyright in the Knowledge Economy – Comments by the Max Planck Institute for Intellectual Property and Tax Law', *IIC*, p. 319.

[51] Declaration on a balanced interpretation of the Three-Step Test in Copyright Law, *IIC* 2008, p. 707. On this declaration, *see* Geiger, C., Griffiths, J. and Hilty, R.M., 'Towards a Balanced Interpretation of the "Three-Step test" in Copyright Law', *supra* note 33. This declaration can be consulted and signed online at the following address: www.ip.mpg.de. The declaration was published (or will be published) in the Netherlands (Auteurs-, Media- & Informatierecht (AMI) 2009, 8), in Germany (*GRUR Int.* 2008, 822), in France (*Propr. intell.* 2008, 399), in Belgium (Auteurs et Médias 2008, 516), in Spain (Actas de derecho industrial y derecho de autor 2007–2008, Vol. 28, 1509), in Italy (Diritto informazione e informatica 2009, 159), in Portugal (Direito da Sociedade da Informação), in Brazil (Revista Trimestral de Direito Civil, July–September 2008, Vol. 35, 239) and in Japan

test' to its original role as a relatively flexible standard precluding clearly unreasonable encroachments upon an author's rights without interfering unduly with the ability of legislatures and courts to respond to the challenges presented by shifting commercial and technological contexts in a fair and balanced manner'.[52] This declaration starts by recalling that the three-step test constitutes an indivisible entirety and that the three steps are to be considered together and as a whole in a comprehensive overall assessment (Article 1). It also clarifies that the requirement of having a 'certain special case' does not prevent legislatures from introducing open-ended limitations and exceptions, so long as the scope of such limitations and exceptions is reasonably foreseeable (Article 3). It also proposes to adopt a normative understanding of the concept of normal exploitation in taking into account the justification of the limitation as well as the payment of an adequate compensation for the use of the work (Article 4). And, finally, it also clearly states that interests deriving from human rights and fundamental freedoms, as well as interests in competition and other public interests (scientific progress, cultural, social, or economic development), must be taken into account when interpreting the three-step test (Article 6). This declaration has been analysed and, since then, some additional but compliant interpretations have been proposed in the specific context of the TRIPS Agreement, in order, for example, to extend the balancing exercise in all areas of IP.[53]

(Digital Content Association of Japan (DCAJ), 'Research on the Introduction of Fair-Use Provisions into Japanese Copyright Law', Annual Report of the Digital Content Association of Japan 2009, 69).

52 Geiger, C., Griffiths, J. and Hilty, R.M., 'Towards a Balanced Interpretation of the 'Three-Step test' in Copyright Law', *supra* note 33.

53 *See* Kur, A., *supra* note 3, pp. 40 *et seq.* Another reading has been also proposed by He, H. (2009), 'Seeking a Balanced Interpretation for the Three-Step Test: An Adjusted Structure in View of Divergent Approaches', 40 *IIC*, p. 274. Wright, R. (2009), 'The "Three-Step Test" and the Wider Public Interest: Towards a More Inclusive Interpretation', *Journal of World Intellectual Property*, pp. 600–21. Anyhow, the declaration was also subject to some (isolated) critical comments, mainly because it gives too much weight to public interests instead of focusing mainly on right holders and therefore it would be too far away from the legal rationales underlying the three-step test (*see* Lucas, A., *supra* note 26, p. 227).

5. IN CONCLUSION: THE NEED FOR A LEGAL INSTRUMENT IN ORDER TO CLARIFY THE INTERPRETATION OF THE TRIPS AGREEMENT AND ITS LIMITATION AND EXCEPTION PROVISIONS

We have seen that the international framework provides for flexible mechanisms that allow balanced interpretations of the limitation and exceptions provisions in TRIPS such as the three-step test.[54] The existing WTO Panel decisions should therefore not be the only orientation for legislators or judges when understanding international intellectual property law. Other interpretations have been put forward, fully compliant with the general principles ruling the Agreement. However, the question of limitations and exceptions is of such relevance in the current debate on copyright and intellectual property in general[55] that it is recommended that such guidelines of interpretations should somehow be included in the international legal framework. This would help legislators and judges gauge their room to manoeuvre and guarantee a more harmonious use of the three-step test provision in the future, thereby also securing that this provision does not function as an ultimate 'show-stopper' whenever an initiative is taken to rebalance the copyright system in order to take into account important interests of society. Such a clarification would surely enhance legal security.

Of course, the most transparent way would be to amend the TRIPS Agreement in order to reformulate the three-step test in a more balanced manner.[56] Another feasible option could be to add an appendix to the

---

[54] *See* in this sense Chapter 7 by A.F. Christie in this book, 'Maximising Permissible Exceptions to Intellectual Property Rights', proposing to draft an exception in national law using the language and concepts of the three-step test in order to maximise the range of activities permitted.

[55] On the importance of limitations to foster creativity and innovation, *see* Geiger, C. (2010), 'Promoting Creativity through Copyright Limitations: Reflections on the Concept of Exclusivity in Copyright Law', 12 (3) *Vanderbilt Journal of Entertainment & Technology Law*, p. 515.

[56] *See* for example the interesting proposal developed by a group of academics in the framework of the project 'Intellectual Property Rights in Transition' (IPT) of adding a new 'balancing clause' in the Agreement (Art. 8a) in order to operate as a guideline for legislature and courts (Kur, A. (ed.), *Intellectual Property Rights in a Fair World Trade System – Proposals for Reform of TRIPS*, (Cheltenham, UK and Northampton, MA, USA: Edward Elgar, 2011); For a rephrasing of the three-step test in order to better take into account the public interest and to assure an adequate balancing of interests, *see* also Sun, H. (2007), 'Overcoming the Achilles Heel of Copyright Law', *Northwestern Journal of Technology & Intellectual*

TRIPS Agreement or any other legal instrument, allowing the establishment of a guide to the interpretation of the provision on limitations and exceptions, on the model of the Agreed Statement concerning the three-step test in the WIPO Treaty of 1996 (Article 10). According to that statement,

> it is understood that the provisions of Article 10 permit Contracting Parties to carry forward and appropriately extend into the digital environment limitations and exceptions in their national laws which have been considered acceptable under the Berne Convention. Similarly, these provisions should be understood to permit Contracting Parties to devise new exceptions and limitations that are appropriate in the digital network environment.

This Agreed Statement clearly shows that it was not the intention of the drafters of the treaty to understand the three-step test as the ultimate barrier for any legislature adopting new limitations and exceptions.[57] Again, another possibility that has been mentioned previously would be to add a reference to the UDHR in the Preamble of the TRIPS Agreement, clarifying that international human rights treaties have to be taken into account when interpreting the Agreement. In any event, all these hard-law options would need a strong commitment by the member states that seems difficult to achieve in the near future,[58] bearing in mind that some of them are currently more likely to advocate the adoption of TRIPS-plus standards[59] (if one looks at the content of recent bilateral free trade agreements).

To establish such a guide to interpretation, there would therefore be some clear advantages in using soft-law mechanisms (such as declarations, guidelines, resolutions or codes of conduct), as these would not require modification of existing provisions, which is always very difficult

---

Property, p. 265 *sq.*, who pleads for replacing the three-step test by a new test that would fully integrate public interest into its ambit (mainly by reducing the test to its current third step); Suthersanen, U. (2005), 'Human Rights and International Copyright Law', in Griffiths, J. and Suthersanen, U. (eds), *Copyright and Free Speech*, Oxford, Oxford University Press, p. 121; Gervais, D., *supra* note 43, p. 29.

57 *See* Senftleben, M. (2006), in Dreier, T. and Hugenholtz, P. B. (eds), *Concise European Copyright Law*, The Netherlands: Kluwer Law International, WCT, Art. 10, No. 6.

58 *See* in this sense Griffiths, J., *supra* note 41, stating that 'the practical difficulties of achieving any form of solution based on a rewriting of the 'test' are obvious. Copyright reform is a slow and acrimonious process' (at 442).

59 *See* recently on this issue the very interesting book edited by Daniel Gervais, (2007) *Intellectual Property, Trade and Development: Strategies to Optimize Economic Development in a TRIPS-Plus Area*, Oxford: Oxford University Press.

politically.[60] In this spirit, but in a far more ambitious way, such use of soft-law modalities has been advocated by Bernd Hugenholtz and Ruth Okediji in a very interesting report, in order to implement a full international instrument on limitations and exceptions to copyright.[61] Going in the same direction, but one step further, in order to embrace all IP rights, Annette Kur and Henning Grosse Ruse-Khan have proposed in a recent paper introducing 'ceiling rules' which would provide for a binding maximum of protection at the international level and have advocated mandatory 'limitations'.[62]

Any initiative in the direction of a more adequate international framework on limitations and exceptions must of course be encouraged, from the more modest to the most ambitious. Anyhow, in the meantime, we legal scholars, not bound by private interests and lobby groups, have

---

[60] For a very interesting analysis of the various options from an institutional perspective, *see* A. Bakardjieva Engelbrekt, 'Factoring Limitations into the System: Institutional Choice and Design', Paper presented at the Conference 'Enough is Enough!: Ceiling on Intellectual Property Rights', New York University, New York, 1 May 2009. More generally, *see also* from the same author: 'Copyright from an Institutional Perspective: Actors, Interests, Stakes and the Logic of Participation', 4 (2), *Review of Economic Research on Copyright Issues* 2007, p. 65.

[61] Hugenholtz, P.B. and Okediji, R., 'Conceiving an International Instrument on Limitations and Exceptions to Copyright, Final Report', *supra* note 3, p. 49, referring to soft-law mechanisms such as Joint Recommendations of WIPO's Standing Committee or, in the context of TRIPS, to the Doha Declaration adopted at the Fourth Ministerial Conference in November 2001. According to these scholars, the advantages of using soft-law models are numerous: first, soft law has been influential in international economic law; second, soft law might evolve into hard law and become binding as international customary law; third, states are more willing to negotiate in detail because of limited effects; fourth, avoiding national ratification leads to stronger commitments by states; and fifth, soft law is easier to amend in case of technical and social changes (at 45). *See also* in this sense, Barczewski, M. (2011), 'From Hard to Soft Law: A Requisite Shift in the International Copyright Regime', *IIC*, p. 40, with direct reference to the 'declaration' as a possible model.

[62] Kur, A. and Grosse Ruse-Khan, H., 'Enough is Enough – The Notion of Binding Ceilings in International Intellectual Property Protection', *Max Planck Institute for Intellectual Property Research Paper Series* No. 09-01 (also available in Kur, A. (ed.), *Intellectual Property Rights in a Fair World Trade System – Proposals for Reform of TRIPS*, Cheltenham, UK and Northampton, MA, USA: Edward Elgar, 2011). In their paper, the concept of 'limitations' is understood very broadly, including 'binding obligations – inside and outside the IP Framework – to give effect to interests distinct from those of IP right holders and their exploitation of protected subject matter' (at 5). See also Kur, A. (2009), 'International Norm-Making in the Field of Intellectual Property: A shift towards Maximum Rules?', *WIPOJ* 27.

one – very small but maybe not to be underestimated – power left in today's debate on copyright limitations: to provide independent and balanced interpretations of existing legal instruments.[63] It would therefore be a pity not to use it.

---

[63] *See*, in the context of European copyright law, Geiger, C. (2009), 'Drafting the Appropriate and Balanced Scope of Copyright Protection in the European Union – What Language can Contribute to the Debate', in Gendreau, Y. and Drassinower, A. (eds), *Language and Copyright/Langues et droit d'auteur*, Québec and Brussels: Carswell and Bruylant, p. 59. *See also* Carter, E.L. (2009), 'Harmonization of Copyright Law in Response to Technological Change: Lessons from Europe about Fair Use and Free Expression', 30 (2) *University of La Verne Law Review* 313, with direct reference to the 'Declaration of the Three Step Test' as a response to changes brought about by technology and harmonization and a 'method for the rescue of public interest within copyright' (at 325).

14. The concept of sustainable development in international IP law – new approaches from EU Economic Partnership Agreements?

Henning Grosse Ruse-Khan*

> The international intellectual property system cannot operate in isolation from broader public policy questions such as how to meet human needs as basic health, food and a clean environment. (Pascal Lamy)[1]

In international law, the concept of sustainable development has an ambiguous meaning and several distinct connotations. Amongst those, the principle of integration and reconciliation of economic, social and environmental aspects functions as its core element. This principle finds support in several general (as well as IP-related) provisions of the first comprehensive Economic Partnership Agreement (EPA), signed in October 2008 between the European Community and its member states and the CARIFORUM group of Caribbean Countries. This agreement may serve as a template: not only for EPA-negotiations with other regional groups of African, Caribbean and Pacific (ACP) countries; but equally for other

* Senior Research Fellow, Max Planck Institute for Intellectual Property and Competition Law, Munich (Germany); email: henning-gr-khan@ip.mpg.de. This chapter has been prepared within the framework of a MPI project on reforming the international intellectual property system. It is based on a policy paper for the International Centre for Trade and Sustainable Development (ICTSD) and the article 'A Real Partnership for Development? Sustainable Development as Treaty Objective in European Economic Partnership Agreements and Beyond', published in the *Journal of International Economic Law*, 13(1) (2010).

[1] Director General of the World Trade Organisation (WTO), speech delivered at the WIPO Conference on Intellectual Property and Public Policy Issues, Geneva, 14 July 2009 – online available at http://www.wipo.int/meetings/en/2009/ip_gc_ge/presentations/lamy.html.

free trade agreements (FTAs) Europe is currently pursuing with India, South Korea, ASEAN countries and states in South and Central America. Given the continuous malfunctioning of multilateral negotiations under the WTO Doha Round, the standards set by FTAs are the most important benchmarks which are likely to be 'multilateralised' later on. Against this background, the agenda pursued and the provisions accepted by one of the most important trading blocs are particularly relevant. In the IP context, they not only consist of the obvious 'TRIPS-plus' standards to be expected from North–South FTAs, but also several interesting norms which address and are affected by the concept of sustainable development discussed in this chapter. In a nutshell, the sustainable development objective indicates the development dimension of the EU–ACP relationship. Examining its operation in the IP context therefore might deliver interesting results. In the wider context of this book, the concept of sustainable development underlines that 'one size does not fit all' – instead, its operation may provide policy space to tailor national IP laws to the domestic development needs.

This chapter begins with a brief analysis of the role of sustainable development in international law (below, section 1). Against this background, section 2 examines the role this concept can play as a treaty objective. It does so by taking the EC – CARIFORUM EPA as an example. This agreement claims to establish a 'trade partnership for sustainable development' and incorporates sustainable as a central objective which must be 'applied and integrated at every level of their economic partnership'.[2] Whether and how this can be done in relation to the IP provisions of the agreement is further examined in section 3. The focus here is less on individual substantive provisions requiring the contracting parties to protect IP rights. Instead, the chapter examines three general provisions setting out the 'context', 'objectives' and the 'nature and scope' of IP obligations in the agreement. The concluding section 4 finally makes observations on how to operationalise the concept of sustainable development as a treaty objective in international IP agreements.

1. THE CONCEPT OF SUSTAINABLE DEVELOPMENT IN INTERNATIONAL LAW

In the famous 'Brundtland' Report of the World Commission on Environment and Development, the term sustainable development is described as 'development that meets the needs of the present without

---

2 See Art.3 (1) of the EC – CARIFORUM EPA.

compromising the ability of future generations to meet their own needs'.[3] Since then, the term has featured prominently in various international forums, agreements and declarations in distinct contexts and with different connotations.

First, several multilateral, regional and bilateral trade agreements contain sustainable development as their object and purpose. On the multilateral level, for example the 1994 Marrakesh Agreement Establishing the World Trade Organization (WTO) recognises the objective of sustainable development in its preamble.[4] WTO Members confirmed the importance of this objective in the 2001 Doha Declaration that kicked off the Doha 'Development' Round of trade negotiations by reaffirming their 'commitment to the objective of sustainable development, as stated in the Preamble to the Marrakesh Agreement'.[5] Also in regional trade agreements such as the North American Free Trade Agreement (NAFTA)[6] and the predecessor to the EPAs, the Cotonou Agreement,[7] sustainable development is heralded in the preamble[8] or features prominently as

---

[3] See United Nations, *Our Common Future – Report of the World Commission on Environment and Development*, UN Doc. A/42/427 – Annex (4 August 1987), chapter 2, I.

[4] 'Recognizing that their relations in the field of trade and economic endeavour should be conducted with a view to raising standards of living, ensuring full employment and a large and steadily growing volume of real income and effective demand, and expanding the production of and trade in goods and services, *while allowing for the optimal use of the world's resources in accordance with the objective of sustainable development*, seeking both to protect and preserve the environment and to enhance the means for doing so in a manner consistent with their respective needs and concerns at different levels of economic development. . .' (emphasis added). See WTO, Legal Texts – The Uruguay Round Agreements, Marrakesh Agreement Establishing the World Trade Organization (WTO Agreement), available online at http://www.wto.org/english/docs_e/legal_e/legal_e.htm. This language differs significantly from the original GATT preamble that encouraged GATT contracting parties to engage in a 'full use of the resources of the world'.

[5] See WTO, Ministerial Declaration, Ministerial Conference – Fourth Session, Doha, Qatar (14 November 2001), WTO Doc. WT/MIN(01)/DEC/W/1, at para.6, available online at http://www.wto.org/english/thewto_e/minist_e/min01_e/mindecl_e.htm.

[6] North American Free Trade Agreement (NAFTA) – available online at http://www.nafta-sec-alena.org/.

[7] Partnership Agreement between Members of the African, Caribbean and Pacific Group of States (ACP countries) and the European Community and its Member States (Cotonou Agreement) –available online at http://ec.europa.eu/development/icenter/repository/agr01_en.pdf.

[8] The NAFTA preamble states that 'the Government of Canada, the Government of the United Mexican States and the Government of the United

a main treaty objective.[9] Sustainable development further serves as an important principle in the legal foundations of regional economic (and social) integration projects such as the European Union:[10] The Treaty on the European Union (EU Treaty)[11] expresses the determination of Member States to 'promote economic and social progress for their peoples, taking into account the principle of sustainable development' in its preamble; and lists as its objective *inter alia* to 'work for the sustainable development of Europe' internally and to 'contribute to (. . .) the sustainable development of the Earth' in its external relations.[12] In international environmental law, for example, the United Nations Framework Convention on Climate Change (UNFCCC)[13] and the United Nations Convention on Biological Diversity (CBD)[14] enshrine the concept of sustainable development, its key principle of reconciling economic, social and environmental priorities and the sustainable use of biodiversity as key objectives.[15]

States of America, resolved to: (. . .) PROMOTE sustainable development (. . .) HAVE AGREED as follows: (. . .)' (emphasis in the original).

9 The second paragraph of Art.1 of the Cotonou Agreement explains that 'the partnership shall be centred on the objective of reducing and eventually eradicating poverty consistent with the objectives of sustainable development and the gradual integration of the ACP countries into the world economy'.

10 On the role of sustainable development in EC law, see Prost, Mario (2005), 'Is European Law Becoming More Sustainable?' in Cordonier Segger, Marie-Claire and Gehring, Markus (eds), *Sustainable Development in World Trade Law*, The Hague: Kluwer Law International, pp. 411–59; Schrijver, Nico J. (2007), 'The Evolution of Sustainable Development in International Law: Inception, Meaning and Status', *Recueil des Cours*, pp. 217–412, at 314–16.

11 See Consolidated Version of the Treaty on the European Union, OJ 2006 C 321 E, 5-36, available online at http://eur-lex.europa.eu/LexUriServ/LexUriServ.do?uri=OJ:C:2006:321E:0001:0331:EN:PDF.

12 See Art.2 sec.3, 5 of the EU Treaty, as amended by the Lisbon Treaty – see OJ 2007 C 306/12, 10-42 (at 13), available online at http://eur-lex.europa.eu/JOHtml.do?uri=OJ:C:2007:306:SOM:en:HTML.

13 United Nations Framework Convention on Climate Change, ILM 1992, Vol.XXXI, 849 – UN Doc. FCCC/INFORMAL/84 GE.05-62220 (E) 200705 (1992), available online at http://unfccc.int/resource/docs/convkp/conveng.pdf.

14 United Nations Convention on Biological Diversity, ILM 1992, Vol.XXXI, 818, available online at http://www.cbd.int/doc/legal/cbd-un-en.pdf.

15 In the UNFCCC, sustainable development appears as a key concept which is addressed in the preamble (recognising the aim to 'achieve sustainable social and economic development') and in the Conventions' objectives in Art.3, including the goal 'to enable economic development to proceed in a sustainable manner' and further recognising that 'the Parties have a right to, and should, promote sustainable development'. The CBD describes its objectives in Art.1 as 'the conservation of biological diversity, the sustainable use of its components and the

Sustainable development also appears to be a key concept in several important, albeit non-binding, declarations and agreed action programmes of the global community of nations such as the Agenda 21[16] and the 1992 Rio Declaration on Environment and Development.[17] The latter embodies a list of 27 principles which *inter alia* focus on integration and the interrelation of social and economic development and environmental protection.[18] In 2002, the World Summit on Sustainable Development (WSSD) placed the notion of sustainable development at the centre of global attention as the main idea to resolve the environment/development dichotomy. The Summit produced the Johannesburg Declaration on Sustainable Development[19] and the Johannesburg Plan of Implementation.[20] In the former, all participating states assumed

---

fair and equitable sharing of the benefits arising out of the utilization of genetic resources'. The Convention further defines 'Sustainable use' in Art.2 as 'the use of components of biological diversity in a way and at a rate that does not lead to the long-term decline of biological diversity, thereby maintaining its potential to meet the needs and aspirations of present and future generations'. Finally, Art.10 on 'Sustainable Use of Components of Biological Diversity' contains the principle of integration in the form of a binding legal obligation for each contracting party 'as far as possible and as appropriate' to 'integrate consideration of the conservation and sustainable use of biological resources into national decision-making'.

[16] Agenda 21 comprises a wide-ranging plan of action for the achievement of sustainable development worldwide – available online at http://www.unep.org/Documents.Multilingual/Default.asp?DocumentID=52.

[17] United Nations, Report of the United Nations Conference on Environment and Development – Annex I: Rio Declaration on Environment and Development, UN Doc. A/CONF.151/26 Vol. I, (12 August 1992), available online at http://www.un.org/documents/ga/conf151/aconf15126-1annex1.htm.

[18] See United Nations, Rio Declaration, *supra* note 17, at principle 4: 'In order to achieve sustainable development, environmental protection shall constitute an integral part of the development process and cannot be considered in isolation from it' and principle 25: 'Peace, development and environmental protection are interdependent and indivisible'.

[19] Johannesburg Declaration on Sustainable Development, adopted at the 17th plenary meeting of the World Summit on Sustainable Development, on 4 September 2002 – available online at http://www.un.org/esa/sustdev/documents/WSSD_POI_PD/English/POI_PD.htm.

[20] The Johannesburg Plan of Implementation (available online at http://www.un.org/esa/sustdev/documents/WSSD_POI_PD/English/POIToc.htm) built on the achievements made since the Rio Summit and aimed to expedite the realisation of the remaining goals. To this end, states committed themselves to undertaking concrete measures promoting the integration of the three components of sustainable development – economic development, social development and environmental protection – as interdependent and mutually reinforcing pillars.

> a collective responsibility to advance and strengthen the interdependent and mutually reinforcing pillars of sustainable development — economic development, social development and environmental protection — at the local, national, regional and global levels.[21]

In the same year, the International Law Association (ILA), based on the work of its Committee on Legal Aspects of Sustainable Development,[22] adopted a Declaration of Principles of International Law Related to Sustainable Development.[23] The Declaration *inter alia* contained 'the principle of integration and interrelationship, in particular in relation to human rights and social, economic and environmental objectives'. It considers this principle on integration as 'essential to the achievement of sustainable development' and states that all levels of governance and all sectors of society are encouraged to implement it.[24]

Finally, various international courts and tribunals have relied on the concept of sustainable development. In several key decisions, the notion of integration and reconciliation concerning socio-economic development and protection of the environment has performed a central function. The concept of sustainable development played just such a conflict-resolution and balance of interest role in the *Gabcikovo – Nagymaros* case decided by the International Court of Justice (ICJ);[25] in the Arbitral Award of the Permanent Court of Arbitration for the *Arbitration Regarding the Iron Rhine ('Ijzeren Rijn') Railway;*[26] and in the decisions of the WTO dispute settlement Panel and Appellate Body in the *US – Shrimp*[27] case.

---

21 Johannesburg Declaration, *supra* note 19 above, at 5.

22 The work of the Committee, in particular its two reports, is available online at http://www.ila-hq.org/en/committees/index.cfm/cid/25.

23 International Law Association, Declaration of Principles of International Law Related to Sustainable Development, Resolution 3/2002 adopted at the 70th Conference of the International Law Association, held in New Delhi, India, 2–6 April 2002 (UN Doc. A/CONF.199/8, 9 August 2002). For an analysis of the principles of the ILA Declaration, see Cordonier Segger, Marie-Claire and Khalfan, Ashfaq (2004), *Sustainable Development Law: Principles, Practices & Prospects*, Oxford: Oxford University Press, pp. 96–171.

24 International Law Association, *supra* note 23, at 7.2.

25 *Gabcikovo-Nagymaros Project* (*Hungary v. Slovakia*), Judgment of 25 September 1997, ICJ Reports 1997, 7–84 –available online at http://www.icj-cij.org/docket/files/92/7375.pdf.

26 *Arbitration Regarding the Iron Rhine ('Ijzeren Rijn') Railway* (Belgium/the Netherlands), Permanent Court of Arbitration – Award of the Arbitral Tribunal (24 May 2005) –available online at http://www.pca-cpa.org/showpage.asp?pag_id=1155.

27 See Appellate Body Report, *United States — Import Prohibition of Certain Shrimp and Shrimp Products*, WT/DS58/AB/R, adopted 6 November 1998 and

From this brief overview it follows that basically all documents relating to sustainable development in international law emphasise the principle of integration and reconciliation. The ILA committee described it 'as the very backbone of the concept of sustainable development'[28] and others have identified it as a core principle inherent in that concept.[29] The Brundtland Report clarified that sustainable development requires the '*balanced reconciliation and integration of economic, environmental and social priorities*'.[30] It is this principle of integration which will be at the forefront of further analysis into the role of sustainable development as a treaty objective.

2. EUROPE'S ECONOMIC PARTNERSHIP AGREEMENTS – TRADE PARTNERSHIPS *FOR* SUSTAINABLE DEVELOPMENT?

On 15 October 2008, the European Community (EC), its Member States and the CARIFORUM[31] group of Caribbean countries signed a comprehensive Economic Partnership Agreement (EPA). This EC – CARIFORUM EPA (CEPA)[32] is the first amongst several EPAs which the EC currently negotiates with different regional groups of African Caribbean and Pacific

---

Panel Report *United States – Shrimp – Recourse to Article 21.5 by Malaysia,* WT/DS58/RW, adopted 15 June 2000.

28 International Law Association, *supra* note 23, at 7.

29 See Sands, P. (1994), 'International Law in the Field of Sustainable Development', 65 *British Yearbook of International Law*, pp. 303–81 (at 336); Schrijver, Nico J., *supra* note 10, at 362.

30 Cordonier Segger, Marie-Claire and Gehring, Markus (2005), 'Introduction', in Cordonier Segger, Marie-Claire and Gehring, Markus (eds), *Sustainable Development in World Trade Law*, The Hague: Kluwer Law International, pp. 1–24, at 5 (emphasis added). In the Brundtland Report, this key principle of 'merging environment and economics in decision making' appears *inter alia* as one of seven 'critical objectives' that follow from the principle of sustainable development (see United Nations, *Our Common Future*, *supra* note 3, at para.72: 'The common theme throughout this strategy for sustainable development is the need to integrate economic and ecological considerations in decision making').

31 The group of CARIFORUM countries includes Antigua and Barbuda, Bahamas, Barbados, Belize, Dominica, the Dominican Republic, Grenada, Guyana, Haiti, Jamaica, Saint Lucia, Saint Vincent and the Grenadines, Saint Kitts and Nevis, Suriname, and Trinidad and Tobago – acting as individual states. While neither Haiti nor Guyana initially signed CEPA, Guyana signed on 20 October. The Agreement is provisionally applied as of 29 December 2008.

32 Economic Partnership Agreement between the CARIFORUM States, of the one part, and the European Community and its Member States, of the other part (CEPA) signed in Bridgetown (Barbados) on 15 October 2008, OJ 2008 L

(ACP) countries. Historically, CEPA builds on the Cotonou Agreement[33] signed between the EC, its Member States and ACP countries in 2000. The Cotonou Agreement itself has to be seen in the context of the special economic relationships between the EC Member States and their former colonies in Africa, the Caribbean and in the Pacific. It continued a regime of preferential access for specific products from ACP countries to the EC market which dispute settlement panels in the early 1990s had found to be in conflict with the General Agreement on Tariffs and Trade (GATT).[34] Since the last waiver to 'legalise' the preferential treatment for ACP countries expired on 31 December 2007, ACP countries recognised their need to negotiate GATT-compatible regional trade agreements with the EC in order to maintain a preferential level of market access.[35] The EC used this bargaining tool to press for comprehensive trade agreements which generally go beyond WTO obligations in scope and substance. Against this background, it is not surprising that CEPA addresses not only trade in goods and services, but a broad list of trade-related matters and is backed by a dispute settlement mechanism as well as an institutional structure.[36] Since it is likely to serve as a template for the further EPAs currently under negotiation, CEPA provides a first look at how the EU and its Members as well as around 80 other countries in Africa, the Caribbean and the Pacific region will conduct their trade and development relations in the future.

CEPA considers itself a 'Trade Partnership *for* Sustainable Development'[37] – emphasising that the overarching objective is sustainable

---

289/I/3 – available online at http://trade.ec.europa.eu/doclib/docs/2008/february/tradoc_137971.pdf.

33 Partnership Agreement between Members of the African, Caribbean and Pacific Group of States and the European Community and its Member States (Cotonou Agreement), OJ 2000 L 317/3 –available online at http://eur-lex.europa.eu/LexUriServ/LexUriServ.do?uri=OJ:L:2000:317:0003:0003:EN:PDF, amended OJ 2005 L 287/1.

34 See Panel Report, *EEC – Member States' Import Regime for Bananas*, DS32/R, 3 June 1993 (unadopted) and Panel Report, *EEC – Member States' Import Regime for Bananas,* DS/38/R, 11 February 1994 (unadopted).

35 Lorand Bartels (2007), For a detailed analysis of the EC's trade relationship with ACP countries, see, 'The Trade and Development Policy of the European Union', 18 (4) *European Journal of International Law*, pp. 715–56.

36 The agreement covers not only traditional trade-related matters like investment, competition, intellectual property and public procurement, but also a chapter on environment, social aspects (labour standards) and the protection of personal data; see CEPA (*supra* note 31), Part II, Titles I–III and especially IV, as well as Parts III and V.

37 See the heading of Part I of the EC – CARFORUM EPA which contains the objectives and principles of the agreement (emphasis added).

development of the parties to the partnership.[38] The EC Commission even hails CEPA as 'a new kind of free-trade agreement as sustainable development is the presiding principle governing the whole agreement'.[39] Since several other international (trade) agreements contain a sustainable development objective, the innovative character of CEPA may be called into question. This section hence examines the potential of the sustainable development objective in CEPA to affect the implementation and interpretation of CEPA obligations.

Next to the preamble and Art.1 of CEPA, the objective of sustainable development is emphasised and defined in Art.3, which bears the heading 'Sustainable Development': According to section 1, this objective

> is to be *applied and integrated at every level of their economic partnership,* in fulfilment of the overarching commitments set out in Articles 1, 2 and 9 of the Cotonou Agreement, and especially the general commitment to reducing and eventually eradicating poverty in a way that is consistent with the objectives of sustainable development.[40]

Art.3 (1) sets out the function of a sustainable development treaty objective: as an interpretative tool, it affects the understanding of all treaty provisions. This draws support from CEPA's call to operationalise this objective '*at every level of the economic partnership*'. Secondly, the words '*is to be* applied and integrated'[41] make clear that such action has yet to take place. Art.3 (1) therefore primarily addresses national legislators and other actors in the process of implementing CEPA provisions. The application and integration of the sustainable development goal hence is not a process which has been exhaustively performed during the negotiations and drafting of CEPA. The substantive CEPA provisions as such do not represent the full and final implementation of the sustainable development objective. Instead, the real operational value of Art.3 (1) lies in its ability to give effect to the sustainable development objective in the process of CEPA implementation.

CEPA's demand for comprehensive implementation and application

---

38 See Art.1 (a) and Art.3 CEPA.

39 EC Commission DG Trade, CARIFORUM – EU Agreement: An Overview (Brussels, 2008), at 3.

40 See Art.3 (1) (emphasis added). Under Art.1 of the Cotonou Agreement, the partnership between the EC and ACP countries 'shall be centred on the objective of reducing and eventually eradicating poverty consistent with the objectives of sustainable development and the gradual integration of the ACP countries into the world economy'.

41 Art.3 (1) CEPA (emphasis added).

of the sustainable development objective can be of particular relevance in defining the scope of substantive obligations in CEPA and may support arguments in favour of balancing economic interests with other social or environmental interests in the process of CEPA implementation. Its role, however, crucially depends on the meaning and scope of the term 'sustainable development' as used in CEPA. Under Art.3 (2), this term is further defined:

> The Parties understand this objective to apply in the case of the present Economic Partnership Agreement as a commitment that:
> a) the application of this Agreement shall fully take into account the human, cultural, economic, social, health and environmental best interests of their respective population and of future generations;
> b) decision-taking methods shall embrace the fundamental principles of ownership, participation and dialogue.

Here, the terms 'commitment' and especially the word 'shall' in para. a) make clear that at issue is a binding obligation. Art.233:5 CEPA further confirms this by stating that contracting parties 'shall ensure that they comply with the objectives laid down in this Agreement'. Secondly, the meaning of the sustainable development objective as defined in Art.3 (2) a) is equivalent to a general understanding of the principle of integration as the core element of sustainable development: in CEPA, it requires the contracting parties to 'fully take into account the human, cultural, economic, social, health and environmental best interests of their respective population and of future generations'. In international law, the principle of integration and interrelationship demands reconciliation of social, economic, financial and human rights aspects, as well as the needs of current and future generations. The drafters of CEPA therefore clearly had the principle of integration in mind when they defined the obligation relating to the sustainable development objective in Art.3 (2) a).

The CEPA provision also aligns with the general opinion in international legal scholarship that an integrated approach cannot and does not demand one specific result or outcome – but rather a duty to adopt *procedures* which balance all relevant elements.[42] This follows especially

[42] Jodoin, Sébastien (2005), 'The Principle of Integration and Interrelationship in Relation to Human Rights and Social, Economic and Environmental Objectives', *CISDL Legal Working Papers* (Montreal), at 9 –available online at http://www.cisdl.org/pdf/sdl/SDL_Integration.pdf (accessed 20 January 2009). See also Lowe, Vaughan (1999), 'Sustainable Development and Unsustainable Arguments', in Boyle, A. and Freestone, D. (eds), *Sustainable Development and International Law: Past Achievements and Future Challenges*, Oxford: Oxford University Press,

from the verbs 'shall fully take into account' in Art.3 (2) a) CEPA which demand an integrative process instead of a particular sustainable development outcome. An obligation to take an integrative procedural approach at all relevant levels of decision-making in applying CEPA further implies *policy space* as to the outcome of the balancing process. This discretion is also underlined by the Art.3 (2) b) language, according to which the reconciliation must be performed by the contracting parties according to the 'best interests of their respective population'. Since determining what is in the best interests will vary according to domestic circumstances, and because such a determination can hardly be imposed from external actors, the CEPA obligation for an integrative approach implies policy space on the domestic level.

In sum, the obligations the contracting parties undertook with regard to the implementation of CEPA's sustainable development objective under Art.3 CEPA align with and support the general function of a sustainable development objective in international treaties.[43] Its main role is to empower and oblige all actors involved in the application of the treaty to take an integrative approach in the process of decision-making. Given the *constructive ambiguity* of the principle of integration,[44] paired with the formal function of treaty objectives as providing interpretative guidance, sustainable development allows (various forms of) concrete integration – *if* it is indeed constructively utilised at the domestic level. Hence, to operationalise sustainable development as a treaty objective means that its core principle of integration guides the interpretation of individual treaty provisions.

From the rules of treaty interpretation in international law[45] then

---

p. 36, who focuses on judicial decision-making processes; and Boyle, Alan and Freestone, David (1999), 'Introduction', in Boyle, A. and Freestone, D. (eds), *International Law and Sustainable Development*, Oxford: Oxford University Press, p. 17, which refer to ample state practice as well as the ICJ decision in *Gabcikovo – Nagymaros Project* (*supra* note 25) as evidence that the principle of integration should be understood as *procedural integration* requiring development decisions to be the outcome of a process which integrates economic, social and environmental concerns and so promotes sustainable development.

43 For an extensive discussion of this general role of sustainable development as a treaty objective, see Grosse Ruse-Khan, H. (2010), 'A Real Partnership for Development? Sustainable Development as Treaty Objective in European Economic Partnership Agreements and Beyond', *Journal of International Economic Law*, 13(1), pp. 139–80.

44 Ibid.

45 See in particular Arts.31–3 of the Vienna Convention on the Law of Treaties (VCLT); in particular Art.31 (1), which provides: 'A treaty shall be interpreted in

follows that a sustainable development objective will have its prime importance where broad and open treaty terms are at stake. Their openness or ambiguity *a priori* lends itself to assuming a margin of appreciation in the interpretation and implementation process. Sustainable development as a treaty objective is well equipped to guide this discretion towards self-determined, integrative outcomes as the result of (domestic) decision-making processes. Surely, the outcome will differ depending on the domestic circumstances, priorities and value judgements. The boundaries for such national diversity, however, are ordinary meaning and context relevant to the international treaty obligation at stake: the more precise and concrete an international norm is, the less room there is for domestic integrative approaches in its implementation. If, however, the norm is sufficiently open, the concept of sustainable development can direct treaty interpretation towards a variety of possible meanings which allow the reconciliation and integration economic, social and environmental concerns affected by the operation of that norm.

The obligation to integrate first and foremost concerns states and their relevant domestic institutions when implementing CEPA. In this regard, they have a certain amount of policy space when balancing the economic, environmental or social interests at stake. Unless specific CEPA provisions demand a particular form of integration, no specific integrative outcome or result is owed; and the interests to be reconciled can equally be determined by domestic institutions. The amount of discretion then depends on the individual treaty provision and the relative importance of the interpretative role of the treaty objective *vis-à-vis* ordinary meaning and context. Under its Art.3 (2) b), CEPA further qualifies the obligation to adopt an integrative approach by requiring this decision-making process to incorporate the principles of ownership, participation and dialogue.

3. CEPA'S SUSTAINABLE DEVELOPMENT OBJECTIVE AND THE IP AND INNOVATION CHAPTER

In CEPA Title IV on trade-related matters, chapter 2 deals with 'Innovation and Intellectual Property'. As one might expect from an IP chapter of a trade agreement negotiated by the EC whose major industries rely on IP protection, CEPA contains obligations which go beyond those of

good faith in accordance with the ordinary meaning to be given to the terms of the treaty in their context and in the light of its object and purpose'.

the TRIPS Agreement and other international IP treaties. In particular, Art.145 on geographical indications and its subsection 3 on IP enforcement are significantly 'TRIPS-plus'. These rather obvious candidates for IP provisions in an FTA will not be further examined here. Instead, this section takes a closer look at some of the general provisions in the IP and Innovation chapter of CEPA and its section on intellectual property in particular.

The chapter on 'Innovation and Intellectual Property'[46] contains in Art.131 and 132 CEPA two general provisions which set out common 'Context' and 'Objectives' for the section on Innovation as well as the one on IP. In the section on 'Intellectual Property', Art.139 CEPA on the 'Nature and Scope of Obligations' is equally relevant for all substantive provisions on IP protection. These provisions and their relation to the sustainable development objective are addressed below. A further focus will be on assessing the impact of CEPA's objective on the substantive IP obligations in CEPA.

As a starting point, it is useful to recognise the generally accepted overarching goal of IP protection and emphasise its potential role to balance and individually tailor the scope and extent of protection to the domestic needs (by means of interpretation and implementation of broad and open terms in IP provisions).[47] IP protection generally aims to further the scientific, technological and cultural development and progress of a society (and not primarily to reward creators and inventors).[48] In a market envi-

---

[46] Spence, M., 'Innovation and Technology Transfer: Lessons from the CARIFORUM EPA Experience', Draft Paper – CEMAC Regional Dialogue on EPAs, IPRs, Innovation and Sustainable Development (ICTSD, ACDIC, April 2008), at 5 – available online at http://www.iprsonline.org/ictsd/Dialogues/2008-04-28/Spence_Paper2.pdf (accessed 3 March 2009) emphasises the importance of this heading as a 'small but important step in changing the paradigm within which the subject of intellectual property is dealt with in trade negotiations' towards a focus on innovation as opposed to plainly the protection of IP.

[47] An example of an interpretative approach in the TRIPS context is a normative understanding of the terms such as 'normal' exploitation or 'unreasonable' in the three-step test; see Grosse Ruse-Khan, H. (2008), 'Proportionality and Balancing within the Objectives of Intellectual Property Protection', in Torremanns, P. (ed.), *Intellectual Property and Human Rights*, Alpen aan der Rijn: Kluwer; Ricketson, S. (2003), 'WIPO Study on Limitations and Exceptions of Copyright and Related Rights in the Digital Environment', Geneva – online available at http://www.wipo.int/edocs/mdocs/copyright/en/sccr_9/sccr_9_7.pdf (accessed January 2010).

[48] See for example Art.7 TRIPS and Art.1 Section 8 of the US Constitution according to which Congress has legislative authority to, *inter alia* '(. . .) *promote the Progress of Science and useful Arts*, by securing for limited Times to Authors

ronment, 'limited' exclusivity secures an incentive to develop and produce innovative and creative goods and services. Without such an incentive, the argument is that either no innovation/creation takes place or their results are kept secret. The incentive hence ensures long-term dissemination and diffusion of innovations/creations in a society. In order for such diffusion to take place, the exclusivity must be sufficiently limited in time and in scope. If the limitations to value-addition and (follow-up) innovation caused by (too) stringent exclusivity regimes outweigh the quantity and quality of further creations and inventions based on the reward incentive, then the IP objectives demand less protection.[49] The overarching aim to promote societal progress hence demands a level of IP protection which takes all relevant interests into account and finds a balance between them. This approach is equally inherent in the concept of sustainable development.[50] Based on these arguments, both the sustainable development objective as well as the overall goal of IP protection provide further justification for a balanced and tailored implementation of IP-related obligations under CEPA. But there are limits to the role of the overall IP goals and the sustainable development objective in determining the outcome of interpretation and implementing individual IP provisions. As an interpretative tool, it also cannot override IP protection which follows from explicit and straightforward ordinary meanings of provisions setting out the level of protection. However, as much terminology allows, the sustainable development objective should be used to enlarge the domestic policy space in tailoring the IP regime to domestic needs.

3.1. The Context

Explicitly dubbed 'Context', Art.131 of the IP and Innovation chapter arguably sets out the wider framework within which the promotion of innovation and protection of IP operates. In particular, it emphasises how the contracting parties envision the chapter on innovation and IP protection to promote the overall goal of sustainable development. Given its title, one could further argue that the norm plays a specific role as interpretative context in line with Art.31 (1) VCLT and hence should be given specific weight when interpreting and implementing individual provisions of this chapter. Based on its link to the general sustainable development

---

and Inventors the exclusive Right to their respective Writings and Discoveries (. . .)' (emphasis added).

[49] Compare Geiger, C. (2007), 'Copyright and the Freedom to Create, A Fragile Balance', 38 *IIC*, p. 707.

[50] See Sections 1 and 2 above.

objective, such an interpretation would re-emphasise the importance of that objective for the understanding of individual CEPA provisions in the IP and Innovation chapter.

In Art.131, the parties agree that

> fostering innovation and creativity *improves competitiveness* and is *a crucial element* in their economic partnership, *in achieving sustainable development*, promoting trade between them and ensuring the gradual integration of CARIFORUM States into the world economy.[51]

In relation to IP in particular, they recognise that

> the protection and enforcement of *intellectual property plays a key role in fostering creativity, innovation and competitiveness*, and are determined to *ensure increasing levels of protection appropriate to their levels of development*.[52]

The common denominator in these two sections is the promotion of creativity, innovation and competitiveness as a *means* of achieving the goal of sustainable development. Beyond this, the protection of IP is no end in itself, but merely an (important) tool for achieving those means.[53] This focus on the overarching CEPA goal implements the general obligation to 'apply and integrate' the objective of sustainable development at 'every level of the EPA'.[54] Against this background, Art.131 (1) supports an implementation and interpretation of CEPA IP obligations which leaves reasonable policy space and flexibility to the domestic legislator. Given the general recognition that in choosing a system of IP protection 'one size does not fit all',[55] the individual circumstances in the implementing

---

[51] Art.131 (1) CEPA (emphasis added).

[52] Art.131 (2) CEPA (emphasis added).

[53] Compare Spence, M. (*supra* note 46, p. 5) who further stresses that Art.131 places innovation and creativity *before* the protection of IP rights.

[54] See Art.3 (1) CEPA.

[55] See UNCTAD, *The Least Developed Country Report 2007 – Knowledge, Technological Learning and Innovation for Development* (Geneva, 2007), at 105–107; World Bank, *Global Economic Prospects and the Developing Countries 2002* (Washington, DC, 2001), at 129; on the historical evidence for tailoring national IP policy and regulation to the domestic economic, technological and development needs of a country, see further Commission on Intellectual Property Rights (CIPR), *Integrating Intellectual Property and Development Policy* (London, 2002), at 18–20 (available online at www.iprcommission.org) and especially the two related background papers Z. Khan, 'Study Paper 1a: Intellectual Property and Economic Development: Lessons from American and European History'; and N. Kumar, 'Study Paper 1b: Intellectual Property Rights, Technology and Economic

country determine the most appropriate level of IP protection for facilitating that country's (sustainable) economic, technological and cultural development. This 'tailoring' of course must further be balanced against security and predictability in trade relations, which demands a certain degree of harmonisation amongst all contracting parties.[56] Reconciling these interests is inherent in the concept of sustainable development and its core principle of integration.[57] In the process of implementation, contracting parties hence must balance economic interests for a secure and predictable trading environment against the (economic and social) need to tailor the IP regime to domestic needs.

The second paragraph of Art.131 further sets out two rather contradictory aims. An interpretation relying on Art.132 (2) as the general context[58] for the IP and innovation provisions demands the reconciliation of the following (potentially) conflicting elements in particular: on the one hand, paragraph 2 calls for *increasing* levels of protection – thereby building on the assumption that a continuous increase in IP protection is in all cases beneficial and positive.[59] On the other hand, this phrase is subject to the condition that such (increasing) protection must be *appropriate to the levels of development* of the contracting parties. The latter reinforces the recognition that 'one size does not fit all' which has been already deducted from the general objective of sustainable development: IP protection must be tailored to meet the needs of the domestic economy and in particular reflect the comparative advantage (in innovation or imitation) of the country concerned.[60]

Development: Experiences of Asian Countries'. For an economic and trade theory justification, see Trebilcock, M. and Howse, R. (2005), *The Regulation of International Trade*, 3rd ed., London: Routledge, pp. 397–401.

56 In the WTO context, see Art.3:2 of the DSU which embodies the goal of 'providing security and predictability to the multilateral trading system'.

57 As section 1) explained, a key function of this concept is to integrate and balance different economic, social and environmental concerns in a mutually reinforcing way.

58 Compare the argument above that the term 'Context' used as heading for Art.131 refers to its specific role as interpretative context in the meaning of Art.31 (1) VCLT.

59 For a general debate on minimum standards and increasing levels of protection and binding limitations, see Kur, A. and Grosse Ruse-Khan, H. (2010), 'Enough is Enough – The Notion of Binding Ceilings in International Intellectual Property Protection', *Max Planck Papers on Intellectual Property, Competition & Tax Law, Research Paper* No.09-01; available online at http://ssrn.com/abstract=1326429 (accessed 3 March 2009).

60 Compare Trebilcock, M. and Howse, R., *supra* note 55, pp. 400–01: whenever the *comparative advantage* of a country in a specific industry or field of

One way to resolve this tension would be to adopt a broader understanding of the term 'protection' – thus encompassing also the protection of the interests of IP users, competitors and the public domain. Such an understanding would find support in the overall goal of IP protection to promote societal progress. Also the relation between CEPA's sustainable development objective and the Innovation and IP chapter as a means of its implementation[61] speak in favour of a broader, more balanced understanding which integrates all affected interests. Another approach would be to perceive the individual level of development as a general qualification for (increasing) IP protection.[62] Increases must be justified in such a way that they are 'appropriate to [the contracting parties'] levels of development'.[63] In any case, for CEPA the term 'increasing levels of protection' is not a stand-alone dogma nor an end in itself. Instead, the overall sustainable development objective via Art.3 (1) and Art.131 (1)

---

technology lies more in production based on imitation than innovation, trade and economic theory suggest that such a country should adopt an IP regime which allows (some extent of) imitation. A general explanation of the theory of comparative advantage, with its origins in Adam Smith's and David Ricardo's work, its main argument for specialisation and (free) international trade and its current implications, can be found in Van der Bossche, P. (2005), *The Law and Policy of the World Trade Organization*, Cambridge: Cambridge University Press, pp. 19–24 For an economist's perspective see Brakman, S., Garretsen, H., van Marrewijk, C. and van Witteloostuijn, A. (2006), *Nations and Firms in the Global Economy*, Cambridge: Cambridge University Press, pp. 63–95.

61 See Art.131 (1) and (2) CEPA, which underline that promoting innovation and protecting IP is a means to achieve sustainable development.

62 See Spence, M. (*supra* note 46, p. 5), who sees herein a general link between the amount of IP protection and level of development. Musungu, S., 'Innovations and Intellectual property in the EC – CARIFORUM EPA: Lessons for other ACP Regions' (GTZ, 2008) – available online at http://www2.gtz.de/dokumente/bib/gtz2008-0393en-cariforum-innovation.pdf (accessed 3 March 2009) fears that a general dependency between increases in IP protection and levels of development is an insufficient safeguard against increases which inhibit innovation or creativity: 'The reason is that in cases where explicit elaboration of what this means is lacking, there is a general assumption that increased levels of IP protection automatically result in innovation and creativity'. He therefore demands 'to be explicit regarding the need for flexibility within the rules and standards and the need to balance the costs and benefits of protection (. . .)'. This balance however is inherent in the sustainable development objective and – as Art.3 (1) CEPA demands – to be 'applied and integrated at every level' of CEPA. Taking these objectives seriously then makes an explicit mention of flexibilities not necessary whenever CEPA language is sufficiently open for an integrative approach at the domestic level (compare section 4 below). An explicit balancing within CEPA provisions (such as is the case in Art.139 (2) CEPA; see below) may, however, be preferred for reasons of clarity and predictability.

63 Art.131 (2) CEPA.

CEPA, as well as the condition 'appropriate to their levels of development' in Art.131 (2), inform its meaning. As an operational provision, the role of Art.131 (2) should be limited to serving as a mandate for future negotiations on IP protection. Here, demands for increases in the amount of protection (if understood in the traditional, narrow sense of increasing right holders' interests) must be in accordance with individual development levels. Demanders thus must bring evidence of any supportive relation – arguably for all contracting parties.

3.2. The Objectives of the Innovation and IP Chapter

The CEPA chapter on Innovation and IP contains one general provision on the objectives of this chapter. Since neither the innovation section nor the IP section within that chapter include further provisions laying out particular objectives, Art.132 applies to both sections and *inter alia* describes the specific objectives of IP protection under CEPA. As a systemic matter, the question arises of what is the relation between the general CEPA objective of sustainable development and the special objectives of the Innovation and IP chapter. On the one hand, the principle of *lex specialis* may suggest that the objectives of Art.132 are alone decisive for the interpretation of IP-related CEPA provisions. On the other hand, Art.31 (1) VCLT refers to the treaties' object and purpose as decisive for treaty interpretation – not to those of individual provisions or sections within that treaty.[64] While the specific IP objectives may still be considered as the relevant interpretative context under Art.31 (2) VCLT, it is the overall treaty object and purpose which is relevant as the third element of treaty interpretation.

Further arguments from CEPA provisions themselves underline the prevalence of the general sustainable development objective for the purpose of interpretation and implementation of CEPA's IP provisions: First, Art.3 (1) contains an obligation to apply and integrate the sustainable development objective at every level of CEPA. It must hence inform the understanding of the specific IP objectives. Secondly, Art.131 confirms the overall role and function of IP protection as a means to promote sustainable development. Against this background, the individual IP provisions must equally be understood in the light of the sustainable development objective.

---

64 Art.31 (1) VCLT states: 'A treaty shall be interpreted in good faith in accordance with the ordinary meaning to be given to the terms of the treaty in their context and in the light of *its* object and purpose.' (emphasis added).

Art.132 of the IP and Innovation chapter contains a list of objectives, including the aims:

- to 'promote the process of innovation, including eco-innovation' and foster competitiveness of (especially micro-, small- and medium) enterprises;
- to 'achieve an adequate and effective level of protection and enforcement of intellectual property rights';
- to 'contribute to the promotion of technological innovation and to the transfer and dissemination of technology and know-how';
- to encourage 'cooperative research, development and production activities in science and technology', as well as in the 'creative industries'.[65]

With regard to the second and third bullet points, these objectives resemble the TRIPS preamble[66] and Art.7 TRIPS[67] respectively. While the aim of 'adequate and effective levels' of IP protection does at first sight appear to emphasise the need for 'strong' IP rights, this does not stand up to more detailed scrutiny. First, the term '*adequate*' implies an assessment on the basis of an individual situation and tailored to the specific circumstances of the case at hand.[68] This is supported by Art.131 (2)[69] and Art.139 (2)[70] which both make the level of IP protection (or its increase) dependent on the individual development needs of the contract-

---

65 See Art.132 (a), (b), (d), (e), (f), (g) CEPA.

66 In its relevant corresponding part, the TRIPS preamble recognises the need for new rules on: (b) the provision of adequate standards and principles concerning the availability, scope and use of trade-related intellectual property rights; and (c) the provision of effective and appropriate means for the enforcement of trade-related intellectual property rights, taking into account differences in national legal systems.

67 Art.7 TRIPS, also called 'Objectives', states: 'The protection and enforcement of intellectual property rights should contribute to the promotion of technological innovation and to the transfer and dissemination of technology, to the mutual advantage of producers and users of technological knowledge and in a manner conducive to social and economic welfare, and to a balance of rights and obligations'.

68 For an analysis of the equivalent terms in the TRIPS preamble, see Grosse Ruse-Khan, H., *supra* note 47, at 171–2.

69 Under Art.132 (2), contracting parties 'are determined to ensure increasing levels of protection *appropriate to their levels of development*.' (emphasis added). For a discussion of this norm, see the section above.

70 Art.139 (2) *inter alia* states that 'the Parties also agree that an adequate and effective enforcement of intellectual property rights should take account of

ing parties. Secondly, the level of IP protection and enforcement must be '*effective*'. This emphasises the need for domestic protection of IP which is efficient, successful or has an effect[71] – both on the substantive – as well as the enforcement level. However, the effectiveness, success or efficiency so required has no complete meaning in itself but must be related to the underlying policy objectives of CEPA provisions on Innovation and IP.[72] Here, Art.131 (1), (2) make clear that IP protection (and enforcement) is a means to foster innovation and creativity, which in turn are means to achieve sustainable development. IP protection under CEPA thus needs to be *effective in achieving the sustainable development objective*.[73] This implies that effectiveness must be measured by the ability of IP protection to support the economic and social development of the contracting states and allows them to integrate other relevant concerns such as the protection of the environment.[74] That in turn again entails sufficient policy space to tailor IP protection to the domestic development needs and to integrate all relevant societal concerns in the implementation process.

Regarding the objective to 'contribute to the promotion of technological innovation and to the transfer and dissemination of technology and know-how' in Art.132 (e) CEPA, the same paradigm as laid down in Art.7 TRIPS demands attention: IP protection must achieve a balance between promoting technological innovation one the one hand and transfer of technology and know-how on the other. An equilibrium between IP exclusivity as a necessary incentive for innovation and the dissemination and diffusion of knowledge to achieve societal progress must be found. Such a balance should give due regard to all interests involved, including those

---

the development needs of the CARIFORUM States.' (emphasis added). For a discussion of this norm, see below.

71 See *Chambers Dictionary* (Edinburgh, 1993), 535.

72 For a similar argument on the identical term in the TRIPS preamble, see ICTSD/UNCTAD, *Resource Book on TRIPS and Development: An Authoritative and Practical Guide to the TRIPS Agreement* (Geneva, 2005), Part One, sec.1 – available online at www.iprsonline.org/unctadictsd/ResourceBookIndex.htm (visited on 8 January 2008); Correa, C. (2007), *Trade Related Aspects of Intellectual Property Rights*, Oxford: Oxford University Press, p. 101; and Grosse Ruse-Khan, H., *supra* note 47, p. 172.

73 The need to consider the objective of IP protection follows not only from the term 'effective' itself, which has no real meaning if not considered in relation to a specific goal or success to achieve. It is also confirmed by Art.31 (1) VCLT which calls for the effectiveness criteria (like any other term or provision of a treaty) to be understood 'in light of its objective and purpose'; compare also section 3.2 above.

74 For a detailed examination of the meaning of the sustainable development objective in treaty law in general and in CEPA in particular, see Grosse Ruse-Khan, H., *supra* note 43.

of right holders, IP users and the public at large.[75] In a way comparable to the operation of the sustainable development objective above, the question arises as to who is entitled to perform this balancing – whether it is embodied in the individual CEPA provisions or still to be performed by the contracting parties in the process of implementation. In general, the individual CEPA provisions on IP protection are surely an expression of how the contracting parties wished to achieve this balance. However, various arguments support significant discretion for the contracting parties to 'fine-tune' the overall equilibrium set by the CEPA IP chapter to fit the domestic development needs:

1. The overarching objective of sustainable development (and the call to apply and integrate it at all levels of CEPA) demands policy space in the interpretation and implementation of CEPA provisions which have a sufficiently open and broad meaning. This discretion must be utilised in line with the integrative approach inherent in the sustainable development objective. It calls upon states to implement IP protection obligations in a way which aims to reconcile all the economic, social and environmental interests at stake.[76]
2. In the Innovation and IP chapter, Art.131 reinforces the overarching goal of sustainable development and emphasises the role of IP protection in fostering its achievement. Together with Art.139 (2) it further stresses the need to tailor the level of IP protection to the individual level of development. As examined above, these provisions offer additional argumentative support for domestic discretion in calibrating IP protection to domestic development needs and to balance all interests involved.
3. The aim for adequate and effective IP protection equally sustains the argument in favour of policy space: while 'adequateness' must by definition be determined in relation to the individual domestic circumstances, 'effectiveness' must be measured in relation to the ability of IP protection to support the sustainable development of the contracting parties.

Some have expressed concern[77] over the limited incorporation of Art.7 TRIPS which is generally perceived as crucial to the flexibility of the

[75] In light of this broader understanding of IP protection, continuously increasing protection (as demanded by Art.131 (2)), does not necessarily mean increasing the scope and extent of IP exclusivity but could equally mean extended protection of IP users (which are often potential future IP producers); compare section 3.1.

[76] Compare the analysis in section 1 above.

[77] See Musungu, S., *supra* note 62, pp. 17, 19.

TRIPS Agreement.[78] However, Art.139 (2) CEPA on the 'Nature and Scope of Obligations' in the IP section does incorporate the additional elements of Art.7 – albeit not in identical language.[79] In fact, as the analysis in Section 3.3 below indicates, Art.139 (2) CEPA goes significantly beyond what Art.7 and 8 TRIPS can offer. Furthermore, the overarching sustainable development objective in CEPA is well equipped to fulfil the balancing role Art.7 TRIPS performs.[80] The related obligation to apply and integrate that CEPA goal at every level of the economic partnership (hence also in relation to the Innovation and IP chapter) again goes beyond TRIPS and clarifies that the balancing advocated is not exhaustively inherent in the treaty provisions, but is (also) to be performed in the process of implementation.

Another critique is that the objectives of the Innovation and IP chapter do not address the need for 'availability and access of products of innovation in various sectors'.[81] Is there hence a missing objective in Art.132 CEPA relating to access as a key element for innovation which allows innovators to 'stand on the shoulders of giants' without having to 'reinvent the wheel'? The reasoning above does not sufficiently take into account the paradigm in Art.132 (e) between innovation incentives and dissemination of the resulting technology and know-how. Dissemination arguably includes the ability to access the IP-protected material – although

---

78 Compare para.5 a) of the Doha Declaration (*supra* note 5).

79 The missing element from Art.7 TRIPS (that the protection and enforcement of intellectual property rights should contribute 'to the mutual advantage of producers and users of technological knowledge and in a manner conducive to social and economic welfare, and to a balance of rights and obligations') can be equated with the parties' agreement in Art.139 (2) 'that an adequate and effective enforcement of intellectual property rights should (. . .) provide a balance of rights and obligations between right holders and users'. The element which remains missing here ('in a manner conducive to social and economic welfare') is arguably covered by the substantively similar phrase in Art.8 TRIPS (allowing Members to 'promote the public interest in sectors of vital importance to their socio-economic and technological development') whose principles apply by virtue of Art.139 (2) as well.

80 For a detailed analysis of the balancing objectives in Art.7 TRIPS, see Grosse Ruse-Khan, H., *supra* note 47. For a comparative examination of the role of the WTO sustainable development objective for TRIPS, see Grosse Ruse-Khan, H. (2008), 'A Comparative Analysis of Policy Space in WTO Law', *Max Planck Papers on Intellectual Property, Competition & Tax Law Research Paper* No. 08-02, available at SSRN: http://ssrn.com/abstract=1309526 – also in Levin, M. and Kur, A. (eds) (2011), *Intellectual Property Rights in a Fair World Trade System*, Cheltenham, UK and Northampton, MA, USA: Edward Elgar Publishing.

81 Musungu, S., *supra* note 62, pp. 17, 19.

not necessarily free of charge or without further conditions attached. Furthermore, in relation to the availability of essential goods such as medicines or food, the right of the contracting parties to 'protect public health and nutrition' arguably implies the right to make these goods available even if this limits the rights of IP right holders.[82]

In sum, the objectives of the IP and Innovation chapter of CEPA therefore encourage the contracting parties to implement the CEPA IP provisions and fine-tune their IP systems in accordance with their domestic development needs. Given the influence of the overarching sustainable development objective, this calls for all relevant economic, social and environmental interests affected by the implementation to be reconciled. The equilibrium between providing an incentive for the creation of new innovations through rewards (usually via negative monopolies ensuring artificial exclusivity and market lead) and securing the transfer and diffusion of innovations to the public (via disclosure mechanisms, the idea-expression dichotomy in copyright, and exceptions to exclusive rights) is primarily set by the contracting parties in CEPA provisions. However, where broad and open treaty language allows, IP protection under CEPA should be implemented in accordance with domestic development priorities and balancing all interests involved.

3.3. The Nature and Scope of IP-related Obligations in CEPA

Within the chapter on Innovation and IP, the second section concerns the protection of IP under CEPA. Within that section, subsection 1 is named 'Principles' and *inter alia* contains provisions on the 'Nature and Scope of Obligations',[83] obligations for Least Developed Countries (LDCs),[84] Regional Integration[85] and the Transfer of Technology.[86] While all these horizontal provisions have implications for sustainable development and (to different degrees) implement the sustainable development objective,[87] this section focuses on the principles expressed in Art.139 (2) CEPA as

---

82 Compare the further analysis in section 3.3 below.

83 Art.139 CEPA, discussed below.

84 See Art.140 CEPA which provides for a longer transition period for LDCs to implement the substantive CEPA IP obligations until 2021.

85 See Art.141 CEPA which aims for further regional integration in the protection of IP, mainly via increased regional harmonisation.

86 See Art.142:2 CEPA.

87 In addition to the obvious extended transition periods for LDCs (giving effect to the sustainable development principle of common but differentiated commitments), Art.142:2 in particular takes an integrative approach to the intersection between IP protection, free competition and transfer of technology.

they embody the main horizontal regulation on the integration of IP and other social interests in the section on IP protection.[88]

The provision first calls for an application of the principles of Art.8 TRIPS to the IP section. Entitled 'Principles', Art.8 TRIPS is the only horizontal provision within TRIPS which addresses public interests affected by IP protection and their relation to interests and rights protected under individual TRIPS rules.[89] It states:

> 1. Members may, in formulating or amending their laws and regulations, adopt measures necessary to protect public health and nutrition, and to promote the public interest in sectors of vital importance to their socio-economic and technological development, provided that such measures are consistent with the provisions of this Agreement.
> 2. Appropriate measures, provided that they are consistent with the provisions of this Agreement, may be needed to prevent the abuse of intellectual property rights by right holders or the resort to practices which unreasonably restrain trade or adversely affect the international transfer of technology.

In a nutshell, Art.8:1 TRIPS allows WTO Members to adopt measures 'necessary to protect public health and nutrition' and to promote public interests of vital importance to their socio-economic and technological development. While this phrase places substantial discretion in the hand of WTO Members,[90] its function as a potential defensive shield for domestic public interest measures against inconsistencies with IP obligations under TRIPS is severely limited by a crucial further requirement: any such measures must be 'consistent with the provisions of this Agreement'. This qualification (which was only added in the final stages of negotiations on the text of the TRIPS Agreement)[91] prevents Art.8:1

---

88 For an analysis of the general exception provisions as tools to integrate social, economic and environmental concerns and their application to IP protection, see Grosse Ruse-Khan, H., *supra* note 43.

89 For a comparative analysis on Art.8:1 TRIPS and equivalent provisions addressing the consistency of domestic public interest measures with international WTO obligations under the rules on trade in goods and services, see Grosse Ruse-Khan, H., *supra* note 80.

90 Compare Correa, C., *supra* note 72, pp. 105–07; ICTSD/UNCTAD, *supra* note 71, Part I, chapter 6, section 3.

91 While the so-called 'Brussels Draft' (Trade Negotiations Committee, Draft final act embodying the results of the Uruguay Round of Multilateral Trade Negotiations (MTN.TNC/W/35/REV.1), 3 December 1990) retained most of the original language from the initial developing countries' proposal (*Communication from Argentina, Brazil, Chile, China, Colombia Cuba, Egypt, India, Nigeria, Peru, Tanzania and Uruguay*, Applicability of the Basic Principles of the GATT and of Relevant International Intellectual Property Conventions (MTN.GNG/

from functioning as a general exception to obligations for IP protection under TRIPS. Art.8:1 does not allow any measures which would conflict with other obligations in TRIPS.[92] In the same vein, Art.8:2 allows domestic measures against the abuse of IP rights and restrains on trade or technology transfer only when they 'are consistent with the provisions of this Agreement'.

Applying the principles of Art.8 TRIPS to the CEPA IP section means that all measures taken in reliance on these principles must be consistent with the provisions in the CEPA IP section. Operationalising these principles in CEPA hence cannot authorise overriding any substantive obligations to protect IP.[93] Art.139 (2) however goes significantly beyond Art.8 (1) TRIPS as it states:

> The Parties also agree that an adequate and effective enforcement of intellectual property rights should *take account of the development needs* of the CARIFORUM States, provide a *balance of rights and obligations* between rightholders and users and *allow* the EC Party and the Signatory CARIFORUM States *to protect public health and nutrition. Nothing in this Agreement* shall be construed as to impair the capacity of the Parties and the Signatory CARIFORUM States to promote access to medicines. (Emphasis added.)

NG11/W/71), 14 May 1990) on what now is Art.8:1, that draft added the further requirement of 'TRIPS consistency'. For an analysis of the history of that provision, see Grosse Ruse-Khan, H., *supra* note 80.

[92] While a majority of commentators seem to agree on this point (see Gervais, D. (2003), *The TRIPS Agreement – Drafting History and Analysis*, 2nd ed., London: Sweet & Maxwell p. 2.84; Blakeney, M. (1996), *Trade Related Aspects of Intellectual Property Rights: A Concise Guide to the TRIPS Agreement*, London: Sweet & Maxwell, at 3.09; ICTSD/UNCTAD, *supra* note 72, Part I, chapter 6, section 3.2), the role of Art.8:1 (especially after its endorsement in the Doha Declaration) remains hotly debated; see for example Yusuf, A. (1998), 'TRIPS: Background, Principles and General Provisions', in Correa, C. and Yusuf, A. (eds), *Intellectual Property and International Trade*, London: Kluwer Law International, p. 13; Correa, C., *supra* note 72, p. 108; ICTSD/UNCTAD, *supra* note 72, Part I, chapter 6, section 3.2.

[93] Misleading therefore is the statement in the CIEL paper ('Intellectual Property in European Union Economic Partnership Agreements with African, Caribbean and Pacific Countries: What Way Forward after the CARIFORUM EPA and the Interim EPAs?' (Center for International Environmental Law, Geneva, April 2008 – available online at http://www.ciel.org/Publications/Oxfam_TechnicalBrief_5May08.pdf (accessed 3 March 2009), which merely mentions a 'right to take measures to protect public health and nutrition'. One could further debate any interpretative role of these principles as foreseen by para.4, 5 a) of the Doha Declaration (*supra* note 5). On this role in the TRIPS context, see Grosse Ruse-Khan, H., *supra* note 80.

This provision contains three distinct elements. At first, it again emphasises the necessity to *take account of the development needs* – this time specifically linked to IP enforcement.[94] As this provision is part of the section dealing exclusively with IP (instead of Innovation and IP), the reinforcement of the conceptual link between the levels of obligations and domestic development needs explained above pre-empts any arguments that the concept might relate only to the Innovation section rather than the IP section. In this instance, it is also not related to the issue of further increasing levels of IP protection, but establishes a general link between the enforcement of IP protection and development needs.[95] Second, the parties agree that adequate and effective IP enforcement should provide a *balance of rights and obligations* between right holders and users. This language borrows from Art.7 TRIPS and is in line with objectives in Art.132 (d) and (e) CEPA.[96] The call for a balance of rights and obligations could, *inter alia*, support the argument that 'increasing levels of protection'[97] do not necessarily relate to strengthened exclusivity, but also include rights of users as outlined above. Based on the above arguments regarding context in Art.131 and objectives in Art.132 of CEPA, the further emphasis on crucial elements of these provisions in Art.139 (2) effectively supports the existence of domestic policy space to address domestic development needs and integrate all the relevant social, economic and environmental interests at stake.

Thirdly, and arguably most importantly, Art.139 (2) substantively widens the public interest principle of Art.8:1 TRIPS. The contracting parties also 'agree that an adequate and effective enforcement of intellectual property rights should (. . .) *allow* the EC Party and the Signatory CARIFORUM States *to protect public health and nutrition*'. Further, '*[n]othing in this Agreement* shall be construed as to impair the capacity of the Parties and the Signatory CARIFORUM States to promote access to medicines' (emphasis added). The first element worth stressing is that both sentences address domestic public interest measures – in particular those relating to public health, nutrition and access to medicines. While the scope of measures covered is hence more limited than in Art.8:1 TRIPS,[98]

---

94 Compare also Art.131 (2) and the analysis in section a) above.

95 See also Spence, M. (2008), 'Trade and Innovation in the EPAs: Another Step towards Re-framing TRIPS', 7 (5), *Trade Negotiations Insights*, June, p. 6, who stresses that the contracting parties in the negotiation process aimed to achieve an appropriate balance between the level of development and the level of IP protection.

96 Compare section 3.2 above.

97 See Art.131 (2) CEPA.

98 One may recall that Art.8:1 covers 'measures necessary to protect public

the crucial point is that measures under Art.139 (2) CEPA do *not* have to be otherwise consistent with the CEPA provisions on IP protection.

At first sight, this may entail a right of the contracting parties to adopt public health or nutrition-protecting measures even if these measures are inconsistent with individual IP obligations. Or it might mean that such individual obligations – as part of 'an adequate and effective enforcement of intellectual property rights'[99] – must be interpreted and implemented in a way that allows domestic measures to protect public health and nutrition.[100] This would find support in the objectives embodied in Art.132 (d) CEPA which equally aim to 'achieve an adequate and effective protection and enforcement of intellectual property rights'.[101] Also the title of Art.139 – 'Nature and Scope of Obligations' – speaks for a role and function of Art.139 (2) that determines the nature and scope of the individual IP obligations in CEPA. Their nature and scope must be so that they allow the protection of public health and nutrition and must not impair access to medicines. This latter understanding seems preferable. It takes into account the general exception provision in Art.224 CEPA which allows contracting parties to take measures otherwise inconsistent with individual CEPA obligations – including those from the IP and Innovation chapter – for example, if such measures 'are necessary to protect human, animal or plant life or health'.[102] In order to avoid overlap and reducing the necessity test embodied in Art.224 CEPA to redundancy,[103] Art.139 (2) should not be viewed as an authorisation to override individual IP obligations under CEPA. The principle of effectiveness (*effet utile*)[104] hence demands such an understanding – as it is the most appropriate way to give effect to all the terms of the treaty without rendering one meaningless, null or void. In

---

health and nutrition, and to promote the public interest in sectors of vital importance to their socio-economic and technological development'.

[99] Art.139 (2).

[100] On the need for an equivalent understanding of Art.8:1 TRIPS in the context of para.4, 5 (a) of the Doha Declaration (*supra* note 5), see Grosse Ruse-Khan, *supra* note 80.

[101] See Art.132 (d) CEPA.

[102] Art.224 CEPA.

[103] Art.139 (2) does not contain the requirement that measures must be 'necessary' to achieve a specific aim (such as access to medicines). This requirement however is a crucial element in the WTO case law on Art.XX GATT and Art. XIV GATS – provisions which CEPA drafters have transplanted almost in their entirety into Art.224 CEPA.

[104] On the principle of effectiveness, see *United States – Standards for Reformulated and Conventional Gasoline*, Appellate Body Report WT/DS24/AB/R, at 21; *Japan — Taxes on Alcoholic Beverages* (WT/DS8/AB/R), Appellate Body report (4 October 1996) at 96 (106).

comparison to the general exception clause, Art.139 (2) thus functions as an IP-specific filter mechanism which obliges those interpreting and implementing CEPA to develop an understanding of the individual provisions which supports the public interests set out in Art.139 (2). In this way, it truly defines the nature and scope of IP obligations in CEPA.

In sum, Art.139 (2) contains the main horizontal provision in the CEPA section on IP protection which explicitly addresses intersections between the interests of IP right holders and other societal concerns – here in form of public health, nutrition and access to medication.[105] In terms of international sustainable development law, Art.139 (2) adopts an integrative approach by reconciling economic and social interests within an international agreement. This provision therefore implements CEPAs sustainable development objective and its core principle of integration at the international level. Based on the general analysis on the principle of integration above,[106] Art.139 (2) CEPA would prevent the contracting parties from taking an integrative approach in the implementation of CEPA provisions which depart from the substance of Art.139 (2). The limitation on discretion to integrate IP protection and public health, nutrition and access to medicines on the domestic level is, however, rather theoretical. The broad language[107] itself implies significant policy space as *how* to protect public health and nutrition and to promote access to medication in relation to IP protection. Against this background, the most important aspect of Art.139 (2) – if not of the whole sub-section 1 on 'Principles' of IP protection under CEPA – is its function to determine the nature and scope of CEPA's obligations relating to IP. Their nature and scope must be so that they allow the protection of public health and nutrition and must not impair access to medicines.

4. OPERATIONALISING A SUSTAINABLE DEVELOPMENT OBJECTIVE IN INTERNATIONAL IP TREATIES

This chapter has examined general international law and the EC – CARIFORUM EPA in order to identify the role a sustainable development objective might play as an element in reforming international IP law.

---

[105] Other more specific provisions addressing such 'intersections' are Arts.142 (2), 144 F, 146 C (3), 147 B, 149 (1), 150 and 155 (3) CEPA.

[106] Compare Section 1 above.

[107] Art.139 (2), essentially allowing contracting parties to protect public health and nutrition and to promote access to medication without any further qualification.

In international law, basically all documents relating to sustainable development emphasise the *principle of integration and reconciliation* as its core element. The focus hence is on balancing economic, social and environmental aspects and integrating them in all (governmental, judicial and administrative) decision-making processes. That, however, gives rise to ambiguities and unresolved questions. What types of issues must be balanced (i.e. where there is an intersection between economic, social and environmental issues) is context-dependent and driven by normative preferences. The principle as such also does not specify, for any given intersection, a concrete integrated outcome. Instead, the focus is on adopting an integrative process in decision-making. Finally, integration has to take place both at international and national levels, with ample tools to do so. The more specific the integrative approach adopted internationally, the smaller the policy space available for balancing domestically. In essence, sustainable development must therefore be understood as an overarching integrative and holistic approach: a call for reconciliation of all relevant economic, environmental and social concerns in decision-making processes.

Giving effect to sustainable development *as a treaty objective* means that its core principle of integration guides the interpretation of individual treaty provisions. Based on the notion of *pacta sunt servanda*, this balancing must primarily be performed in the process of treaty implementation by states as the main addressees of a sustainable development treaty objective. Here, the ambiguous nature of the integration principle secures policy space when states implement treaty provisions in light of the sustainable development objective. Since it cannot operate as a norm which constrains state conduct in a way that prescribes one specific integrative outcome, states inevitably retain substantial discretion in giving effect to a sustainable development objective. International courts and tribunals have to recognise this domestic policy space to balance economic, social and environmental concerns. Hence they must exercise deference when assessing a disputed implementation of provisions originating from treaties with a sustainable development objective.

Of course, states' discretion is limited and cannot amount to a rewriting of individual treaty provisions. Defining the boundaries of this policy space therefore is crucial. One decisive factor is whether the treaty at stake does already contain relevant provisions which perform a *specific integration on the international plane*. If this is the case, an integrative implementation at the domestic level must comply with the balancing chosen by the contracting parties at international level. Another crucial element concerns the general interplay between treaty objectives and the other main elements of interpretation and how that works out in the case at hand. The former will have central importance where the ordinary meaning and context of the treaty provision at hand does not offer concrete results and so allows focusing on the treaties' objective. That is in particular the case where the *interpretation of broad and open legal concepts* is at stake. Their openness or ambiguity *a priori* lends itself to assuming a margin of appreciation, flexibility or policy space in the interpretation and implementation process. Sustainable development as a treaty objective is well equipped to guide and direct the utilisation of this discretion towards a reconciliation of all relevant economic, social and environmental in domestic decision-making processes. It is here where the significant potential for reforming the international IP system lies: treaty objectives which focus on overreaching and inclusive goals such as sustainable development and a balance of all interests involved can re-shape the interpretation and implementation of specific (IP) provisions. In this way, these objectives determine the overall scope and substance of an international obligation to give effect to treaty law.

The EC – CARIFORUM EPA has been called a 'Trade Partnership for Sustainable Development' where 'sustainable development is the presiding principle governing the whole agreement'.[108] The analysis above has shown that the general objectives and principles of CEPA do allow the concept of sustainable development to play such a role – if the contracting parties are able and willing to use its potential. The obligations the contracting parties undertook in Art.3 CEPA with regard to the implementation of CEPA's sustainable development objective align with the general understanding of the function of a sustainable development objective in international treaties: to empower and oblige all actors involved in the application of the treaty to take an integrative approach to the process of decision-making. CEPA further qualifies the obligation to adopt an integrative approach by requiring this decision-making process to incorporate the principles of ownership, participation and dialogue.

A scrutiny of the main provisions of the Innovation and IP chapter setting out the context and objectives, as well as the nature and scope of obligations relating to IP protection in CEPA, further confirms the conclusion on the general CEPA objectives: IP protection is a means to achieve sustainable development and should be tailored to the level of development. Art.139 (2) on the 'Nature and Scope of Obligations' implements CEPA's sustainable development objective by adopting an integrative approach that reconciles economic and social interests within CEPA's IP section. Its main function truly is to determine nature and scope of the

---

108 EC Commission and DG Trade, *supra* note 39.

CEPA obligations relating to IP. Their nature and scope must be so such as to allow the protection of public health and nutrition and must not impair access to medicines.

What can we learn from this in terms of a reform of the International IP system? Countries, international organisations and other relevant actors should acknowledge the need for a comprehensive integration of economic, social and environmental concerns in all areas of decision-making. Incorporating sustainable development as a treaty objective in international agreements on the protection of IP can function as a tool to overcome the structural bias and self-contained nature of international IP regulation. This requires action on the international and the national level: the concept gives negotiators in the treaty-drafting process; domestic actors in the course of treaty implementation; and international courts and tribunals when settling disputes over the proper treaty application an option to address intersections between economic, social and environmental interests.

Negotiators are encouraged to identify and regulate such intersections by determining a (self-determined) balance between IP and other interests at stake at the *international level*. The WIPO Development Agenda and the ongoing negotiations on the relationship between TRIPS and the Convention on Biological Diversity (CBD) in the WTO can be good forums for action. Discourses, views and results 'from the outside' such as the Intergovernmental Working Group on Public Health, Innovation and Intellectual Property (IGWG) and the ongoing negotiations on climate change, the transfer of 'green' technology and IP in the framework of the UNFCCC should be taken into account. Issues so far not addressed within the IP system but with a significant impact on or relation to IP protection must be integrated and reconciled with IP rules. *If it wishes to retain relevance and credibility, the IP system cannot be silent on today's global problems such as climate change, food security and eradication of poverty*. Intersections like the transfer of 'green' technology to reduce carbon emissions and patent protection or securing sustainable, local agricultural production and plant variety or patent protection must be looked at.

While multilateral approaches – especially to global problems such as climate change and food security – are certainly to be preferred, regional and bilateral negotiations should equally implement the concept of sustainable development and its core principle of integration. CEPA does seem to offer some positive examples here as it includes chapters on the environment, social aspects (dealing primarily with the protection of core workers' rights) and the protection of personal data. Especially in regional and bilateral settings one must, however, always be mindful of asymmetric negotiation powers and the impact on key regulatory areas which most likely so far have been in the realm of state autonomy. Regardless of the quality of the substantive obligations, it should be ensured that these 'non-trade issues' in particular actually represent democratic choices of the majority in all countries involved and are not imposed upon these peoples.

At the *domestic level*, countries should develop national IP strategies and align those with their national strategies for sustainable development (NSSD).[109] IP protection should be tailored to domestic needs, and in particular respect social and environmental concerns. This requires connecting the relevant actors and stakeholders in order to identify domestic intersections between IP and 'other' concerns. In the absence of specific 'integrative' treaty provisions on the international level, a sustainable development (treaty) objective should generally offer sufficient freedom to adopt good faith measures which balance IP with other societal interests at stake.

International obligations – especially under TRIPS – should therefore not *a priori* prevent thinking on flexible solutions to integrate all relevant interests affected by IP protection. The policy space flowing from the sustainable development objective in the WTO Agreement by and large offers adequate discretion for a tailored domestic attempt to give effect to public interests. Although not limited to them, the primary provisions with broad and open terms inviting an integrative approach are the various versions of the three-step test regulating the right to foresee exceptions and limitations to IP rights. In Art.13 TRIPS, for example,[110] confining exceptions to '*special*' cases, avoiding conflict with '*normal*' exploitation as well as '*unreasonable*' prejudice of the '*legitimate*' interests of right holders, offers ample room for a normative understanding which recognises public interests:

- '*Special*' cases may include those which address public interests recognised in Art.8:1 or the concept of sustainable development.
- An exploitation could be considered '*normal*' only if it does not significantly interfere with such objectives.[111]

---

[109] *See* Agenda 21, *supra* note 16, at chapter 8 (8.7).

[110] One may recall the wording of Art.13 stating 'Members shall confine limitations or exceptions to exclusive rights to certain special cases which do not conflict with a normal exploitation of the work and do not unreasonably prejudice the legitimate interests of the right holder'.

[111] See the *Declaration on a Balanced Interpretation of the Three Step Test in Copyright Law*, at point 4 (printed in IIC Vol.39, No.6 (2008), 707–713);

- Any prejudice caused by good faith measures (necessary for) protecting those objectives may be understood as not being '*unreasonable*' and '*legitimate*' interests of right holders may only be those which sufficiently reconcile the public interests recognised in the WTO/TRIPS objectives.[112]

Other versions of the three-step test which explicitly call for '*taking account of the legitimate interests of third parties*'[113] provide even more options for reconciling economic with public interests and other (fundamental) rights of third parties.

The WTO/TRIPS balancing objectives support an understanding of the general relationship between IP protection and exceptions to it as one of balance instead of (universal) rule and (minor) exception.[114] In the *US – Shrimp* dispute mentioned above, the Appellate Body developed an overall equilibrium between trade liberalisation and public interests as a guiding principle for interpreting the exceptions relating to obligations on trade in goods.[115] The same can be said of the protection of IP and recog-

---

available online at http://www.ip.mpg.de/ww/de/pub/aktuelles/declaration_on_the_three_step_.cfm (visited 30 September 2008); compare further Ricketson, S., *supra* note 47.

[112] See Kur, A., 'Of Oceans, Islands, and Inland Water -- How Much Room for Exceptions and Limitations under the Three Step-Test?' in Kur, A. (ed.), *Intellectual Property Rights in Fair World Trade System – Proposals for Reform of TRIPS*, Cheltenham, UK and Northampton, MA, USA: Edward Elgar, 2011) who however favours an accumulation of public interest balancing on the third step while at the same time ensuring that the individual steps are not separate units but merge into an overall assessment. *See* also the Declaration on a Balanced Interpretation of the Three Step Test in Copyright Law, *supra* note 111 above, at point 6.

[113] See Art.17, 26:2, 30 TRIPS. Interests could be considered '*legitimate*' *inter alia* if they pursue recognised public policy concerns or other interests addressed in TRIPS or the WTO Agreements' preamble.

[114] *Singularia non sunt extendenda.* see also Godt, C. (2003), 'International Economic and Environmental Law', in Krämer, L. (ed.), *Recht und Um-Welt – Essays in Honour of Prof. Dr. Gerd Winter*, Groningen: Europa Law Publishing, pp. 237–52 (at 242–5), who focuses on the relation between Art.27:1 (establishing the criteria for patent protection and the need to cover all fields of technology) and Art.27:2 (allowing exceptions from patentability based on public policies) as an example where a balancing paradigm, instead of a rule-exception principle should apply.

[115] In the *US – Shrimp* dispute, the WTO Appellate Body stated that the sustainable development objective in the Preamble to the WTO Agreement 'must add colour, texture and shading to our interpretation of the Agreements annexed to the WTO Agreement' (see *US – Shrimp*, *supra* note 27, at para.153).

nition of public interests under TRIPS. Such a general balance does not only follow from the overarching objective of sustainable development in the WTO preamble, but equally from Art.7 and 8 TRIPS. It is further a matter of internal consistency of the WTO as a legal system. Allowing a proper balance in one area but denying it in another threatens legitimacy and acceptance for the latter area and the whole system which will easily be perceived as biased.

Finally, international courts and tribunals called upon to review the consistency of domestic implementation with international IP obligations should also take an integrative approach. While the writings of some scholars and emerging jurisprudence of the ICJ and other tribunals speak in favour of such an approach regardless any specifically applicable treaty language, this must be even more so when sustainable development forms the agreed objective of the treaty whose provisions are subject to interpretation. Here, the WTO Appellate Body has set a useful precedent in the trade and environment context that should guide further WTO dispute settlement decisions relating to all other areas of WTO law, hence including TRIPS. In the words of the Appellate Body, the WTO treaties' objective of sustainable development 'must *add colour, texture and shading* to our interpretation of the Agreements annexed to the WTO Agreement'.[116]

The domestic policy space in treaty implementation emphasised above means that international courts and tribunals must recognise and accept this discretion. They must exercise deference with regard to the integrative approach taken at the domestic level – if that is within the boundaries set by the ordinary meaning and context of the provision at stake. In what is at present the main sphere of operationalising the sustainable development objective in the WTO – the general exception provision of Art.XX GATT – commentators have described the approach of the Appellate Body as a 'disproportionality' test.[117] This type of judicial restraint on

---

[116] *US – Shrimp*, *supra* note 27, at para.152.

[117] Schloemann, H., 'Brazil Tyres: Policy Space Confirmed under GATT Article XX', 12(1), *Bridges Monthly Trade Review*, at 11 (online available at http://www.ictsd.org/monthly/bridges/BRIDGES_12-1.pdf – visited 21 April 2008) observes that 'the "weighing and balancing" test in particular is a thinly veiled proportionality test, miraculously operating rather well without an agreed value system (constitution) to rely on – probably because it comes along with utmost judicial restraint, if not deference to national policy choices. Perhaps "disproportionality" test would therefore be a better word for it'. Compare also the conclusion reached by Andenas, M. and Zleptnig, S. (2007), 'Proportionality and Balancing in WTO Law: A Comparative Perspective', 20(1) *Cambridge Review of International Affairs* (CRIA), pp. 7–18 (at 10) which emphasises not only the

national policy choices which balance all relevant economic, social and environmental interests, however, is only appropriate as long as no specific integration has taken place on the international plane.

flexible balancing approach adopted by the Appellate Body but equally stresses 'a certain degree of subjectivity on the part of the judiciary'. Gerstetter, C. (2006), 'The Appellate Body's Response to the Tensions and Interdependencies between Transnational Trade Governance and Social Regulation', in Joerges, C. and Petersmann, E.-U. (eds), *Constitutionalism, Multilateral Trade Governance and Social Regulation*, Oxford: Hart Publishing, pp. 123–24 further highlights the Appellate Body's deference to the WTO Members' right to balance economic with public interests.

Index